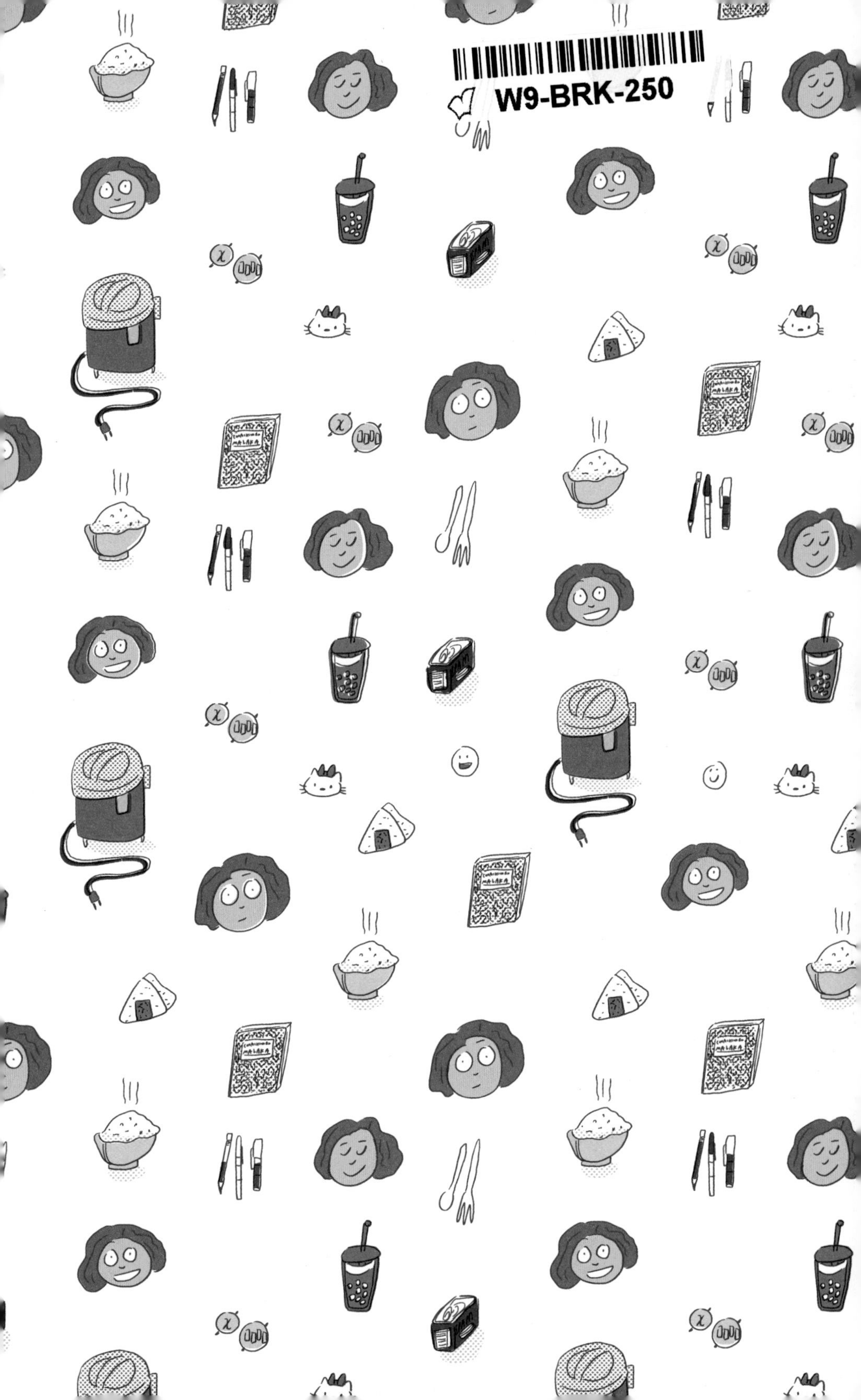

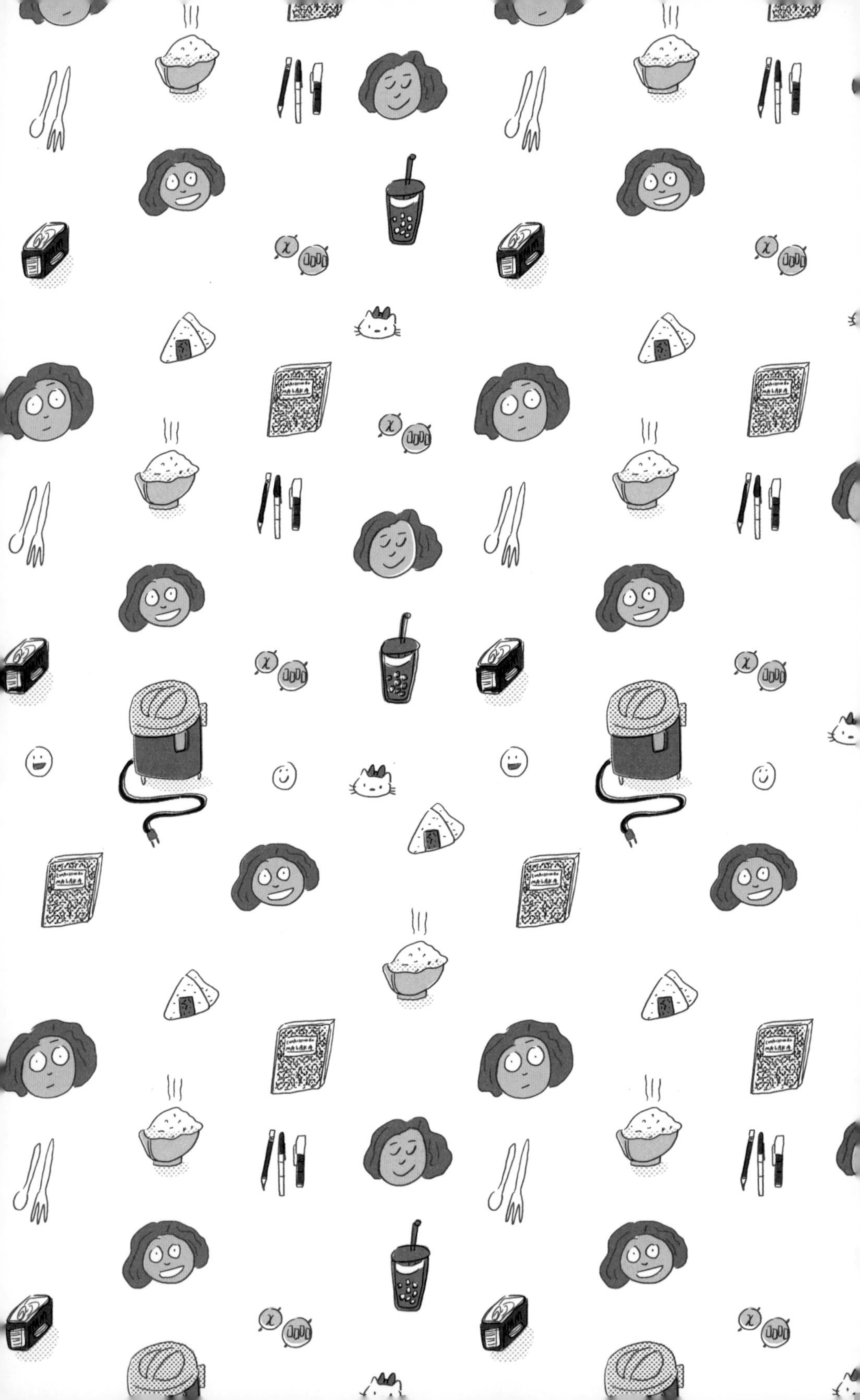

I Was Their American Dream

A GRAPHIC MEMOIR

Malaka Gharib

Clarkson Potter/Publishers
New York

Published in the United States by Clarkson Potter/
Publishers, an imprint of the Crown Publishing Group,
a division of Penguin Random House LLC, New York.

crownpublishing.com
clarksonpotter.com

CLARKSON POTTER is a trademark and POTTER
with colophon is a registered trademark of Penguin
Random House LLC.

ISBN 978-0-525-57511-5

Ebook ISBN 978-0-525-57512-2

Printed in China

Coloring by Toby Leigh

10 9

First Edition

FOR
MOMMY + DADDY

Meet the Fam

MOM

MALAKA'S MOTHER,
WHO WORKS LONG
HOURS TO PROVIDE
FOR THE FAMILY

MALAKA

A CURIOUS GIRL,
JUST TRYING TO
FIND HER PLACE
IN THE WORLD

DAD

MALAKA'S FATHER,
A DISCIPLINED AND
INTELLIGENT MAN

MIN MIN

MALAKA'S SPUNKY
HALF-SISTER WITH
A MIND OF HER OWN

TITO MARO

MALAKA'S MATERNAL
UNCLE, KNOWN FOR
BEING FUN AND A
GREAT COOK

NANAY

MALAKA'S MATERNAL
GRANDMOTHER, WHO
SPENDS LOTS OF TIME
WITH HER GRANDKIDS

TATAY

MALAKA'S MATERNAL GRANDFATHER, WHO ENCOURAGED HER TO READ LOTS OF BOOKS

TITA PINKY

MALAKA'S MATERNAL AUNT AND THE MATRIARCH OF THE FAMILY

TITO ARNEL

PINKY'S HUSBAND, A KIND MAN WHO GIVES GOOD ADVICE

DARREN

THE SWEET, GOOFY SOUTHERNER WHO MALAKA WOULD EVENTUALLY MARRY

HALA

MALAKA'S BELOVED STEPMOTHER, WHO TREATED HER LIKE HER OWN CHILD

SALMA, DONNIA, AHMED

MALAKA'S YOUNGER HALF-SIBLINGS WHO LIVE IN THE MIDDLE EAST

Chapter 1

WHEN I WAS GROWING UP,
MY MOM WOULD ALWAYS SAY:

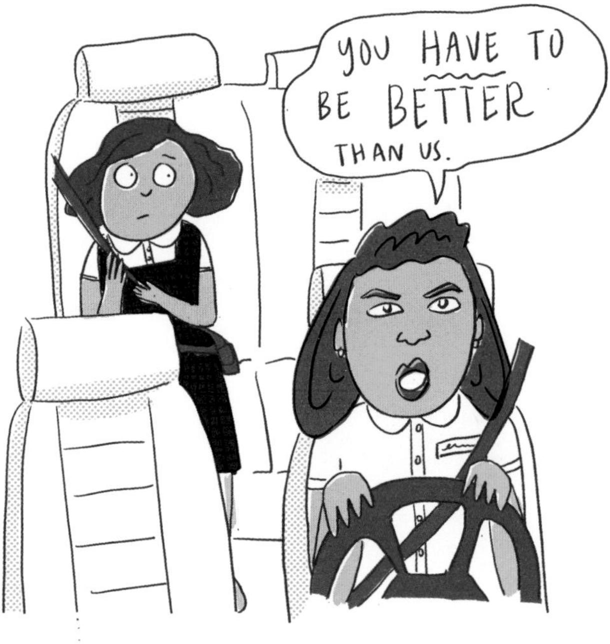
YOU HAVE TO BE BETTER THAN US.

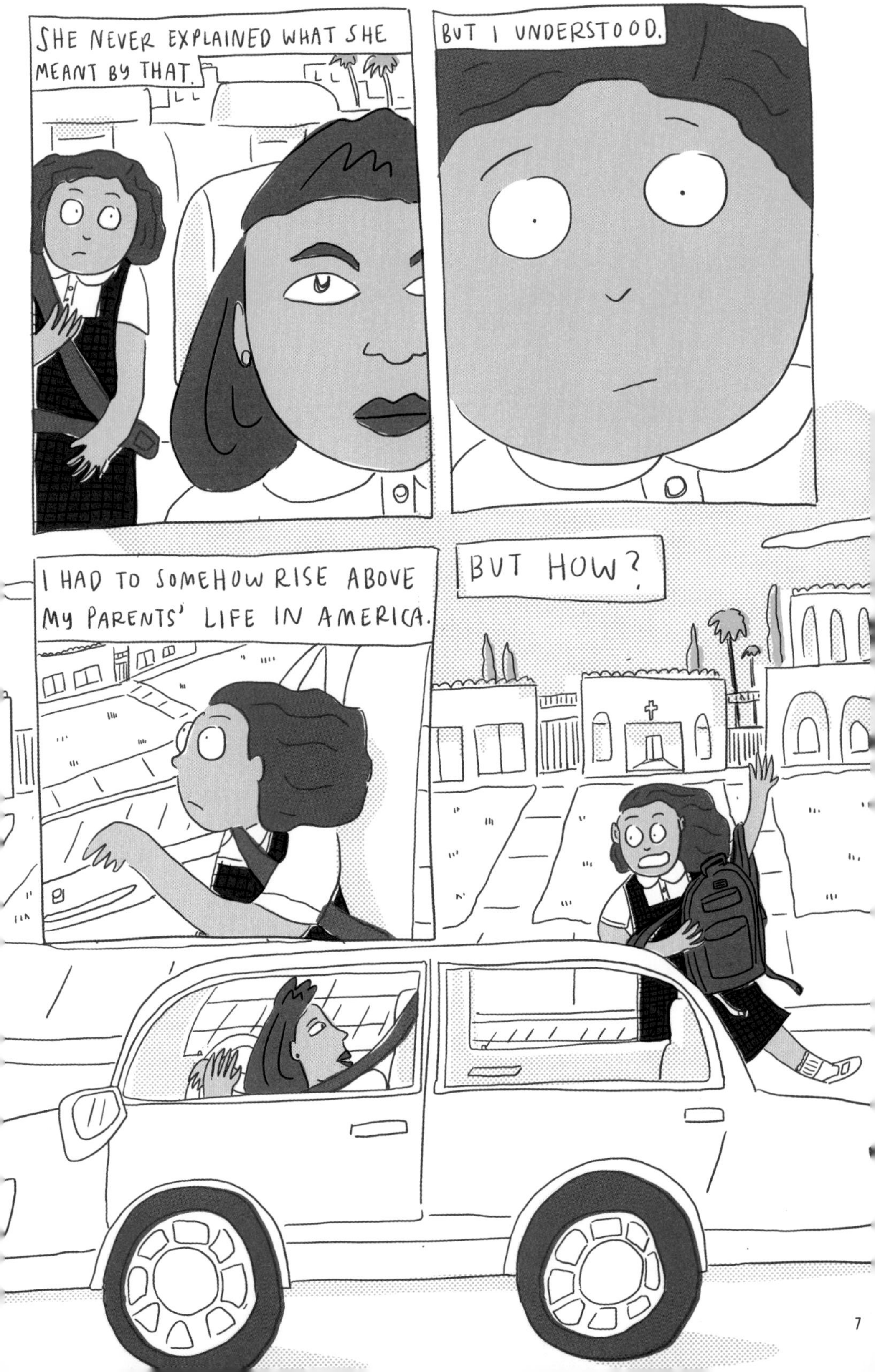
SHE NEVER EXPLAINED WHAT SHE MEANT BY THAT.
BUT I UNDERSTOOD.
I HAD TO SOMEHOW RISE ABOVE MY PARENTS' LIFE IN AMERICA.
BUT HOW?

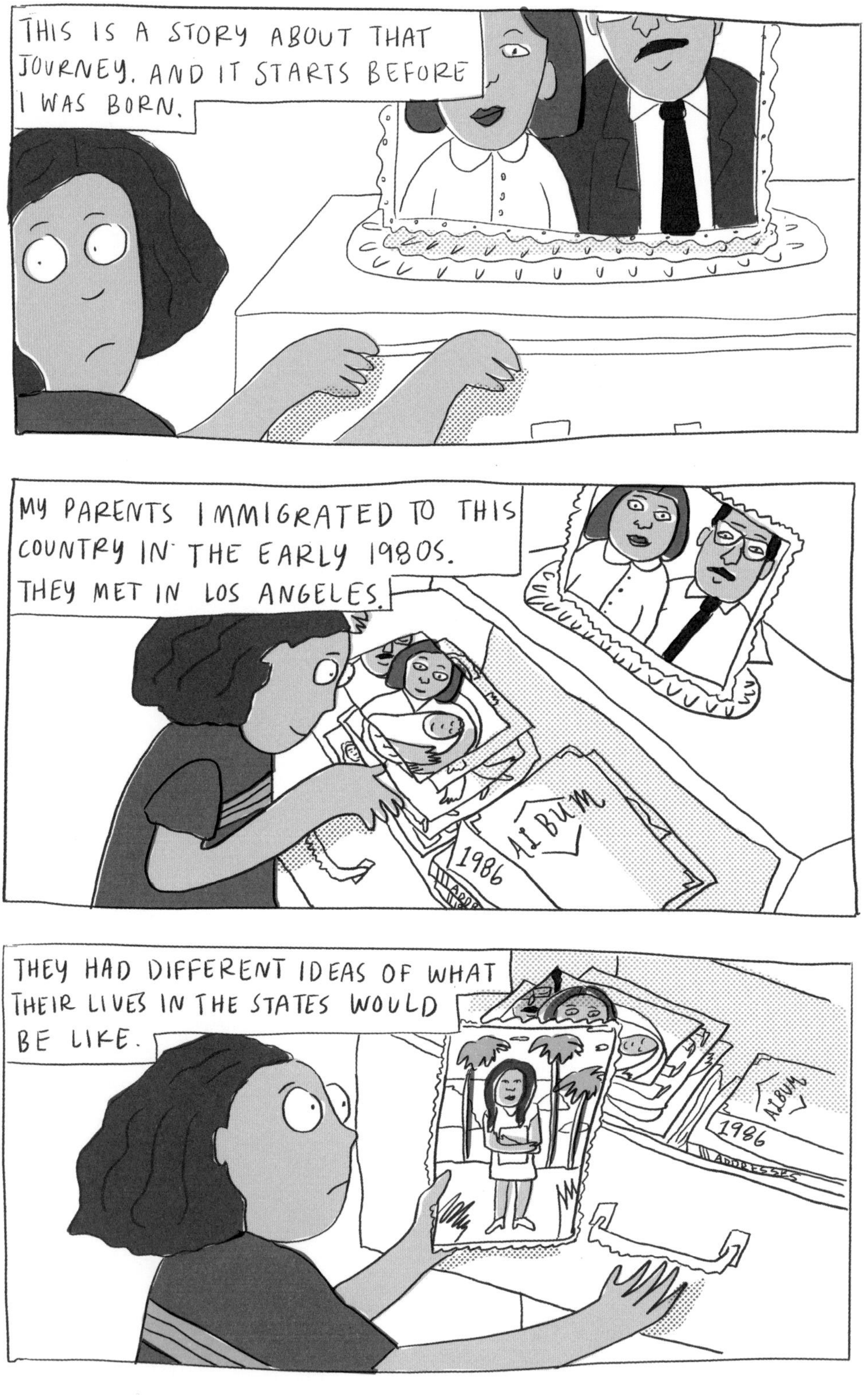
THIS IS A STORY ABOUT THAT JOURNEY. AND IT STARTS BEFORE I WAS BORN.
MY PARENTS IMMIGRATED TO THIS COUNTRY IN THE EARLY 1980S. THEY MET IN LOS ANGELES.
ALBUM
1986
THEY HAD DIFFERENT IDEAS OF WHAT THEIR LIVES IN THE STATES WOULD BE LIKE.
ALBUM
1986

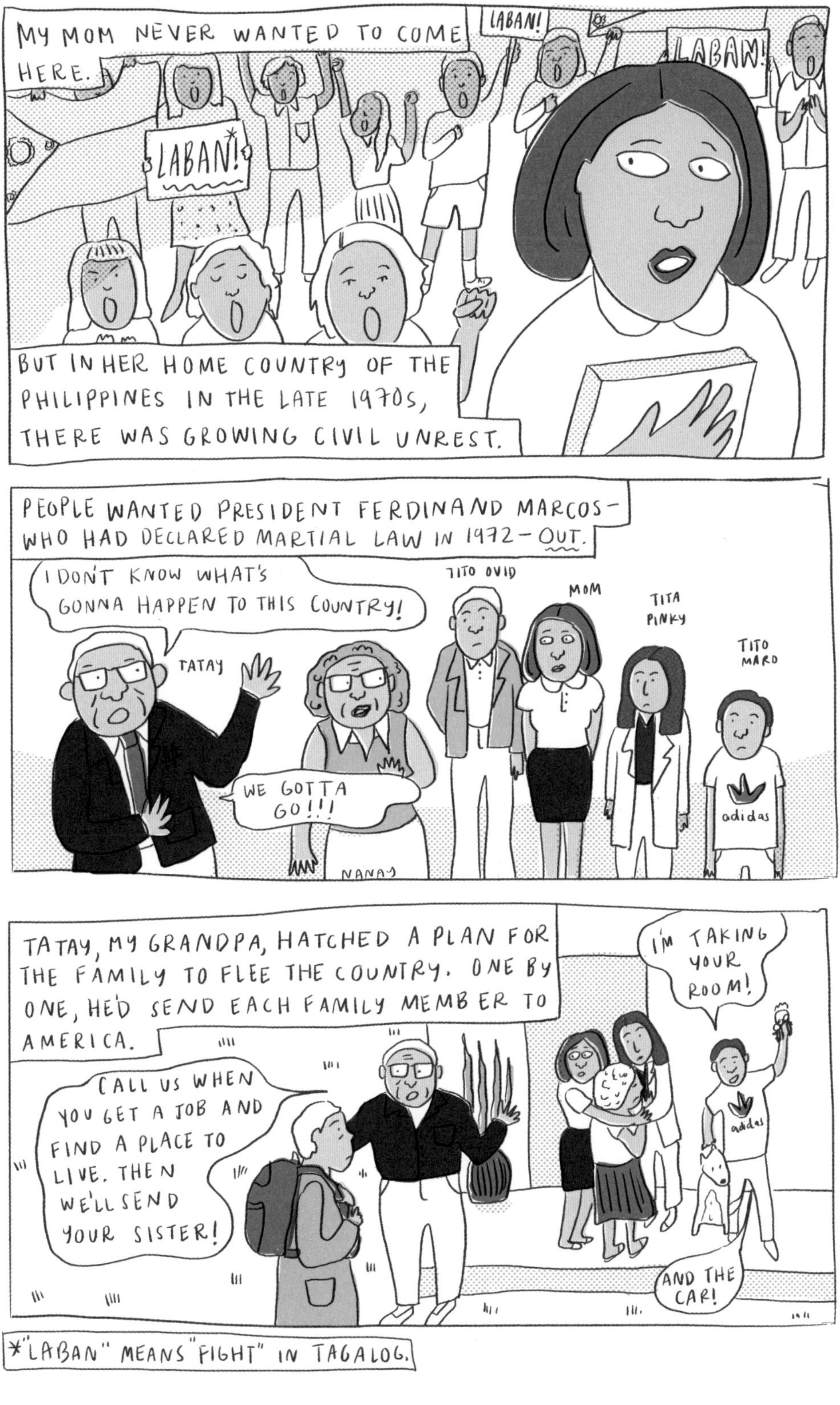
MY MOM NEVER WANTED TO COME HERE.
LABAN!
LABAN!
LABAN!*
BUT IN HER HOME COUNTRY OF THE PHILIPPINES IN THE LATE 1970S, THERE WAS GROWING CIVIL UNREST.
PEOPLE WANTED PRESIDENT FERDINAND MARCOS— WHO HAD DECLARED MARTIAL LAW IN 1972—OUT.
I DON'T KNOW WHAT'S GONNA HAPPEN TO THIS COUNTRY!
TATAY
TITO OVID
MOM
TITA PINKY
TITO MARD
WE GOTTA GO!!!
NANAY
adidas
TATAY, MY GRANDPA, HATCHED A PLAN FOR THE FAMILY TO FLEE THE COUNTRY. ONE BY ONE, HE'D SEND EACH FAMILY MEMBER TO AMERICA.
I'M TAKING YOUR ROOM!
CALL US WHEN YOU GET A JOB AND FIND A PLACE TO LIVE. THEN WE'LL SEND YOUR SISTER!
adidas
AND THE CAR!
*"LABAN" MEANS "FIGHT" IN TAGALOG.

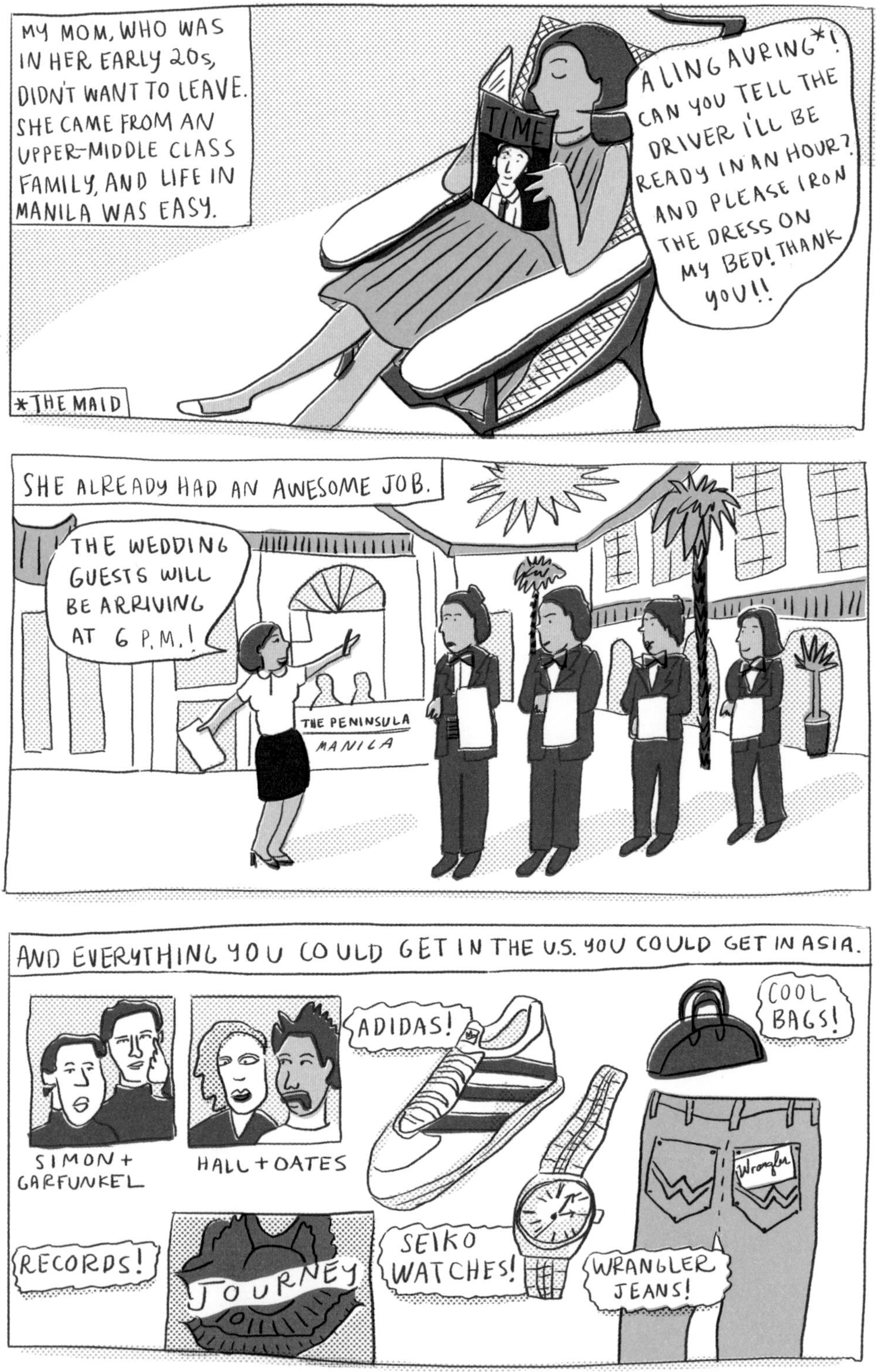
MY MOM, WHO WAS IN HER EARLY 20s, DIDN'T WANT TO LEAVE. SHE CAME FROM AN UPPER-MIDDLE CLASS FAMILY, AND LIFE IN MANILA WAS EASY.
ALING AURING*! CAN YOU TELL THE DRIVER I'LL BE READY IN AN HOUR? AND PLEASE IRON THE DRESS ON MY BED! THANK YOU!!
TIME
*THE MAID
SHE ALREADY HAD AN AWESOME JOB.
THE WEDDING GUESTS WILL BE ARRIVING AT 6 P.M.!
THE PENINSULA MANILA
AND EVERYTHING YOU COULD GET IN THE U.S. YOU COULD GET IN ASIA.
SIMON + GARFUNKEL
HALL + OATES
ADIDAS!
COOL BAGS!
RECORDS!
JOURNEY
SEIKO WATCHES!
WRANGLER JEANS!
Wrangler

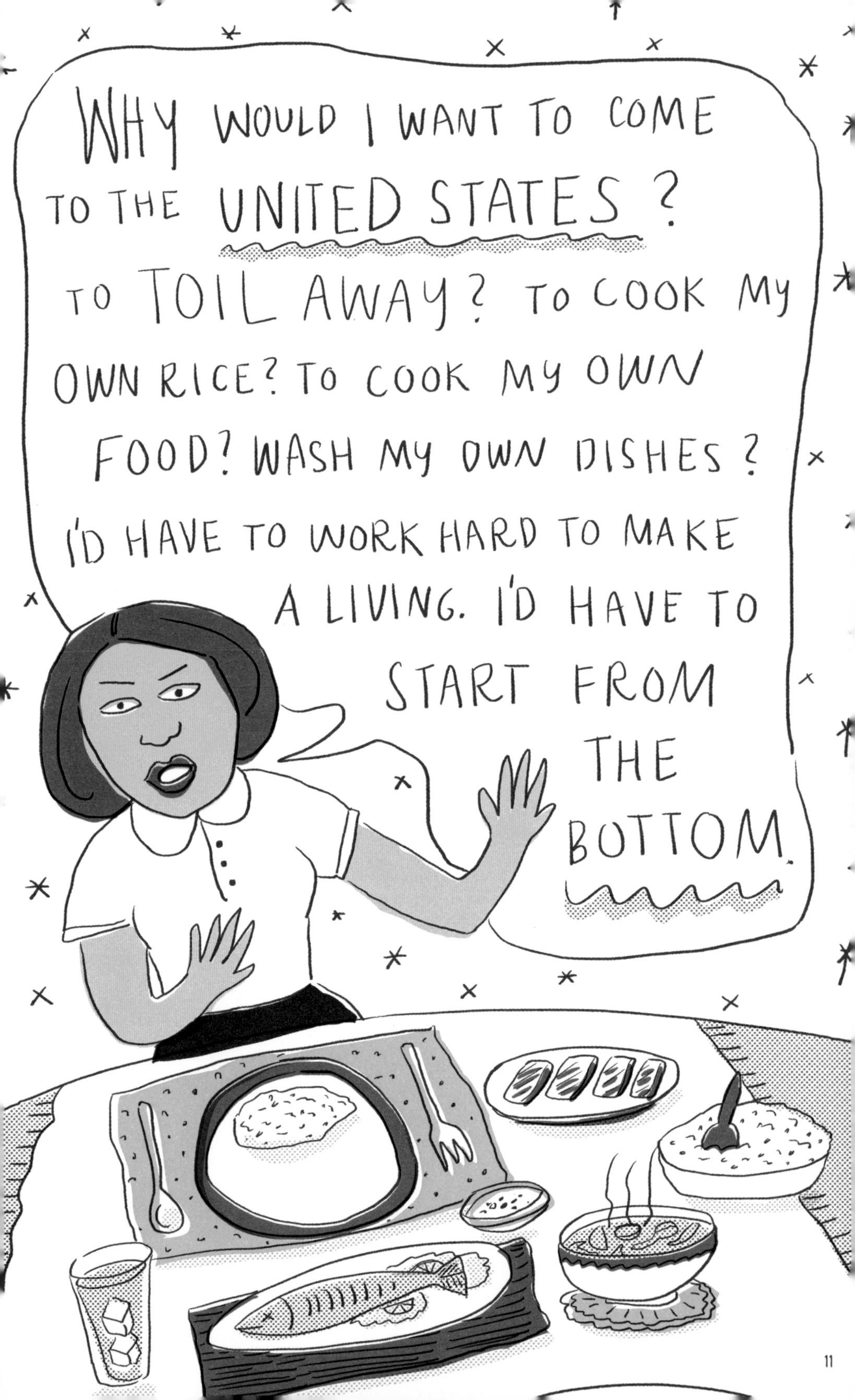
WHY WOULD I WANT TO COME TO THE UNITED STATES? TO TOIL AWAY? TO COOK MY OWN RICE? TO COOK MY OWN FOOD? WASH MY OWN DISHES? I'D HAVE TO WORK HARD TO MAKE A LIVING. I'D HAVE TO START FROM THE BOTTOM.

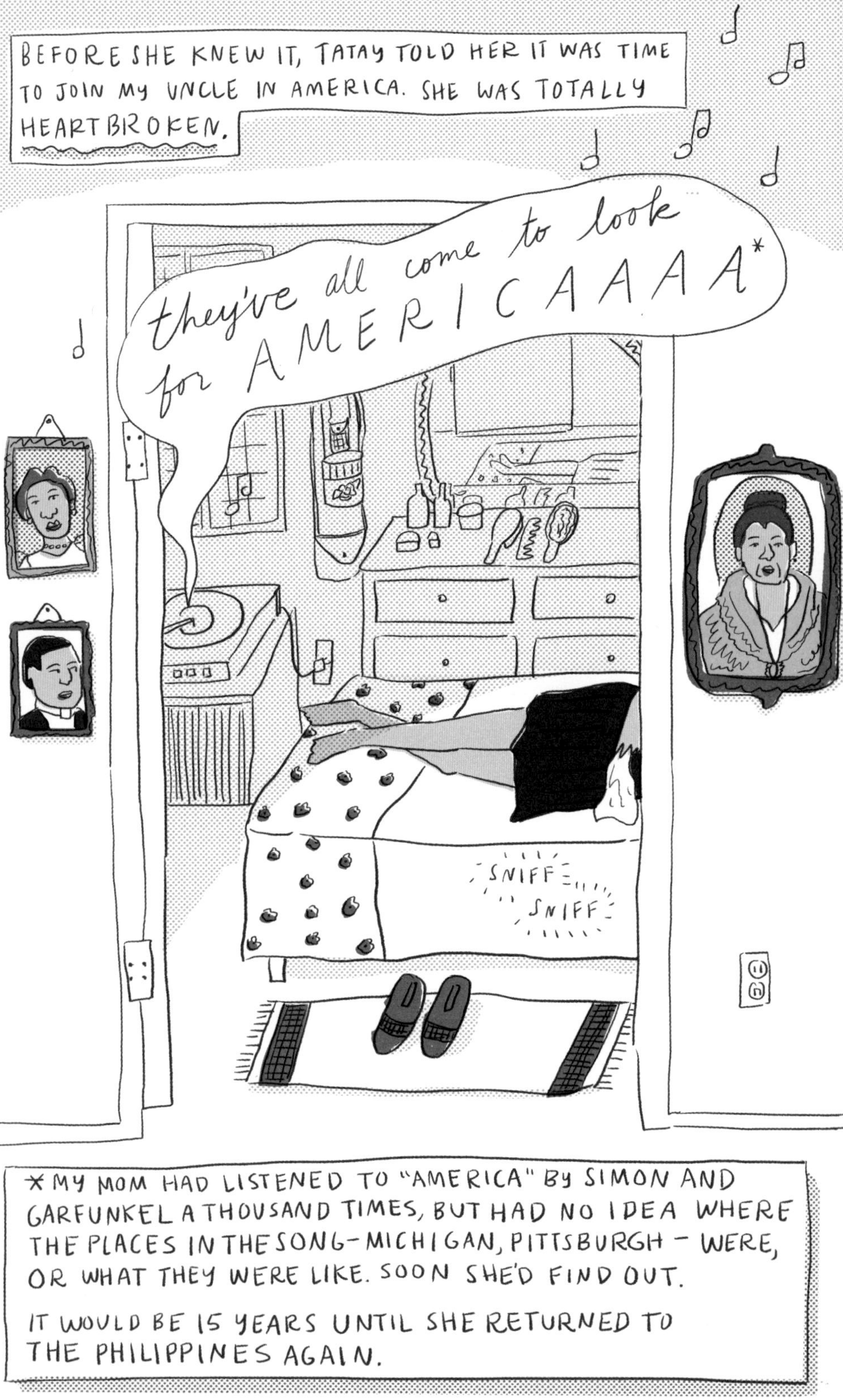
BEFORE SHE KNEW IT, TATAY TOLD HER IT WAS TIME TO JOIN MY UNCLE IN AMERICA. SHE WAS TOTALLY HEARTBROKEN.
they've all come to look for AMERICAAAA*
SNIFF SNIFF
* MY MOM HAD LISTENED TO "AMERICA" BY SIMON AND GARFUNKEL A THOUSAND TIMES, BUT HAD NO IDEA WHERE THE PLACES IN THE SONG - MICHIGAN, PITTSBURGH - WERE, OR WHAT THEY WERE LIKE. SOON SHE'D FIND OUT.
IT WOULD BE 15 YEARS UNTIL SHE RETURNED TO THE PHILIPPINES AGAIN.

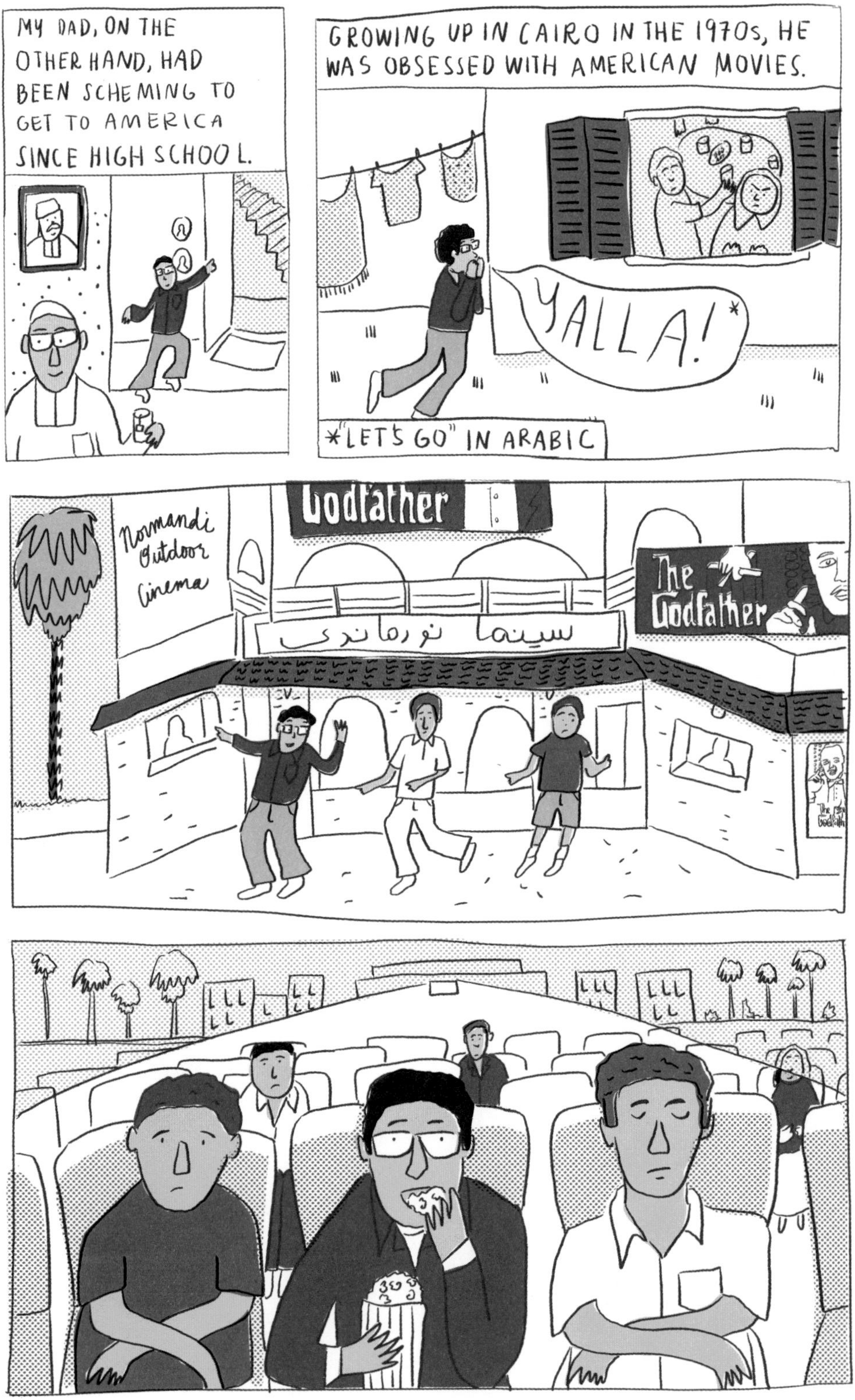
MY DAD, ON THE OTHER HAND, HAD BEEN SCHEMING TO GET TO AMERICA SINCE HIGH SCHOOL.
GROWING UP IN CAIRO IN THE 1970s, HE WAS OBSESSED WITH AMERICAN MOVIES.
YALLA!*
*"LET'S GO" IN ARABIC
Godfather
Normandi Outdoor Cinema
The Godfather
سينما نورماندى

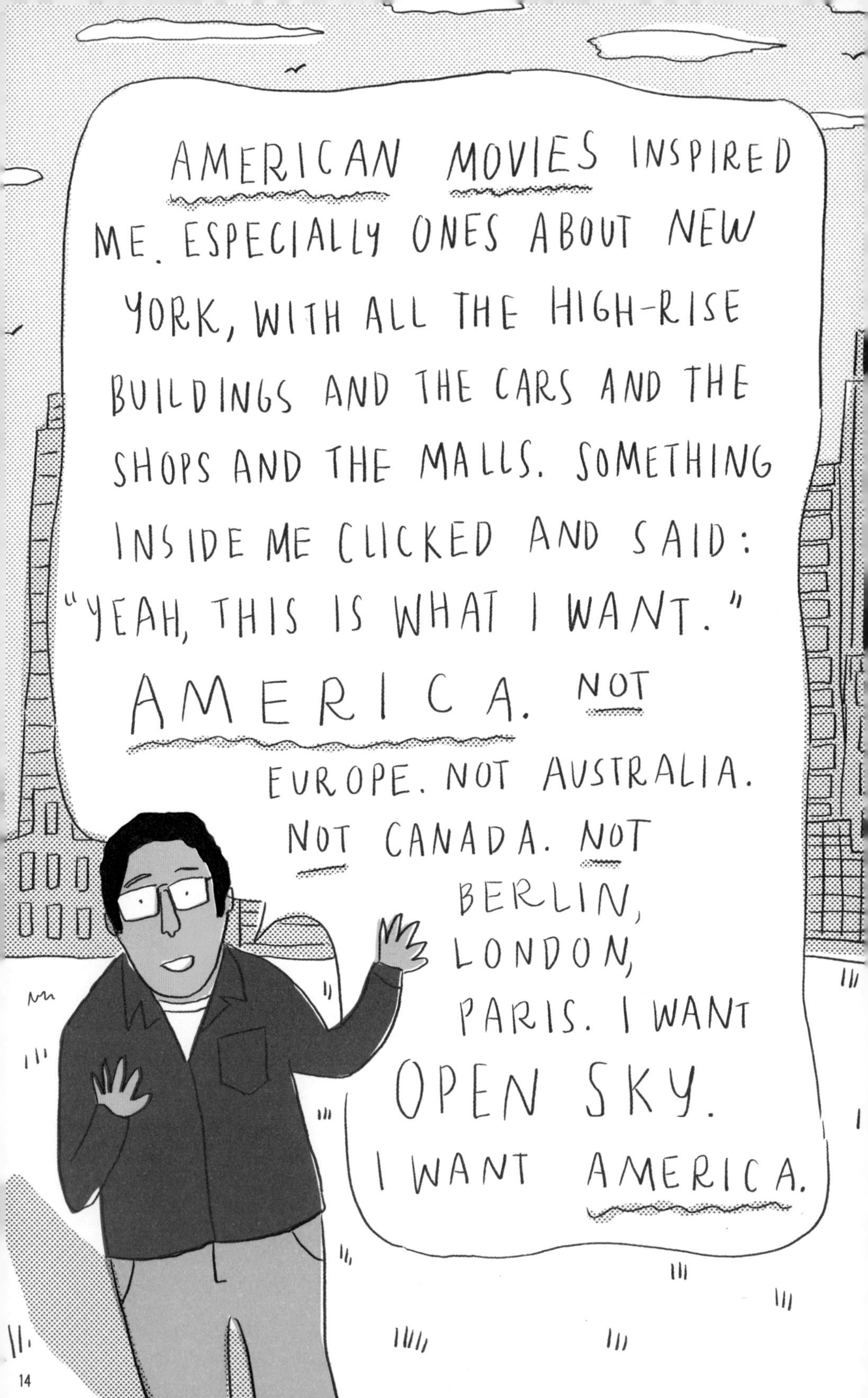
AMERICAN MOVIES INSPIRED ME. ESPECIALLY ONES ABOUT NEW YORK, WITH ALL THE HIGH-RISE BUILDINGS AND THE CARS AND THE SHOPS AND THE MALLS. SOMETHING INSIDE ME CLICKED AND SAID: "YEAH, THIS IS WHAT I WANT." AMERICA. NOT EUROPE. NOT AUSTRALIA. NOT CANADA. NOT BERLIN, LONDON, PARIS. I WANT OPEN SKY. I WANT AMERICA.

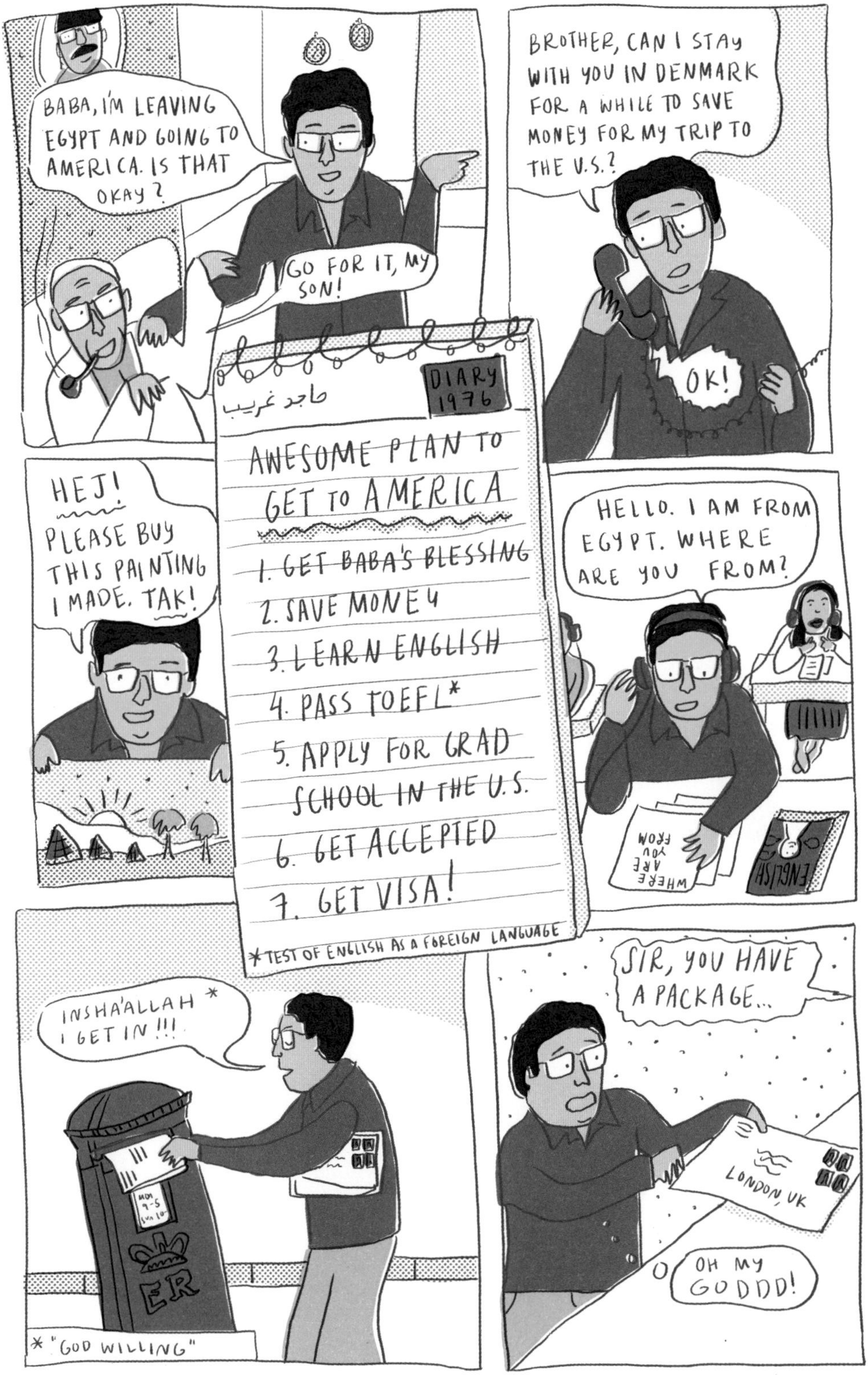

BABA, I'M LEAVING EGYPT AND GOING TO AMERICA. IS THAT OKAY?
GO FOR IT, MY SON!
BROTHER, CAN I STAY WITH YOU IN DENMARK FOR A WHILE TO SAVE MONEY FOR MY TRIP TO THE U.S.?
OK!
ماجد غريب
DIARY 1976
AWESOME PLAN TO GET TO AMERICA
1. GET BABA'S BLESSING
2. SAVE MONEY
3. LEARN ENGLISH
4. PASS TOEFL*
5. APPLY FOR GRAD SCHOOL IN THE U.S.
6. GET ACCEPTED
7. GET VISA!
*TEST OF ENGLISH AS A FOREIGN LANGUAGE
HEJ! PLEASE BUY THIS PAINTING I MADE. TAK!
HELLO. I AM FROM EGYPT. WHERE ARE YOU FROM?
WHERE ARE YOU FROM
ENGLISH
INSHA'ALLAH * I GET IN!!!
ER
*"GOD WILLING"
SIR, YOU HAVE A PACKAGE...
LONDON, UK
OH MY GODDD!

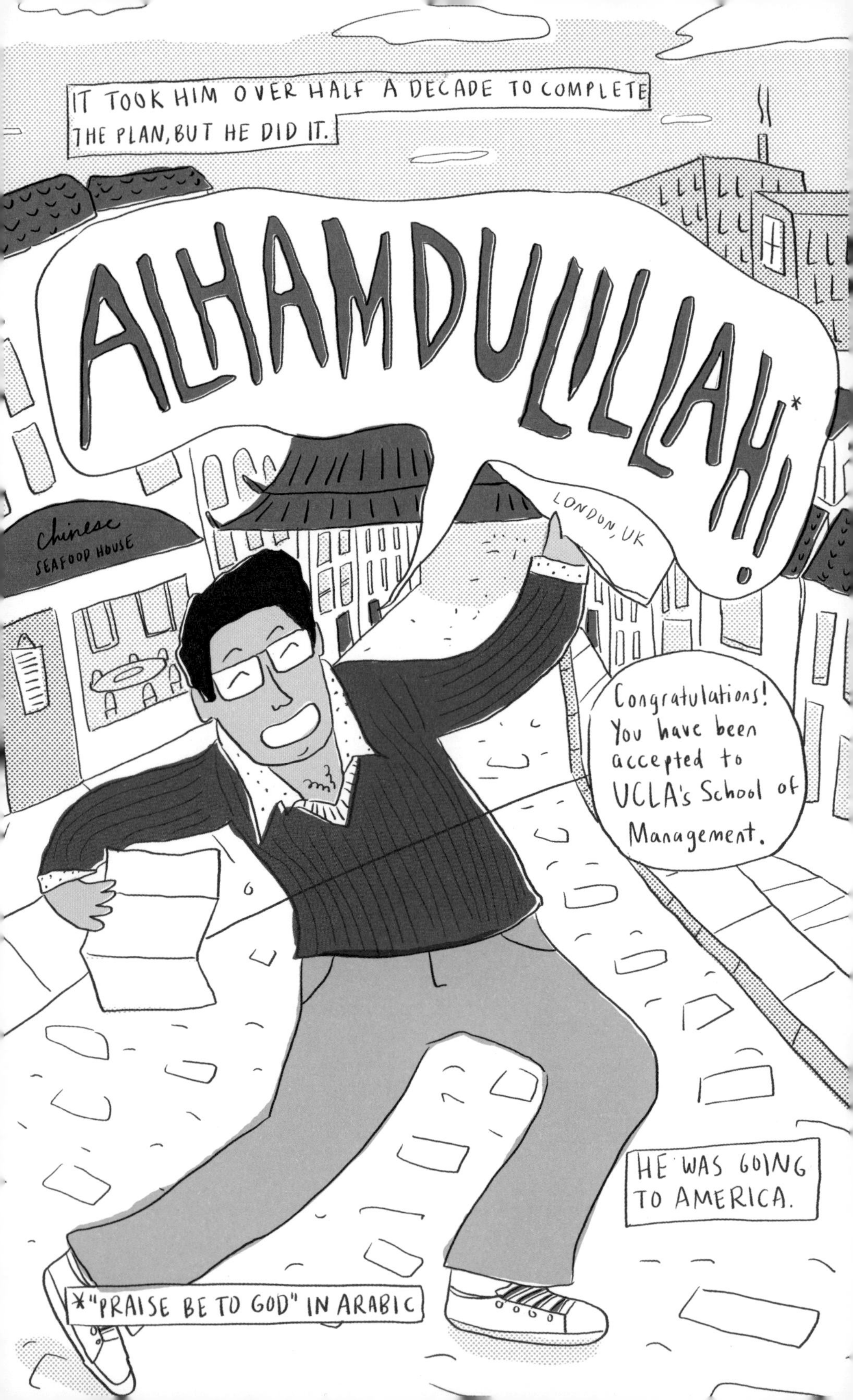
IT TOOK HIM OVER HALF A DECADE TO COMPLETE THE PLAN, BUT HE DID IT.
ALHAMDULILLAH!*
LONDON, UK
Chinese SEAFOOD HOUSE
Congratulations! You have been accepted to UCLA's School of Management.
HE WAS GOING TO AMERICA.
*"PRAISE BE TO GOD" IN ARABIC

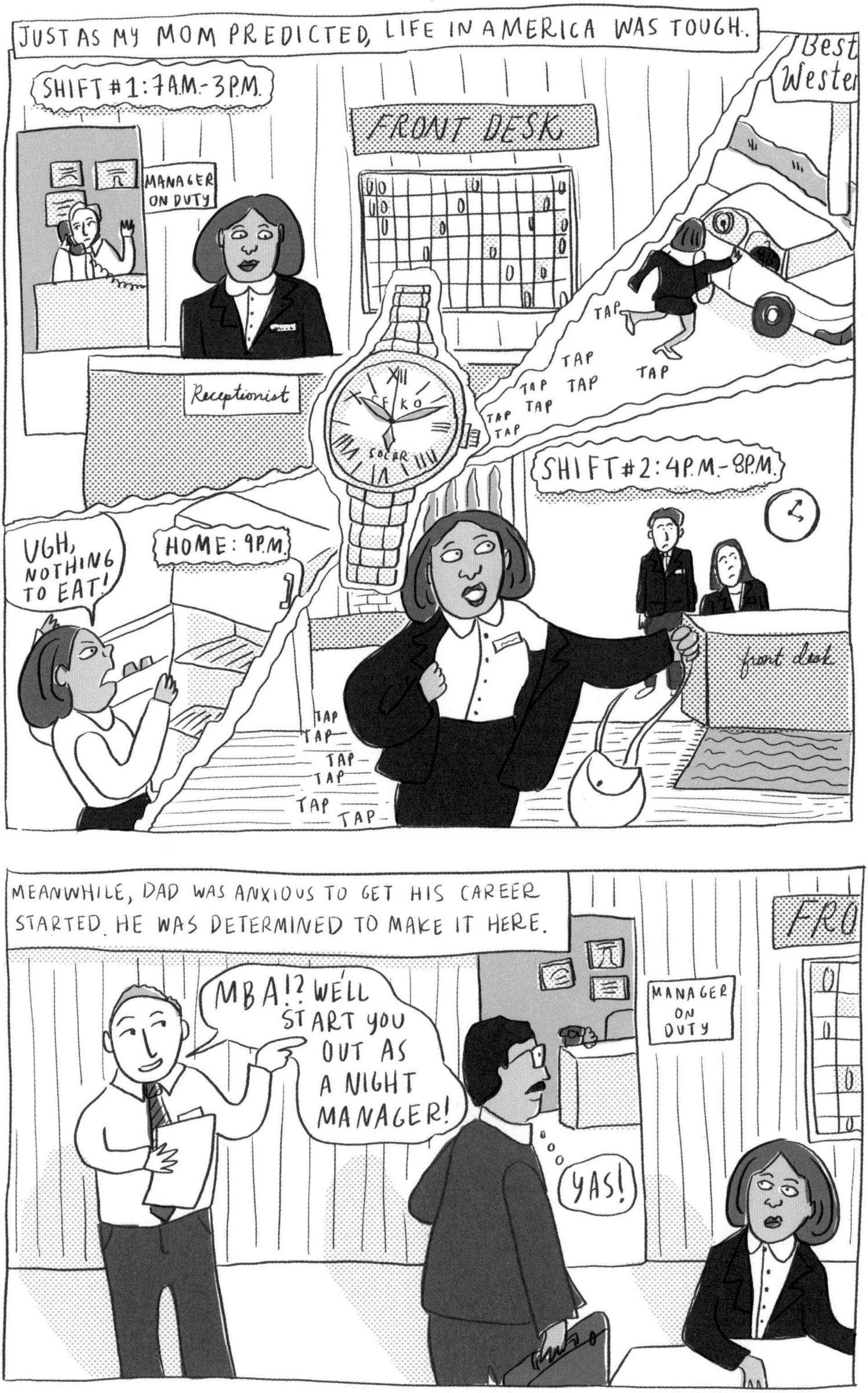
JUST AS MY MOM PREDICTED, LIFE IN AMERICA WAS TOUGH.
SHIFT #1: 7A.M.-3P.M.
FRONT DESK
MANAGER ON DUTY
Receptionist
SEIKO
SOLAR
Best Western
TAP TAP TAP TAP TAP TAP TAP TAP
SHIFT #2: 4P.M.-8P.M.
front desk
TAP TAP TAP TAP TAP TAP
HOME: 9P.M.
UGH, NOTHING TO EAT!
MEANWHILE, DAD WAS ANXIOUS TO GET HIS CAREER STARTED. HE WAS DETERMINED TO MAKE IT HERE.
FRO
MANAGER ON DUTY
MBA!? WE'LL START YOU OUT AS A NIGHT MANAGER!
YAS!

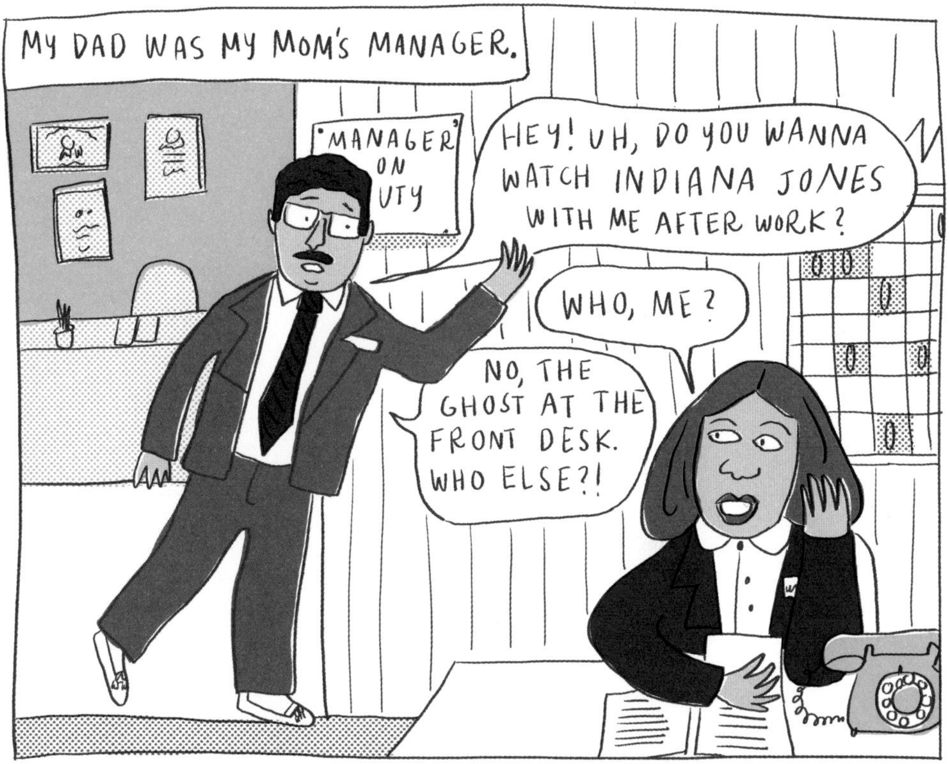
MY DAD WAS MY MOM'S MANAGER.
"MANAGER" ON UTY
HEY! UH, DO YOU WANNA WATCH INDIANA JONES WITH ME AFTER WORK?
WHO, ME?
NO, THE GHOST AT THE FRONT DESK. WHO ELSE?!

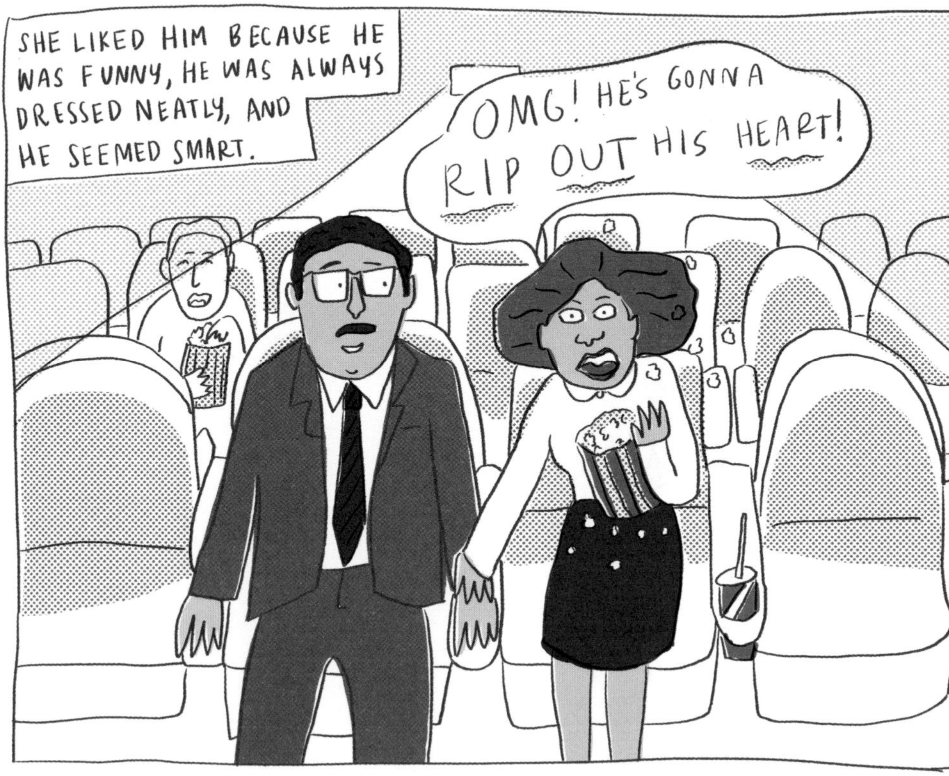
SHE LIKED HIM BECAUSE HE WAS FUNNY, HE WAS ALWAYS DRESSED NEATLY, AND HE SEEMED SMART.
OMG! HE'S GONNA RIP OUT HIS HEART!

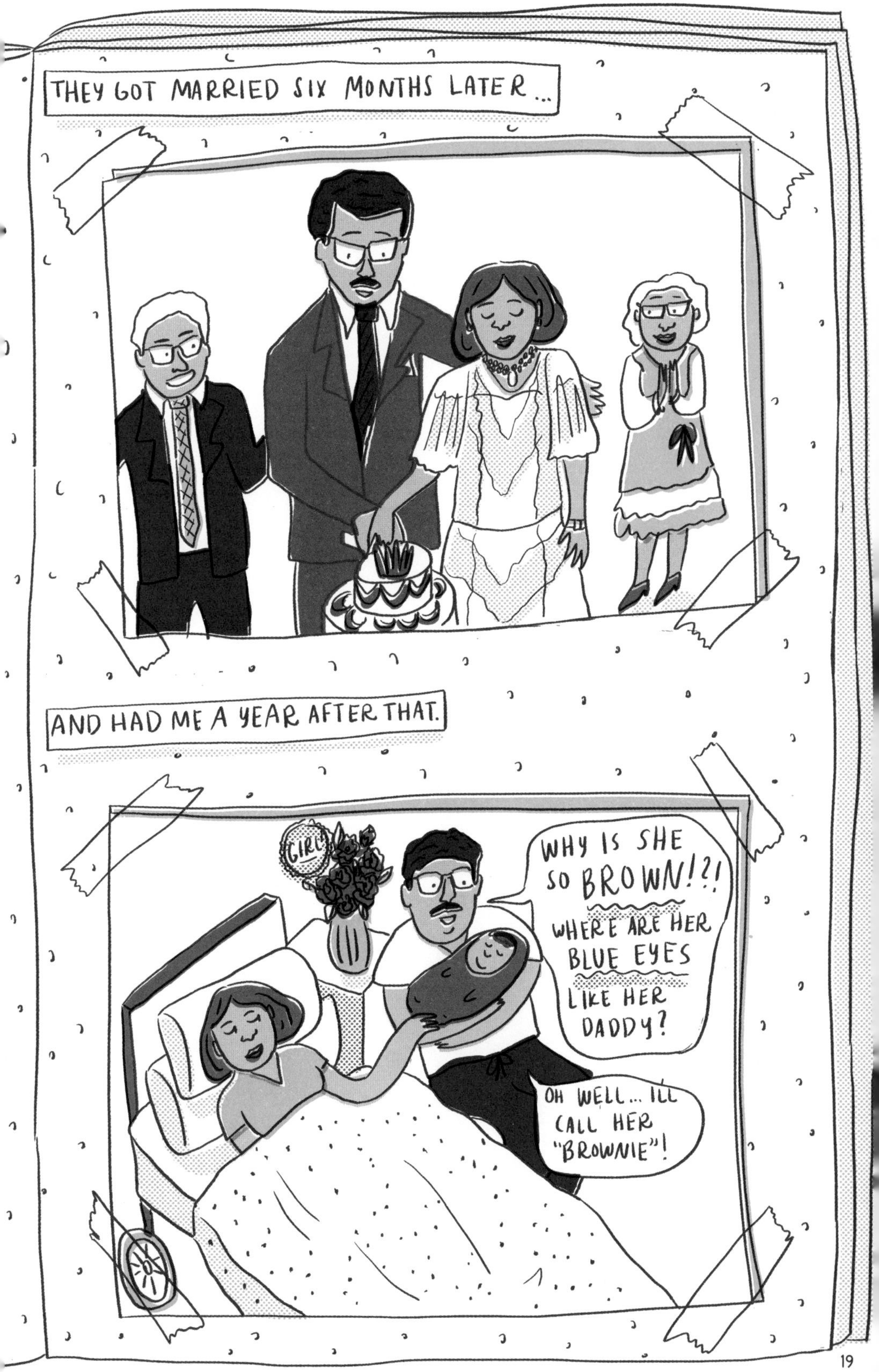
THEY GOT MARRIED SIX MONTHS LATER...
AND HAD ME A YEAR AFTER THAT.
GIRL!
WHY IS SHE SO BROWN!?! WHERE ARE HER BLUE EYES LIKE HER DADDY?
OH WELL... ILL CALL HER "BROWNIE"!

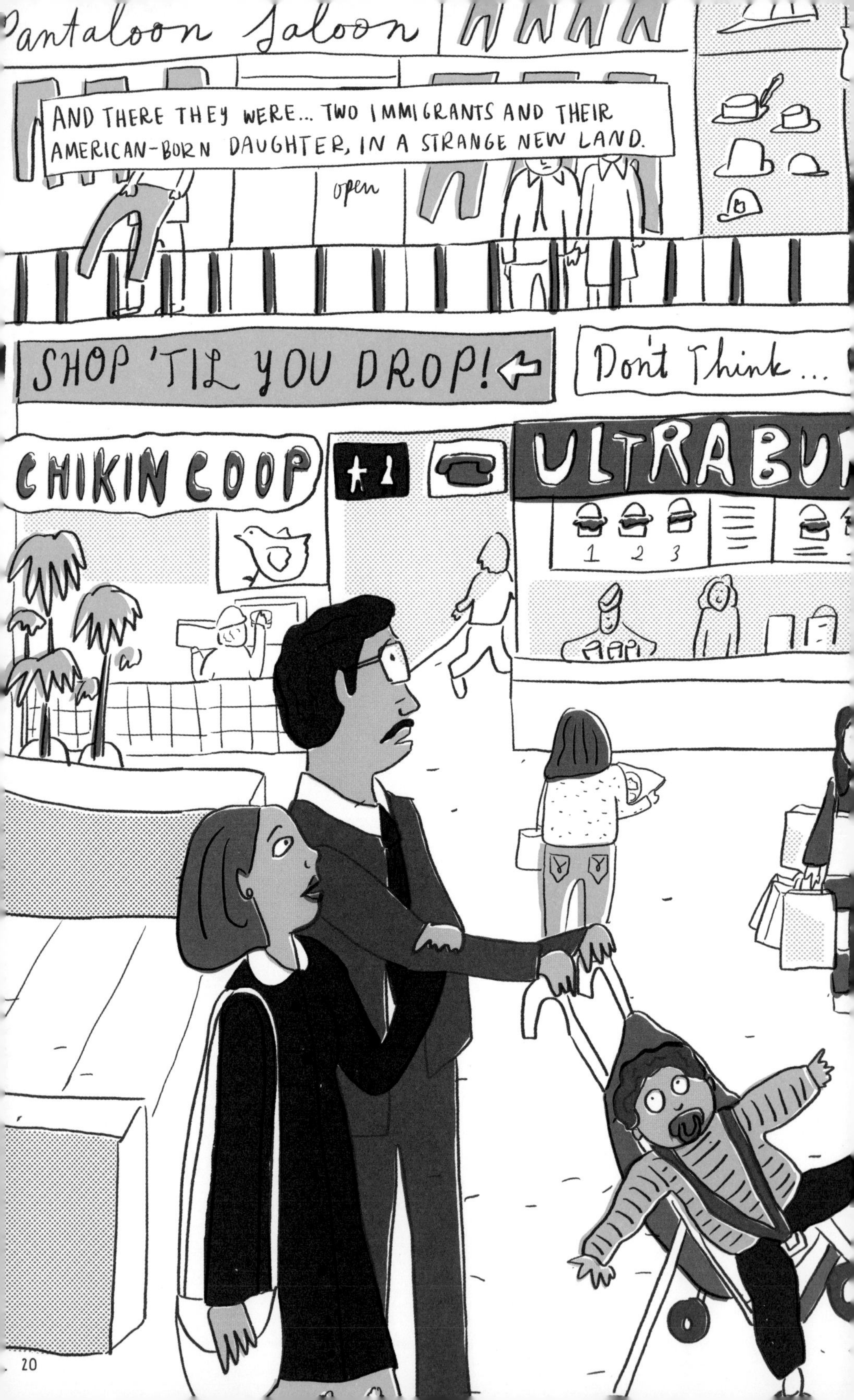
Pantaloon Saloon
AND THERE THEY WERE... TWO IMMIGRANTS AND THEIR AMERICAN-BORN DAUGHTER, IN A STRANGE NEW LAND.
open
SHOP 'TIL YOU DROP!
Don't Think...
CHIKIN COOP
ULTRABU
1 2 3

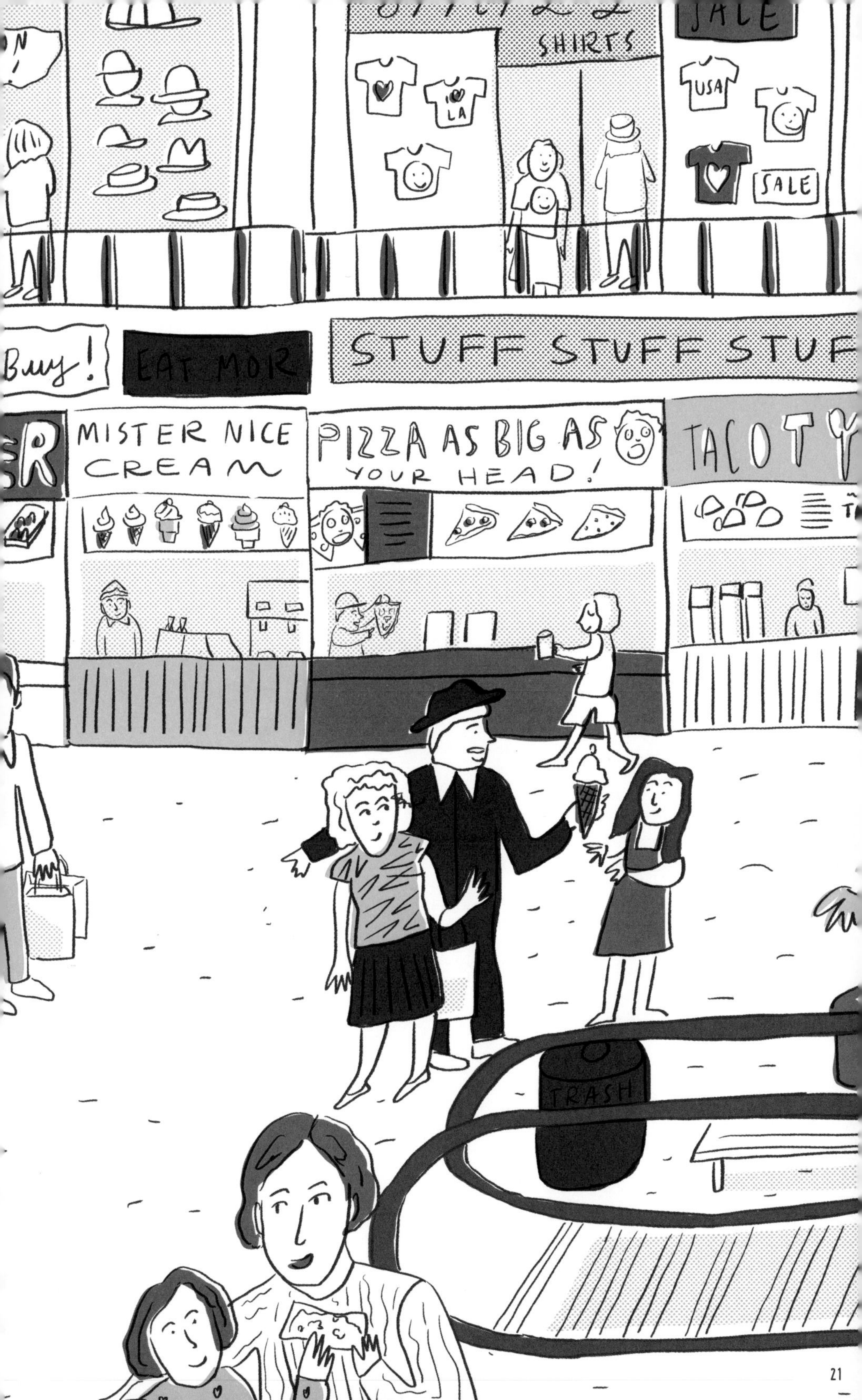
SHIRTS
SALE
I ♥ LA
USA
SALE
Buy!
EAT MOR
STUFF STUFF STUF
MISTER NICE CREAM
PIZZA AS BIG AS YOUR HEAD!
TACOTY
TRASH

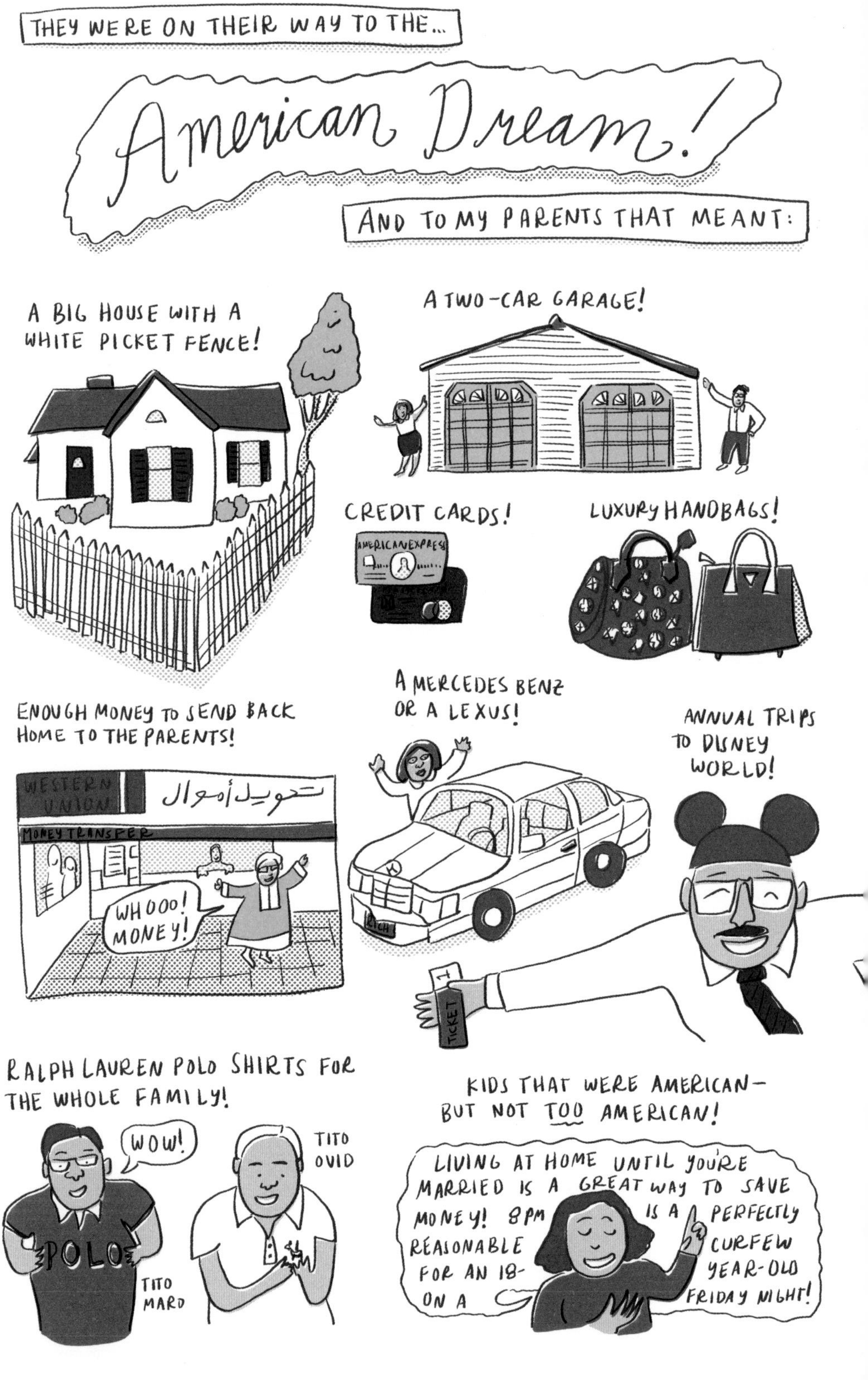
THEY WERE ON THEIR WAY TO THE...
American Dream!
AND TO MY PARENTS THAT MEANT:
A BIG HOUSE WITH A WHITE PICKET FENCE!
A TWO-CAR GARAGE!
CREDIT CARDS!
AMERICAN EXPRESS
LUXURY HANDBAGS!
ENOUGH MONEY TO SEND BACK HOME TO THE PARENTS!
WESTERN UNION
تحويل أموال
MONEY TRANSFER
WHOOO! MONEY!
A MERCEDES BENZ OR A LEXUS!
RICH
ANNUAL TRIPS TO DISNEY WORLD!
TICKET
RALPH LAUREN POLO SHIRTS FOR THE WHOLE FAMILY!
WOW!
POLO
TITO MARD
TITO OVID
KIDS THAT WERE AMERICAN— BUT NOT TOO AMERICAN!
LIVING AT HOME UNTIL YOU'RE MARRIED IS A GREAT WAY TO SAVE MONEY! 8PM IS A PERFECTLY REASONABLE CURFEW FOR AN 18-YEAR-OLD ON A FRIDAY NIGHT!

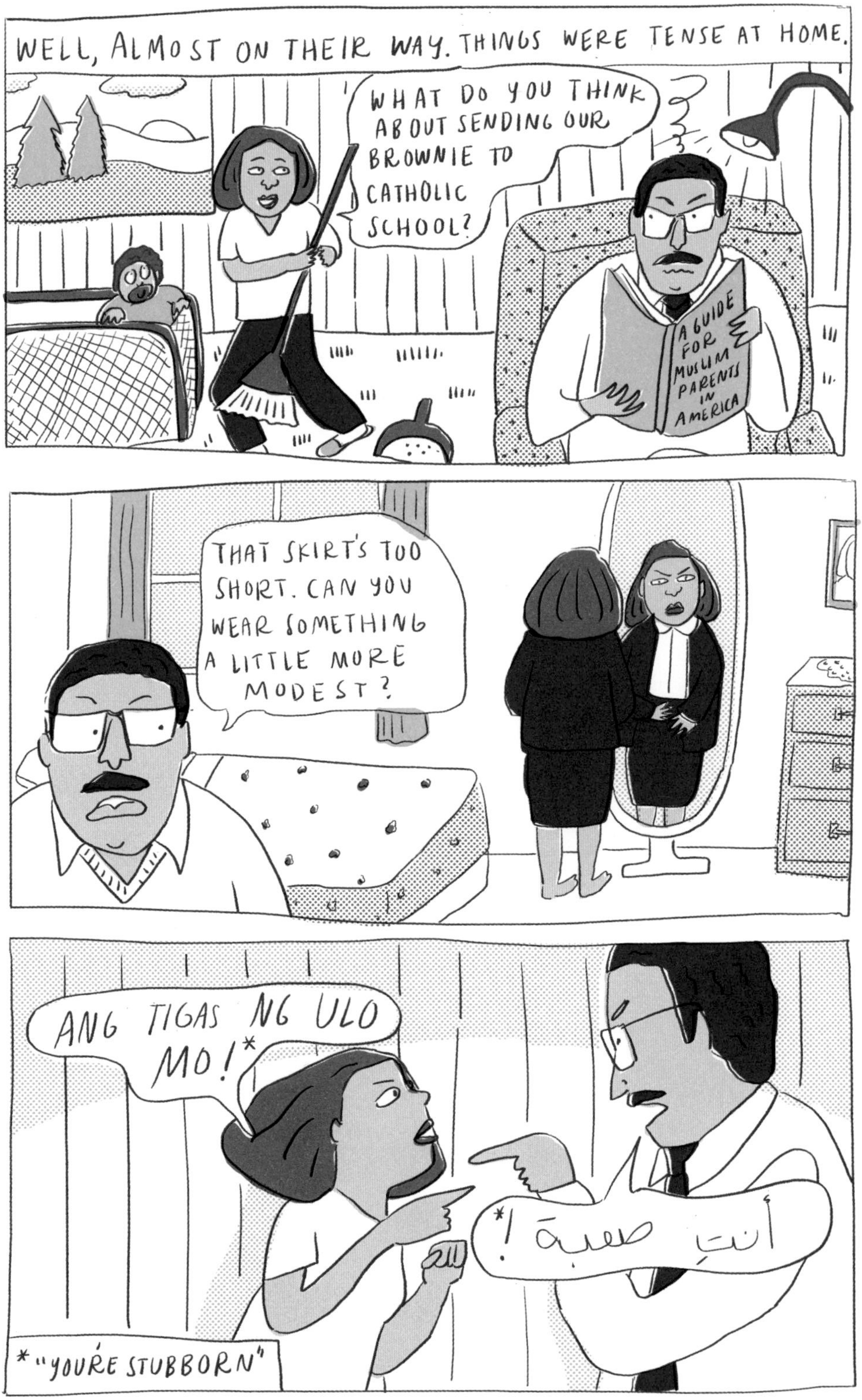
WELL, ALMOST ON THEIR WAY. THINGS WERE TENSE AT HOME.
WHAT DO YOU THINK ABOUT SENDING OUR BROWNIE TO CATHOLIC SCHOOL?
A GUIDE FOR MUSLIM PARENTS IN AMERICA
THAT SKIRT'S TOO SHORT. CAN YOU WEAR SOMETHING A LITTLE MORE MODEST?
ANG TIGAS NG ULO MO!*
أنتِ صعبة!*
*"YOU'RE STUBBORN"

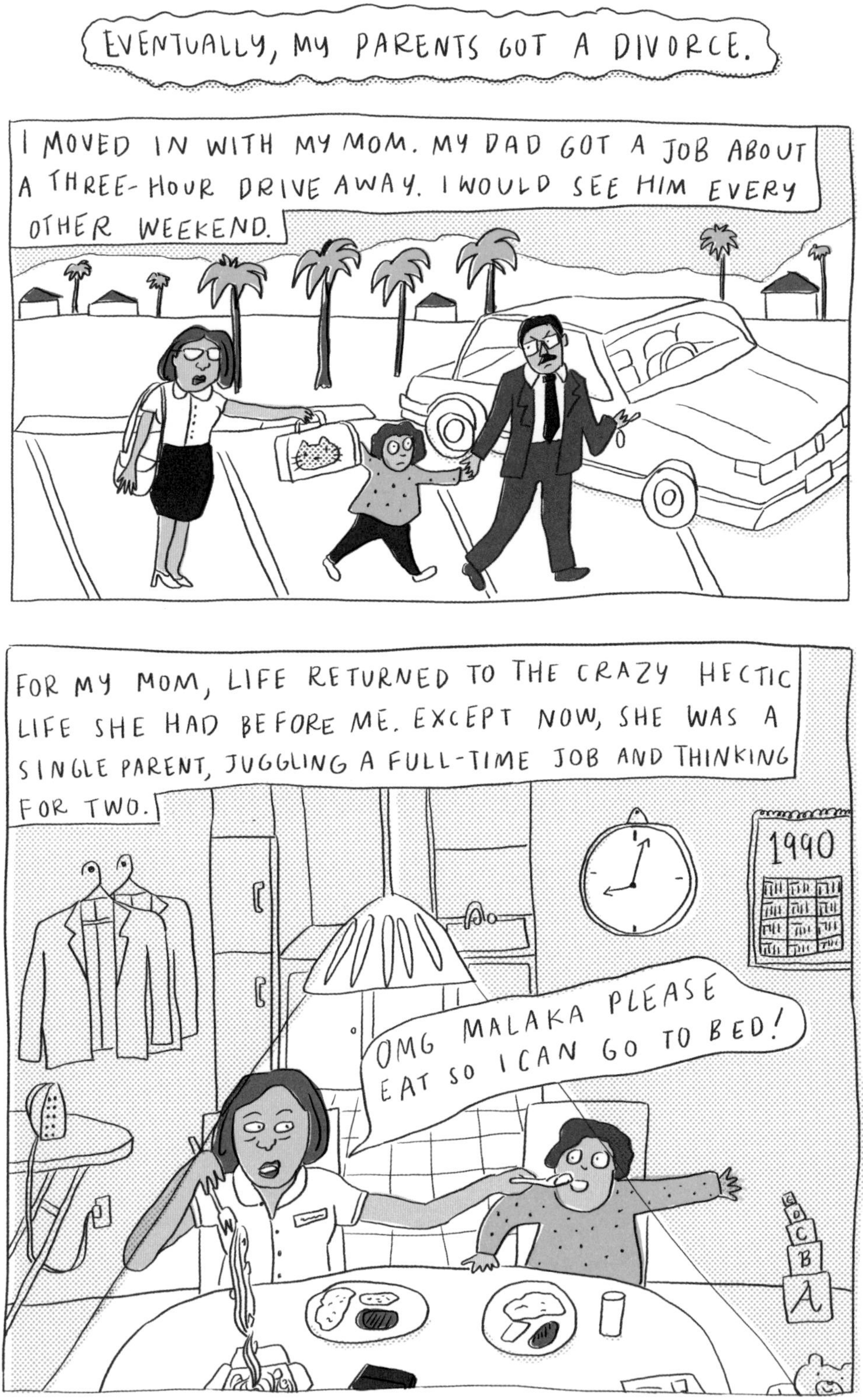
EVENTUALLY, MY PARENTS GOT A DIVORCE.
I MOVED IN WITH MY MOM. MY DAD GOT A JOB ABOUT A THREE-HOUR DRIVE AWAY. I WOULD SEE HIM EVERY OTHER WEEKEND.
FOR MY MOM, LIFE RETURNED TO THE CRAZY HECTIC LIFE SHE HAD BEFORE ME. EXCEPT NOW, SHE WAS A SINGLE PARENT, JUGGLING A FULL-TIME JOB AND THINKING FOR TWO.
1990
OMG MALAKA PLEASE EAT SO I CAN GO TO BED!

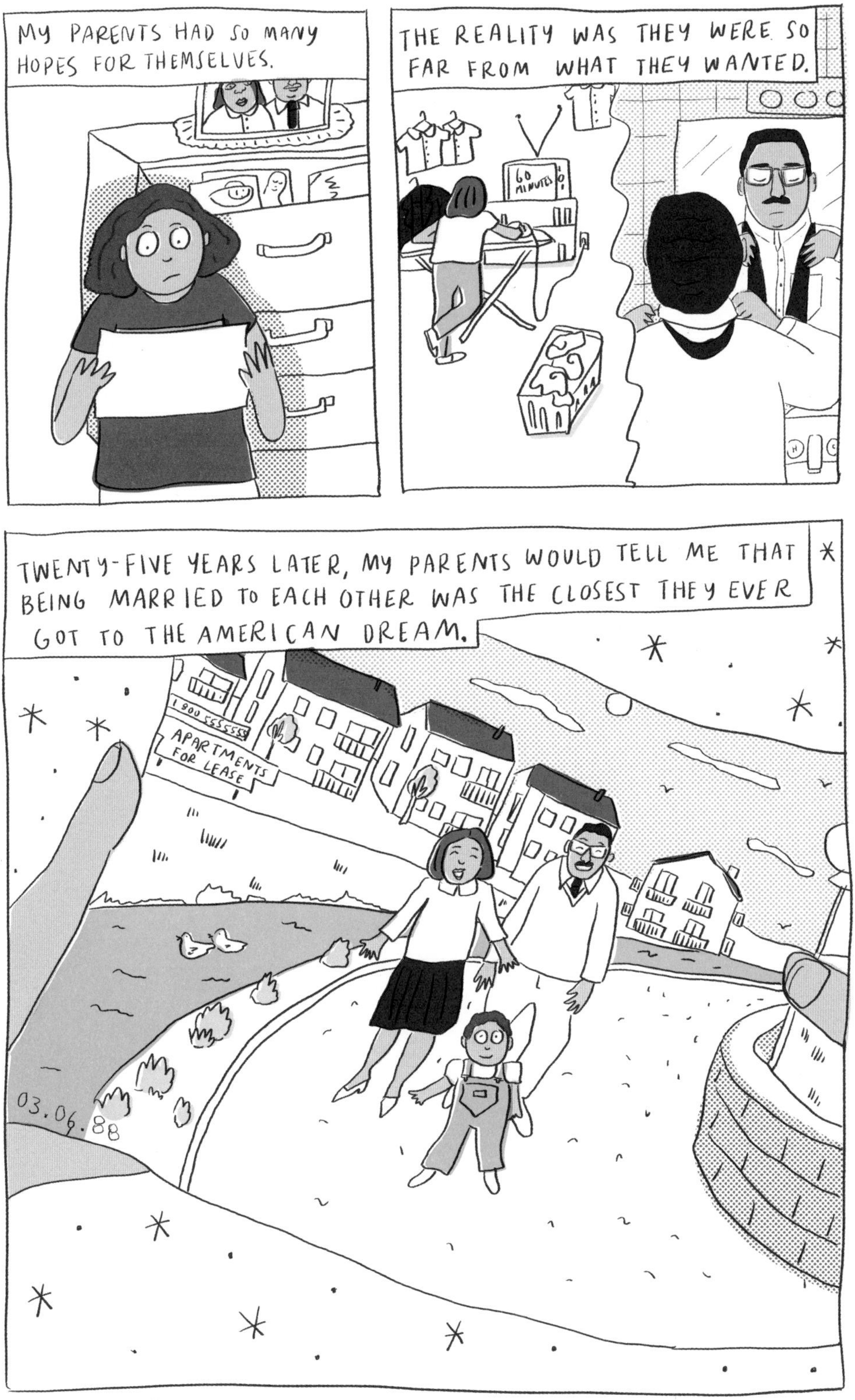
MY PARENTS HAD SO MANY HOPES FOR THEMSELVES.
THE REALITY WAS THEY WERE SO FAR FROM WHAT THEY WANTED.
60 MINUTES
TWENTY-FIVE YEARS LATER, MY PARENTS WOULD TELL ME THAT BEING MARRIED TO EACH OTHER WAS THE CLOSEST THEY EVER GOT TO THE AMERICAN DREAM.
1 800 555555
APARTMENTS FOR LEASE
03.06.88

Chapter 2

MY FAMILY DIDN'T LOOK LIKE THE ONES ON TV.

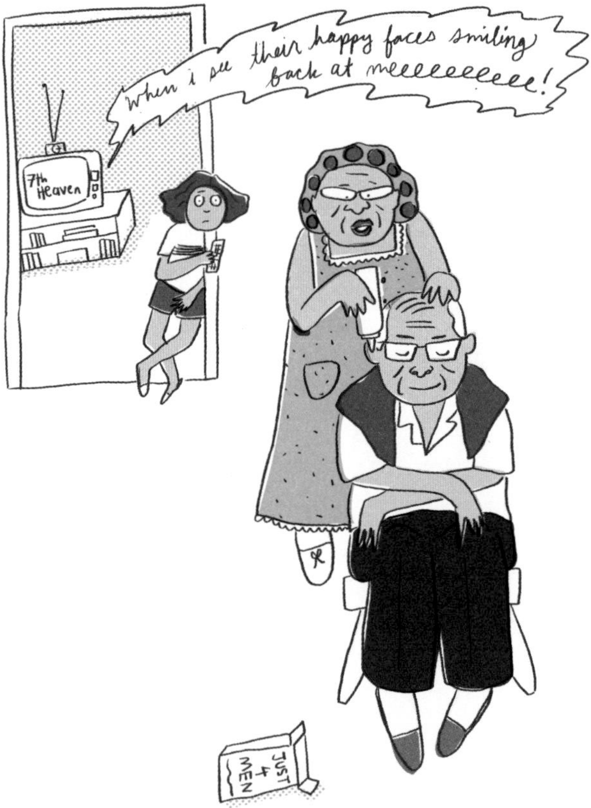
When i see their happy faces smiling back at meeeeeeeee!
7th Heaven
JUST 4 MEN

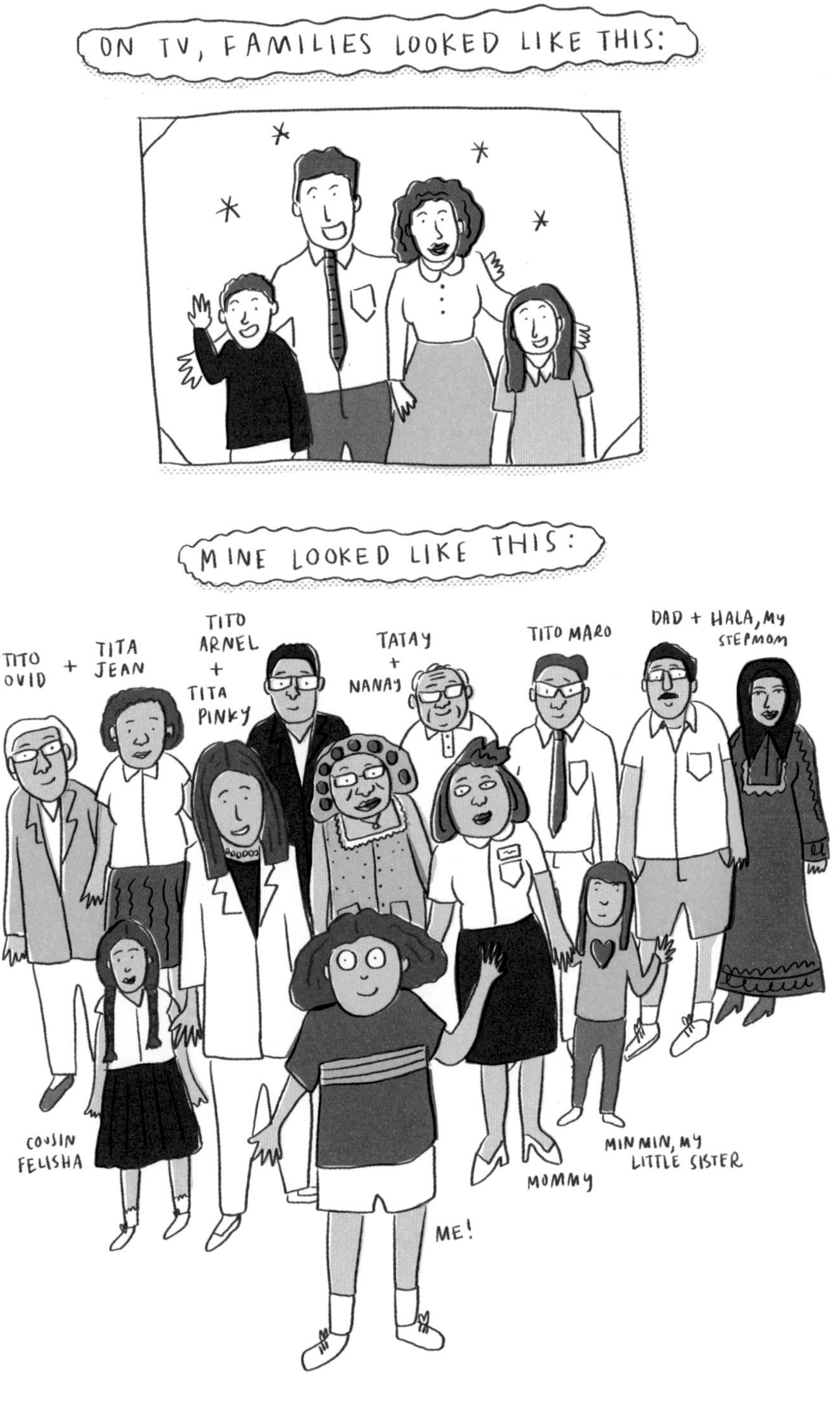
ON TV, FAMILIES LOOKED LIKE THIS:
MINE LOOKED LIKE THIS:
TITO OVID + TITA JEAN
TITO ARNEL + TITA PINKY
TATAY + NANAY
TITO MARO
DAD + HALA, MY STEPMOM
COUSIN FELISHA
MOMMY
MIN MIN, MY LITTLE SISTER
ME!

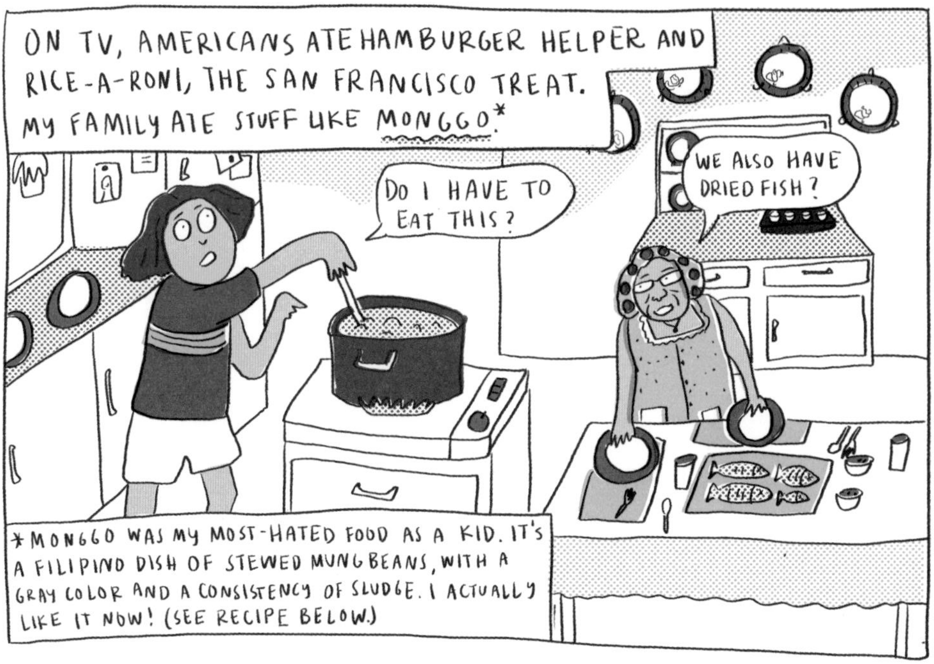
ON TV, AMERICANS ATE HAMBURGER HELPER AND RICE-A-RONI, THE SAN FRANCISCO TREAT. MY FAMILY ATE STUFF LIKE MONGGO*
DO I HAVE TO EAT THIS?
WE ALSO HAVE DRIED FISH?
*MONGGO WAS MY MOST-HATED FOOD AS A KID. IT'S A FILIPINO DISH OF STEWED MUNG BEANS, WITH A GRAY COLOR AND A CONSISTENCY OF SLUDGE. I ACTUALLY LIKE IT NOW! (SEE RECIPE BELOW.)

FABULOUS

Monggo!

Adapted from a recipe by Nora Daza. Serves 6. This is a popular weeknight dish, served with steamed rice and something crispy on the side (like fried fish or pork belly).

INGREDIENTS

1 cup mung beans, soaked overnight
4 cups water
2 cloves garlic, minced
3 tomatoes, chopped
1 onion, chopped
1 tbsp olive oil
2 tbsp shrimp paste
½ c pork, boiled and sliced into bite-size pieces
½ cup shrimp, peeled and sliced
2 cups spinach
fish sauce and pepper to taste

DIRECTIONS

- Boil mung beans in water until tender.
- Sauté garlic, tomatoes, and onion until soft in some oil. Add shrimp and pork and stir for a minute.
- Add mung beans and shrimp paste. Add the 4 cups of water and let simmer for 15 minutes.
- Season with fish sauce and pepper to taste.
- Add spinach and cook until wilted.
- Serve immediately, like this:

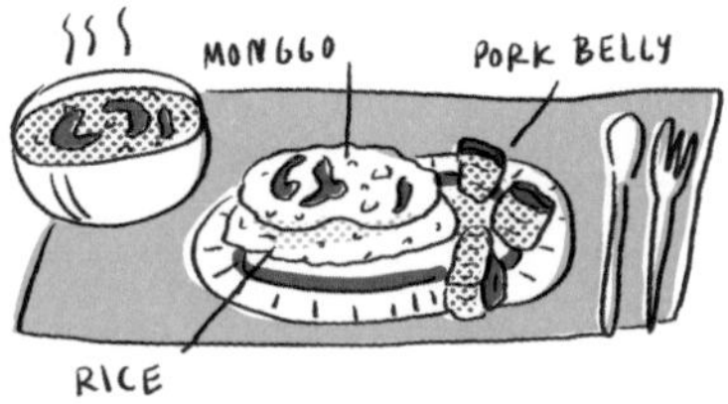
MONGGO
PORK BELLY
RICE

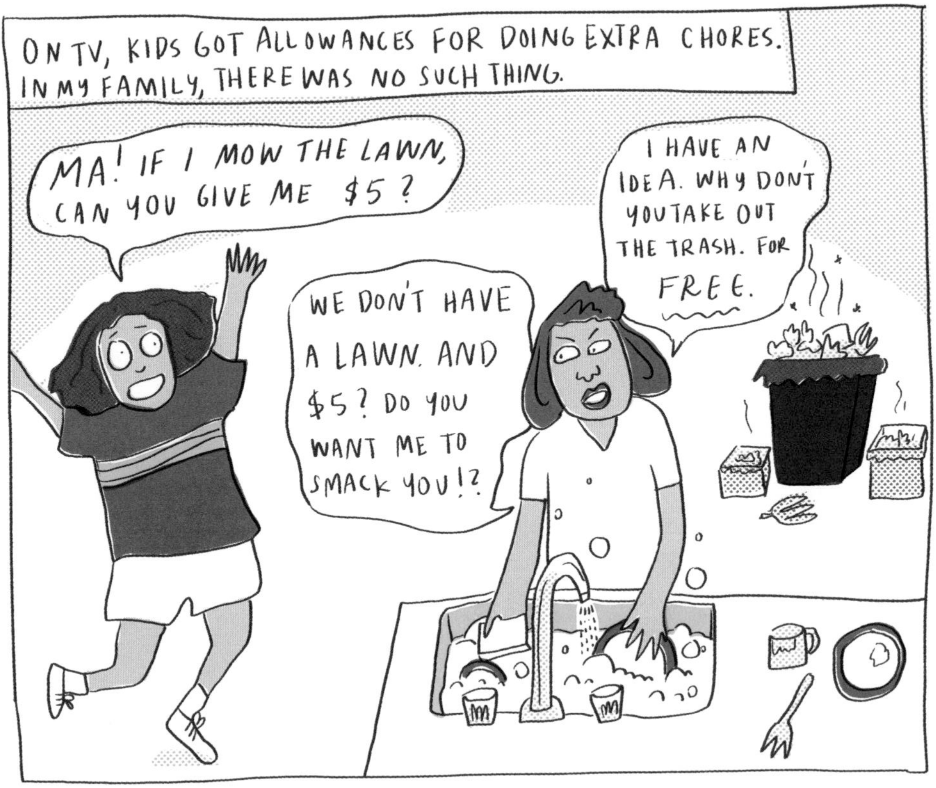
ON TV, KIDS GOT ALLOWANCES FOR DOING EXTRA CHORES. IN MY FAMILY, THERE WAS NO SUCH THING.
MA! IF I MOW THE LAWN, CAN YOU GIVE ME $5?
WE DON'T HAVE A LAWN. AND $5? DO YOU WANT ME TO SMACK YOU!?
I HAVE AN IDEA. WHY DON'T YOU TAKE OUT THE TRASH. FOR FREE.

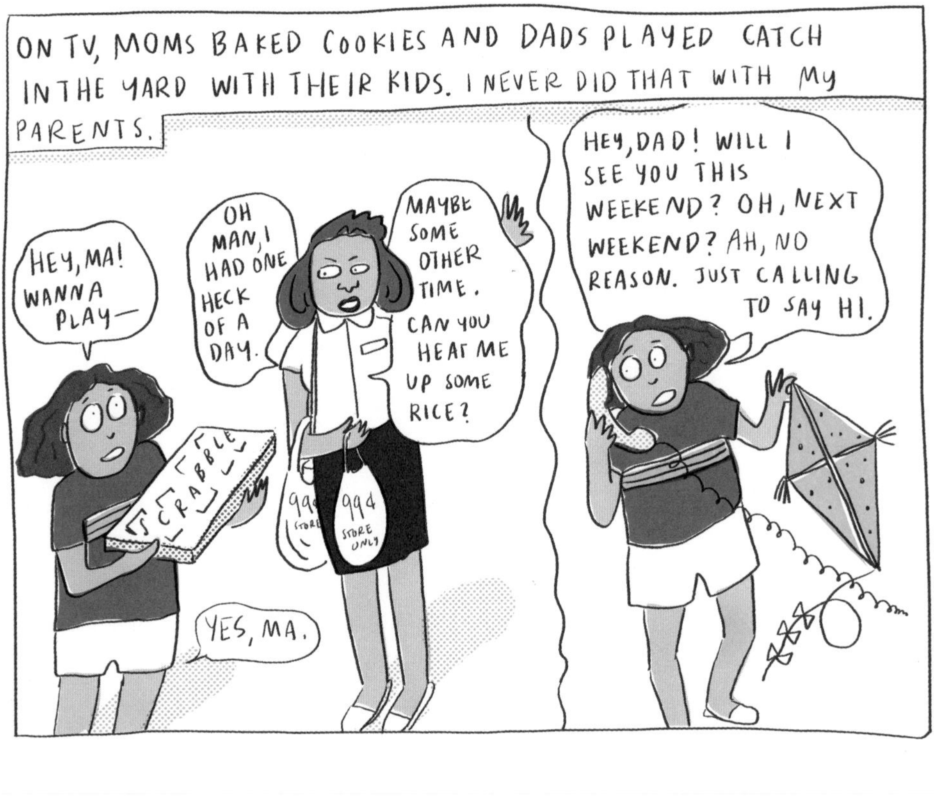
ON TV, MOMS BAKED COOKIES AND DADS PLAYED CATCH IN THE YARD WITH THEIR KIDS. I NEVER DID THAT WITH MY PARENTS.
HEY, MA! WANNA PLAY—
OH MAN, I HAD ONE HECK OF A DAY.
MAYBE SOME OTHER TIME. CAN YOU HEAT ME UP SOME RICE?
SCRABBLE
99¢ STORE ONLY
YES, MA.
HEY, DAD! WILL I SEE YOU THIS WEEKEND? OH, NEXT WEEKEND? AH, NO REASON. JUST CALLING TO SAY HI.

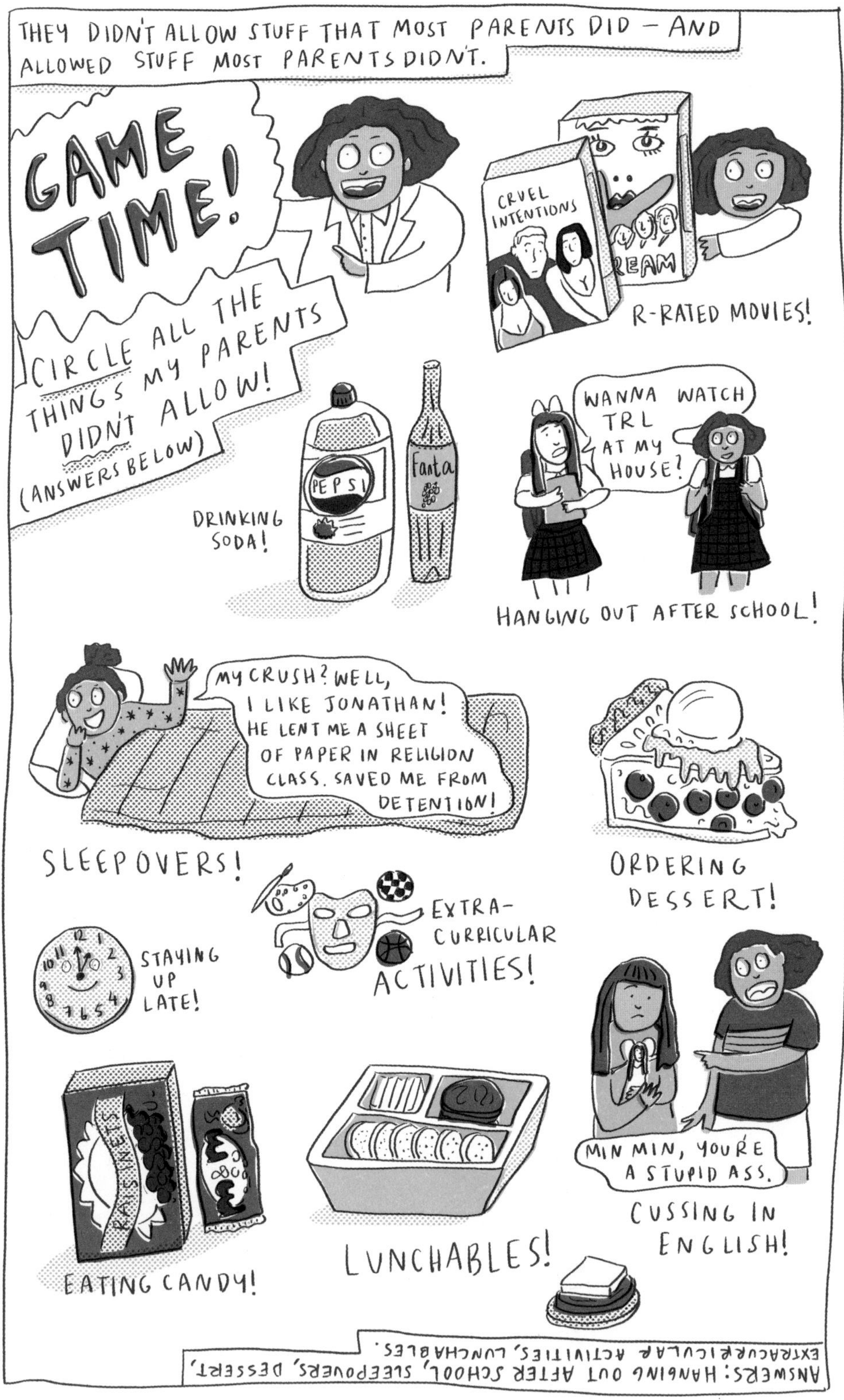

THEY DIDN'T ALLOW STUFF THAT MOST PARENTS DID — AND ALLOWED STUFF MOST PARENTS DIDN'T.
GAME TIME!
CIRCLE ALL THE THINGS MY PARENTS DIDN'T ALLOW! (ANSWERS BELOW)
CRUEL INTENTIONS
SCREAM
R-RATED MOVIES!
PEPSI
Fanta
DRINKING SODA!
WANNA WATCH TRL AT MY HOUSE?
HANGING OUT AFTER SCHOOL!
MY CRUSH? WELL, I LIKE JONATHAN! HE LENT ME A SHEET OF PAPER IN RELIGION CLASS. SAVED ME FROM DETENTION!
SLEEPOVERS!
ORDERING DESSERT!
EXTRA-CURRICULAR ACTIVITIES!
STAYING UP LATE!
MIN MIN, YOU'RE A STUPID ASS.
CUSSING IN ENGLISH!
RAISINETS
EATING CANDY!
LUNCHABLES!
ANSWERS: HANGING OUT AFTER SCHOOL, SLEEPOVERS, DESSERT, EXTRACURRICULAR ACTIVITIES, LUNCHABLES.

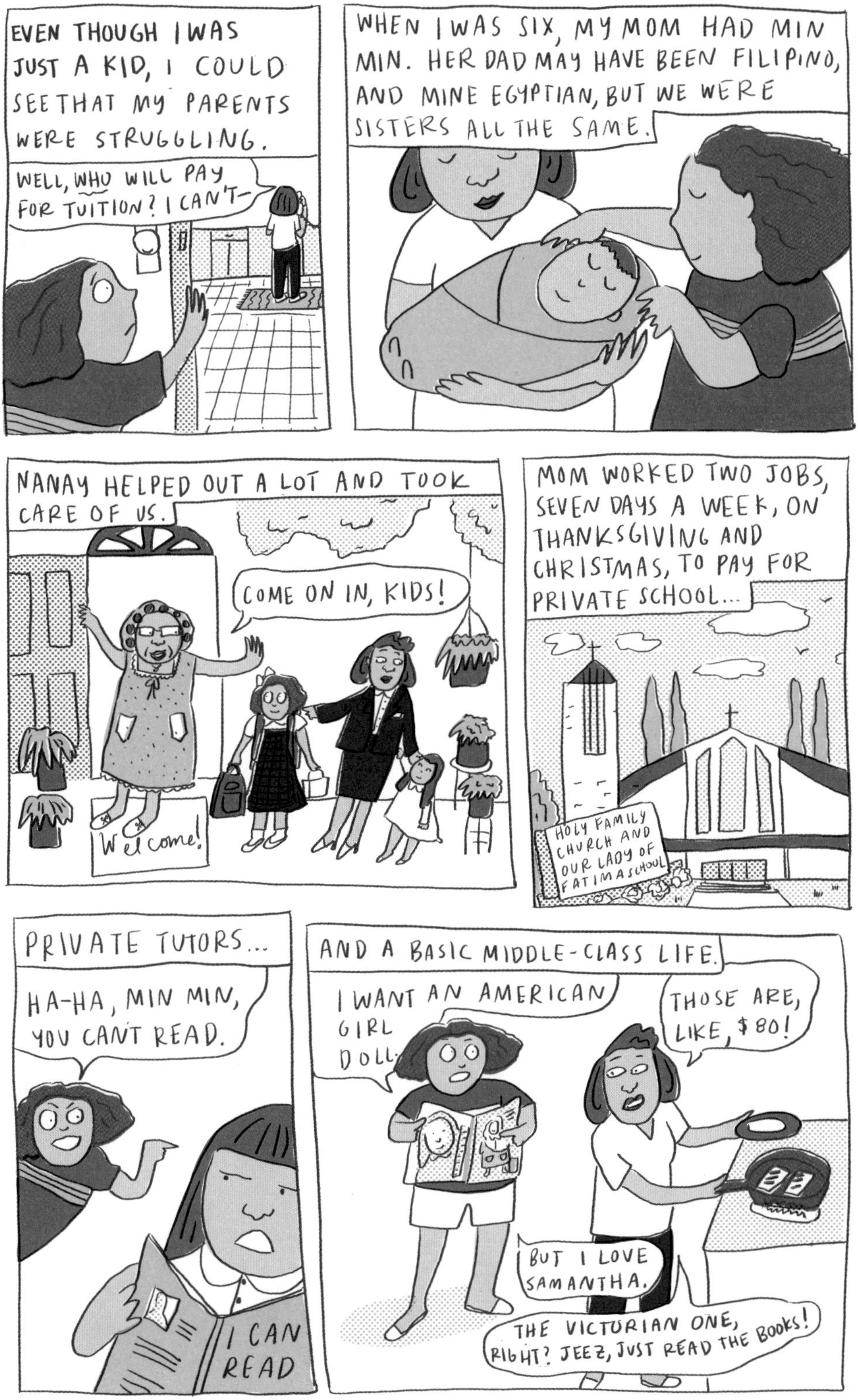
EVEN THOUGH I WAS JUST A KID, I COULD SEE THAT MY PARENTS WERE STRUGGLING.
WELL, WHO WILL PAY FOR TUITION? I CAN'T—
WHEN I WAS SIX, MY MOM HAD MIN MIN. HER DAD MAY HAVE BEEN FILIPINO, AND MINE EGYPTIAN, BUT WE WERE SISTERS ALL THE SAME.
NANAY HELPED OUT A LOT AND TOOK CARE OF US.
COME ON IN, KIDS!
Welcome!
MOM WORKED TWO JOBS, SEVEN DAYS A WEEK, ON THANKSGIVING AND CHRISTMAS, TO PAY FOR PRIVATE SCHOOL...
HOLY FAMILY CHURCH AND OUR LADY OF FATIMA SCHOOL
PRIVATE TUTORS...
HA-HA, MIN MIN, YOU CAN'T READ.
I CAN READ
AND A BASIC MIDDLE-CLASS LIFE.
I WANT AN AMERICAN GIRL DOLL.
THOSE ARE, LIKE, $80!
BUT I LOVE SAMANTHA.
THE VICTORIAN ONE, RIGHT? JEEZ, JUST READ THE BOOKS!

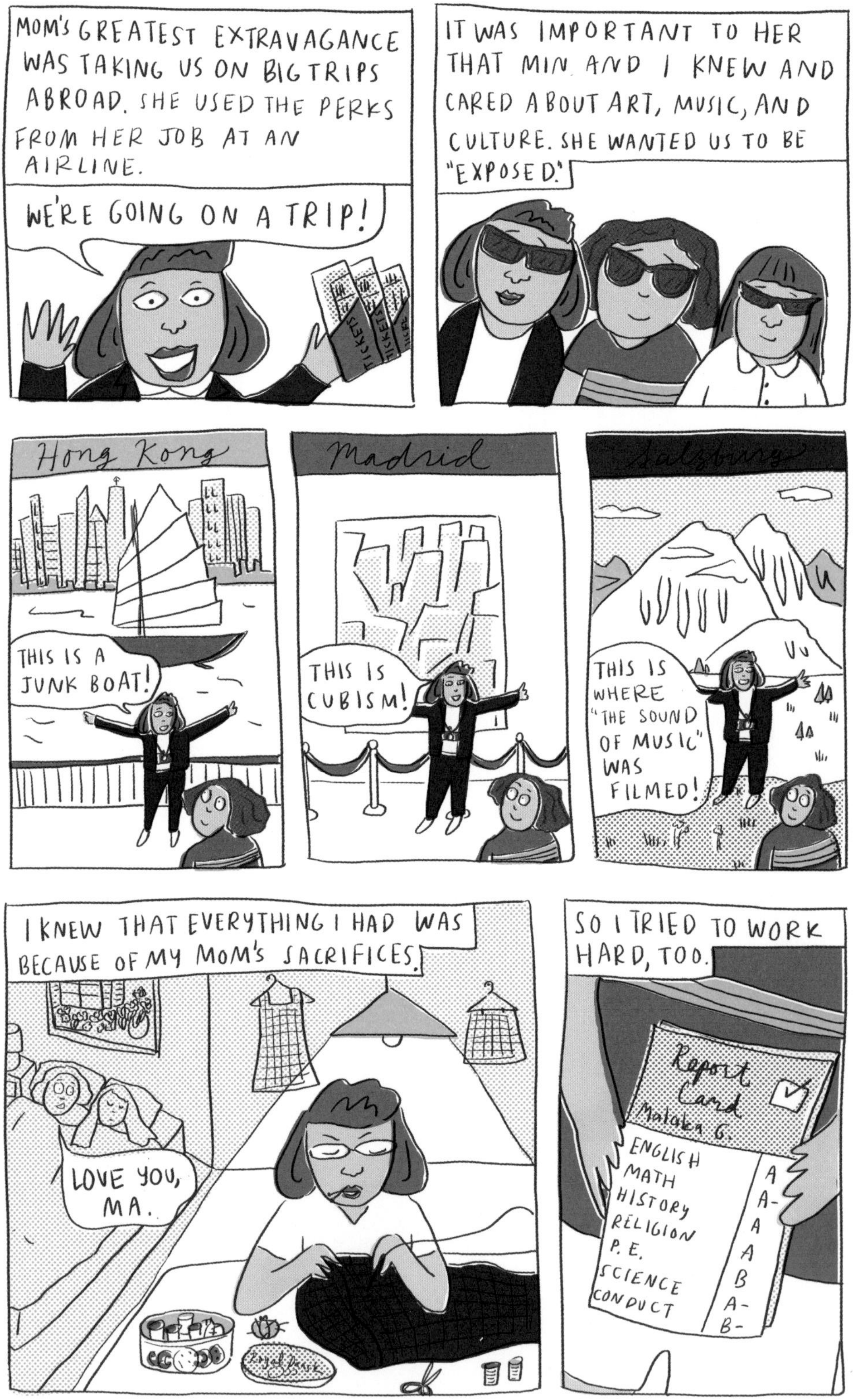
MOM'S GREATEST EXTRAVAGANCE WAS TAKING US ON BIG TRIPS ABROAD. SHE USED THE PERKS FROM HER JOB AT AN AIRLINE.
WE'RE GOING ON A TRIP!
TICKETS
IT WAS IMPORTANT TO HER THAT MIN AND I KNEW AND CARED ABOUT ART, MUSIC, AND CULTURE. SHE WANTED US TO BE "EXPOSED."
Hong Kong
THIS IS A JUNK BOAT!
Madrid
THIS IS CUBISM!
Salzburg
THIS IS WHERE "THE SOUND OF MUSIC" WAS FILMED!
I KNEW THAT EVERYTHING I HAD WAS BECAUSE OF MY MOM'S SACRIFICES.
LOVE YOU, MA.
SO I TRIED TO WORK HARD, TOO.
Report Card
ENGLISH A
MATH A-
HISTORY A
RELIGION A
P. E. B
SCIENCE A-
CONDUCT B-

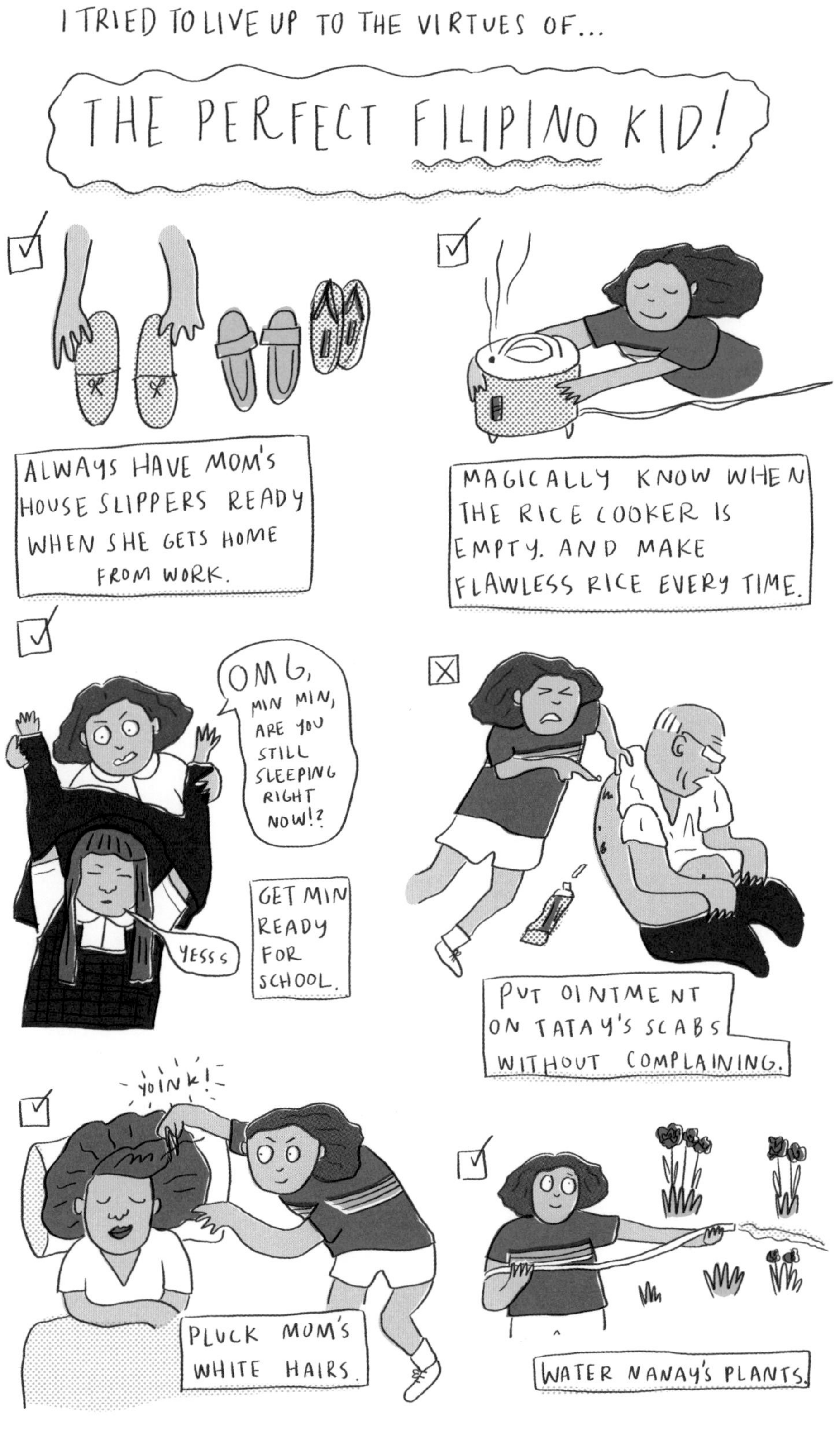
I TRIED TO LIVE UP TO THE VIRTUES OF...
THE PERFECT FILIPINO KID!
ALWAYS HAVE MOM'S HOUSE SLIPPERS READY WHEN SHE GETS HOME FROM WORK.
MAGICALLY KNOW WHEN THE RICE COOKER IS EMPTY. AND MAKE FLAWLESS RICE EVERY TIME.
OMG, MIN MIN, ARE YOU STILL SLEEPING RIGHT NOW!?
YESSS
GET MIN READY FOR SCHOOL.
PUT OINTMENT ON TATAY'S SCABS WITHOUT COMPLAINING.
YOINK!
PLUCK MOM'S WHITE HAIRS.
WATER NANAY'S PLANTS.

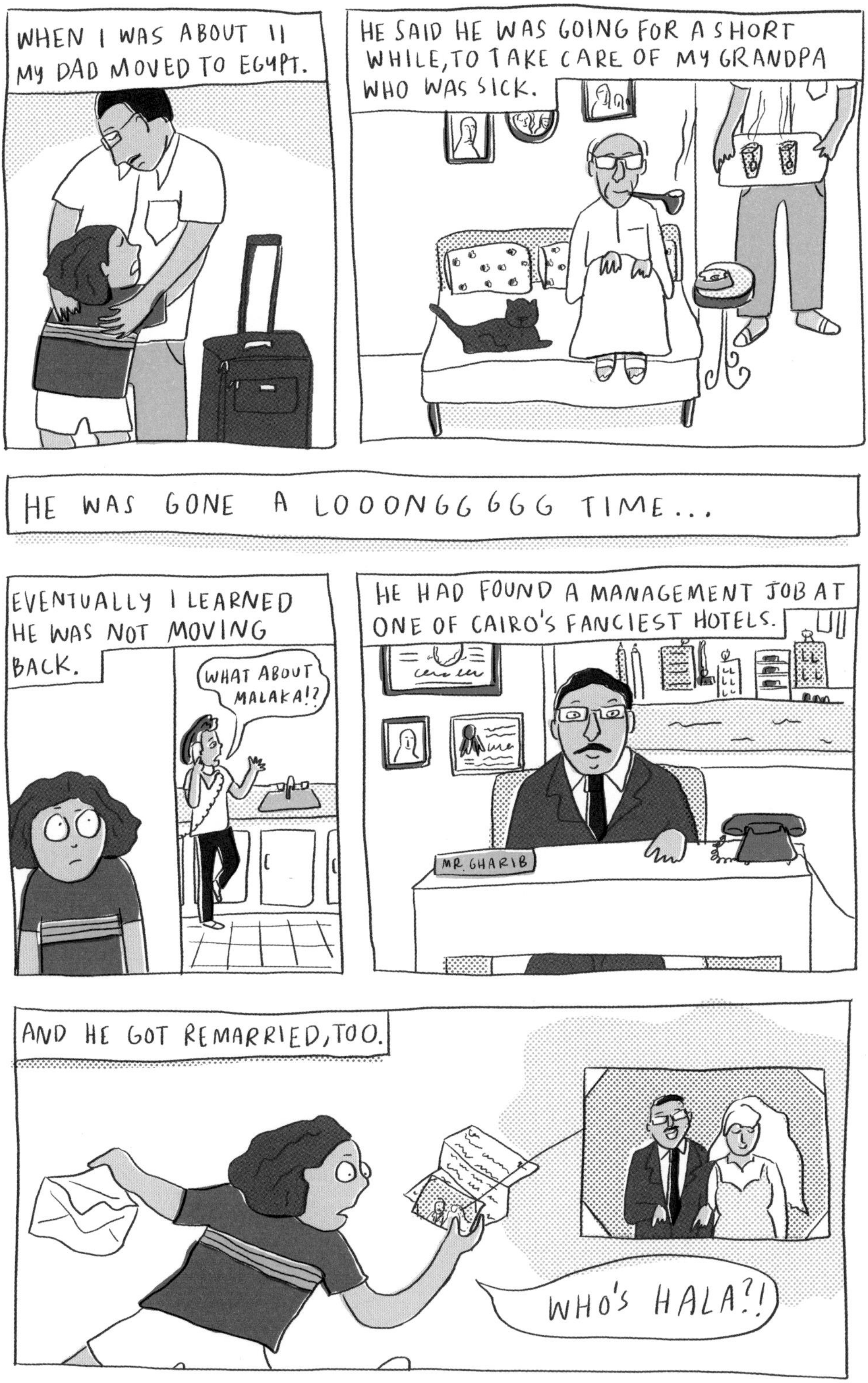
WHEN I WAS ABOUT 11 MY DAD MOVED TO EGYPT.
HE SAID HE WAS GOING FOR A SHORT WHILE, TO TAKE CARE OF MY GRANDPA WHO WAS SICK.
HE WAS GONE A LOOONGGGGG TIME...
EVENTUALLY I LEARNED HE WAS NOT MOVING BACK.
WHAT ABOUT MALAKA!?
HE HAD FOUND A MANAGEMENT JOB AT ONE OF CAIRO'S FANCIEST HOTELS.
MR. GHARIB
AND HE GOT REMARRIED, TOO.
WHO'S HALA?!

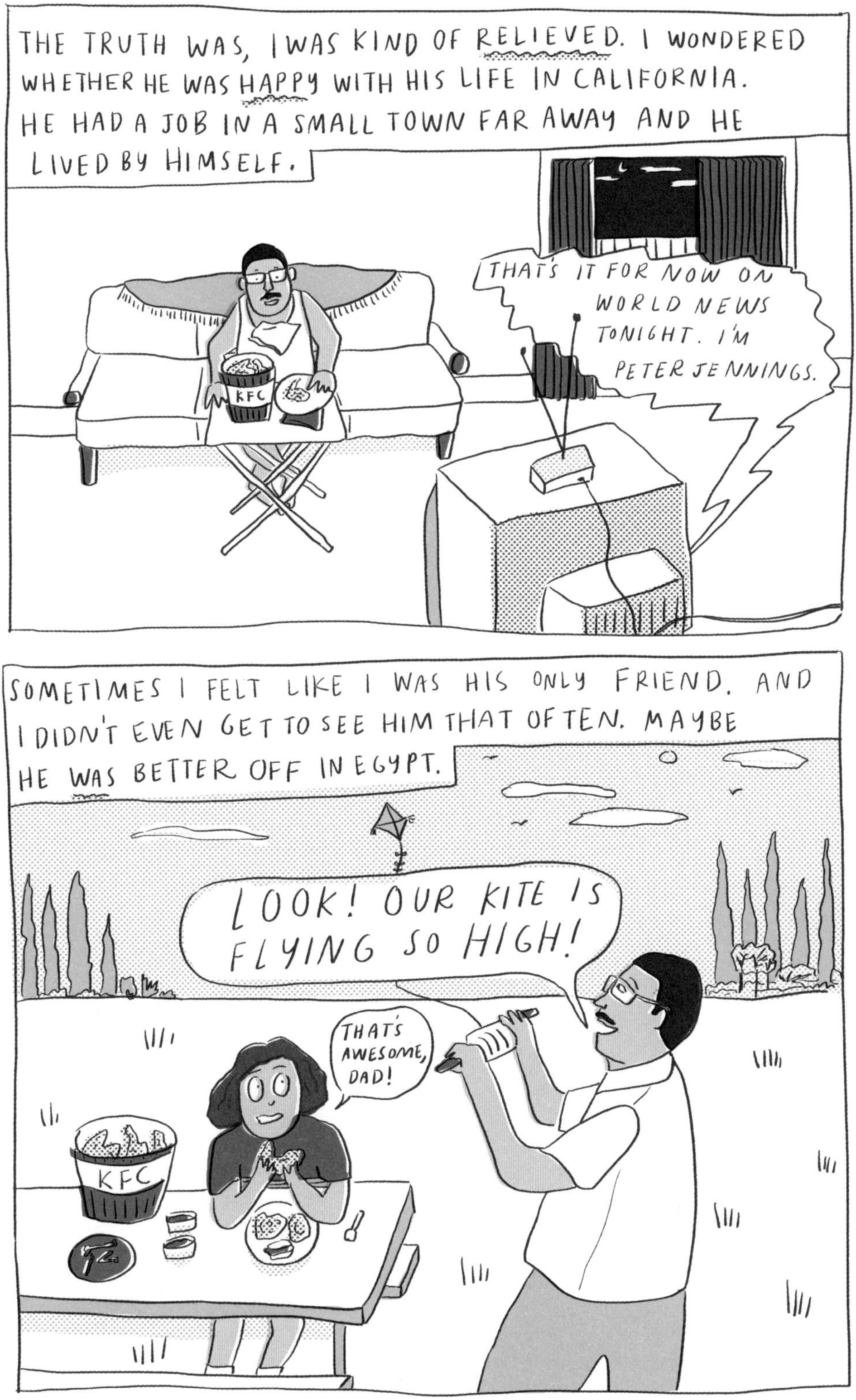
THE TRUTH WAS, I WAS KIND OF RELIEVED. I WONDERED WHETHER HE WAS HAPPY WITH HIS LIFE IN CALIFORNIA. HE HAD A JOB IN A SMALL TOWN FAR AWAY AND HE LIVED BY HIMSELF.
KFC
THAT'S IT FOR NOW ON WORLD NEWS TONIGHT. I'M PETER JENNINGS.
SOMETIMES I FELT LIKE I WAS HIS ONLY FRIEND. AND I DIDN'T EVEN GET TO SEE HIM THAT OFTEN. MAYBE HE WAS BETTER OFF IN EGYPT.
LOOK! OUR KITE IS FLYING SO HIGH!
THAT'S AWESOME, DAD!
KFC

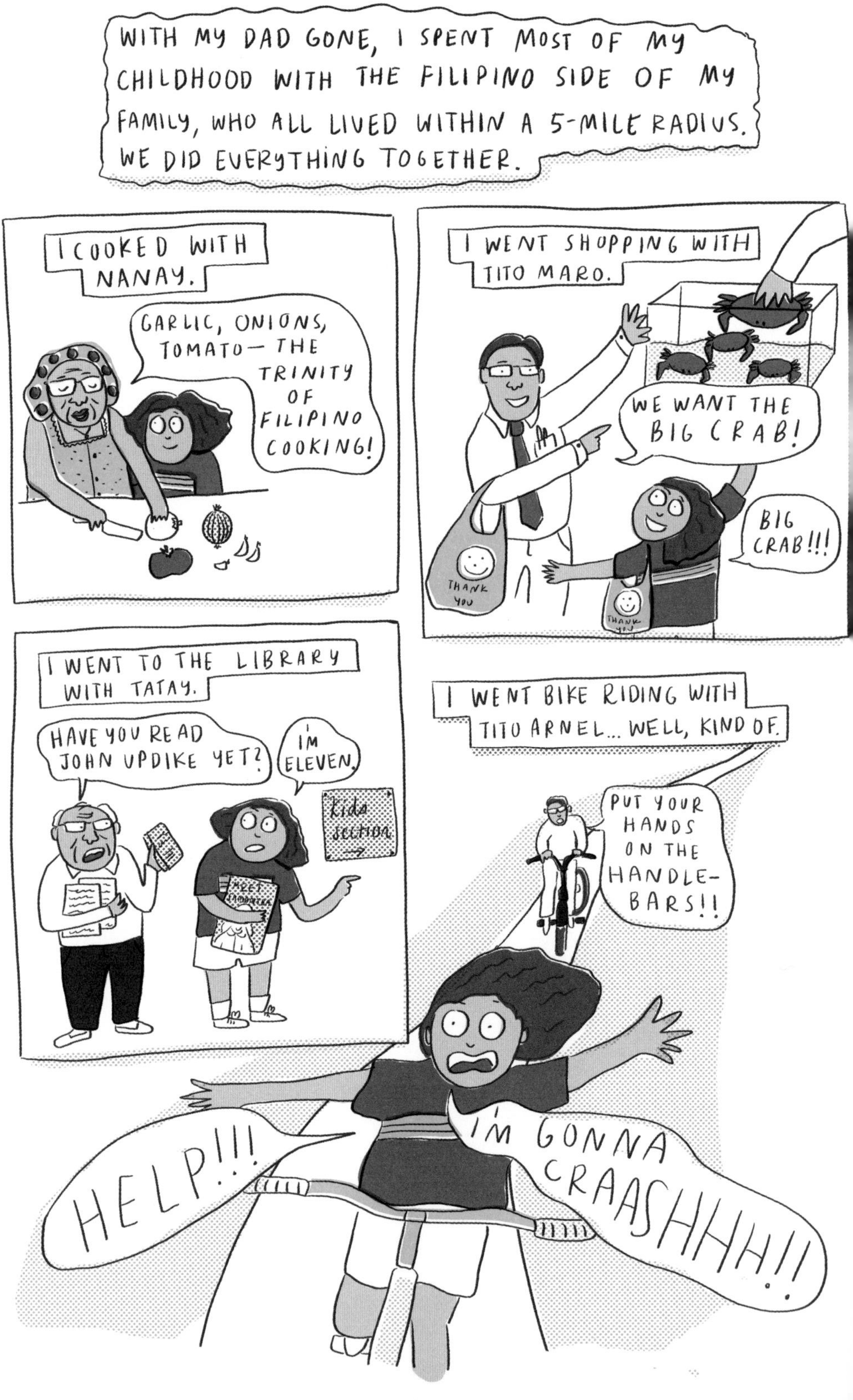
WITH MY DAD GONE, I SPENT MOST OF MY CHILDHOOD WITH THE FILIPINO SIDE OF MY FAMILY, WHO ALL LIVED WITHIN A 5-MILE RADIUS. WE DID EVERYTHING TOGETHER.
I COOKED WITH NANAY.
GARLIC, ONIONS, TOMATO— THE TRINITY OF FILIPINO COOKING!
I WENT SHOPPING WITH TITO MARO.
WE WANT THE BIG CRAB!
BIG CRAB!!!
THANK YOU
THANK YOU
I WENT TO THE LIBRARY WITH TATAY.
HAVE YOU READ JOHN UPDIKE YET?
I'M ELEVEN.
Kids section
I WENT BIKE RIDING WITH TITO ARNEL... WELL, KIND OF.
PUT YOUR HANDS ON THE HANDLE-BARS!!
HELP!!!
I'M GONNA CRAASHHH!!!

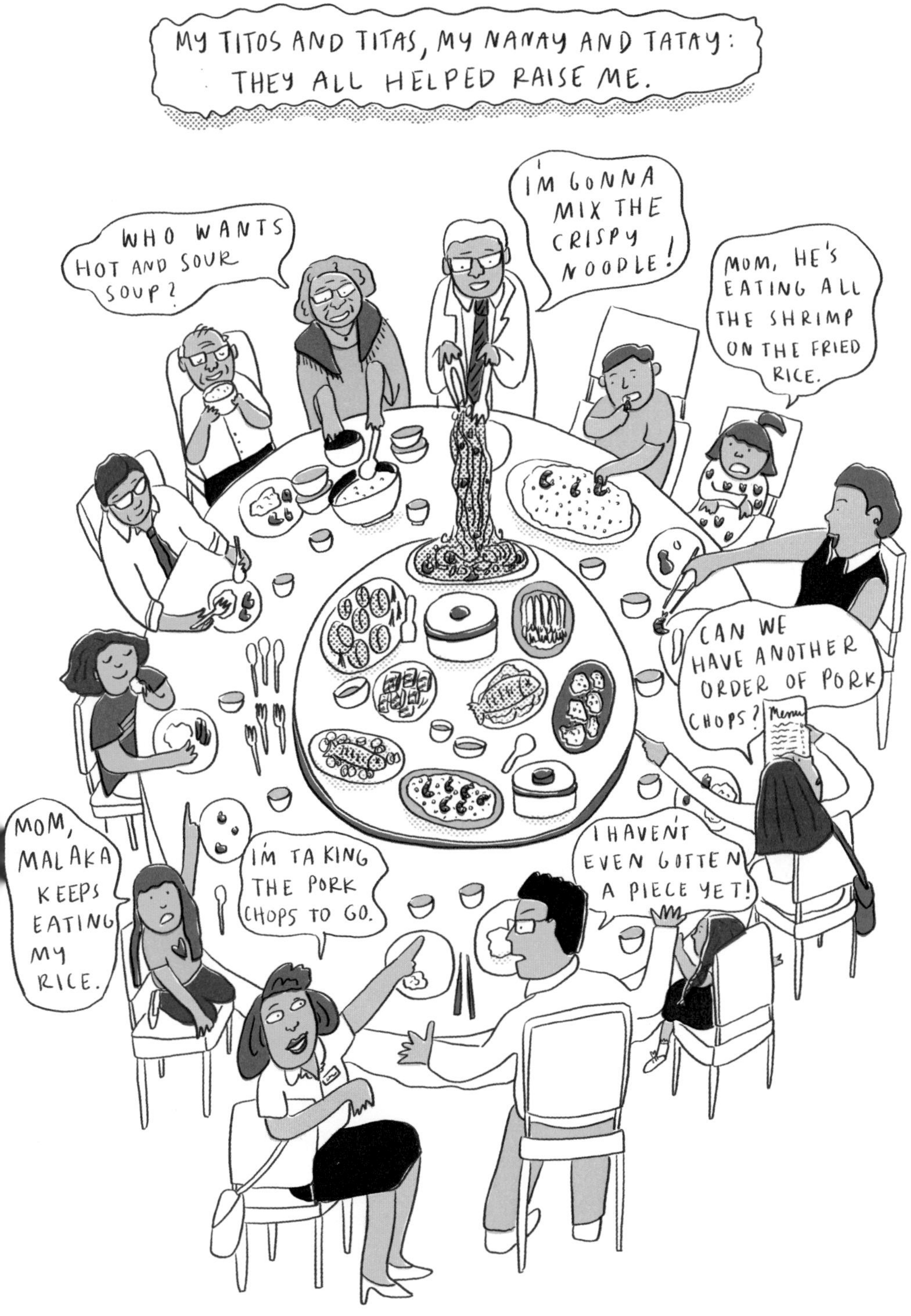
MY TITOS AND TITAS, MY NANAY AND TATAY: THEY ALL HELPED RAISE ME.
WHO WANTS HOT AND SOUR SOUP?
I'M GONNA MIX THE CRISPY NOODLE!
MOM, HE'S EATING ALL THE SHRIMP ON THE FRIED RICE.
CAN WE HAVE ANOTHER ORDER OF PORK CHOPS?
Menu
MOM, MALAKA KEEPS EATING MY RICE.
I'M TAKING THE PORK CHOPS TO GO.
I HAVEN'T EVEN GOTTEN A PIECE YET!

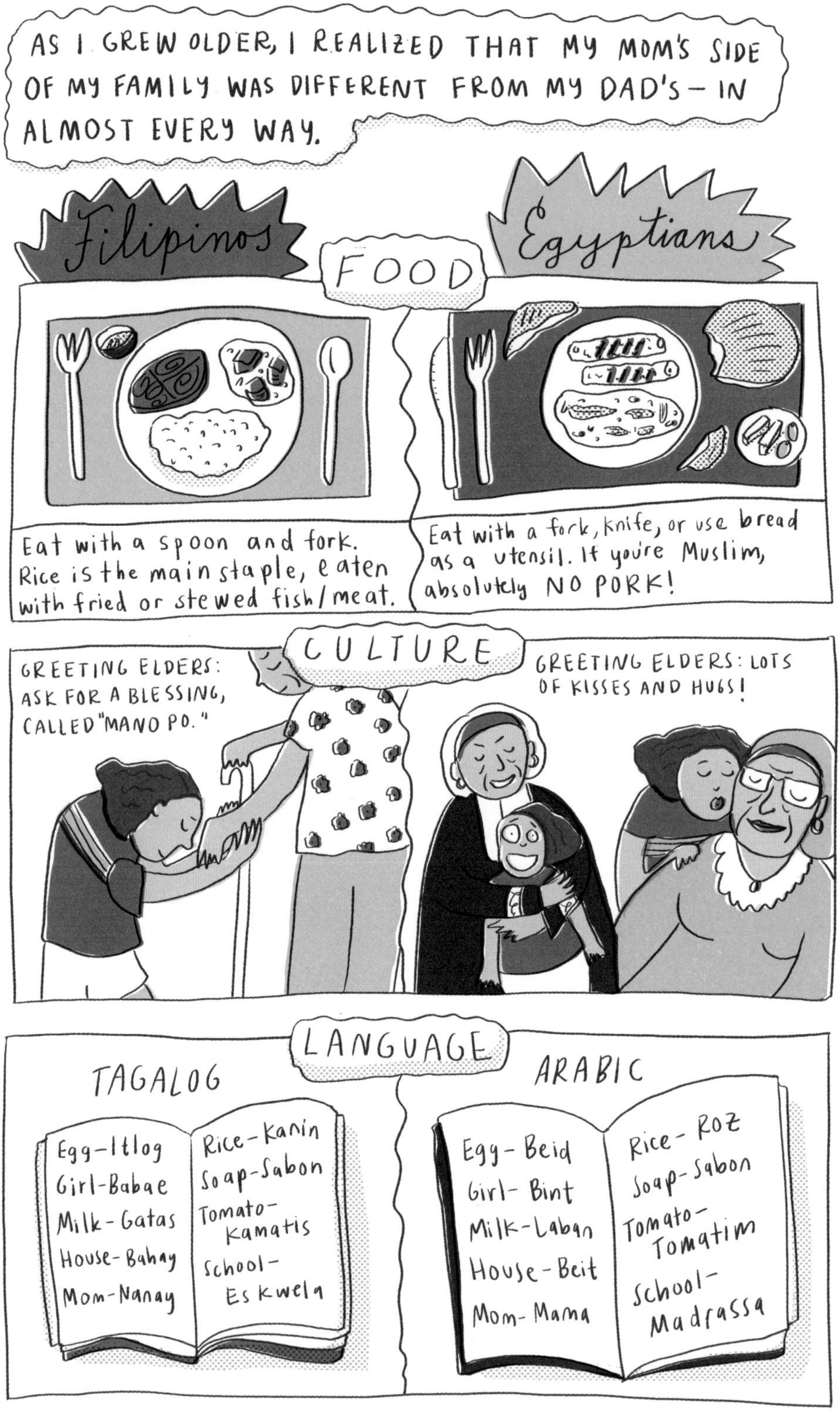
AS I GREW OLDER, I REALIZED THAT MY MOM'S SIDE OF MY FAMILY WAS DIFFERENT FROM MY DAD'S—IN ALMOST EVERY WAY.
Filipinos
FOOD
Egyptians
Eat with a spoon and fork. Rice is the main staple, eaten with fried or stewed fish/meat.
Eat with a fork, knife, or use bread as a utensil. If you're Muslim, absolutely NO PORK!
CULTURE
GREETING ELDERS: ASK FOR A BLESSING, CALLED "MANO PO."
GREETING ELDERS: LOTS OF KISSES AND HUGS!
LANGUAGE
TAGALOG
Egg-Itlog
Girl-Babae
Milk-Gatas
House-Bahay
Mom-Nanay
Rice-Kanin
Soap-Sabon
Tomato-Kamatis
School-Eskwela
ARABIC
Egg-Beid
Girl-Bint
Milk-Laban
House-Beit
Mom-Mama
Rice-Roz
Soap-Sabon
Tomato-Tomatim
School-Madrassa

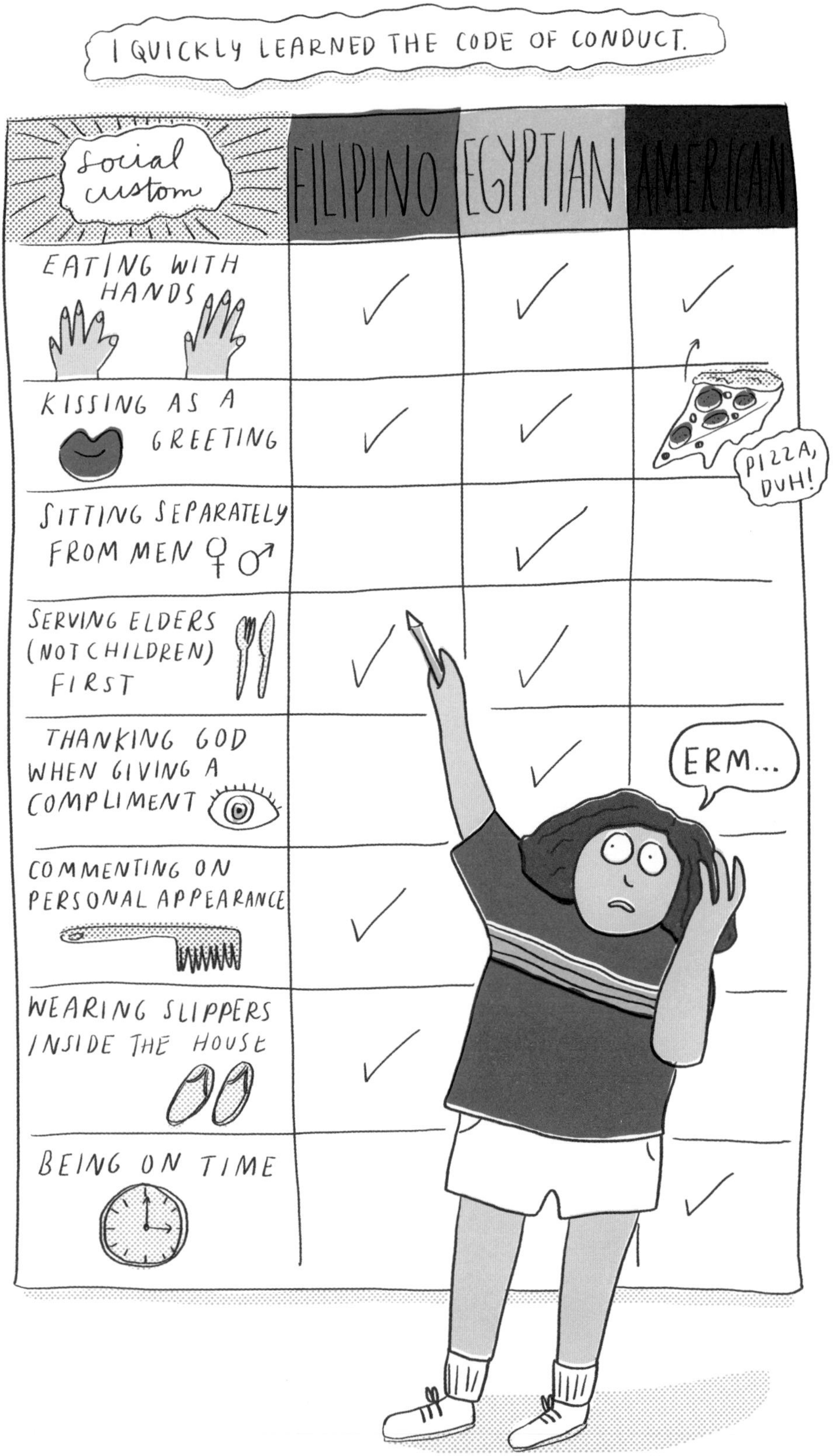

I QUICKLY LEARNED THE CODE OF CONDUCT.
Social custom
FILIPINO
EGYPTIAN
AMERICAN
EATING WITH HANDS
KISSING AS A GREETING
PIZZA, DUH!
SITTING SEPARATELY FROM MEN
SERVING ELDERS (NOT CHILDREN) FIRST
THANKING GOD WHEN GIVING A COMPLIMENT
ERM...
COMMENTING ON PERSONAL APPEARANCE
WEARING SLIPPERS INSIDE THE HOUSE
BEING ON TIME

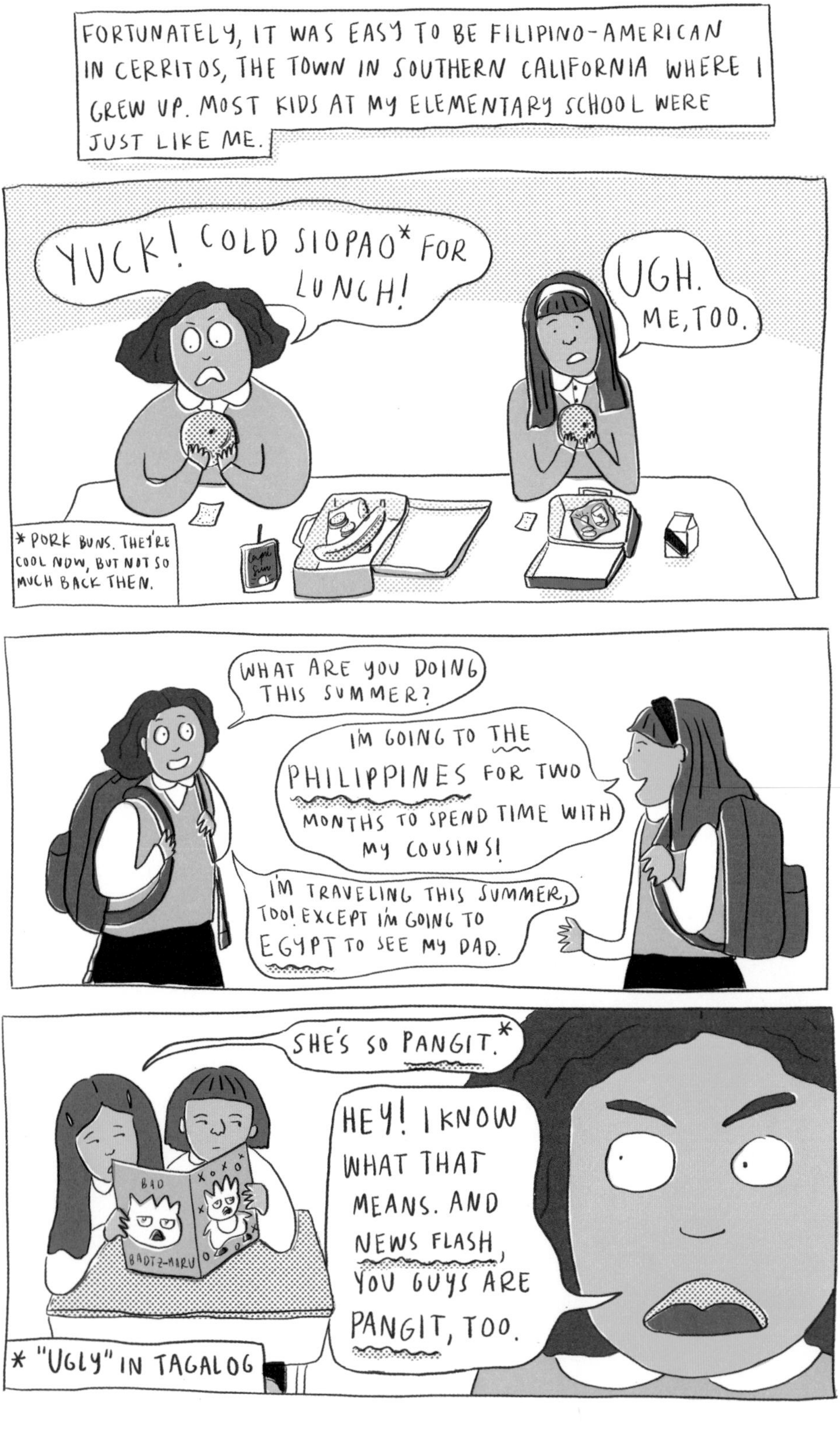
FORTUNATELY, IT WAS EASY TO BE FILIPINO-AMERICAN IN CERRITOS, THE TOWN IN SOUTHERN CALIFORNIA WHERE I GREW UP. MOST KIDS AT MY ELEMENTARY SCHOOL WERE JUST LIKE ME.
YUCK! COLD SIOPAO* FOR LUNCH!
UGH. ME, TOO.
* PORK BUNS. THEY'RE COOL NOW, BUT NOT SO MUCH BACK THEN.
WHAT ARE YOU DOING THIS SUMMER?
I'M GOING TO THE PHILIPPINES FOR TWO MONTHS TO SPEND TIME WITH MY COUSINS!
I'M TRAVELING THIS SUMMER, TOO! EXCEPT I'M GOING TO EGYPT TO SEE MY DAD.
SHE'S SO PANGIT.*
BAD
BADTZ-MARU
HEY! I KNOW WHAT THAT MEANS. AND NEWS FLASH, YOU GUYS ARE PANGIT, TOO.
* "UGLY" IN TAGALOG

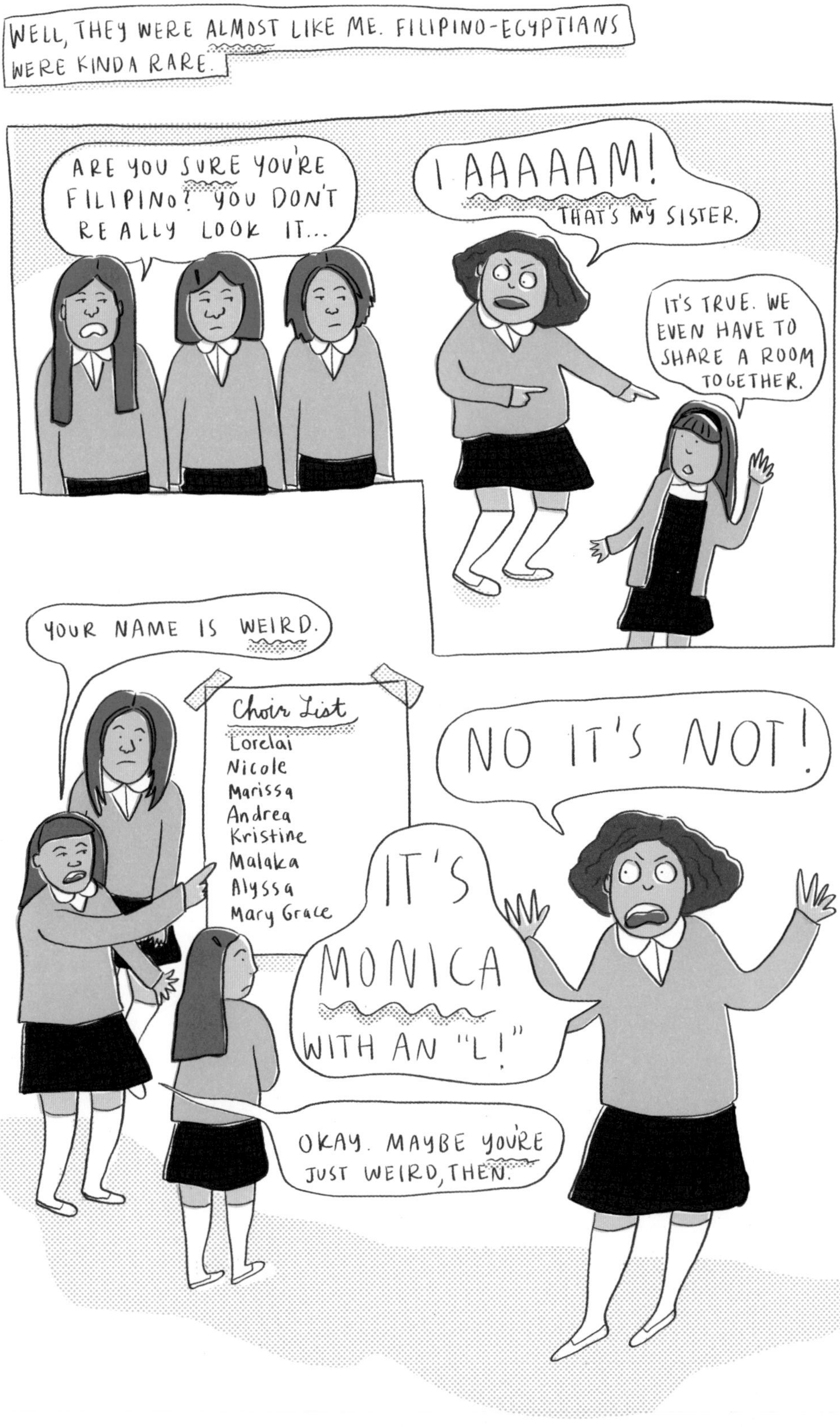
WELL, THEY WERE ALMOST LIKE ME. FILIPINO-EGYPTIANS WERE KINDA RARE.
ARE YOU SURE YOU'RE FILIPINO? YOU DON'T REALLY LOOK IT...
I AAAAAM! THAT'S MY SISTER.
IT'S TRUE. WE EVEN HAVE TO SHARE A ROOM TOGETHER.
YOUR NAME IS WEIRD.
Choir List
Lorelai
Nicole
Marissa
Andrea
Kristine
Malaka
Alyssa
Mary Grace
NO IT'S NOT!
IT'S MONICA WITH AN "L!"
OKAY. MAYBE YOU'RE JUST WEIRD, THEN.

TO ME, NOTHING MIXED ME UP MORE THAN RELIGION.

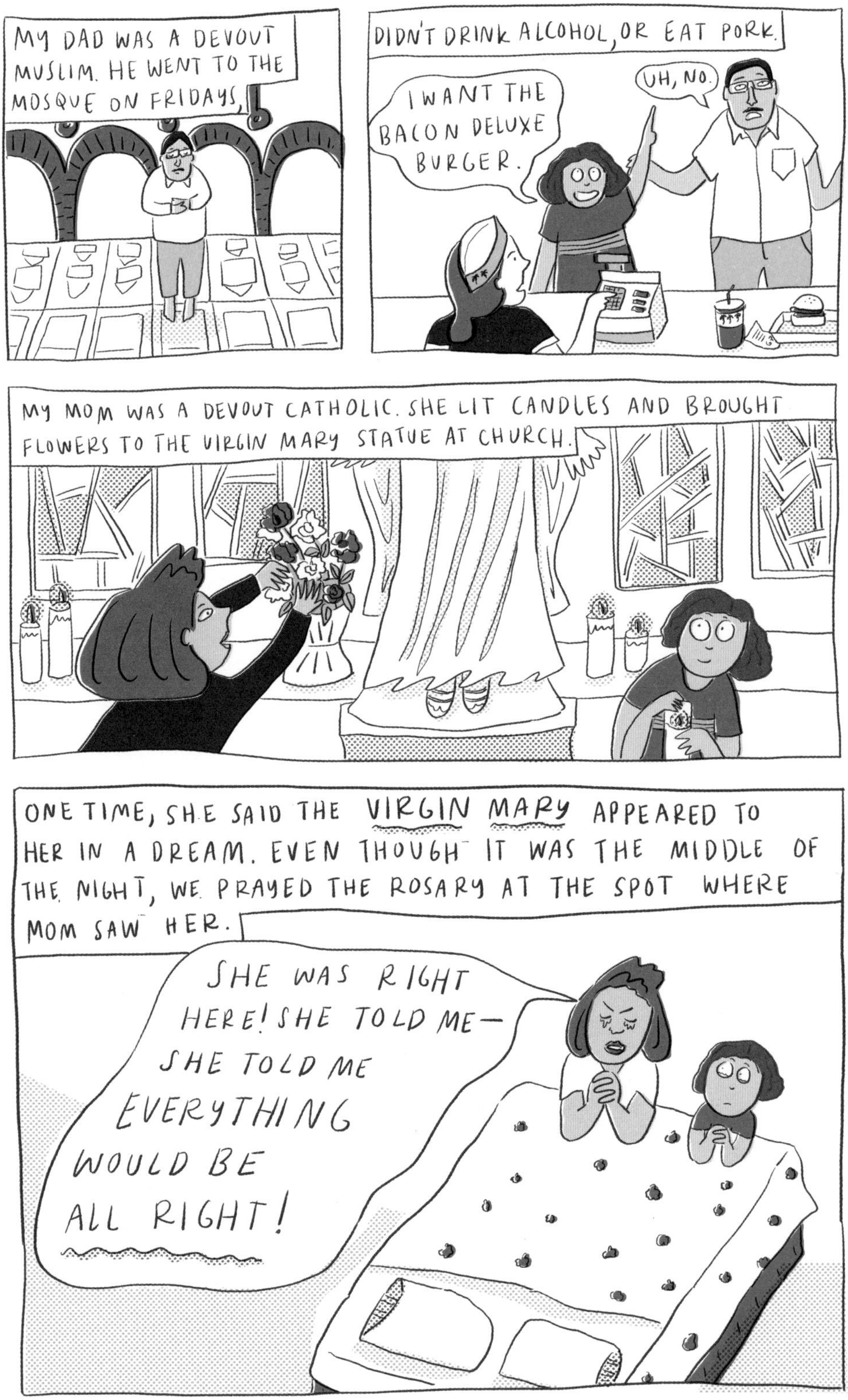
MY DAD WAS A DEVOUT MUSLIM. HE WENT TO THE MOSQUE ON FRIDAYS,
DIDN'T DRINK ALCOHOL, OR EAT PORK.
I WANT THE BACON DELUXE BURGER.
UH, NO.
MY MOM WAS A DEVOUT CATHOLIC. SHE LIT CANDLES AND BROUGHT FLOWERS TO THE VIRGIN MARY STATUE AT CHURCH.
ONE TIME, SHE SAID THE VIRGIN MARY APPEARED TO HER IN A DREAM. EVEN THOUGH IT WAS THE MIDDLE OF THE NIGHT, WE PRAYED THE ROSARY AT THE SPOT WHERE MOM SAW HER.
SHE WAS RIGHT HERE! SHE TOLD ME— SHE TOLD ME EVERYTHING WOULD BE ALL RIGHT!

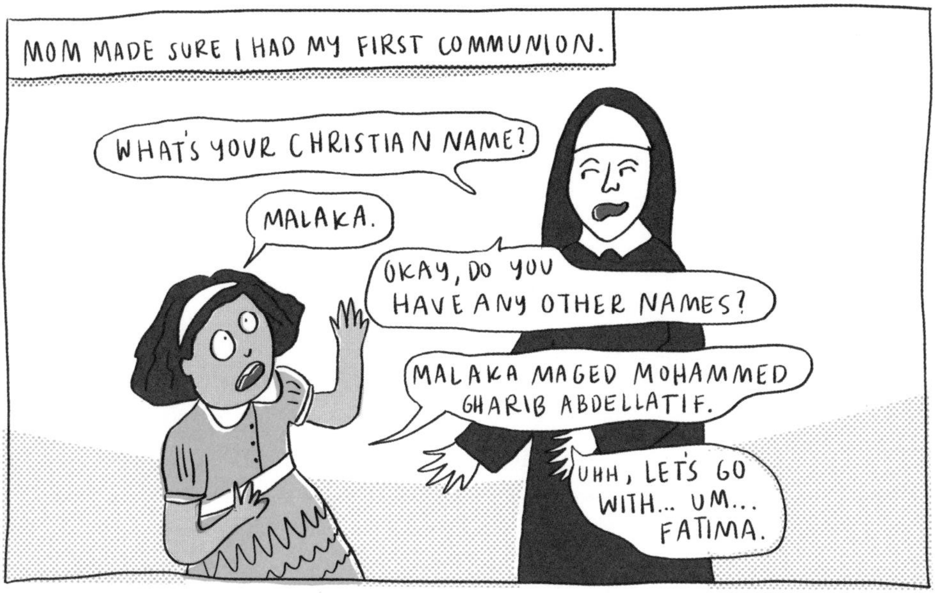
MOM MADE SURE I HAD MY FIRST COMMUNION.
WHAT'S YOUR CHRISTIAN NAME?
MALAKA.
OKAY, DO YOU HAVE ANY OTHER NAMES?
MALAKA MAGED MOHAMMED GHARIB ABDELLATIF.
UHH, LET'S GO WITH... UM... FATIMA.

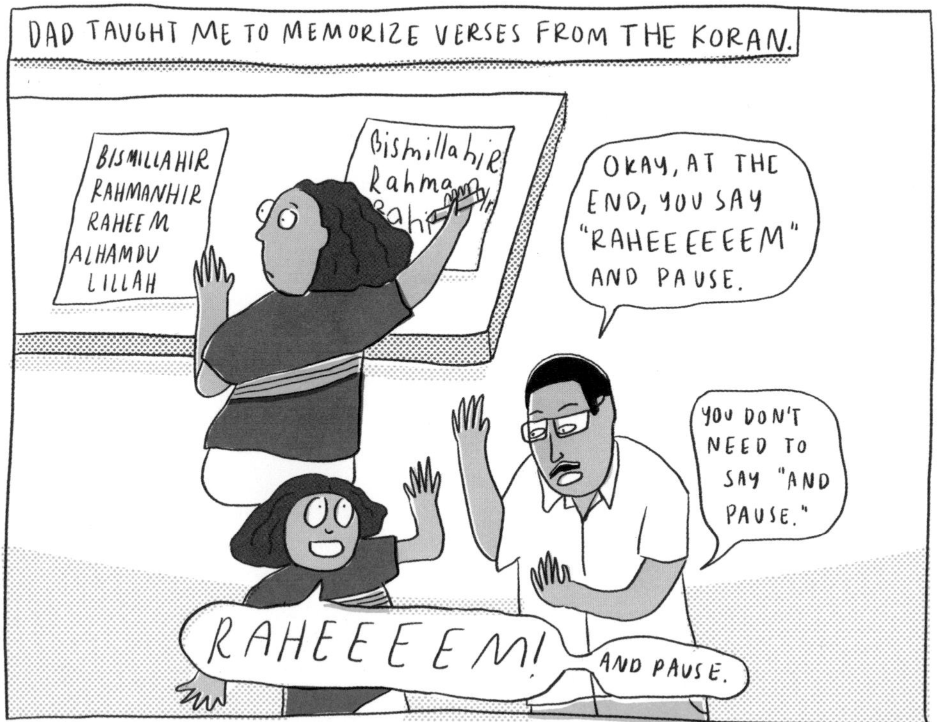
DAD TAUGHT ME TO MEMORIZE VERSES FROM THE KORAN.
BISMILLAHIR RAHMANHIR RAHEEM ALHAMDU LILLAH
Bismillahir Rahma
OKAY, AT THE END, YOU SAY "RAHEEEEEEM" AND PAUSE.
YOU DON'T NEED TO SAY "AND PAUSE."
RAHEEEEEM!
AND PAUSE.

FUN FACT:

DAD USED TO RECORD HIMSELF RECITING VERSES OF THE KORAN ON CASSETTE TAPES.

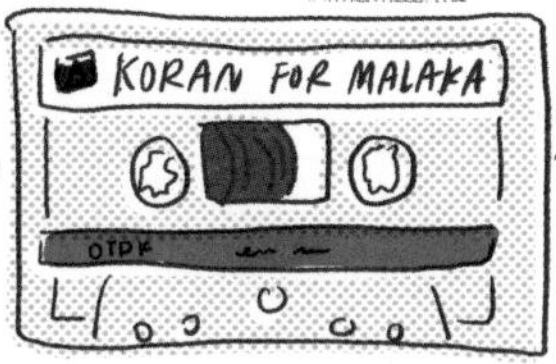
KORAN FOR MALAKA

HE MADE THEM SO I COULD PRACTICE WHEN HE WASN'T AROUND. I JUST LISTENED TO THEM BECAUSE I MISSED THE SOUND OF HIS VOICE..

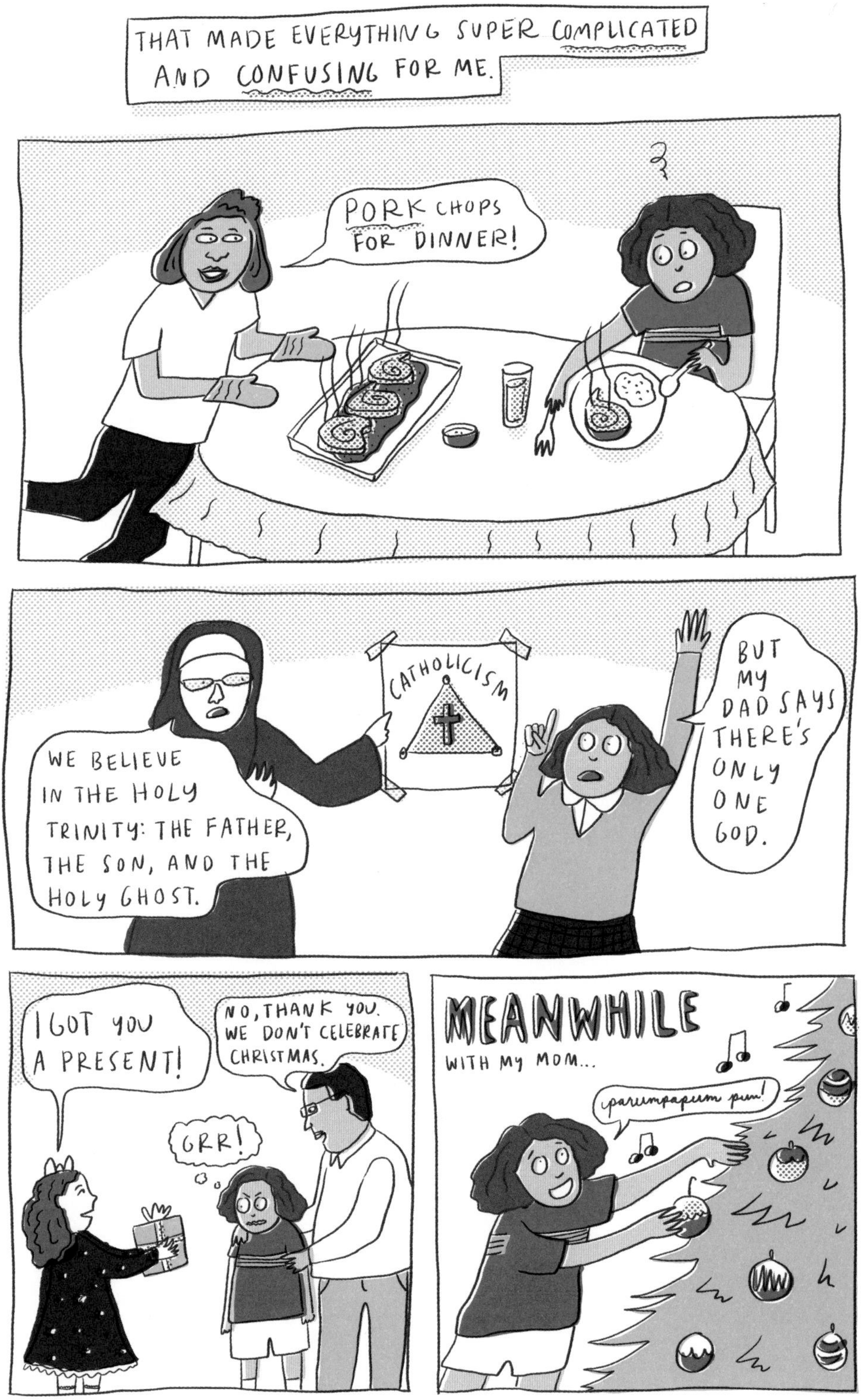
THAT MADE EVERYTHING SUPER COMPLICATED AND CONFUSING FOR ME.
PORK CHOPS FOR DINNER!
CATHOLICISM
WE BELIEVE IN THE HOLY TRINITY: THE FATHER, THE SON, AND THE HOLY GHOST.
BUT MY DAD SAYS THERE'S ONLY ONE GOD.
I GOT YOU A PRESENT!
NO, THANK YOU. WE DON'T CELEBRATE CHRISTMAS.
GRR!
MEANWHILE
WITH MY MOM...
parumpapum pum!

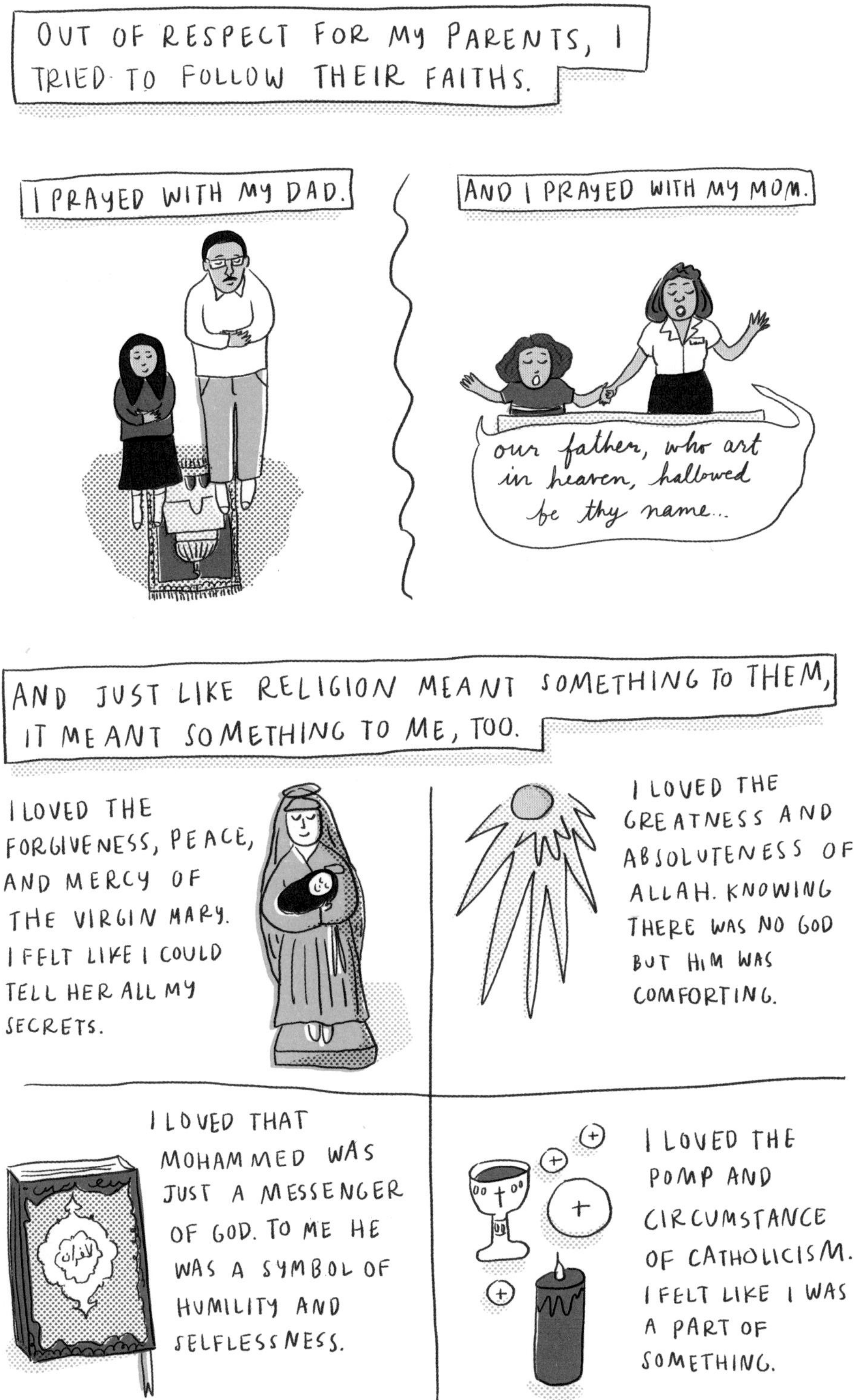
OUT OF RESPECT FOR MY PARENTS, I TRIED TO FOLLOW THEIR FAITHS.
I PRAYED WITH MY DAD.
AND I PRAYED WITH MY MOM.
our father, who art in heaven, hallowed be thy name...
AND JUST LIKE RELIGION MEANT SOMETHING TO THEM, IT MEANT SOMETHING TO ME, TOO.
I LOVED THE FORGIVENESS, PEACE, AND MERCY OF THE VIRGIN MARY. I FELT LIKE I COULD TELL HER ALL MY SECRETS.
I LOVED THE GREATNESS AND ABSOLUTENESS OF ALLAH. KNOWING THERE WAS NO GOD BUT HIM WAS COMFORTING.
I LOVED THAT MOHAMMED WAS JUST A MESSENGER OF GOD. TO ME HE WAS A SYMBOL OF HUMILITY AND SELFLESSNESS.
I LOVED THE POMP AND CIRCUMSTANCE OF CATHOLICISM. I FELT LIKE I WAS A PART OF SOMETHING.

I WISHED THAT I COULD HAVE SMUSHED THEM ALL TOGETHER INTO ONE FAITH. SO... FOR MOST OF MY CHILDHOOD, I DID.

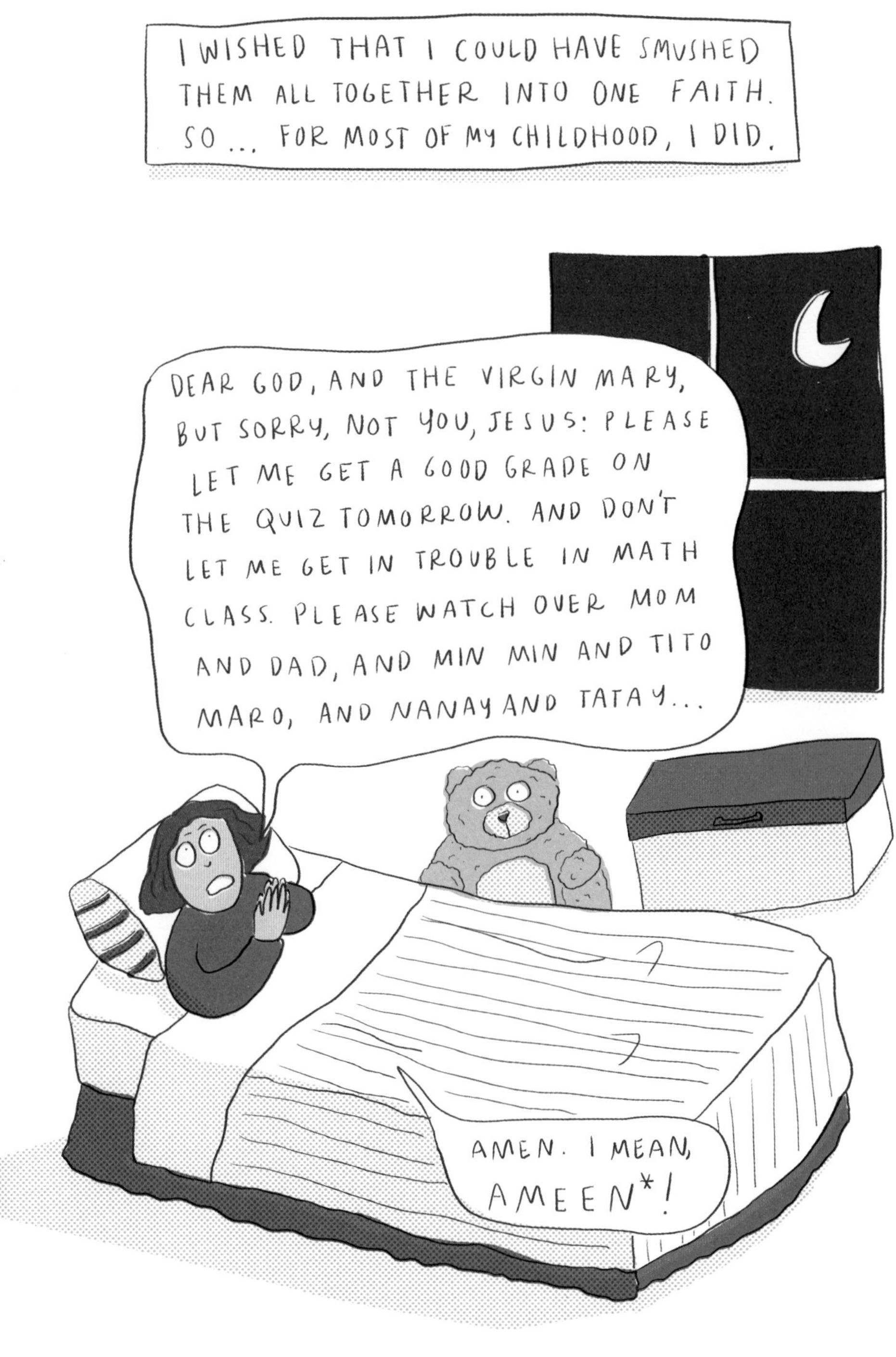
DEAR GOD, AND THE VIRGIN MARY, BUT SORRY, NOT YOU, JESUS: PLEASE LET ME GET A GOOD GRADE ON THE QUIZ TOMORROW. AND DON'T LET ME GET IN TROUBLE IN MATH CLASS. PLEASE WATCH OVER MOM AND DAD, AND MIN MIN AND TITO MARO, AND NANAY AND TATAY...
AMEN. I MEAN, AMEEN*!

*HOW MUSLIMS SAY "AMEN"

Chapter 3

MY PARENTS HAD A DEAL.
SCHOOL WITH MY MOM IN THE STATES,
SUMMERS WITH MY DAD IN EGYPT.

SUMMER IN EGYPT WAS SO DIFFERENT FROM THE LIFE I KNEW IN CALIFORNIA. TIME MOVED SO MUCH SLOWER!

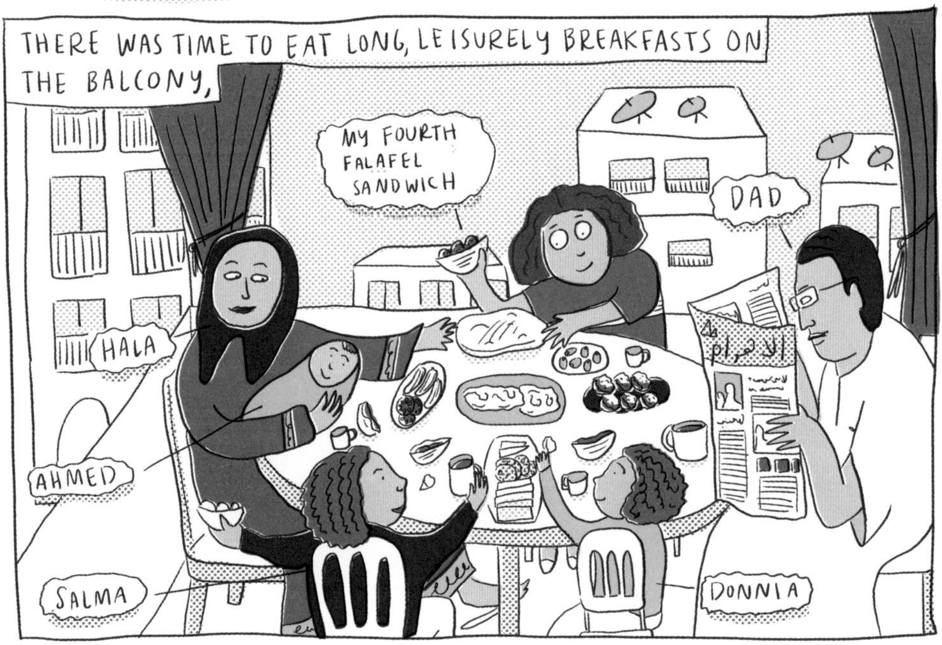
THERE WAS TIME TO EAT LONG, LEISURELY BREAKFASTS ON THE BALCONY,
MY FOURTH FALAFEL SANDWICH
DAD
HALA
AHMED
SALMA
DONNIA

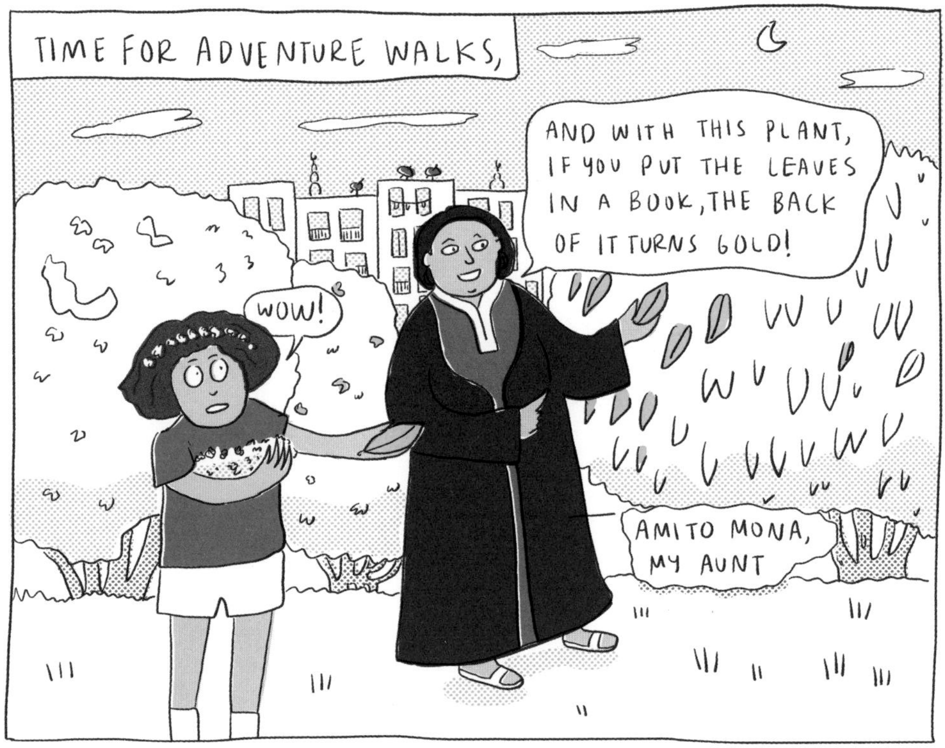
TIME FOR ADVENTURE WALKS,
AND WITH THIS PLANT, IF YOU PUT THE LEAVES IN A BOOK, THE BACK OF IT TURNS GOLD!
WOW!
AMITO MONA, MY AUNT

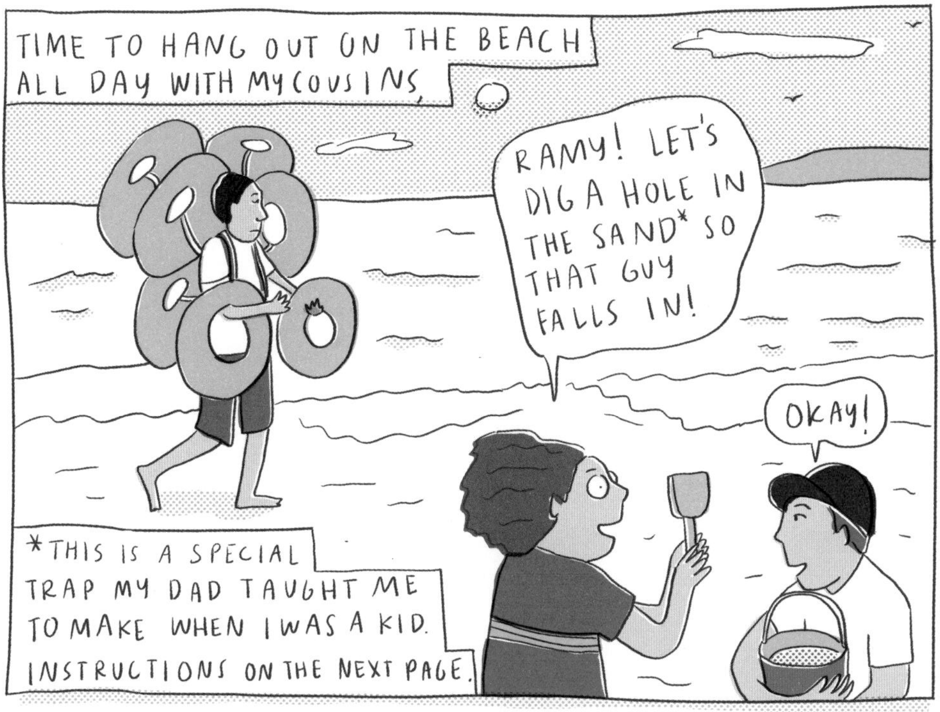
TIME TO HANG OUT ON THE BEACH ALL DAY WITH MY COUSINS,
RAMY! LET'S DIG A HOLE IN THE SAND* SO THAT GUY FALLS IN!
OKAY!
*THIS IS A SPECIAL TRAP MY DAD TAUGHT ME TO MAKE WHEN I WAS A KID. INSTRUCTIONS ON THE NEXT PAGE.

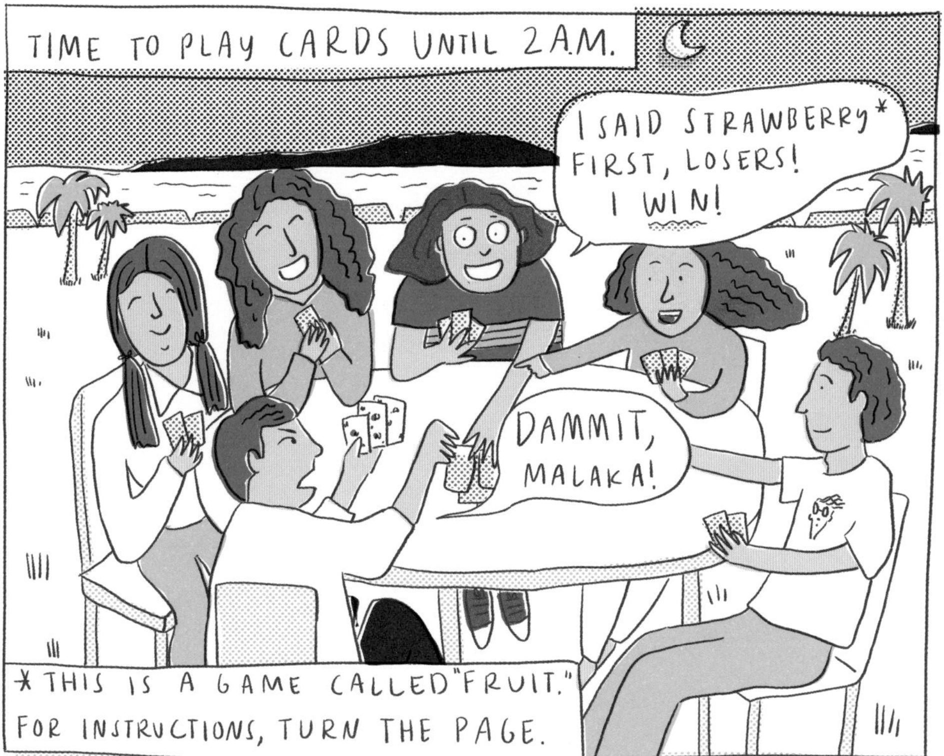
TIME TO PLAY CARDS UNTIL 2 A.M.
I SAID STRAWBERRY* FIRST, LOSERS! I WIN!
DAMMIT, MALAKA!
*THIS IS A GAME CALLED "FRUIT." FOR INSTRUCTIONS, TURN THE PAGE.

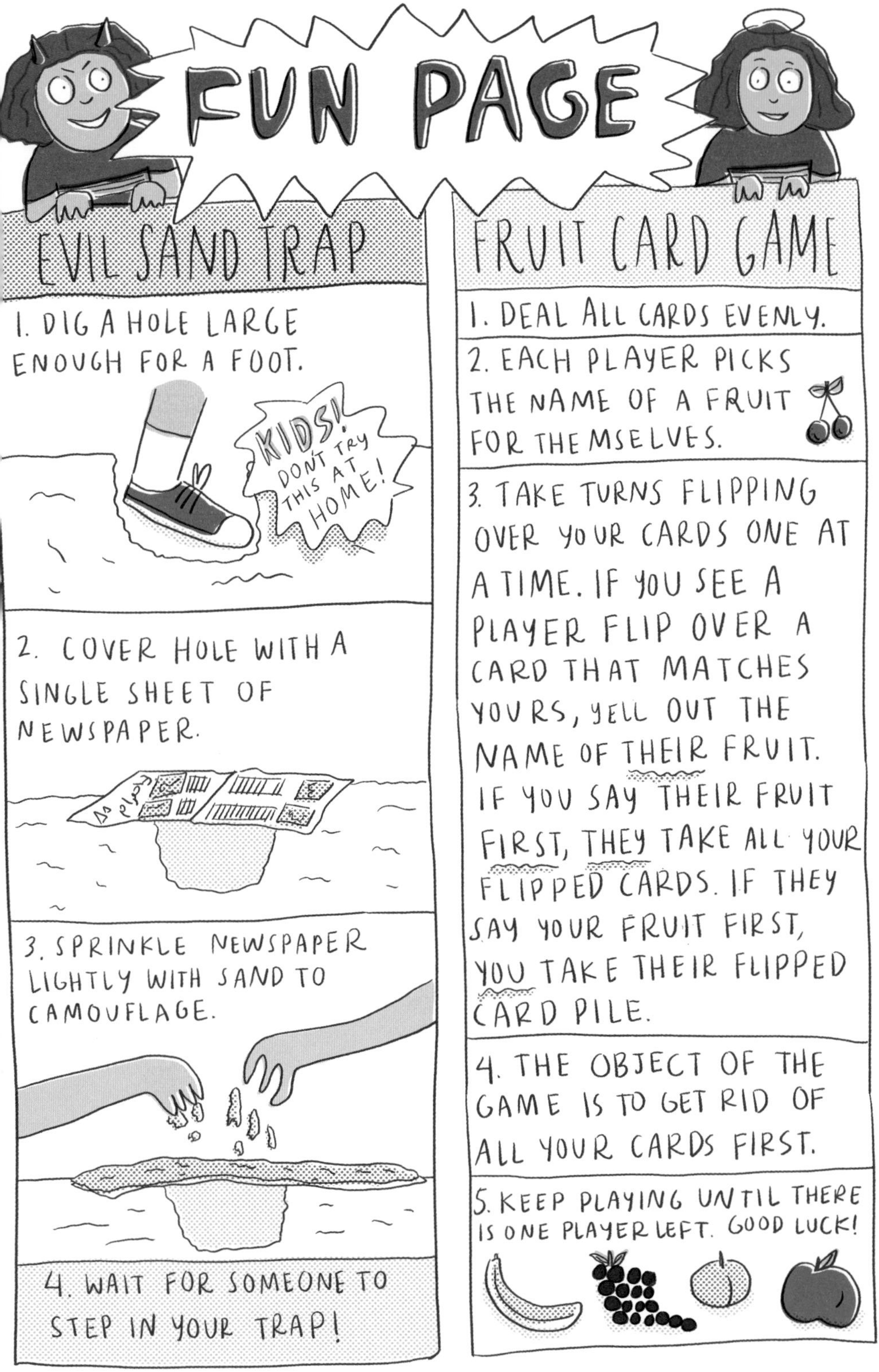
FUN PAGE
EVIL SAND TRAP
1. DIG A HOLE LARGE ENOUGH FOR A FOOT.
KIDS! DON'T TRY THIS AT HOME!
2. COVER HOLE WITH A SINGLE SHEET OF NEWSPAPER.
3. SPRINKLE NEWSPAPER LIGHTLY WITH SAND TO CAMOUFLAGE.
4. WAIT FOR SOMEONE TO STEP IN YOUR TRAP!
FRUIT CARD GAME
1. DEAL ALL CARDS EVENLY.
2. EACH PLAYER PICKS THE NAME OF A FRUIT FOR THEMSELVES.
3. TAKE TURNS FLIPPING OVER YOUR CARDS ONE AT A TIME. IF YOU SEE A PLAYER FLIP OVER A CARD THAT MATCHES YOURS, YELL OUT THE NAME OF THEIR FRUIT. IF YOU SAY THEIR FRUIT FIRST, THEY TAKE ALL YOUR FLIPPED CARDS. IF THEY SAY YOUR FRUIT FIRST, YOU TAKE THEIR FLIPPED CARD PILE.
4. THE OBJECT OF THE GAME IS TO GET RID OF ALL YOUR CARDS FIRST.
5. KEEP PLAYING UNTIL THERE IS ONE PLAYER LEFT. GOOD LUCK!

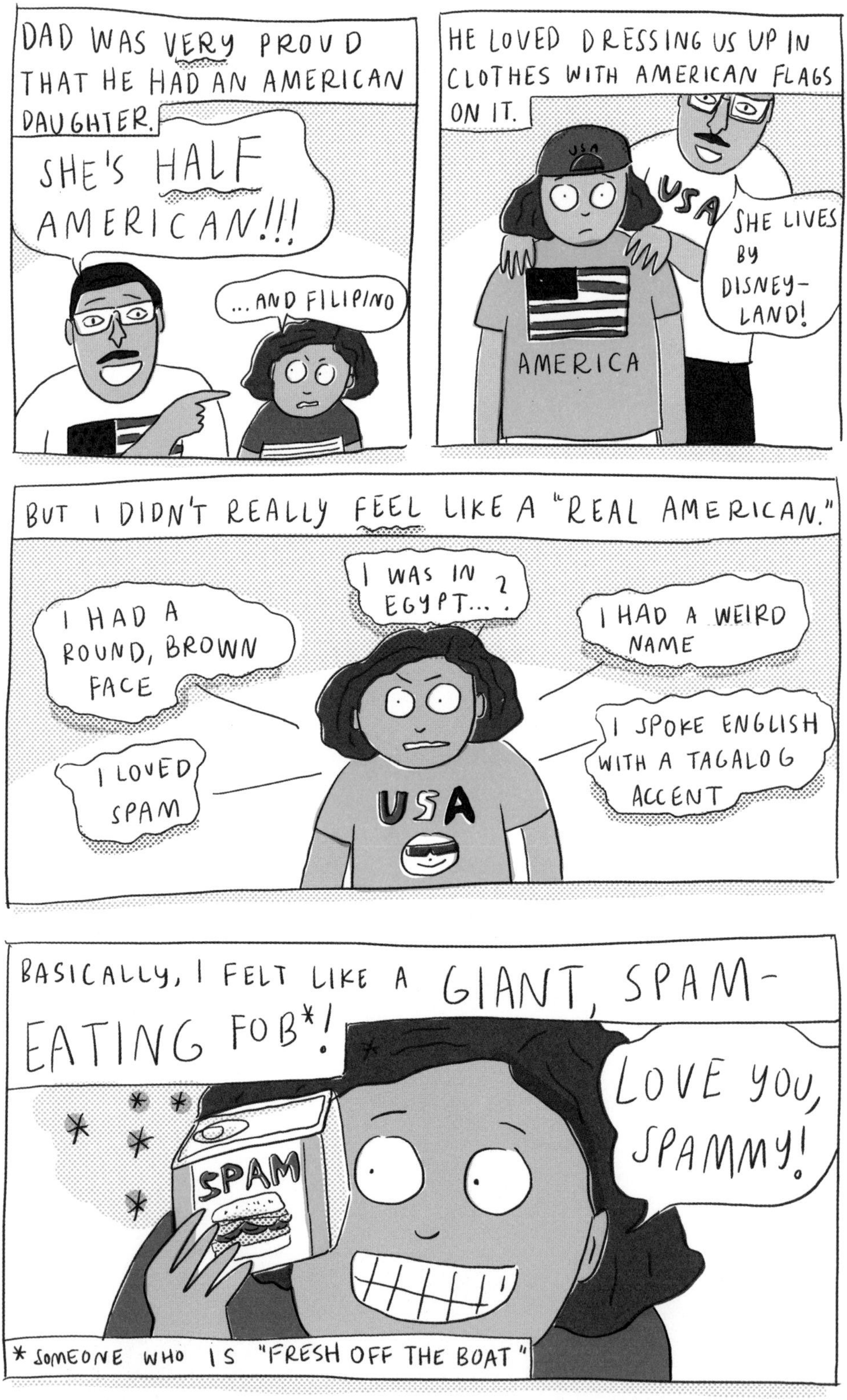
DAD WAS VERY PROUD THAT HE HAD AN AMERICAN DAUGHTER.
SHE'S HALF AMERICAN!!!
...AND FILIPINO
HE LOVED DRESSING US UP IN CLOTHES WITH AMERICAN FLAGS ON IT.
USA
USA
AMERICA
SHE LIVES BY DISNEY-LAND!
BUT I DIDN'T REALLY FEEL LIKE A "REAL AMERICAN."
I WAS IN EGYPT...?
I HAD A ROUND, BROWN FACE
I HAD A WEIRD NAME
I LOVED SPAM
I SPOKE ENGLISH WITH A TAGALOG ACCENT
USA
BASICALLY, I FELT LIKE A GIANT, SPAM-EATING FOB*!
LOVE YOU, SPAMMY!
SPAM
* SOMEONE WHO IS "FRESH OFF THE BOAT"

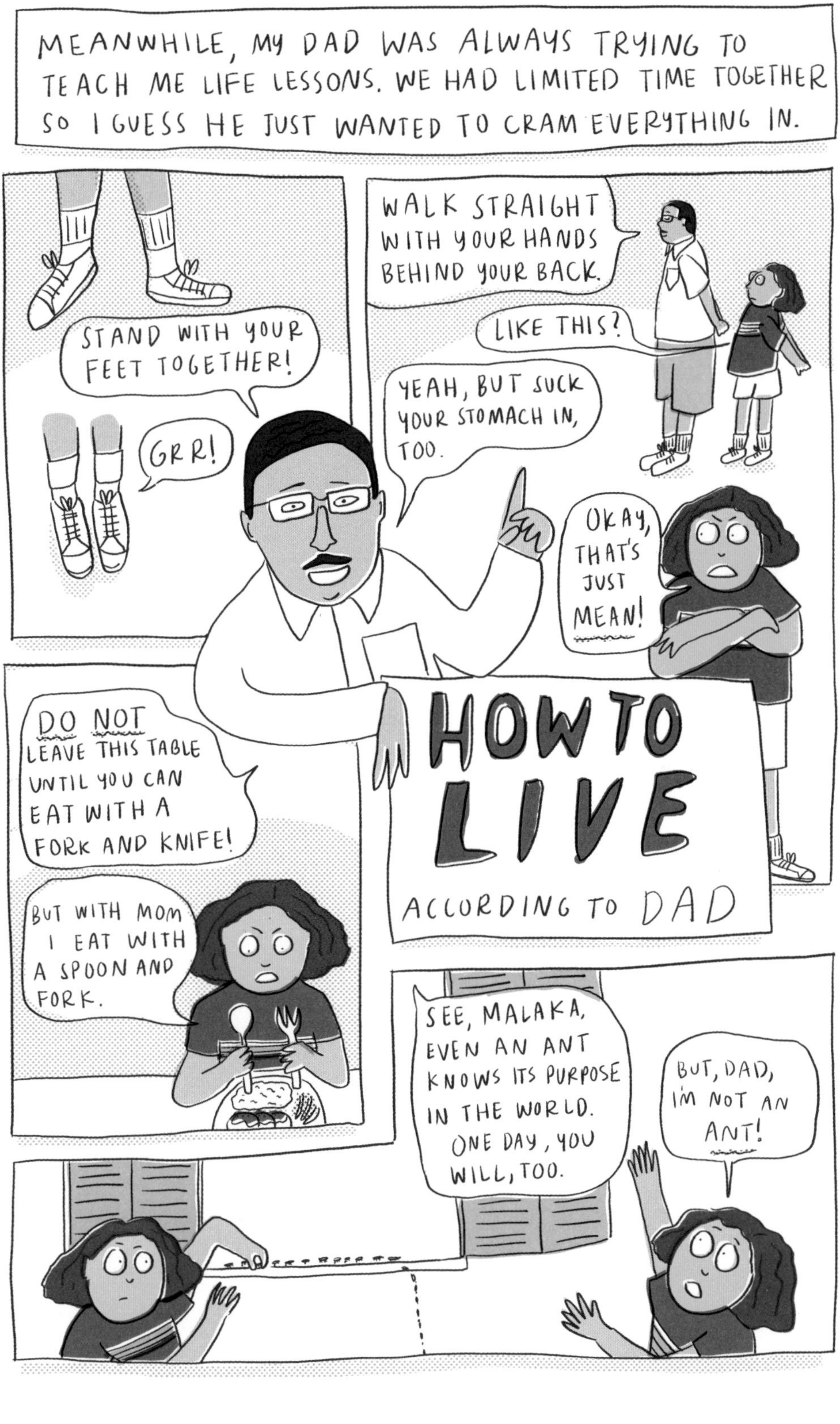
MEANWHILE, MY DAD WAS ALWAYS TRYING TO TEACH ME LIFE LESSONS. WE HAD LIMITED TIME TOGETHER SO I GUESS HE JUST WANTED TO CRAM EVERYTHING IN.
STAND WITH YOUR FEET TOGETHER!
GRR!
WALK STRAIGHT WITH YOUR HANDS BEHIND YOUR BACK.
LIKE THIS?
YEAH, BUT SUCK YOUR STOMACH IN, TOO.
OKAY, THAT'S JUST MEAN!
HOW TO LIVE
ACCORDING TO DAD
DO NOT LEAVE THIS TABLE UNTIL YOU CAN EAT WITH A FORK AND KNIFE!
BUT WITH MOM I EAT WITH A SPOON AND FORK.
SEE, MALAKA, EVEN AN ANT KNOWS ITS PURPOSE IN THE WORLD. ONE DAY, YOU WILL, TOO.
BUT, DAD, I'M NOT AN ANT!

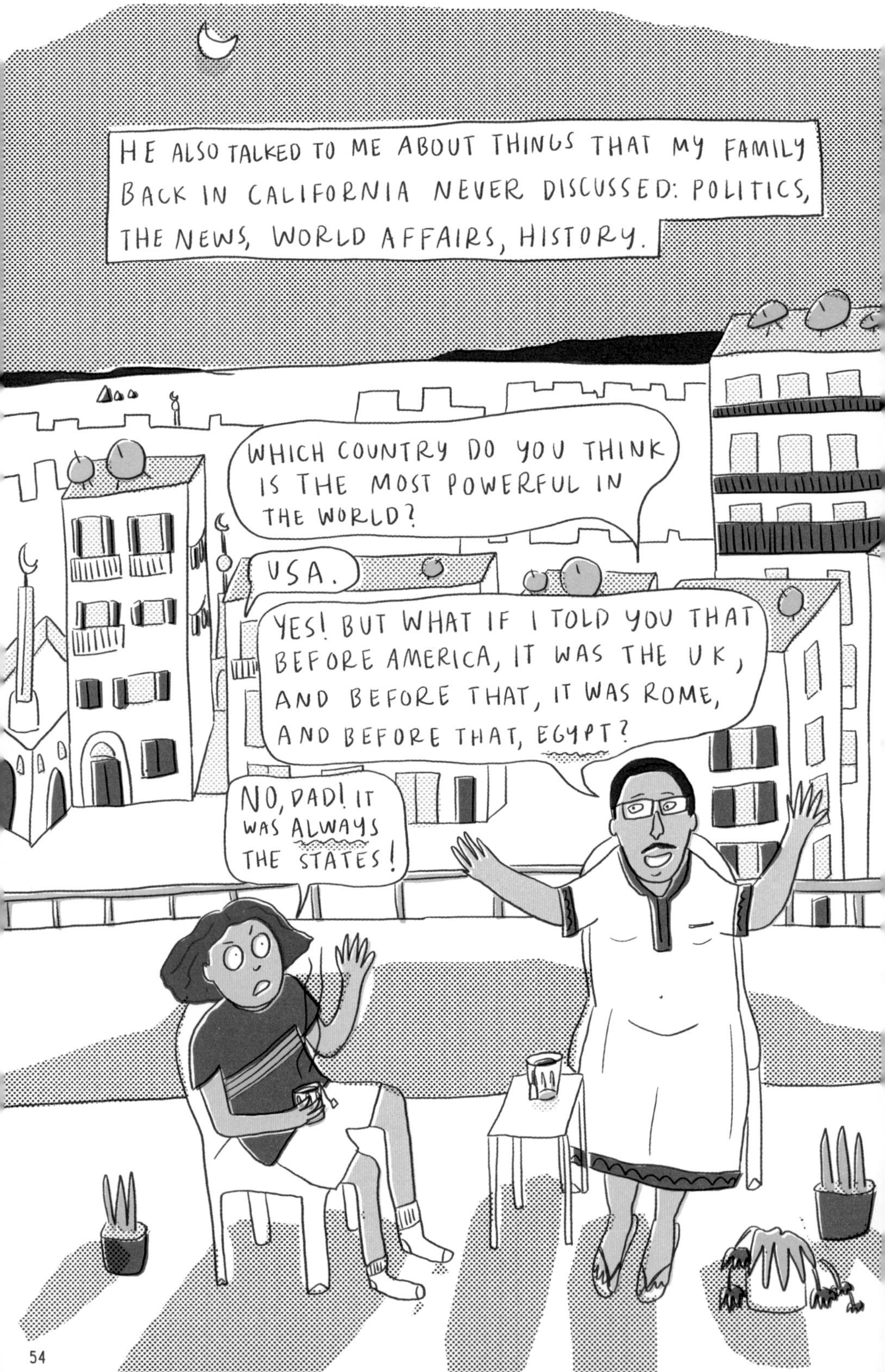
HE ALSO TALKED TO ME ABOUT THINGS THAT MY FAMILY BACK IN CALIFORNIA NEVER DISCUSSED: POLITICS, THE NEWS, WORLD AFFAIRS, HISTORY.
WHICH COUNTRY DO YOU THINK IS THE MOST POWERFUL IN THE WORLD?
USA.
YES! BUT WHAT IF I TOLD YOU THAT BEFORE AMERICA, IT WAS THE UK, AND BEFORE THAT, IT WAS ROME, AND BEFORE THAT, EGYPT?
NO, DAD! IT WAS ALWAYS THE STATES!

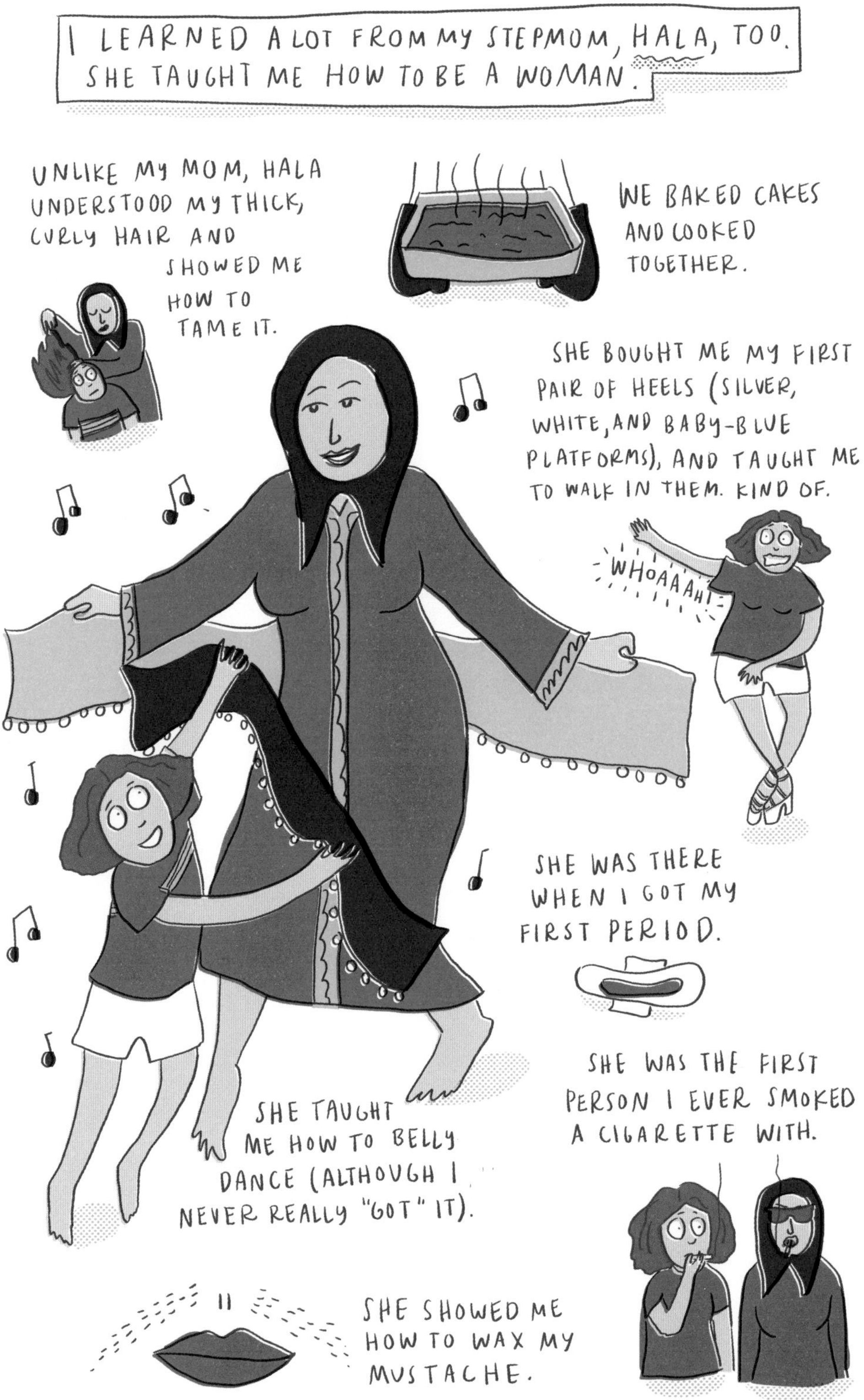
I LEARNED A LOT FROM MY STEPMOM, HALA, TOO. SHE TAUGHT ME HOW TO BE A WOMAN.
UNLIKE MY MOM, HALA UNDERSTOOD MY THICK, CURLY HAIR AND SHOWED ME HOW TO TAME IT.
WE BAKED CAKES AND COOKED TOGETHER.
SHE BOUGHT ME MY FIRST PAIR OF HEELS (SILVER, WHITE, AND BABY-BLUE PLATFORMS), AND TAUGHT ME TO WALK IN THEM. KIND OF.
WHOAAAAH!
SHE WAS THERE WHEN I GOT MY FIRST PERIOD.
SHE TAUGHT ME HOW TO BELLY DANCE (ALTHOUGH I NEVER REALLY "GOT" IT).
SHE WAS THE FIRST PERSON I EVER SMOKED A CIGARETTE WITH.
SHE SHOWED ME HOW TO WAX MY MUSTACHE.

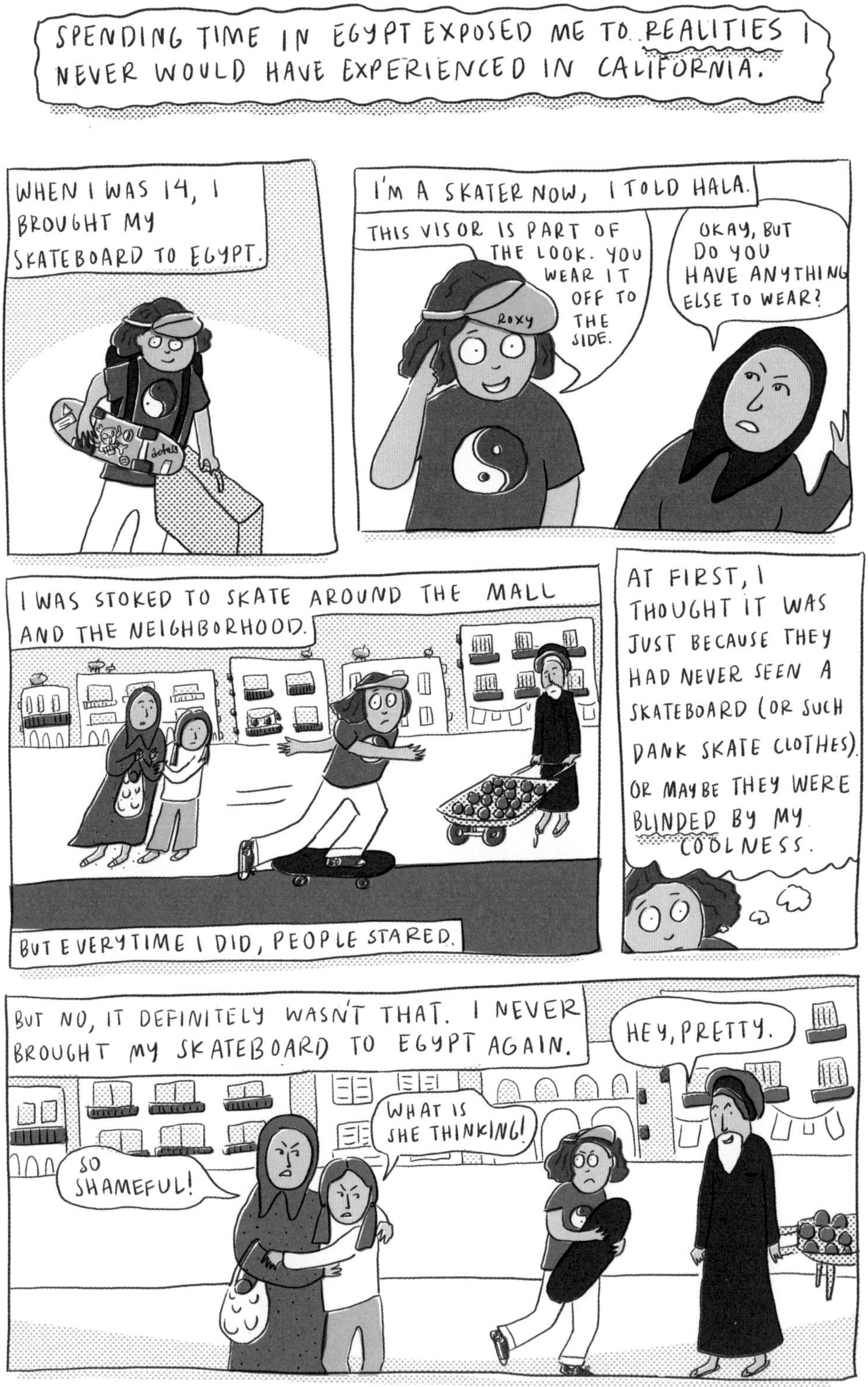
SPENDING TIME IN EGYPT EXPOSED ME TO REALITIES I NEVER WOULD HAVE EXPERIENCED IN CALIFORNIA.
WHEN I WAS 14, I BROUGHT MY SKATEBOARD TO EGYPT.
I'M A SKATER NOW, I TOLD HALA.
THIS VISOR IS PART OF THE LOOK. YOU WEAR IT OFF TO THE SIDE.
ROXY
OKAY, BUT DO YOU HAVE ANYTHING ELSE TO WEAR?
I WAS STOKED TO SKATE AROUND THE MALL AND THE NEIGHBORHOOD.
BUT EVERYTIME I DID, PEOPLE STARED.
AT FIRST, I THOUGHT IT WAS JUST BECAUSE THEY HAD NEVER SEEN A SKATEBOARD (OR SUCH DANK SKATE CLOTHES). OR MAYBE THEY WERE BLINDED BY MY COOLNESS.
BUT NO, IT DEFINITELY WASN'T THAT. I NEVER BROUGHT MY SKATEBOARD TO EGYPT AGAIN.
HEY, PRETTY.
WHAT IS SHE THINKING!
SO SHAMEFUL!

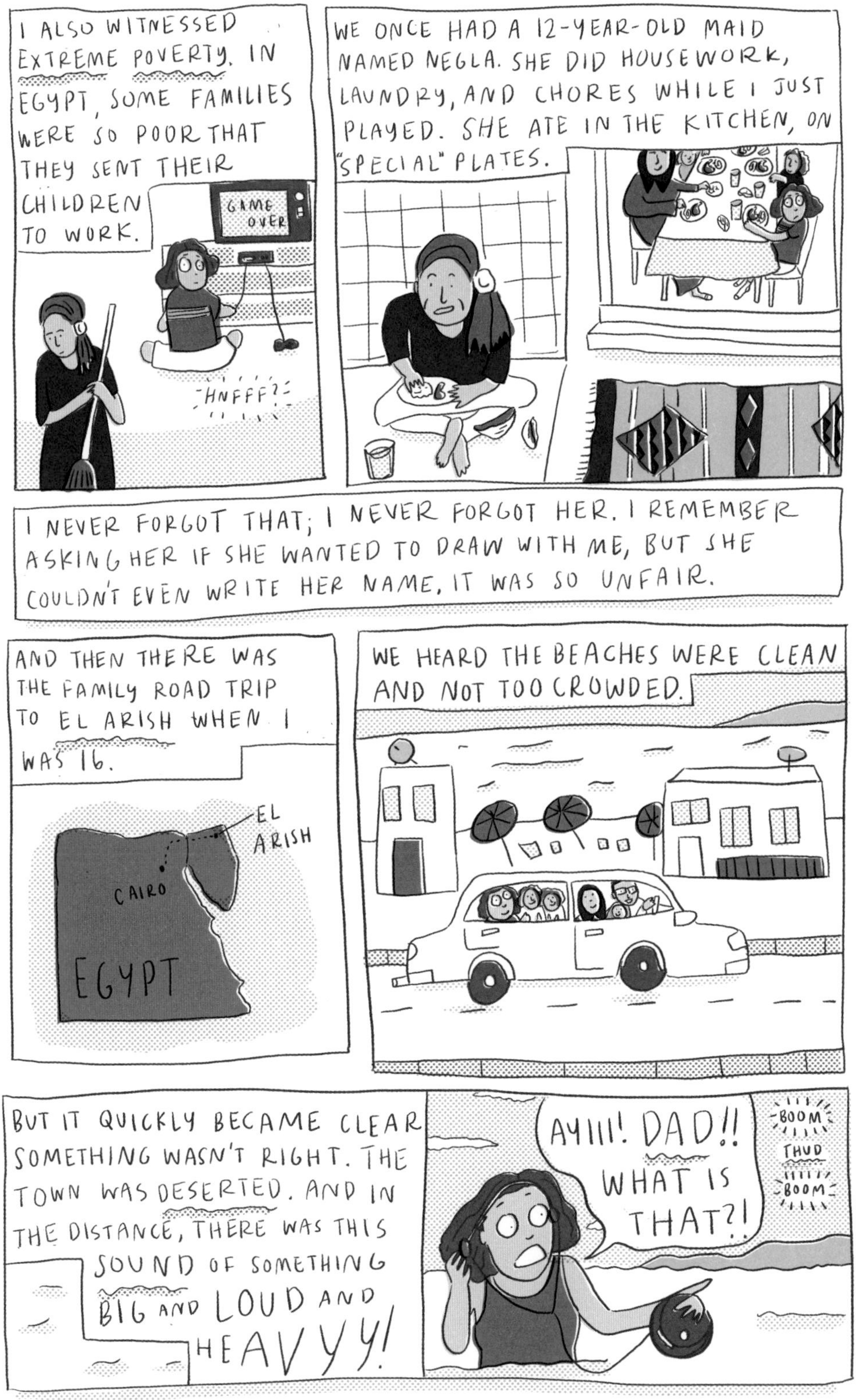
I ALSO WITNESSED EXTREME POVERTY. IN EGYPT, SOME FAMILIES WERE SO POOR THAT THEY SENT THEIR CHILDREN TO WORK.
GAME OVER
HNFFF?
WE ONCE HAD A 12-YEAR-OLD MAID NAMED NEGLA. SHE DID HOUSEWORK, LAUNDRY, AND CHORES WHILE I JUST PLAYED. SHE ATE IN THE KITCHEN, ON "SPECIAL" PLATES.
I NEVER FORGOT THAT; I NEVER FORGOT HER. I REMEMBER ASKING HER IF SHE WANTED TO DRAW WITH ME, BUT SHE COULDN'T EVEN WRITE HER NAME. IT WAS SO UNFAIR.
AND THEN THERE WAS THE FAMILY ROAD TRIP TO EL ARISH WHEN I WAS 16.
EL ARISH
CAIRO
EGYPT
WE HEARD THE BEACHES WERE CLEAN AND NOT TOO CROWDED.
BUT IT QUICKLY BECAME CLEAR SOMETHING WASN'T RIGHT. THE TOWN WAS DESERTED. AND IN THE DISTANCE, THERE WAS THIS SOUND OF SOMETHING BIG AND LOUD AND HEAVYY!
AYIII! DAD!! WHAT IS THAT?!
BOOM
THUD
BOOM

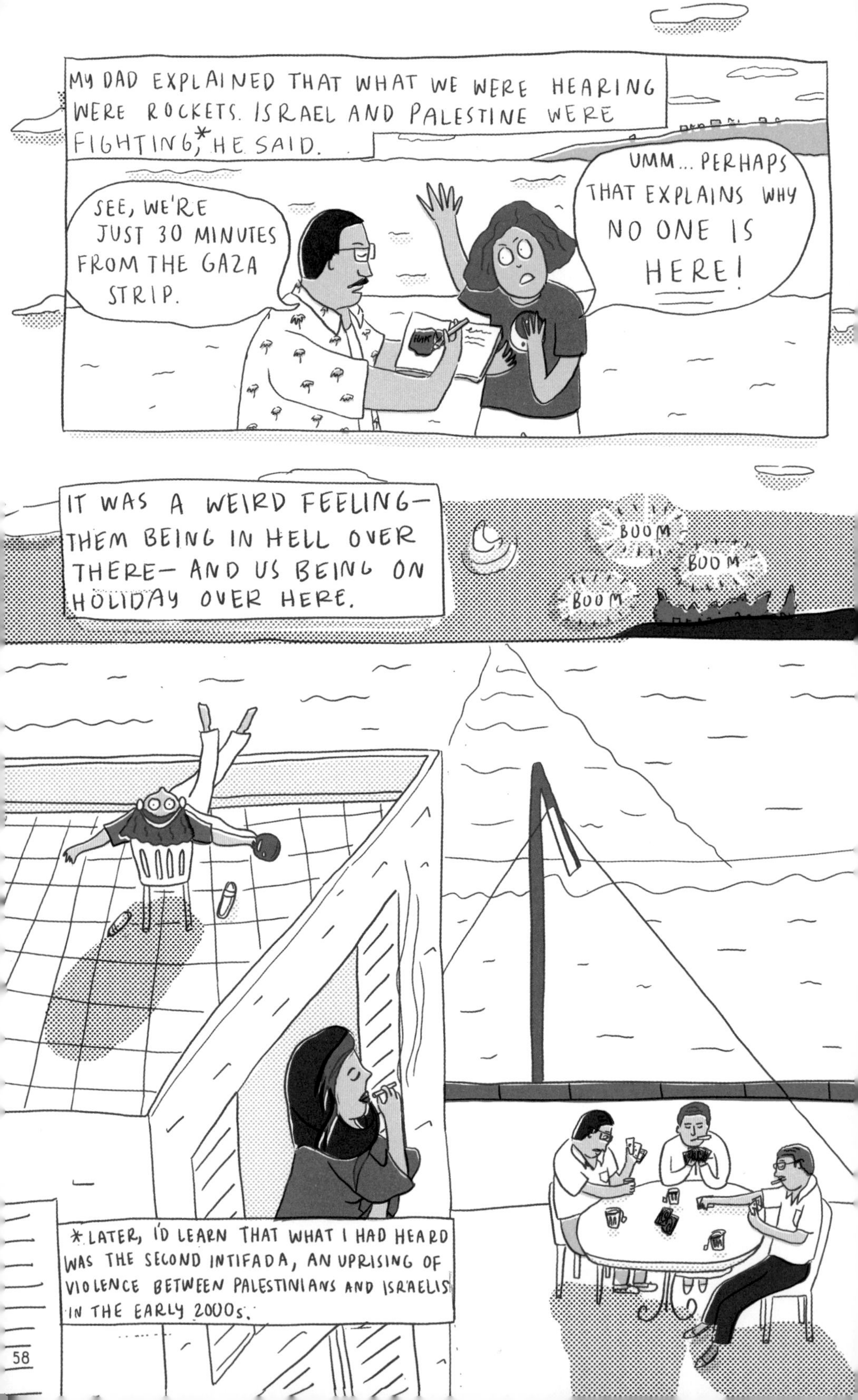
MY DAD EXPLAINED THAT WHAT WE WERE HEARING WERE ROCKETS. ISRAEL AND PALESTINE WERE FIGHTING,* HE SAID.
SEE, WE'RE JUST 30 MINUTES FROM THE GAZA STRIP.
UMM... PERHAPS THAT EXPLAINS WHY NO ONE IS HERE!
IT WAS A WEIRD FEELING—THEM BEING IN HELL OVER THERE—AND US BEING ON HOLIDAY OVER HERE.
BOOM
BOOM
BOOM
* LATER, I'D LEARN THAT WHAT I HAD HEARD WAS THE SECOND INTIFADA, AN UPRISING OF VIOLENCE BETWEEN PALESTINIANS AND ISRAELIS IN THE EARLY 2000s.

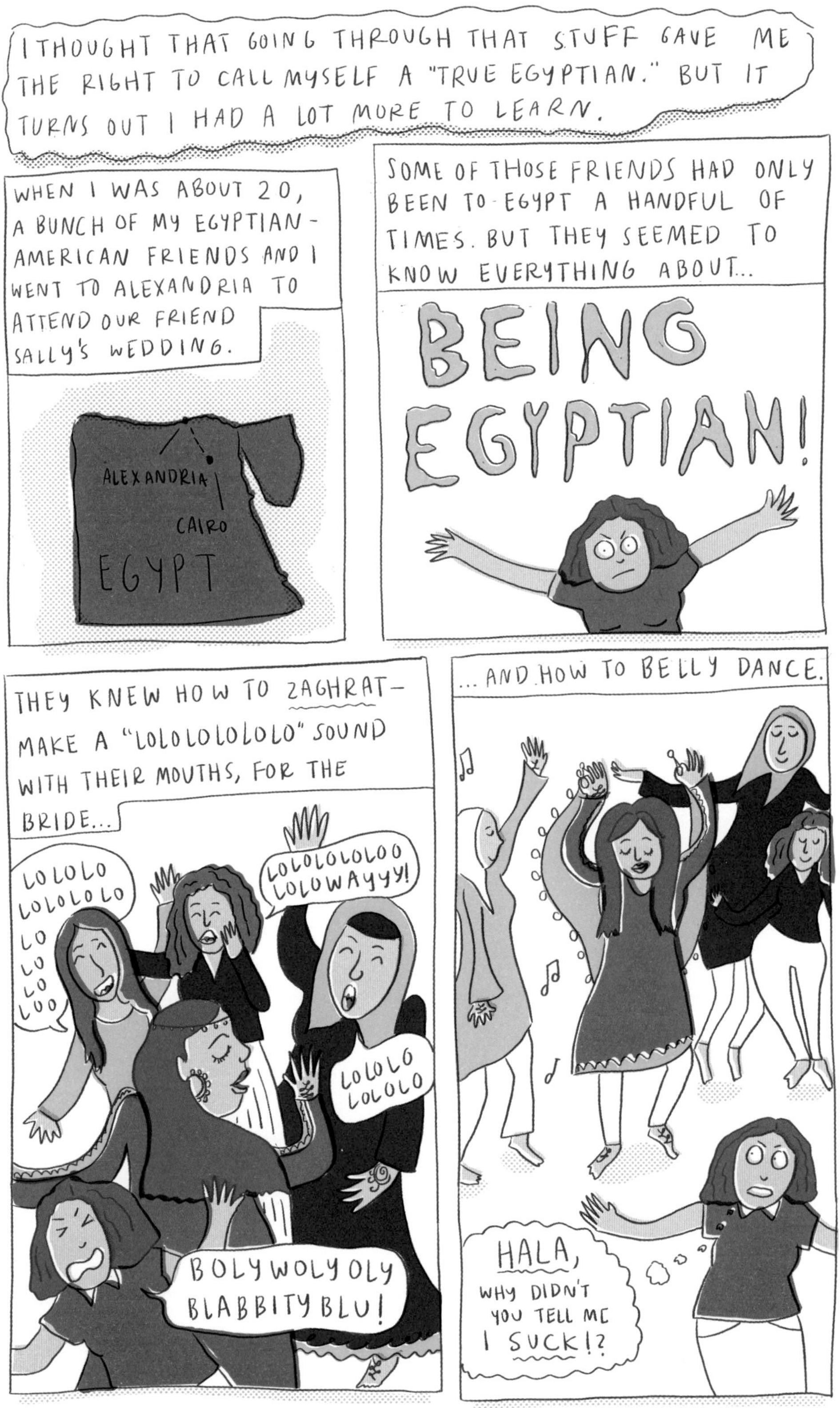
I THOUGHT THAT GOING THROUGH THAT STUFF GAVE ME THE RIGHT TO CALL MYSELF A "TRUE EGYPTIAN." BUT IT TURNS OUT I HAD A LOT MORE TO LEARN.
WHEN I WAS ABOUT 20, A BUNCH OF MY EGYPTIAN-AMERICAN FRIENDS AND I WENT TO ALEXANDRIA TO ATTEND OUR FRIEND SALLY'S WEDDING.
ALEXANDRIA
CAIRO
EGYPT
SOME OF THOSE FRIENDS HAD ONLY BEEN TO EGYPT A HANDFUL OF TIMES. BUT THEY SEEMED TO KNOW EVERYTHING ABOUT...
BEING EGYPTIAN!
THEY KNEW HOW TO ZAGHRAT— MAKE A "LOLOLOLOLOLO" SOUND WITH THEIR MOUTHS, FOR THE BRIDE...
LOLOLO LOLOLOLO LO LO LO LOO
LOLOLOLOLOO LOLOWAYYY!
LOLOLO LOLOLO
BOLYWOLYOLY BLABBITYBLU!
...AND HOW TO BELLY DANCE.
HALA, WHY DIDN'T YOU TELL ME I SUCK!?

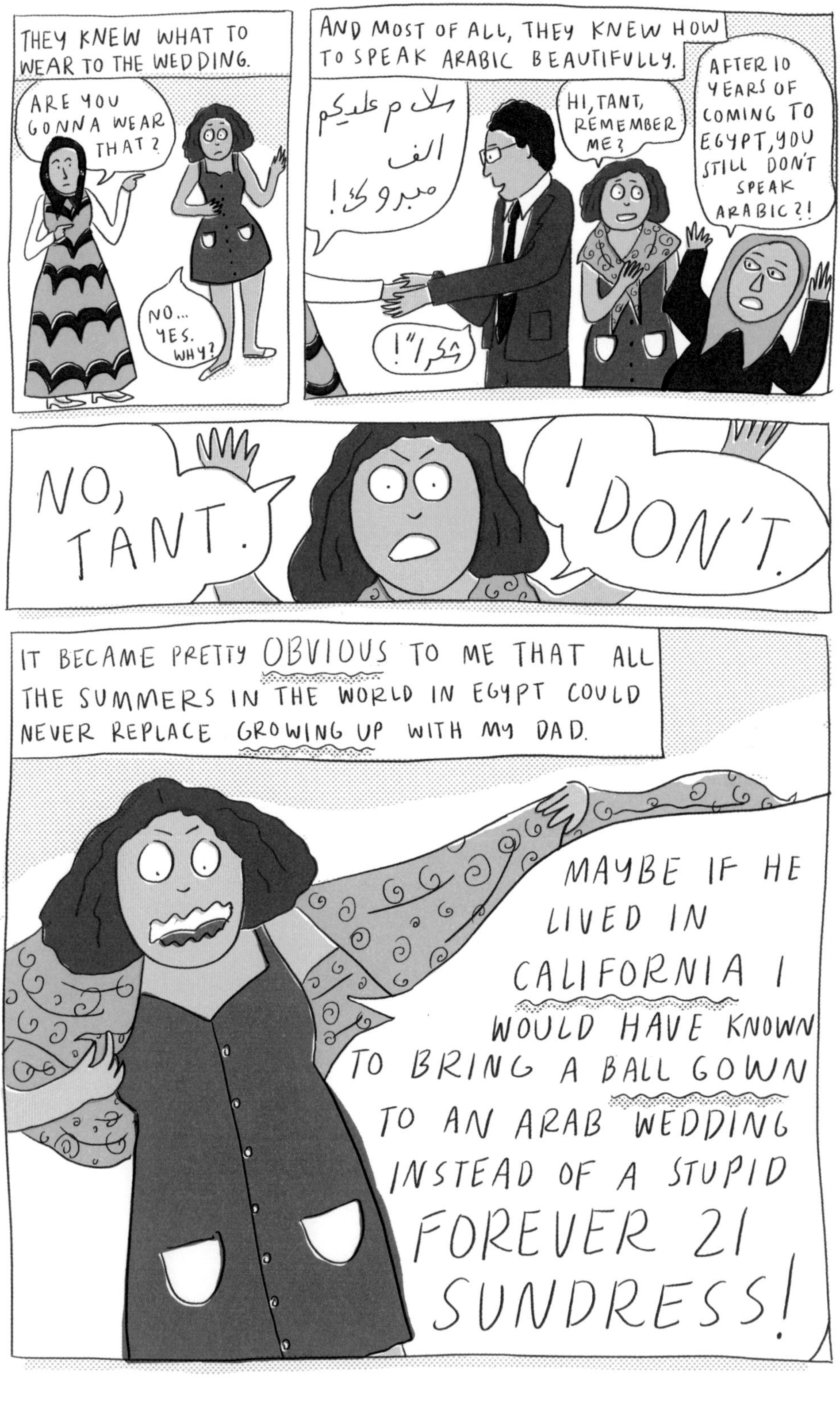

THEY KNEW WHAT TO WEAR TO THE WEDDING.
ARE YOU GONNA WEAR THAT?
NO... YES. WHY?
AND MOST OF ALL, THEY KNEW HOW TO SPEAK ARABIC BEAUTIFULLY.
سلام عليكم الف مبروك!
HI, TANT, REMEMBER ME?
شكرا!
AFTER 10 YEARS OF COMING TO EGYPT, YOU STILL DON'T SPEAK ARABIC?!
NO, TANT.
I DON'T.
IT BECAME PRETTY OBVIOUS TO ME THAT ALL THE SUMMERS IN THE WORLD IN EGYPT COULD NEVER REPLACE GROWING UP WITH MY DAD.
MAYBE IF HE LIVED IN CALIFORNIA I WOULD HAVE KNOWN TO BRING A BALL GOWN TO AN ARAB WEDDING INSTEAD OF A STUPID FOREVER 21 SUNDRESS!

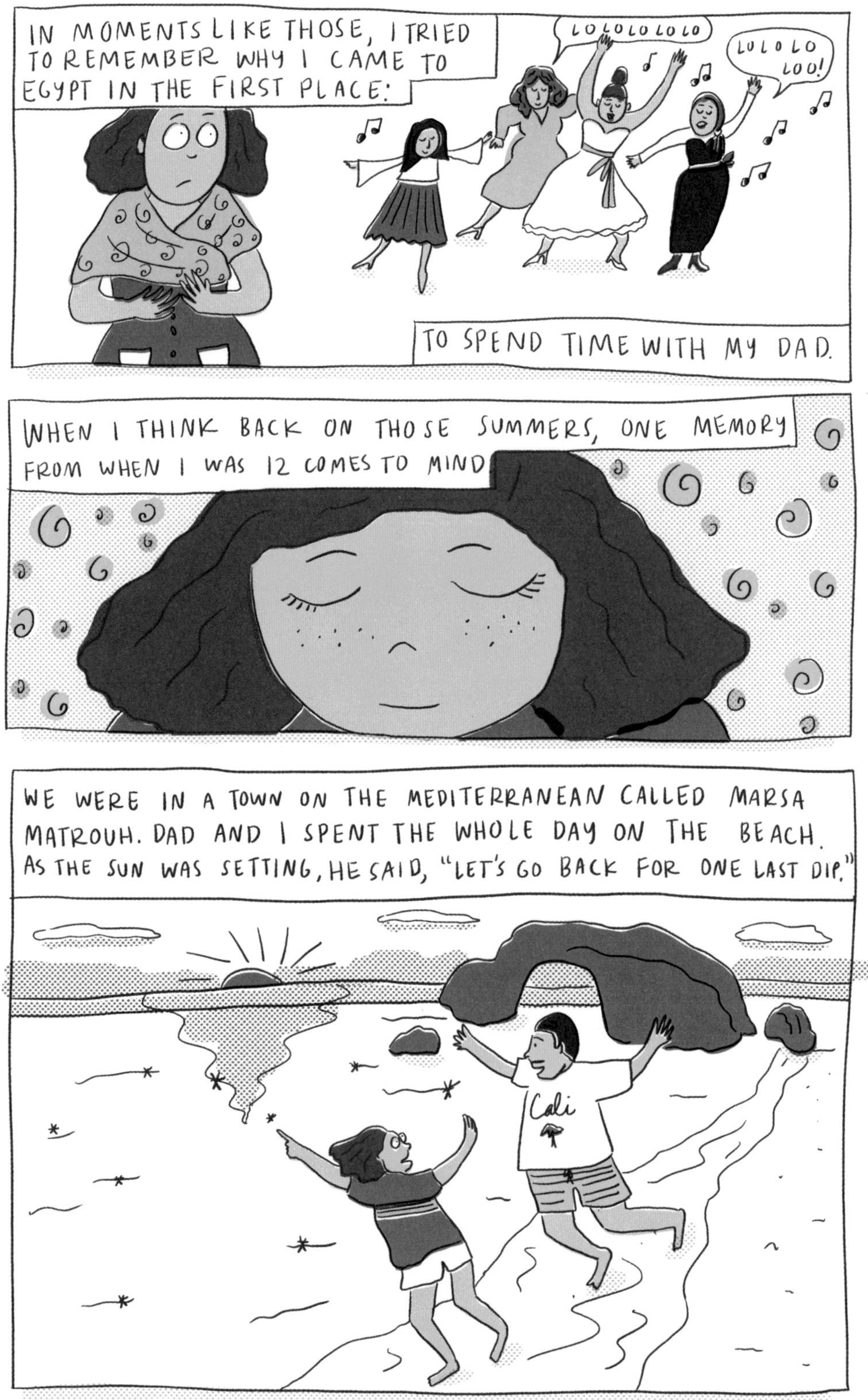
IN MOMENTS LIKE THOSE, I TRIED TO REMEMBER WHY I CAME TO EGYPT IN THE FIRST PLACE:
LOLOLOLOLO
LULOLO LOO!
TO SPEND TIME WITH MY DAD.
WHEN I THINK BACK ON THOSE SUMMERS, ONE MEMORY FROM WHEN I WAS 12 COMES TO MIND.
WE WERE IN A TOWN ON THE MEDITERRANEAN CALLED MARSA MATROUH. DAD AND I SPENT THE WHOLE DAY ON THE BEACH. AS THE SUN WAS SETTING, HE SAID, "LET'S GO BACK FOR ONE LAST DIP."
Cali

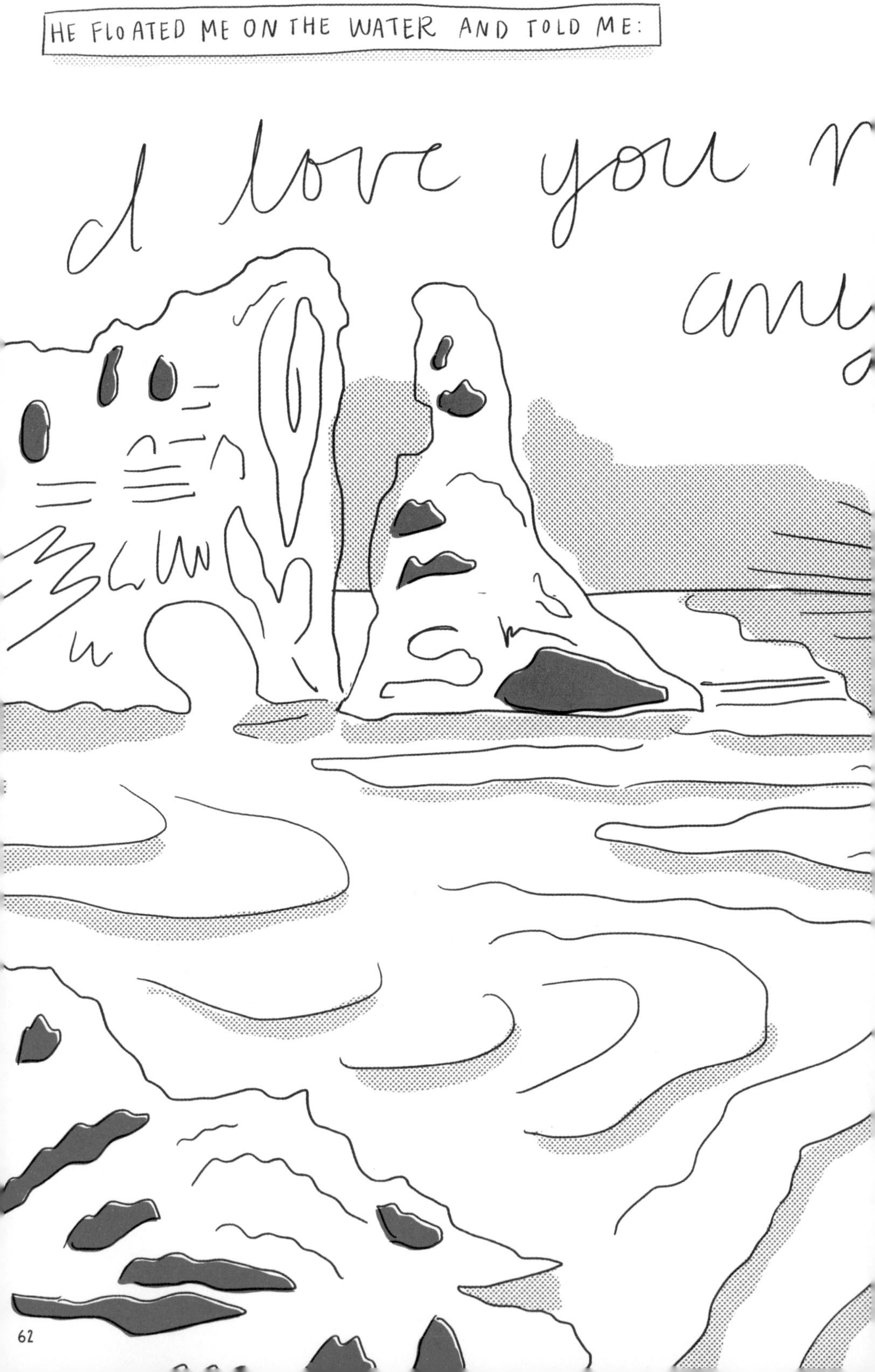
HE FLOATED ME ON THE WATER AND TOLD ME:
I love you

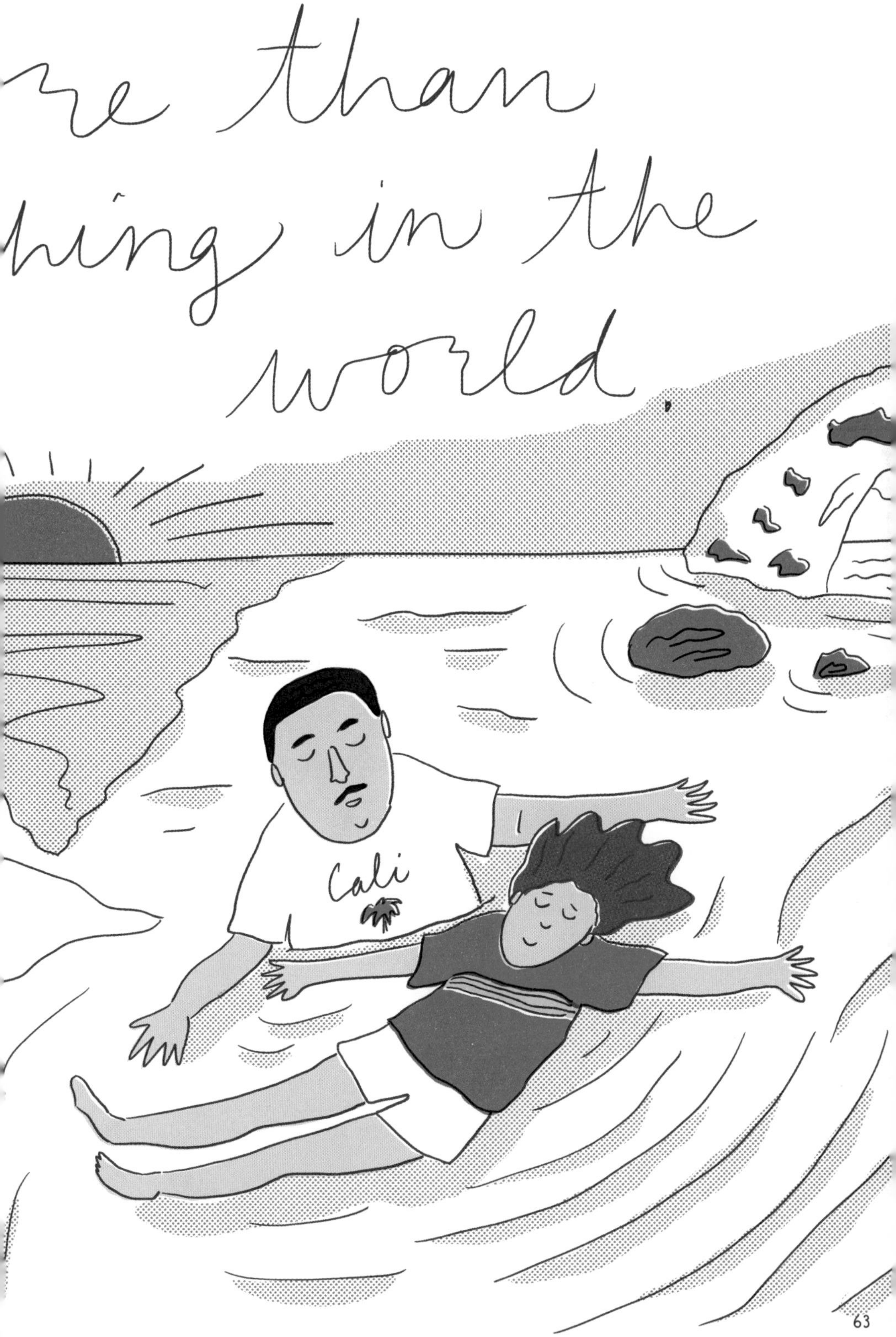
re than
hing in the
world
Cali

Chapter 4

IN MY HIGH SCHOOL,
THE CLASS PRESIDENT WAS KOREAN
AND THE PROM QUEEN, FILIPINO.

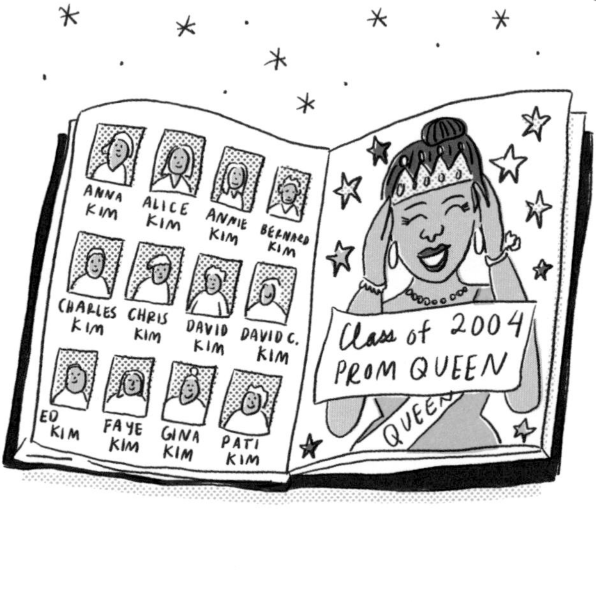

ANNA KIM
ALICE KIM
ANNIE KIM
BERNARD KIM
CHARLES KIM
CHRIS KIM
DAVID KIM
DAVID C. KIM
ED KIM
FAYE KIM
GINA KIM
PATI KIM
Class of 2004
PROM QUEEN
QUEEN

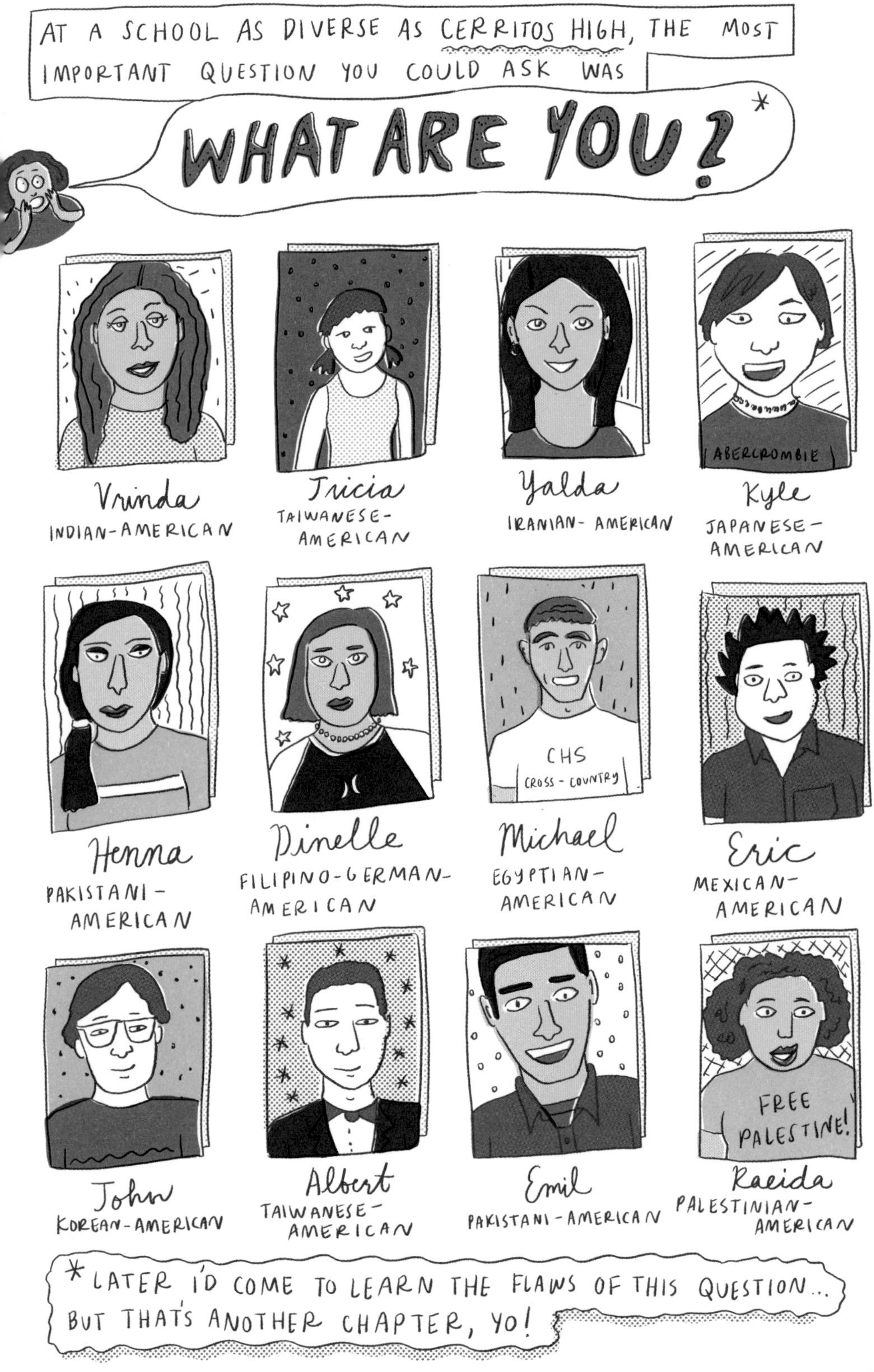
AT A SCHOOL AS DIVERSE AS CERRITOS HIGH, THE MOST IMPORTANT QUESTION YOU COULD ASK WAS
WHAT ARE YOU?*
ABERCROMBIE
Vrinda
INDIAN-AMERICAN
Tricia
TAIWANESE-AMERICAN
Yalda
IRANIAN-AMERICAN
Kyle
JAPANESE-AMERICAN
CHS
CROSS-COUNTRY
Henna
PAKISTANI-AMERICAN
Dinelle
FILIPINO-GERMAN-AMERICAN
Michael
EGYPTIAN-AMERICAN
Eric
MEXICAN-AMERICAN
FREE PALESTINE!
John
KOREAN-AMERICAN
Albert
TAIWANESE-AMERICAN
Emil
PAKISTANI-AMERICAN
Raeida
PALESTINIAN-AMERICAN
*LATER I'D COME TO LEARN THE FLAWS OF THIS QUESTION... BUT THAT'S ANOTHER CHAPTER, YO!

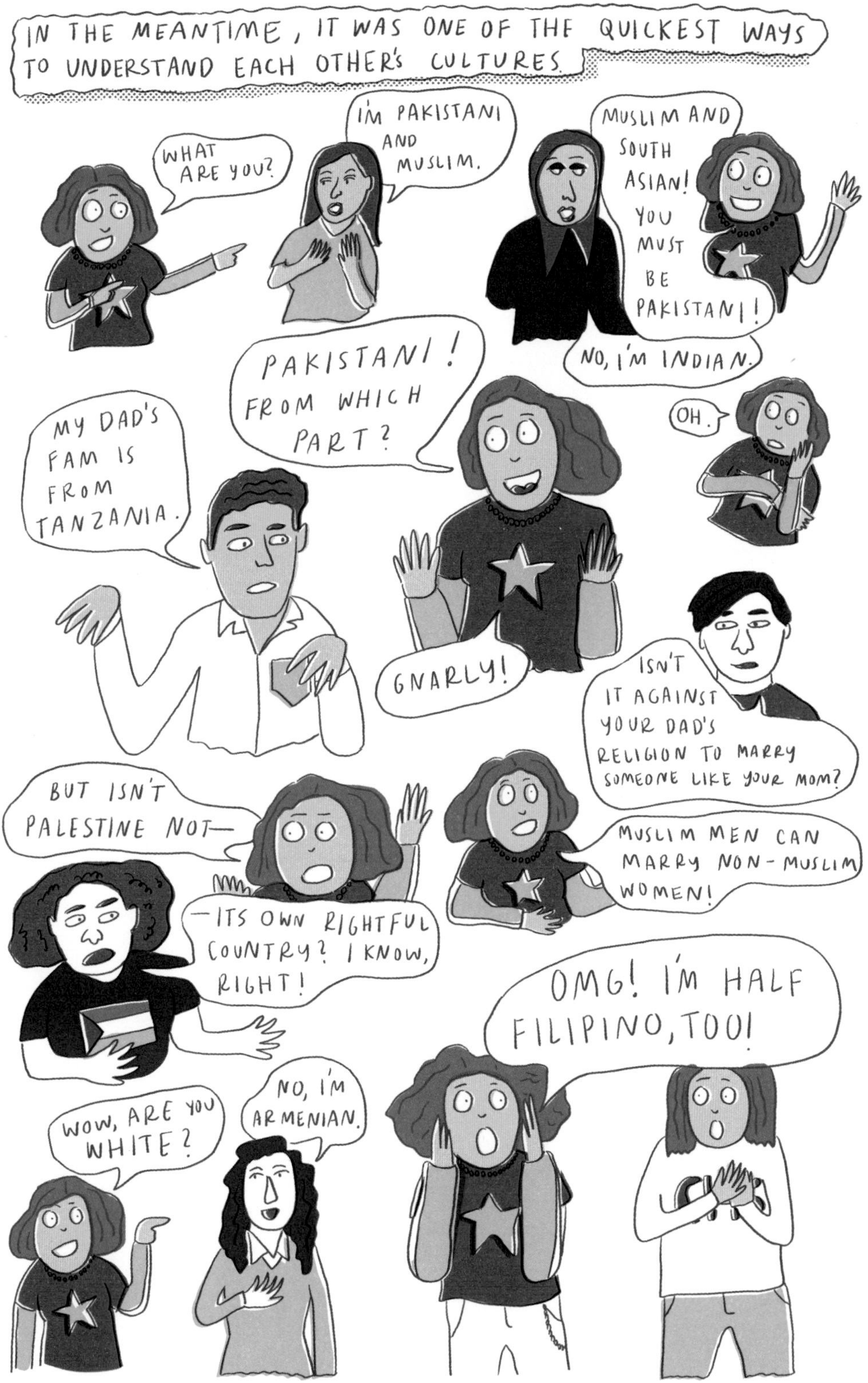
IN THE MEANTIME, IT WAS ONE OF THE QUICKEST WAYS TO UNDERSTAND EACH OTHER'S CULTURES.
WHAT ARE YOU?
I'M PAKISTANI AND MUSLIM.
MUSLIM AND SOUTH ASIAN! YOU MUST BE PAKISTANI!
NO, I'M INDIAN.
OH.
MY DAD'S FAM IS FROM TANZANIA.
PAKISTANI! FROM WHICH PART?
GNARLY!
ISN'T IT AGAINST YOUR DAD'S RELIGION TO MARRY SOMEONE LIKE YOUR MOM?
MUSLIM MEN CAN MARRY NON-MUSLIM WOMEN!
BUT ISN'T PALESTINE NOT—
—ITS OWN RIGHTFUL COUNTRY? I KNOW, RIGHT!
WOW, ARE YOU WHITE?
NO, I'M ARMENIAN.
OMG! I'M HALF FILIPINO, TOO!

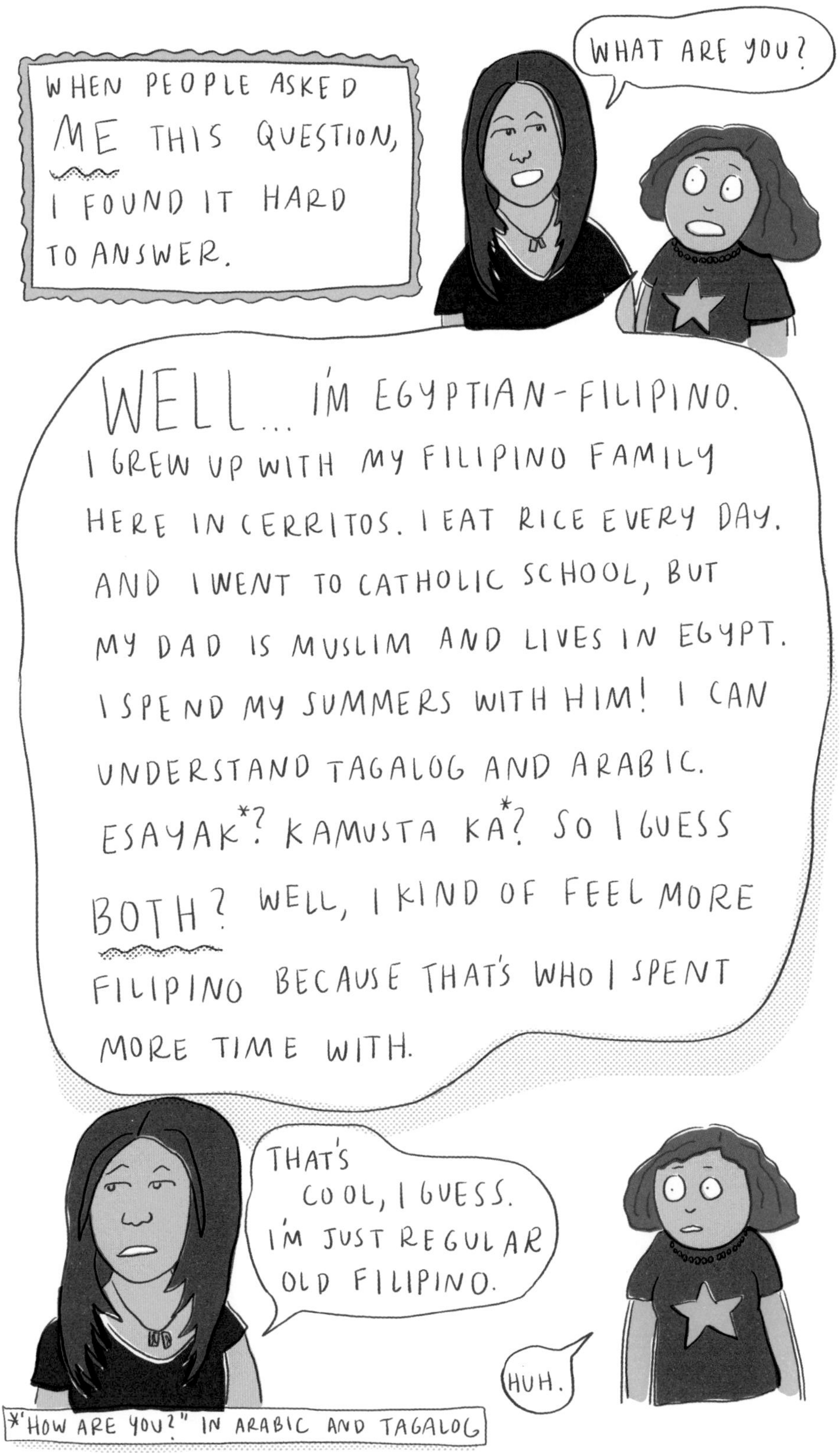
WHEN PEOPLE ASKED ME THIS QUESTION, I FOUND IT HARD TO ANSWER.
WHAT ARE YOU?
WELL... I'M EGYPTIAN-FILIPINO. I GREW UP WITH MY FILIPINO FAMILY HERE IN CERRITOS. I EAT RICE EVERY DAY. AND I WENT TO CATHOLIC SCHOOL, BUT MY DAD IS MUSLIM AND LIVES IN EGYPT. I SPEND MY SUMMERS WITH HIM! I CAN UNDERSTAND TAGALOG AND ARABIC. ESAYAK*? KAMUSTA KA*? SO I GUESS BOTH? WELL, I KIND OF FEEL MORE FILIPINO BECAUSE THAT'S WHO I SPENT MORE TIME WITH.
THAT'S COOL, I GUESS. I'M JUST REGULAR OLD FILIPINO.
HUH.
*"HOW ARE YOU?" IN ARABIC AND TAGALOG

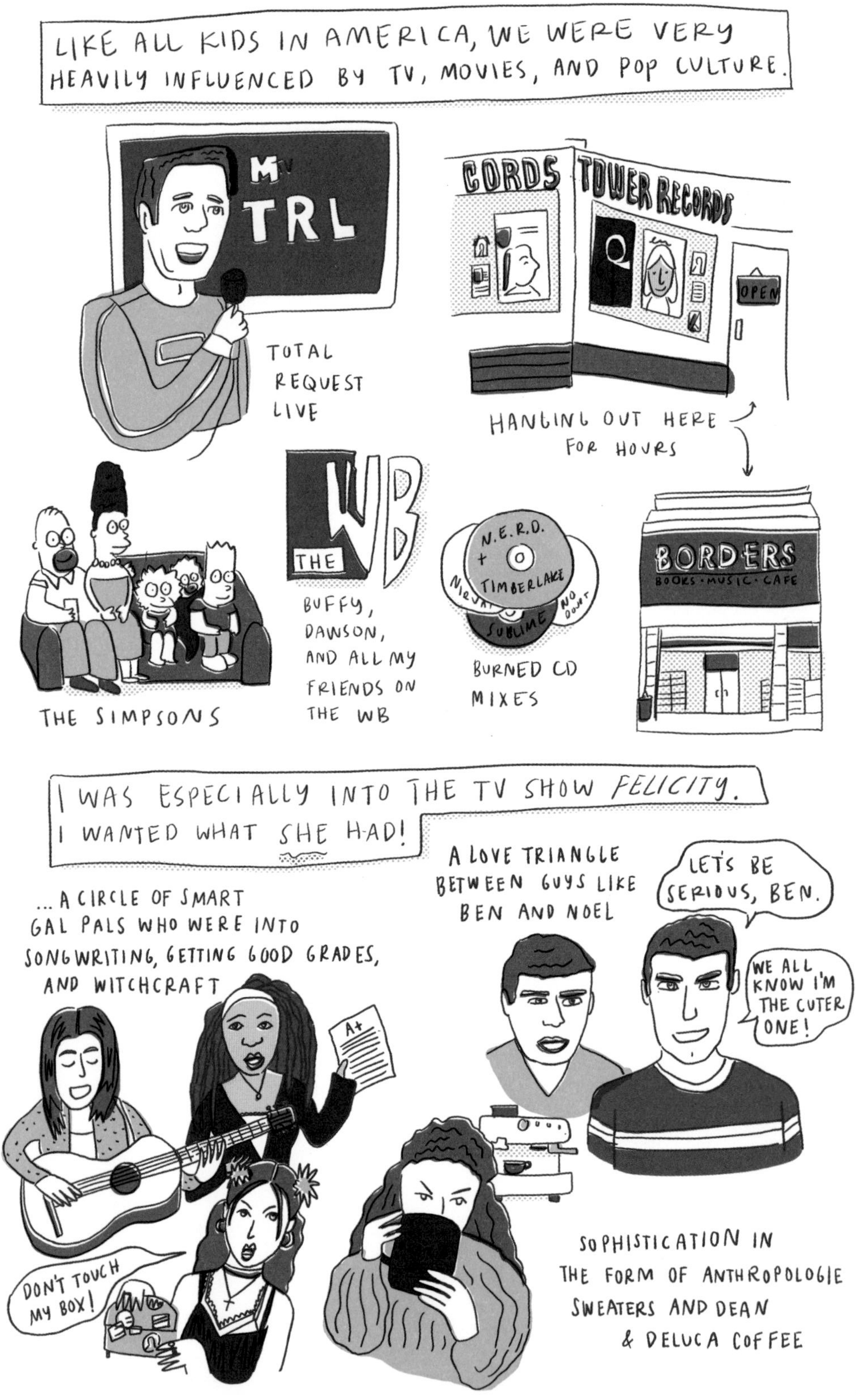
LIKE ALL KIDS IN AMERICA, WE WERE VERY HEAVILY INFLUENCED BY TV, MOVIES, AND POP CULTURE.
MTV TRL
TOTAL REQUEST LIVE
CORDS
TOWER RECORDS
OPEN
HANGING OUT HERE FOR HOURS
BORDERS
BOOKS · MUSIC · CAFE
THE SIMPSONS
THE WB
BUFFY, DAWSON, AND ALL MY FRIENDS ON THE WB
N.E.R.D. + TIMBERLAKE
SUBLIME
BURNED CD MIXES
I WAS ESPECIALLY INTO THE TV SHOW *FELICITY*. I WANTED WHAT SHE HAD!
...A CIRCLE OF SMART GAL PALS WHO WERE INTO SONGWRITING, GETTING GOOD GRADES, AND WITCHCRAFT
A+
DON'T TOUCH MY BOX!
A LOVE TRIANGLE BETWEEN GUYS LIKE BEN AND NOEL
LET'S BE SERIOUS, BEN.
WE ALL KNOW I'M THE CUTER ONE!
SOPHISTICATION IN THE FORM OF ANTHROPOLOGIE SWEATERS AND DEAN & DELUCA COFFEE

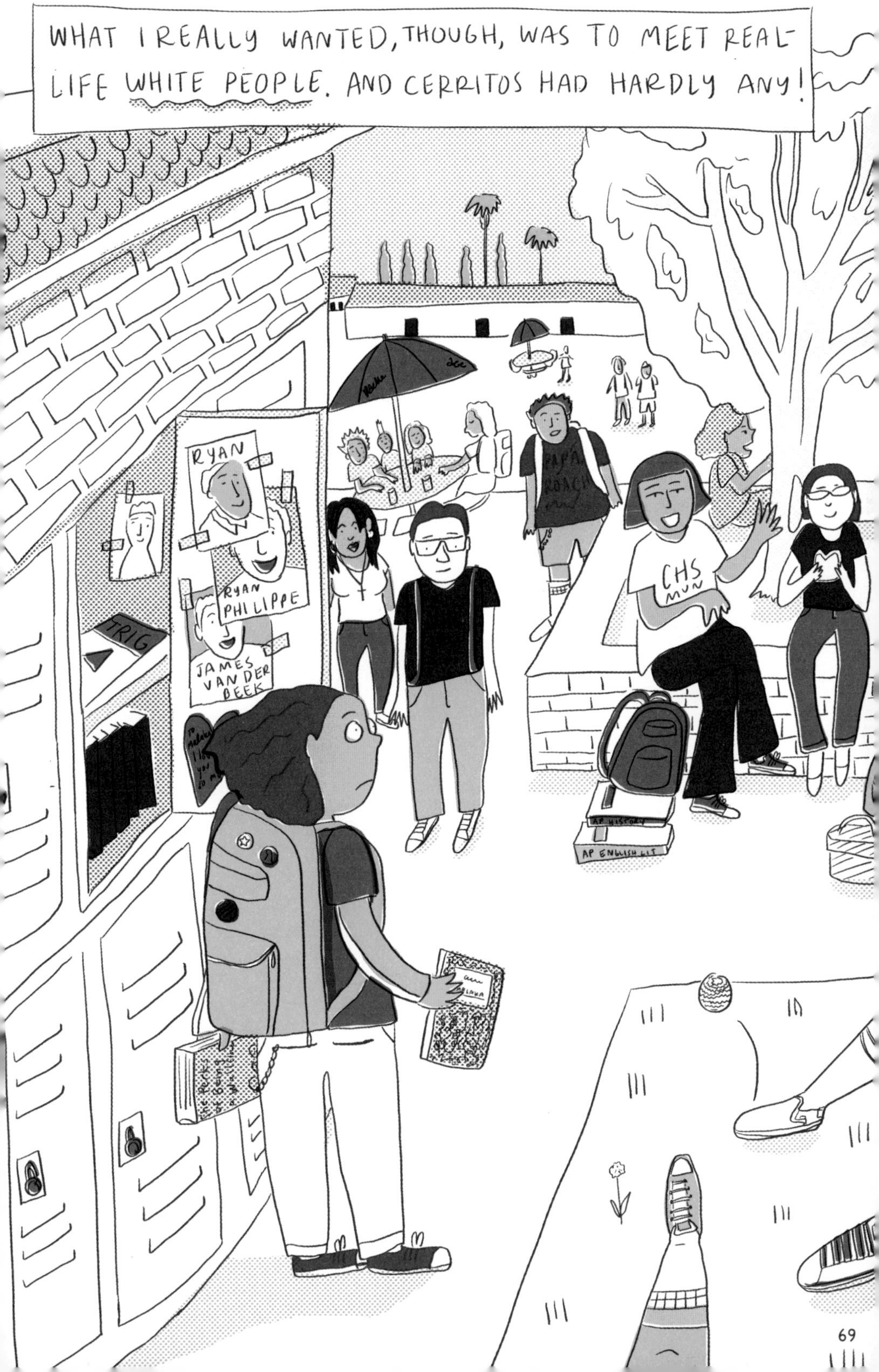
WHAT I REALLY WANTED, THOUGH, WAS TO MEET REAL-LIFE WHITE PEOPLE. AND CERRITOS HAD HARDLY ANY!
RYAN
RYAN PHILIPPE
JAMES VAN DER BEEK
TRIG
PAPA ROACH
CHS MUN
AP HISTORY
AP ENGLISH LIT

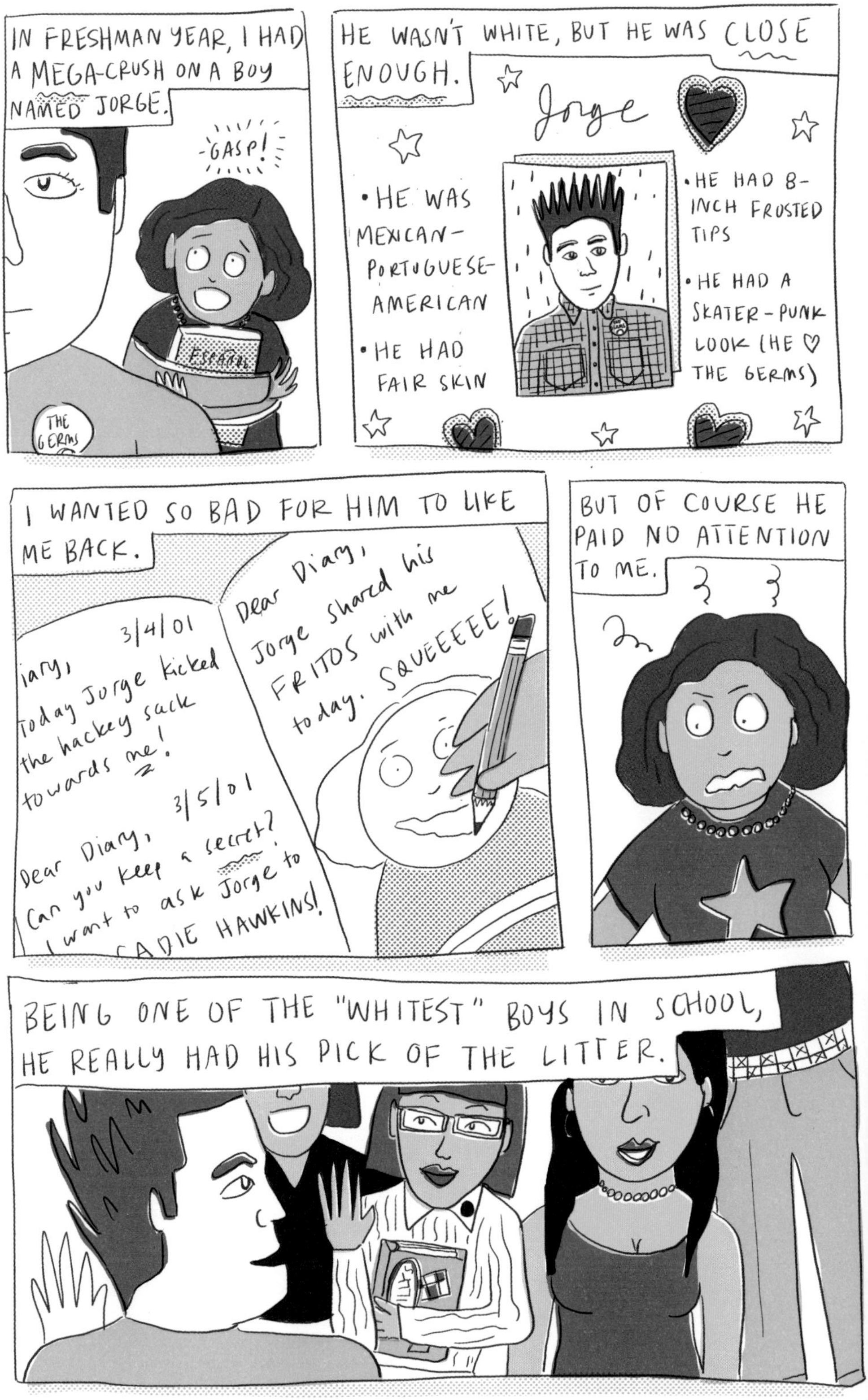
IN FRESHMAN YEAR, I HAD A MEGA-CRUSH ON A BOY NAMED JORGE.
GASP!
ESPAÑOL
THE GERMS
HE WASN'T WHITE, BUT HE WAS CLOSE ENOUGH.
Jorge
• HE WAS MEXICAN-PORTUGUESE-AMERICAN
• HE HAD FAIR SKIN
• HE HAD 8-INCH FROSTED TIPS
• HE HAD A SKATER-PUNK LOOK (HE ♡ THE GERMS)
I WANTED SO BAD FOR HIM TO LIKE ME BACK.
3/4/01
iary, Today Jorge kicked the hackey sack towards me!
3/5/01
Dear Diary, Can you keep a secret? I want to ask Jorge to
ADIE HAWKINS!
Dear Diary, Jorge shared his FRITOS with me today. SQUEEEEE!
BUT OF COURSE HE PAID NO ATTENTION TO ME.
BEING ONE OF THE "WHITEST" BOYS IN SCHOOL, HE REALLY HAD HIS PICK OF THE LITTER.

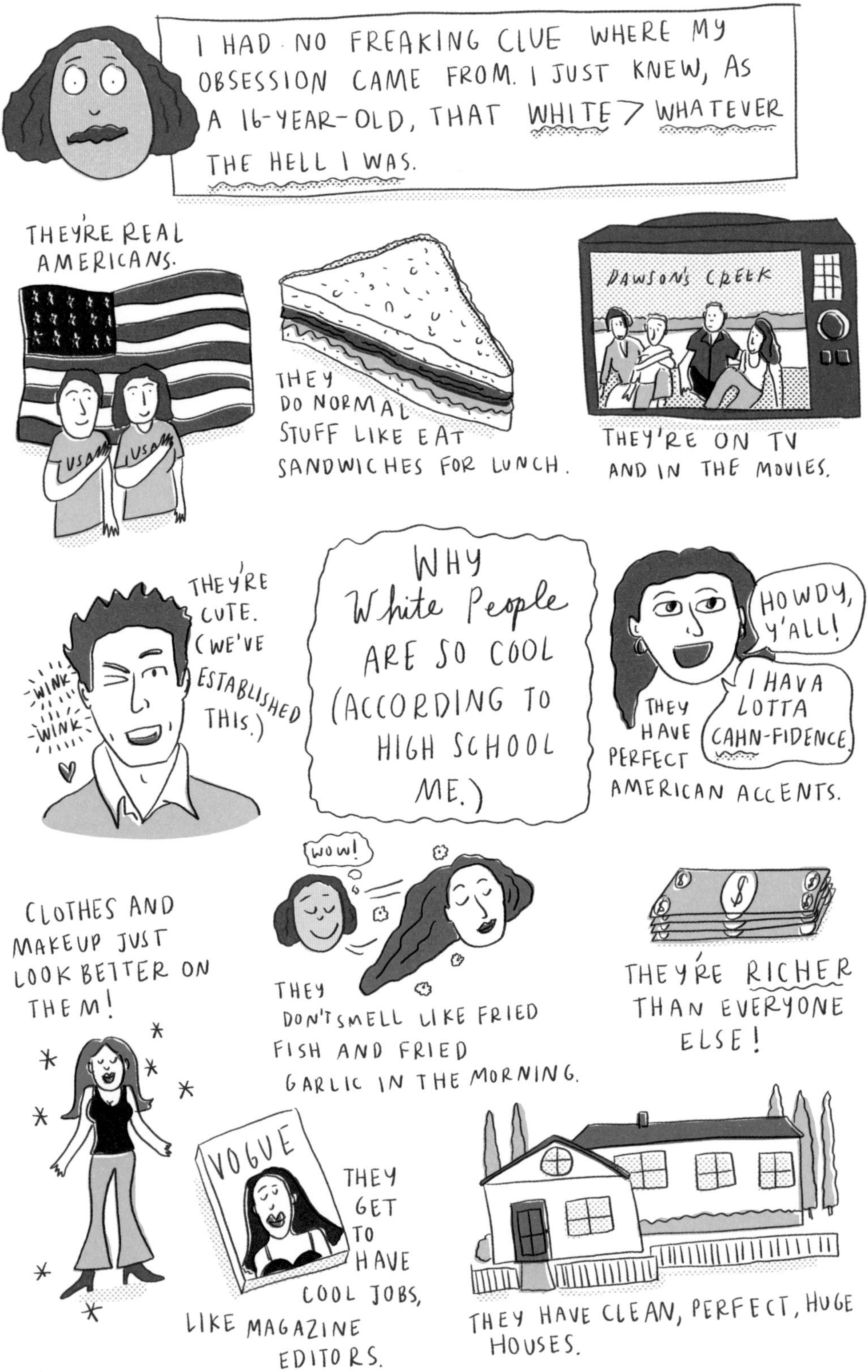
I HAD NO FREAKING CLUE WHERE MY OBSESSION CAME FROM. I JUST KNEW, AS A 16-YEAR-OLD, THAT WHITE > WHATEVER THE HELL I WAS.
THEY'RE REAL AMERICANS.
USA
USA
THEY DO NORMAL STUFF LIKE EAT SANDWICHES FOR LUNCH.
DAWSON'S CREEK
THEY'RE ON TV AND IN THE MOVIES.
THEY'RE CUTE. (WE'VE ESTABLISHED THIS.)
WINK
WINK
WHY White People ARE SO COOL (ACCORDING TO HIGH SCHOOL ME.)
HOWDY, Y'ALL!
I HAVA LOTTA CAHN-FIDENCE.
THEY HAVE PERFECT AMERICAN ACCENTS.
CLOTHES AND MAKEUP JUST LOOK BETTER ON THEM!
WOW!
THEY DON'T SMELL LIKE FRIED FISH AND FRIED GARLIC IN THE MORNING.
THEY'RE RICHER THAN EVERYONE ELSE!
VOGUE
THEY GET TO HAVE COOL JOBS, LIKE MAGAZINE EDITORS.
THEY HAVE CLEAN, PERFECT, HUGE HOUSES.

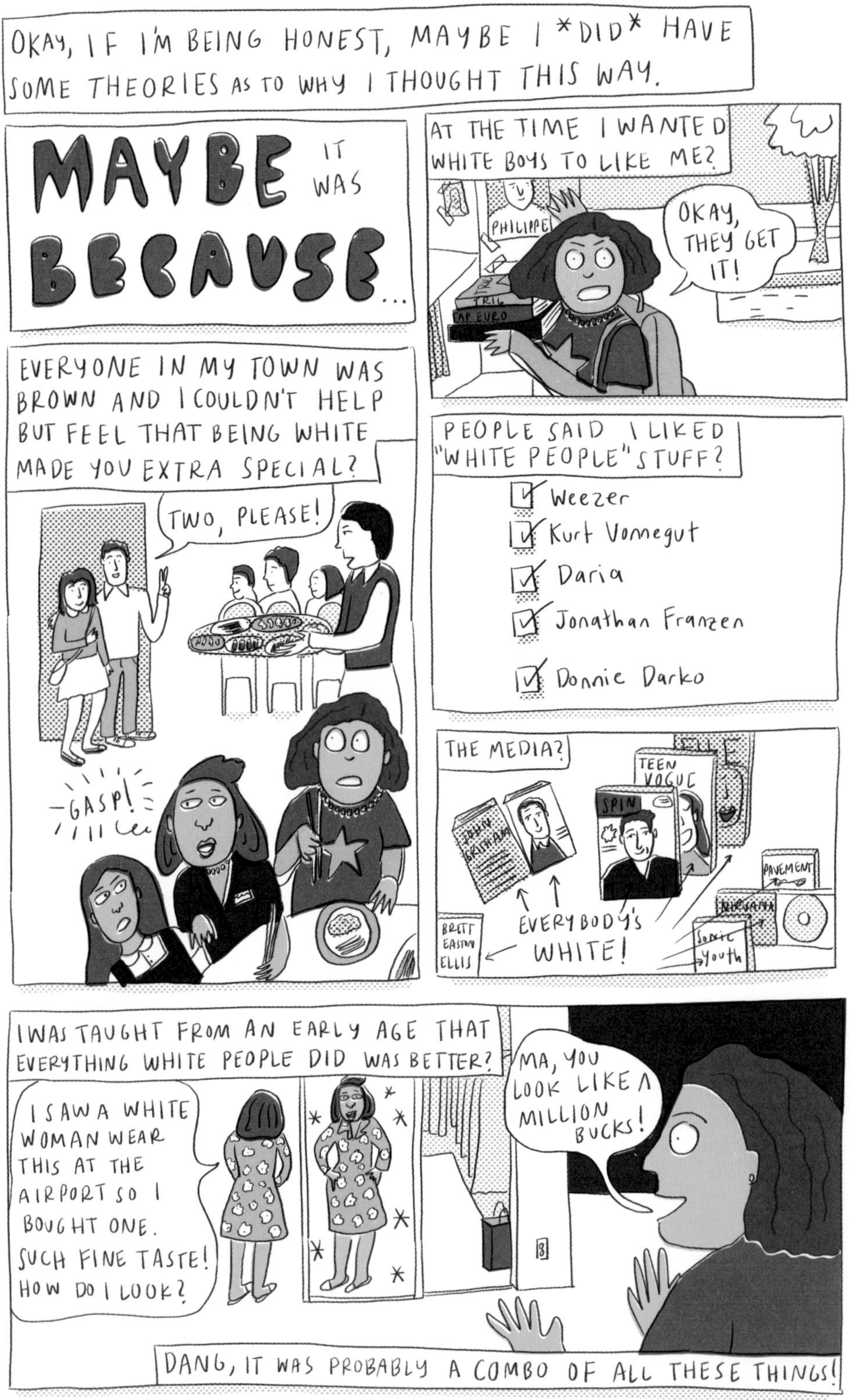
OKAY, IF I'M BEING HONEST, MAYBE I *DID* HAVE SOME THEORIES AS TO WHY I THOUGHT THIS WAY.
MAYBE IT WAS BECAUSE...
AT THE TIME I WANTED WHITE BOYS TO LIKE ME?
PHILIPPE
OKAY, THEY GET IT!
EVERYONE IN MY TOWN WAS BROWN AND I COULDN'T HELP BUT FEEL THAT BEING WHITE MADE YOU EXTRA SPECIAL?
TWO, PLEASE!
GASP!
PEOPLE SAID I LIKED "WHITE PEOPLE" STUFF?
Weezer
Kurt Vonnegut
Daria
Jonathan Franzen
Donnie Darko
THE MEDIA?
TEEN VOGUE
SPIN
PAVEMENT
BRETT EASTON ELLIS
EVERYBODY'S WHITE!
Sonic Youth
I WAS TAUGHT FROM AN EARLY AGE THAT EVERYTHING WHITE PEOPLE DID WAS BETTER?
I SAW A WHITE WOMAN WEAR THIS AT THE AIRPORT SO I BOUGHT ONE. SUCH FINE TASTE! HOW DO I LOOK?
MA, YOU LOOK LIKE A MILLION BUCKS!
DANG, IT WAS PROBABLY A COMBO OF ALL THESE THINGS!

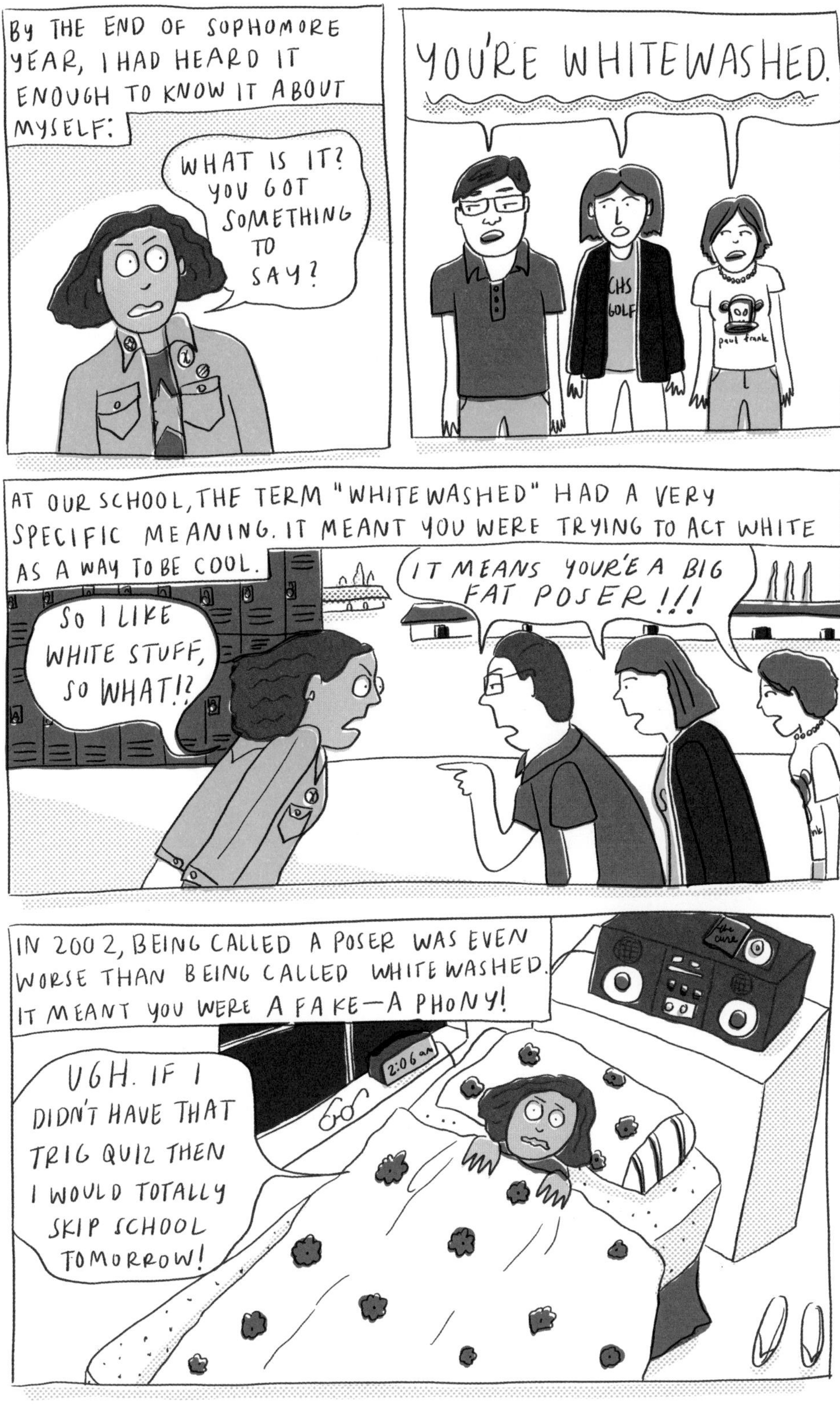

BY THE END OF SOPHOMORE YEAR, I HAD HEARD IT ENOUGH TO KNOW IT ABOUT MYSELF:
WHAT IS IT? YOU GOT SOMETHING TO SAY?
YOU'RE WHITEWASHED.
CHS GOLF
paul frank
AT OUR SCHOOL, THE TERM "WHITEWASHED" HAD A VERY SPECIFIC MEANING. IT MEANT YOU WERE TRYING TO ACT WHITE AS A WAY TO BE COOL.
SO I LIKE WHITE STUFF, SO WHAT!?
IT MEANS YOU'RE A BIG FAT POSER!!!
IN 2002, BEING CALLED A POSER WAS EVEN WORSE THAN BEING CALLED WHITEWASHED. IT MEANT YOU WERE A FAKE—A PHONY!
the cure
2:06 am
UGH. IF I DIDN'T HAVE THAT TRIG QUIZ THEN I WOULD TOTALLY SKIP SCHOOL TOMORROW!

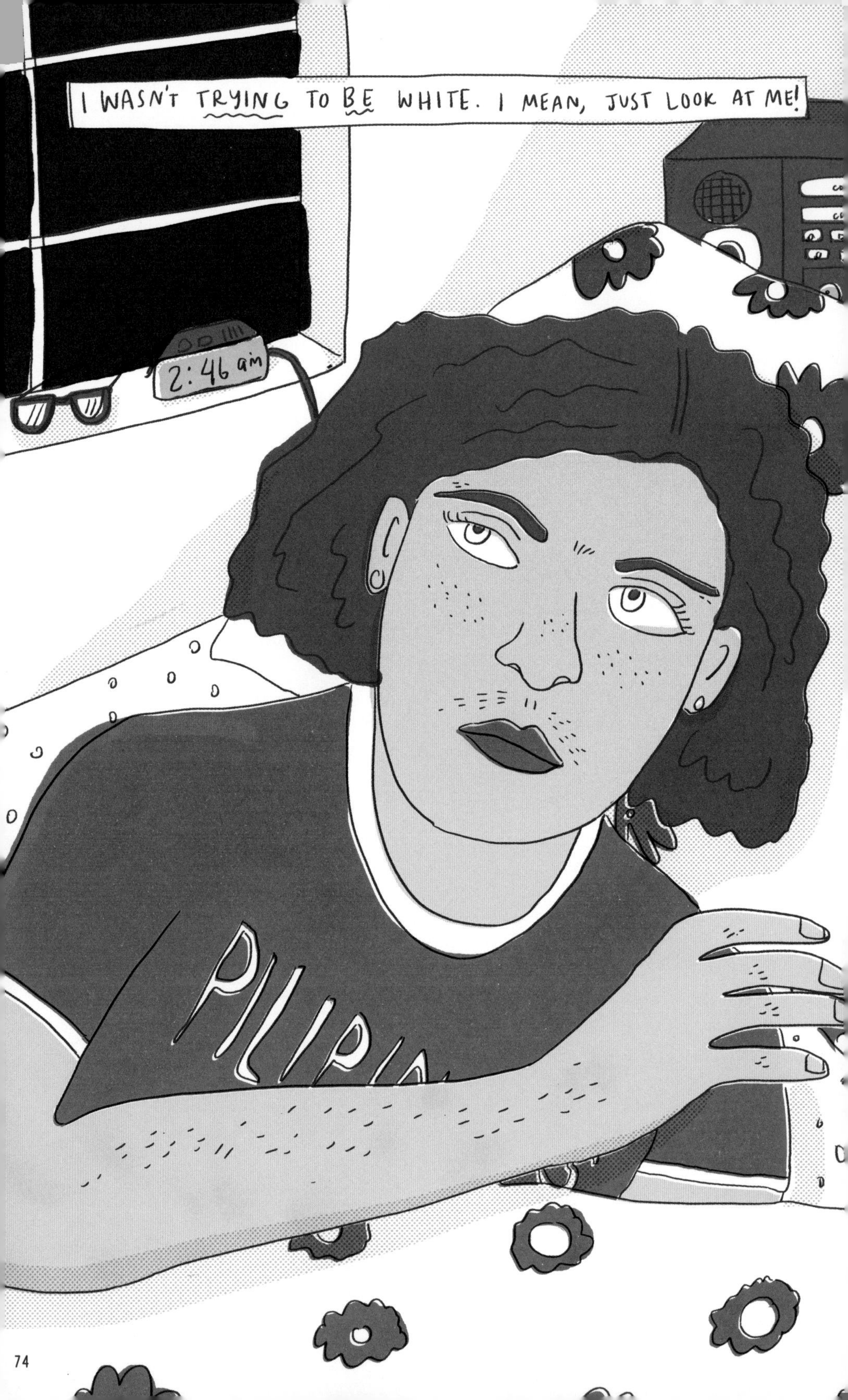
I WASN'T TRYING TO BE WHITE. I MEAN, JUST LOOK AT ME!
2:46 am
PILIPIN

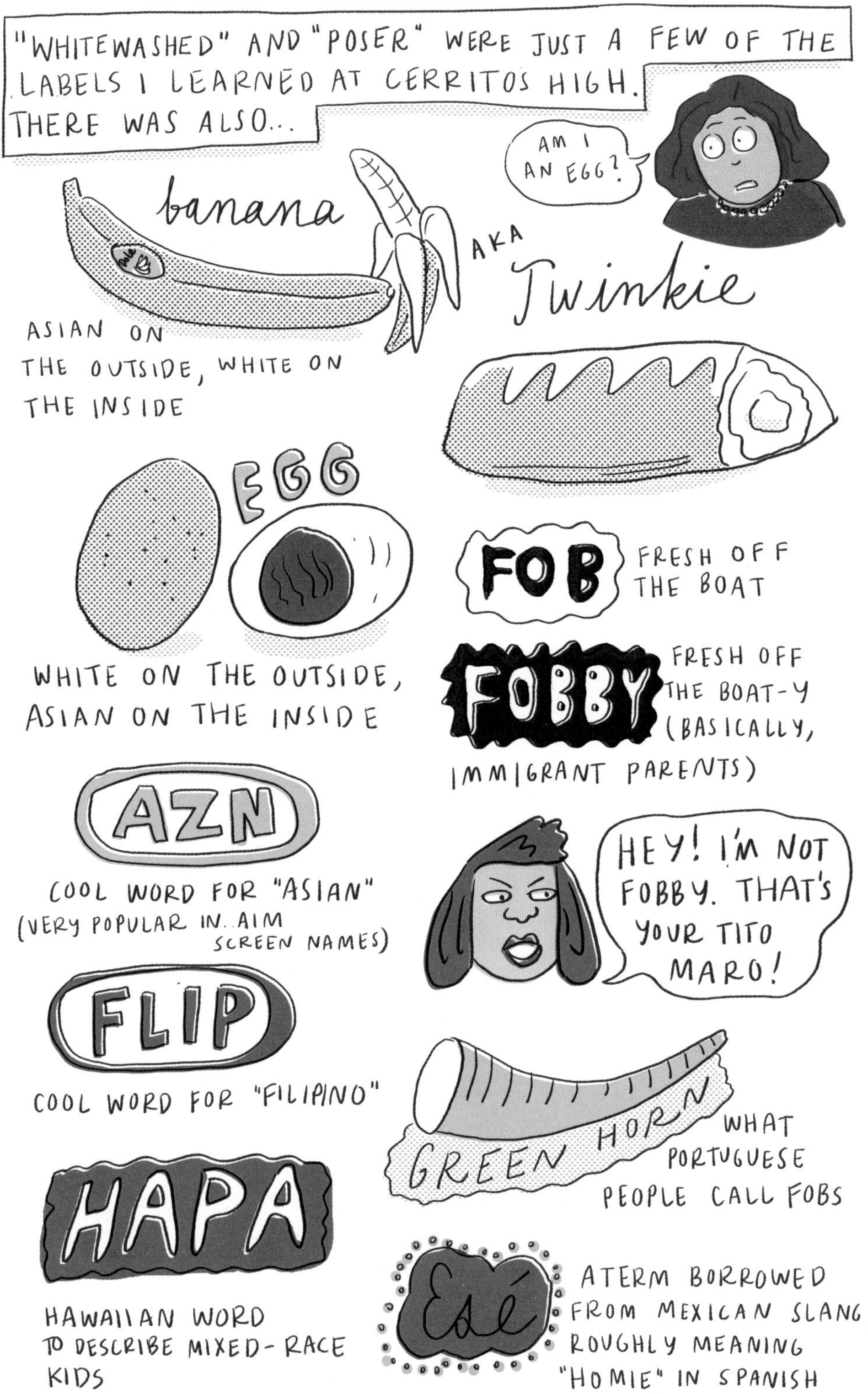

"WHITEWASHED" AND "POSER" WERE JUST A FEW OF THE LABELS I LEARNED AT CERRITOS HIGH. THERE WAS ALSO...
AM I AN EGG?
banana
AKA
Twinkie
ASIAN ON THE OUTSIDE, WHITE ON THE INSIDE
EGG
WHITE ON THE OUTSIDE, ASIAN ON THE INSIDE
FOB
FRESH OFF THE BOAT
FOBBY
FRESH OFF THE BOAT-Y (BASICALLY, IMMIGRANT PARENTS)
AZN
COOL WORD FOR "ASIAN" (VERY POPULAR IN AIM SCREEN NAMES)
HEY! I'M NOT FOBBY. THAT'S YOUR TITO MARO!
FLIP
COOL WORD FOR "FILIPINO"
GREEN HORN
WHAT PORTUGUESE PEOPLE CALL FOBS
HAPA
HAWAIIAN WORD TO DESCRIBE MIXED-RACE KIDS
Esé
A TERM BORROWED FROM MEXICAN SLANG ROUGHLY MEANING "HOMIE" IN SPANISH

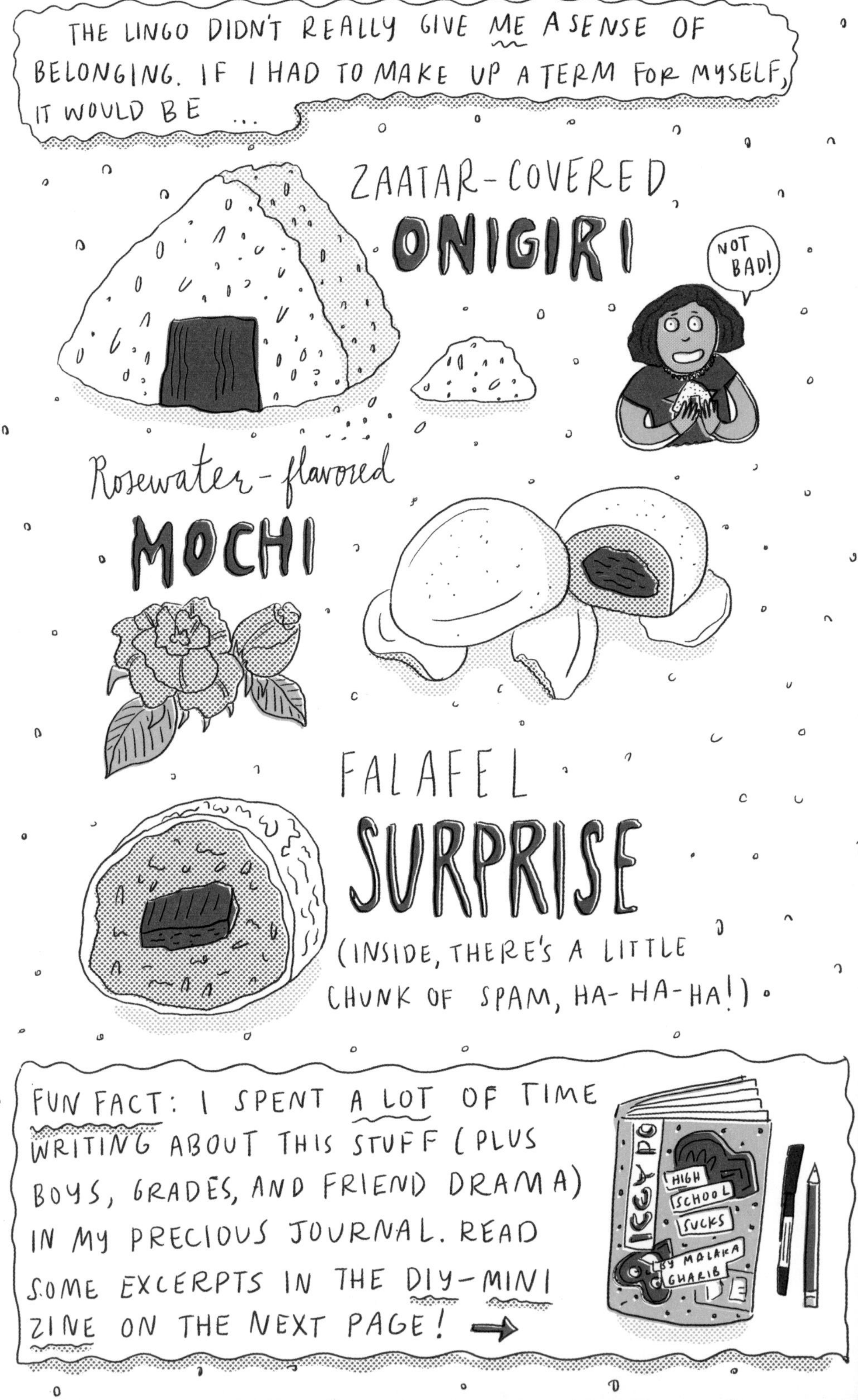
THE LINGO DIDN'T REALLY GIVE ME A SENSE OF BELONGING. IF I HAD TO MAKE UP A TERM FOR MYSELF, IT WOULD BE ...
ZAATAR-COVERED ONIGIRI
NOT BAD!
Rosewater-flavored MOCHI
FALAFEL SURPRISE
(INSIDE, THERE'S A LITTLE CHUNK OF SPAM, HA-HA-HA!)
FUN FACT: I SPENT A LOT OF TIME WRITING ABOUT THIS STUFF (PLUS BOYS, GRADES, AND FRIEND DRAMA) IN MY PRECIOUS JOURNAL. READ SOME EXCERPTS IN THE DIY-MINI ZINE ON THE NEXT PAGE!
HIGH SCHOOL SUCKS
BY MALAKA GHARIB

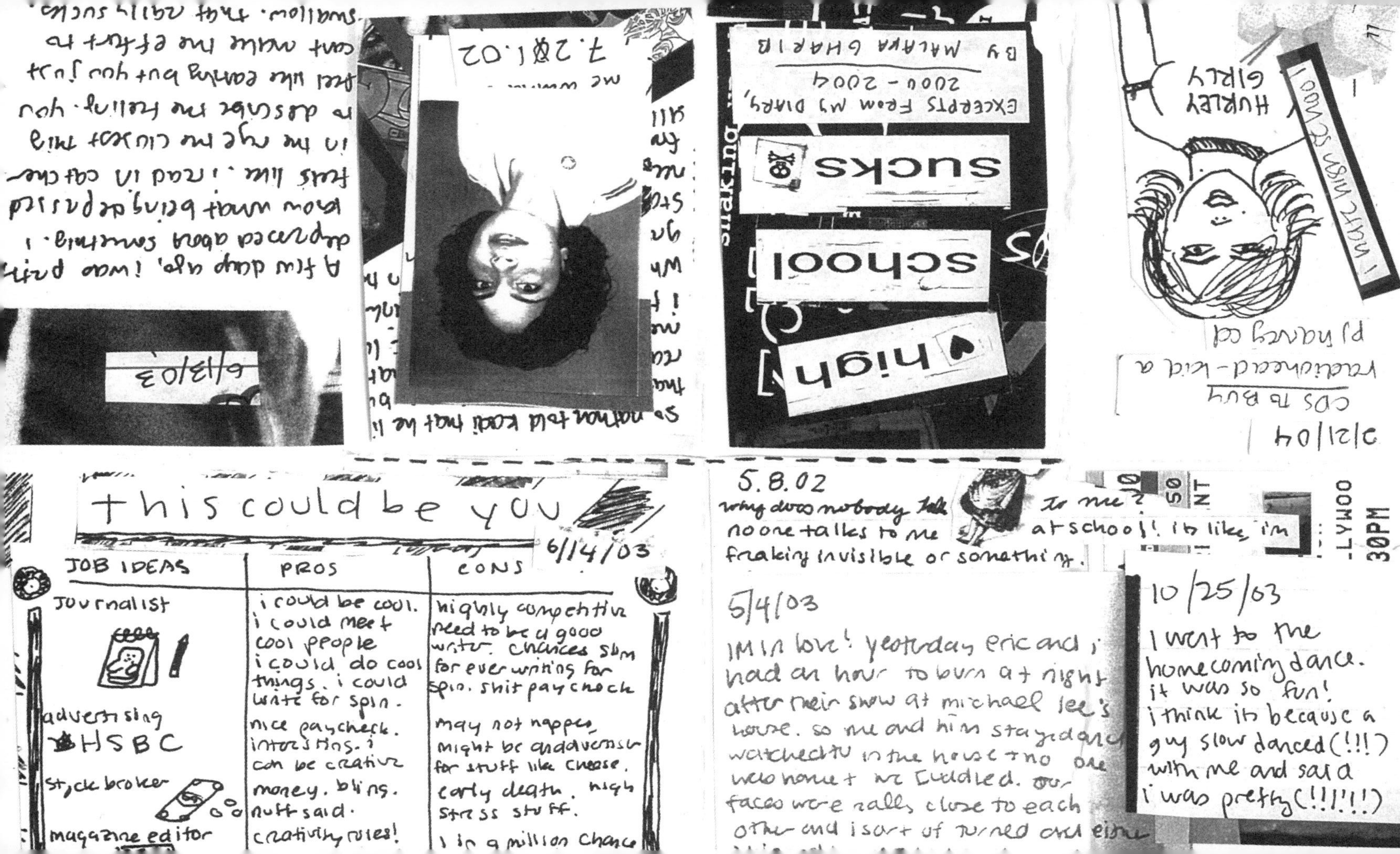
A few days ago, i was pretty depressed about something. i know what being depressed feels like. i read in catcher in the rye the closest thing to describe the feeling. you feel like eating but you just cant make the effort to swallow. that really sucks.
6/13/03
7.20.02
So nathan told kodi that he li
high school sucks
EXCERPTS FROM MY DIARY, 2000-2004
BY MALAKA GHARIB
HURLEY GIRLY
i hate high school
2/21/04
CDS TO BUY
radiohead-kid a
pj harvey cd
this could be you
6/14/03
JOB IDEAS | PROS | CONS
journalist | i could be cool. i could meet cool people i could do cool things. i could write for spin. | highly competitive need to be a good writer. chances slim for ever writing for spin. shit paycheck
advertising HSBC | nice paycheck. interesting. i can be creative | may not happen, might be an advertiser for stuff like cheese.
stock broker | money. bling. nuff said. | early death. high stress stuff.
magazine editor | creativity rules! | 1 in a million chance
5.8.02
why does nobody talk to me?
no one talks to me at school! its like i'm freaking invisible or something.
5/4/03
IM in love! yesterday eric and i had an hour to burn at night after their show at michael lee's house. so me and him stayed and watched TV in the house + no one was home + we cuddled. our faces were really close to each other and i sort of turned and either
10/25/03
I went to the homecoming dance. it was so fun! i think its because a guy slow danced(!!!) with me and said i was pretty(!!!!!)
.LYWOO
30PM

HOW TO MAKE THIS MINI ZINE

1. TEAR THIS PAGE OUT OF THE BOOK (YES, REALLY. DO IT NOW! AND DO IT NEATLY ☺).
2. FOLD THE PAPER INTO EIGHTHS.

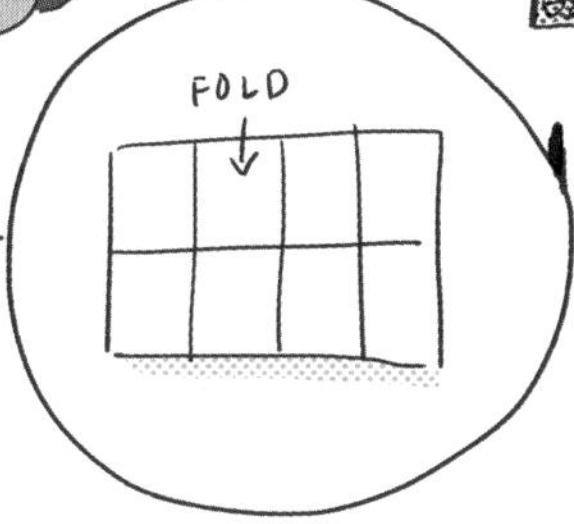
FOLD

3. FOLD THE PAPER IN HALF HAMBURGER-WISE; CUT ALONG THE DOTTED LINES IN THE CENTER.

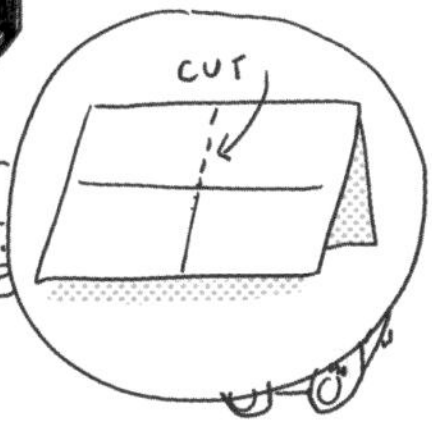
CUT

4. FOLD THE PAGE HOT DOG-WISE AND COLLAPSE THE PAPER INTO A BOOK!

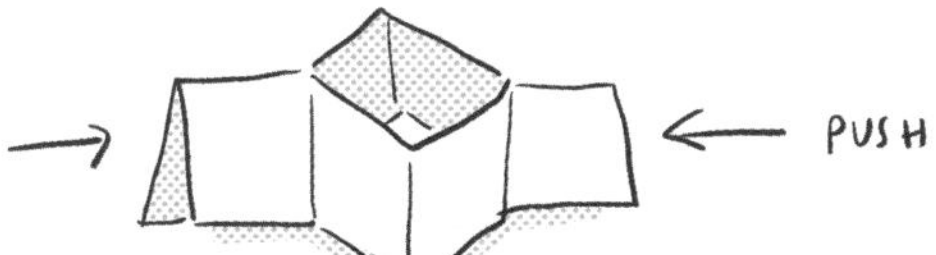
PUSH

5. FOLD IN PLACE. NOW YOU KNOW HOW TO MAKE A MINI ZINE... SO MAKE YOUR OWN!

EVEN AMONGST MINORITIES, I WAS A MINORITY. EVERYONE IN HIGH SCHOOL HUNG OUT WITH PEOPLE BASED ON CLUBS, SPORTS, ETHNICITY. WHO'D BE MY FRIEND?

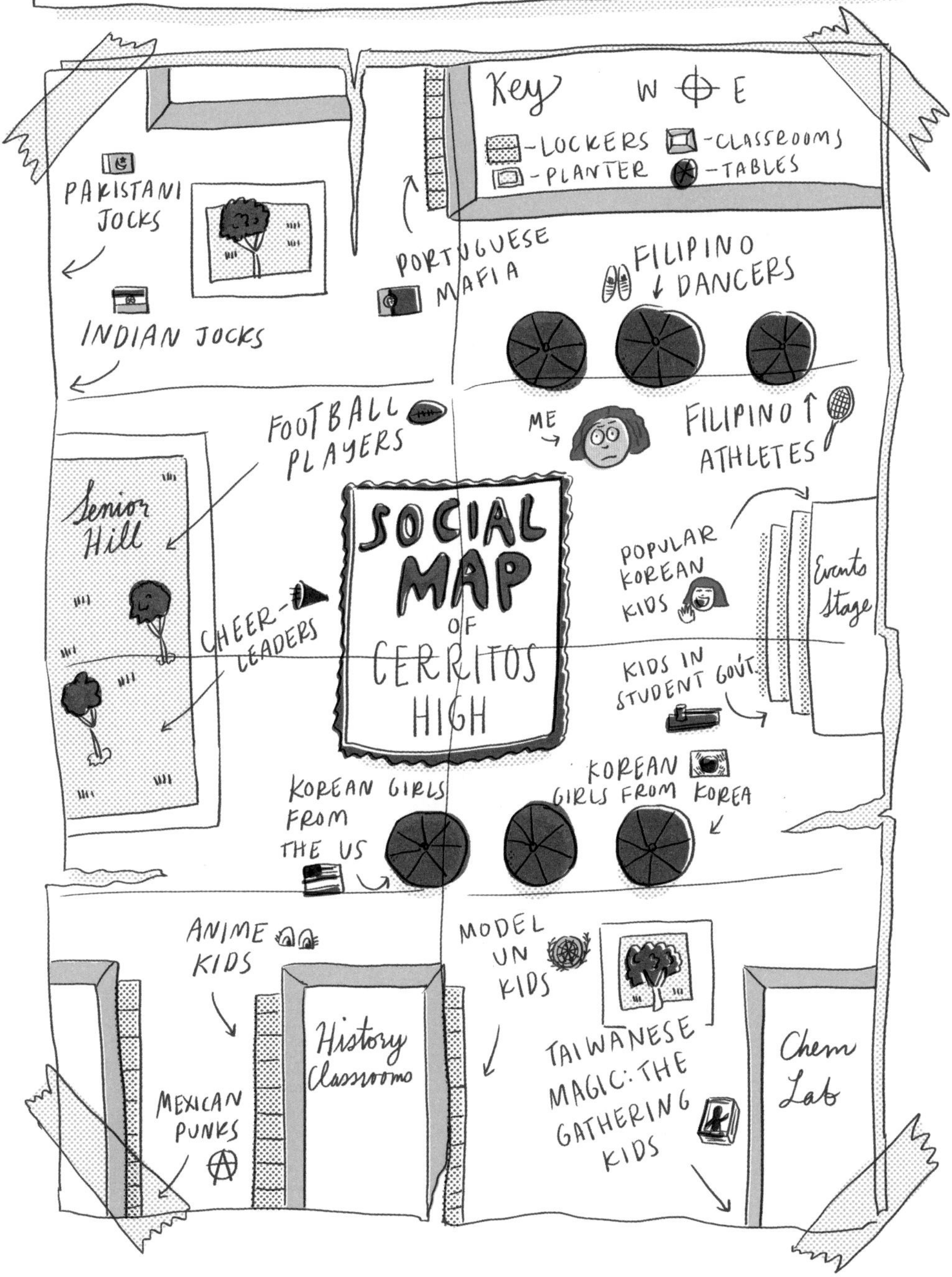

Key
W E
-LOCKERS
-CLASSROOMS
-PLANTER
-TABLES
PAKISTANI JOCKS
PORTUGUESE MAFIA
FILIPINO DANCERS
INDIAN JOCKS
FOOTBALL PLAYERS
ME
FILIPINO ATHLETES
Senior Hill
SOCIAL MAP OF CERRITOS HIGH
CHEER-LEADERS
POPULAR KOREAN KIDS
Events Stage
KIDS IN STUDENT GOV'T
KOREAN GIRLS FROM THE US
KOREAN GIRLS FROM KOREA
ANIME KIDS
MODEL UN KIDS
History Classrooms
MEXICAN PUNKS
TAIWANESE MAGIC: THE GATHERING KIDS
Chem Lab

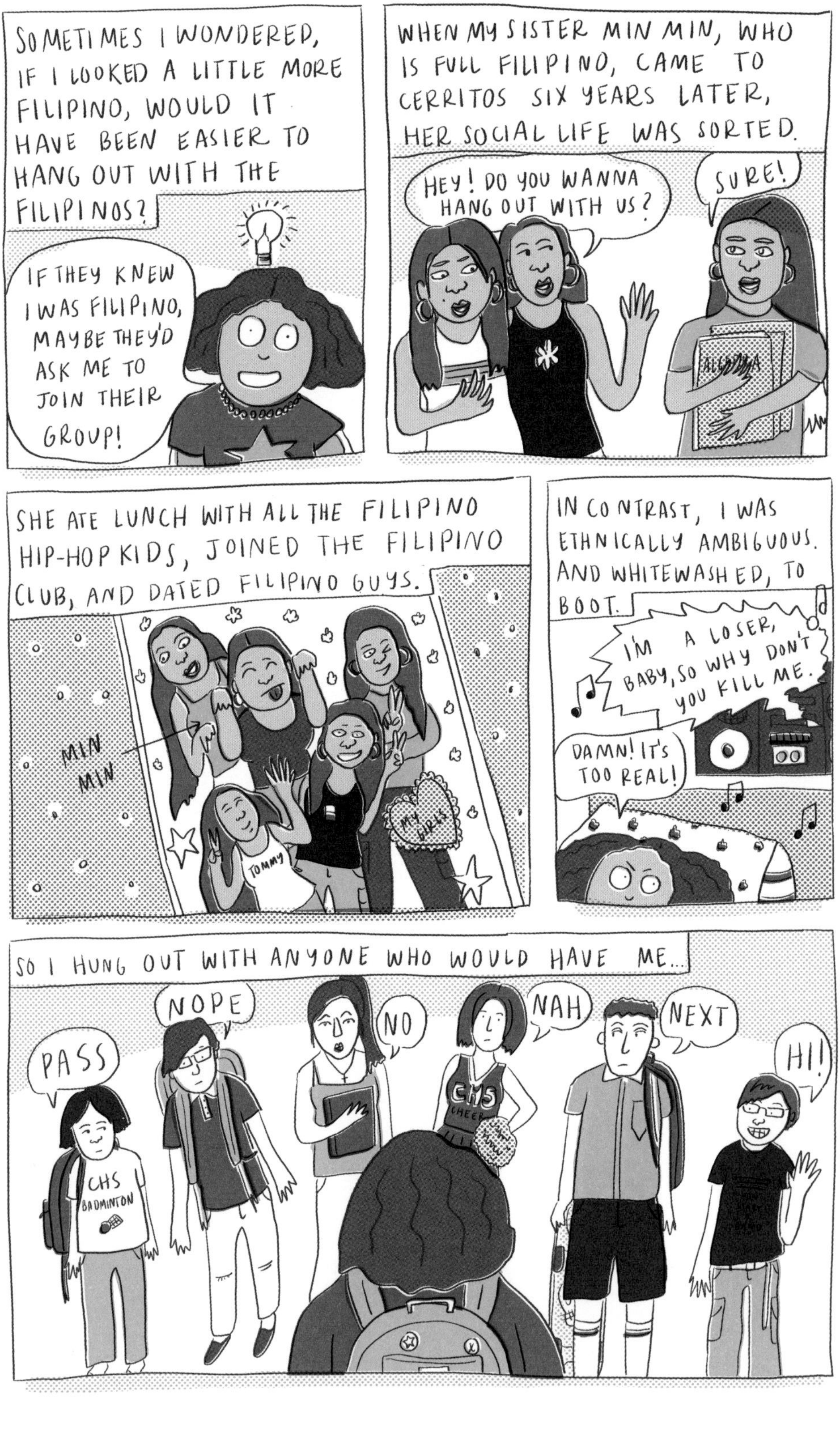
SOMETIMES I WONDERED, IF I LOOKED A LITTLE MORE FILIPINO, WOULD IT HAVE BEEN EASIER TO HANG OUT WITH THE FILIPINOS?
IF THEY KNEW I WAS FILIPINO, MAYBE THEY'D ASK ME TO JOIN THEIR GROUP!
WHEN MY SISTER MIN MIN, WHO IS FULL FILIPINO, CAME TO CERRITOS SIX YEARS LATER, HER SOCIAL LIFE WAS SORTED.
HEY! DO YOU WANNA HANG OUT WITH US?
SURE!
SHE ATE LUNCH WITH ALL THE FILIPINO HIP-HOP KIDS, JOINED THE FILIPINO CLUB, AND DATED FILIPINO GUYS.
MIN MIN
TOMMY
MY GIRLS
IN CONTRAST, I WAS ETHNICALLY AMBIGUOUS. AND WHITEWASHED, TO BOOT.
I'M A LOSER, BABY, SO WHY DON'T YOU KILL ME.
DAMN! IT'S TOO REAL!
SO I HUNG OUT WITH ANYONE WHO WOULD HAVE ME...
PASS
NOPE
NO
NAH
NEXT
HI!
CHS BADMINTON
CHS CHEER

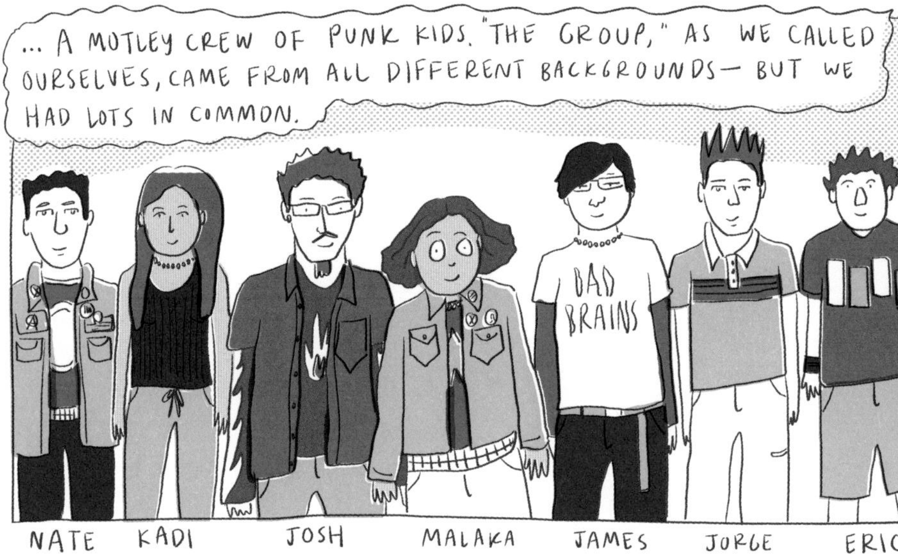
... A MOTLEY CREW OF PUNK KIDS. "THE GROUP," AS WE CALLED OURSELVES, CAME FROM ALL DIFFERENT BACKGROUNDS— BUT WE HAD LOTS IN COMMON.
BAD BRAINS
NATE
KADI
JOSH
MALAKA
JAMES
JORGE
ERIC

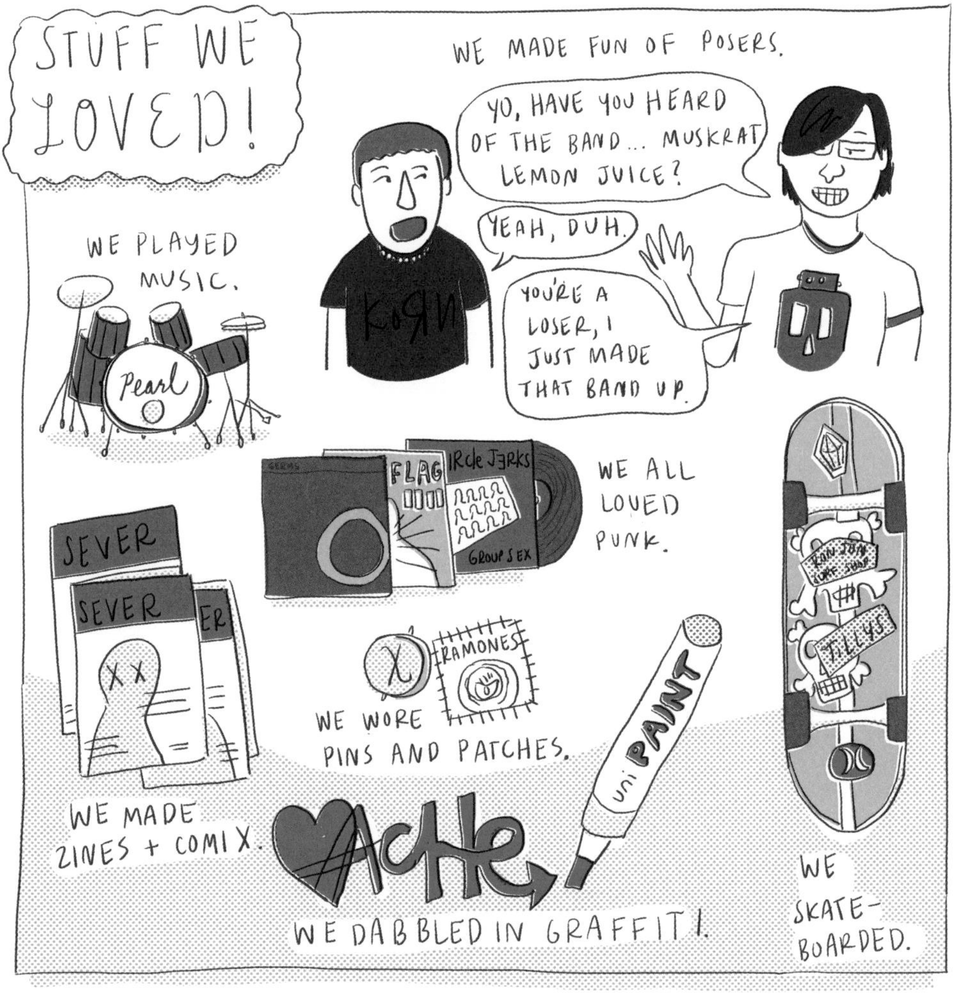
STUFF WE LOVED!
WE MADE FUN OF POSERS.
YO, HAVE YOU HEARD OF THE BAND... MUSKRAT LEMON JUICE?
YEAH, DUH.
YOU'RE A LOSER, I JUST MADE THAT BAND UP.
KoRN
WE PLAYED MUSIC.
Pearl
FLAG
GROUP SEX
WE ALL LOVED PUNK.
SEVER
SEVER
RAMONES
WE WORE PINS AND PATCHES.
uni PAINT
WE MADE ZINES + COMIX.
Ache
WE DABBLED IN GRAFFITI.
WE SKATE-BOARDED.

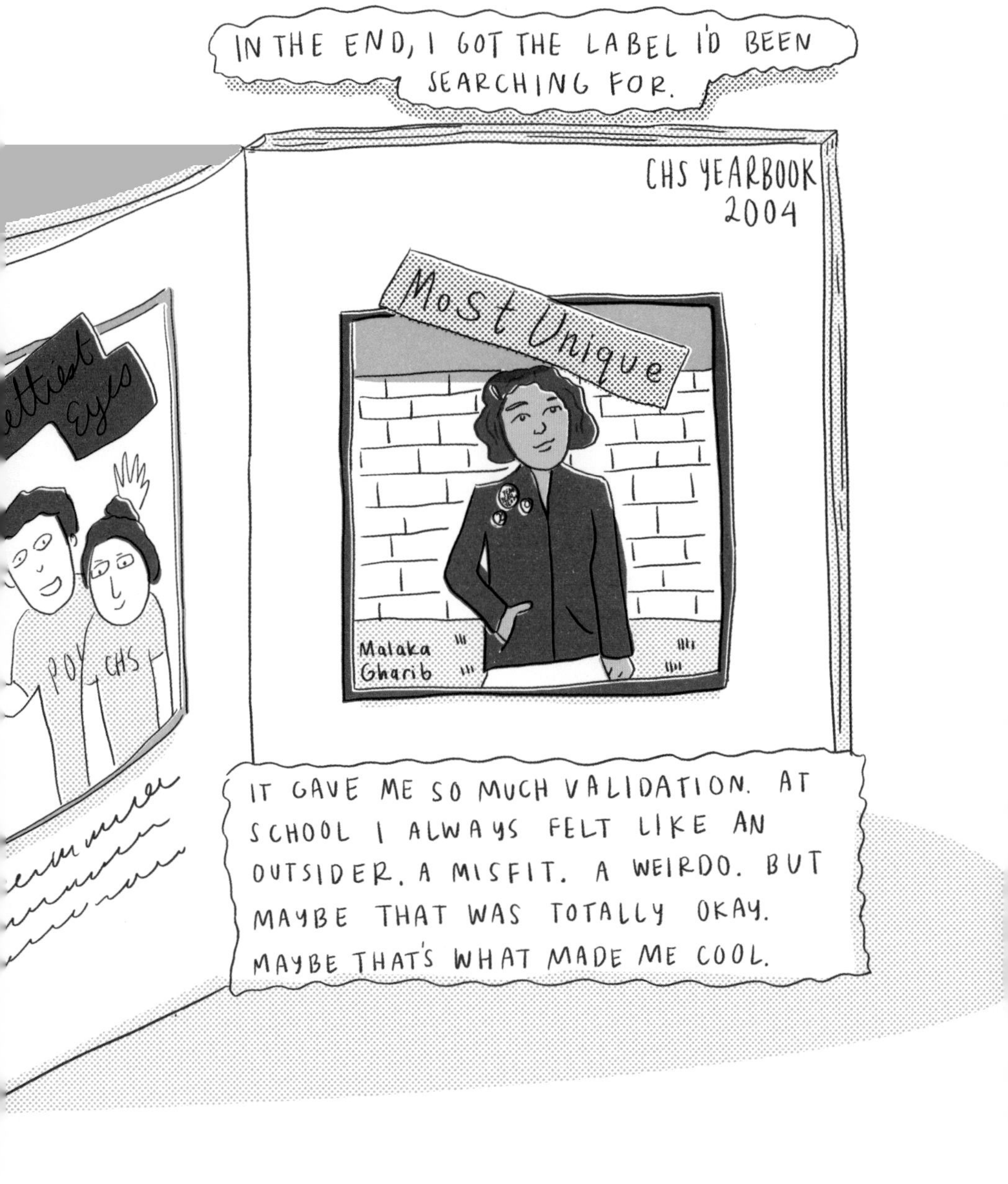
IN THE END, I GOT THE LABEL I'D BEEN SEARCHING FOR.
CHS YEARBOOK 2004
Most Unique
Malaka Gharib
CHS
IT GAVE ME SO MUCH VALIDATION. AT SCHOOL I ALWAYS FELT LIKE AN OUTSIDER. A MISFIT. A WEIRDO. BUT MAYBE THAT WAS TOTALLY OKAY. MAYBE THAT'S WHAT MADE ME COOL.

Chapter 5

I HAD TO GO TO COLLEGE IN NEW YORK.

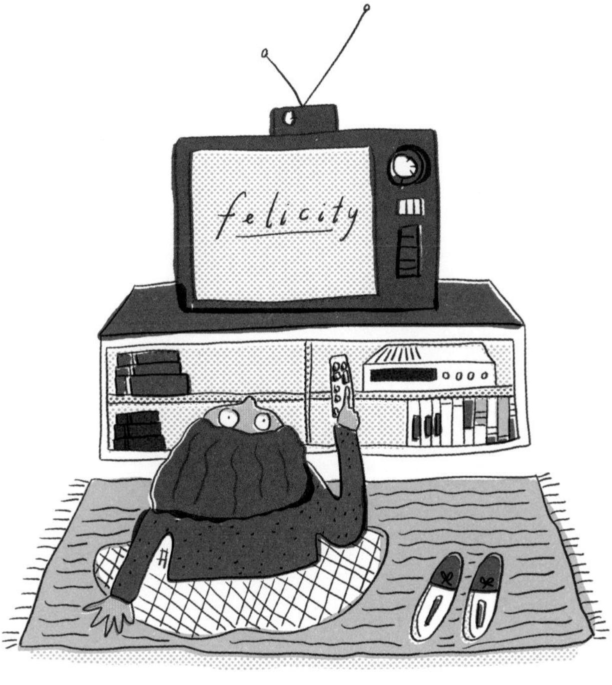
felicity

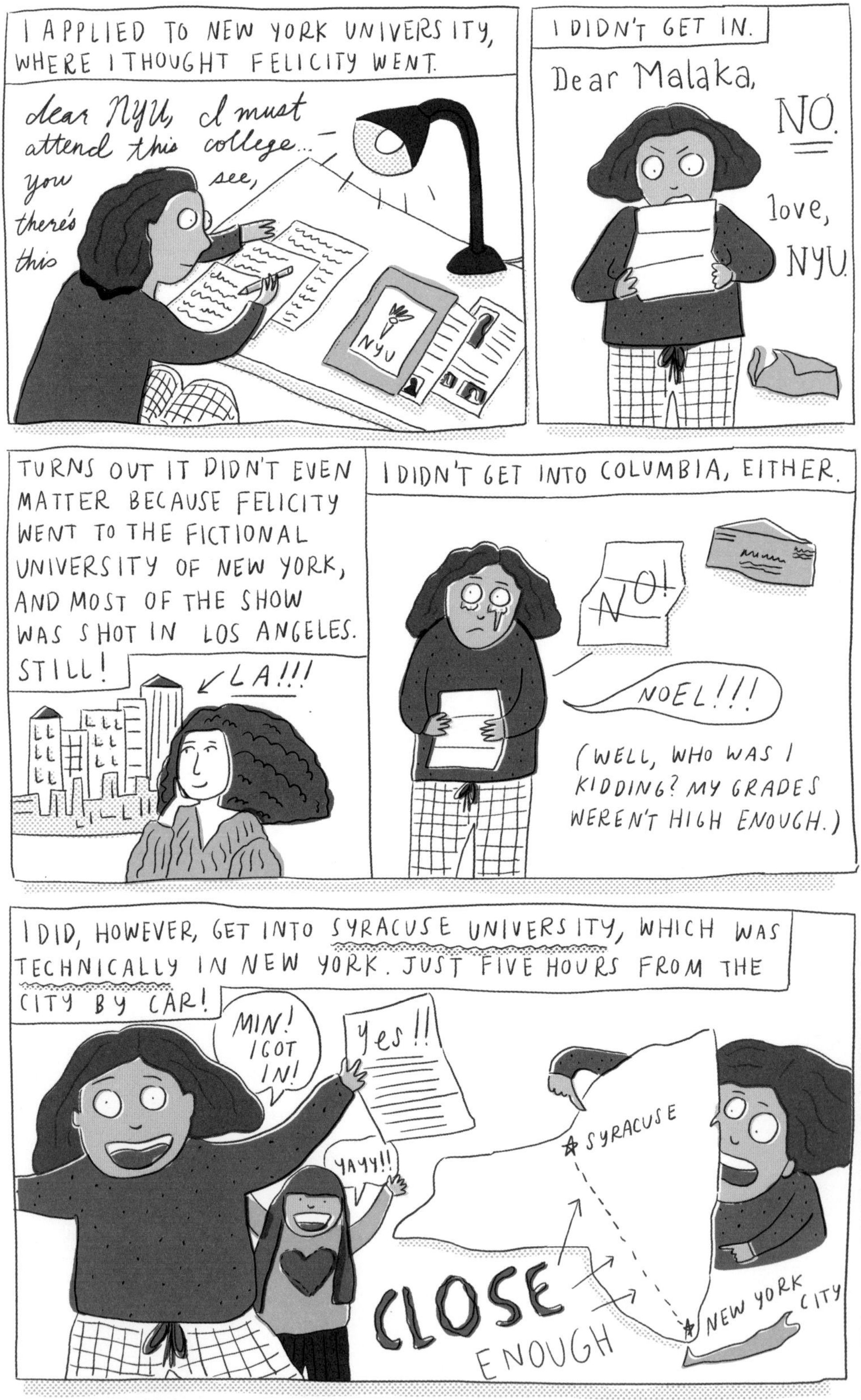
I APPLIED TO NEW YORK UNIVERSITY, WHERE I THOUGHT FELICITY WENT.
dear NYU, I must attend this college... you see, there's this
NYU
I DIDN'T GET IN.
Dear Malaka,
NO.
love,
NYU.
TURNS OUT IT DIDN'T EVEN MATTER BECAUSE FELICITY WENT TO THE FICTIONAL UNIVERSITY OF NEW YORK, AND MOST OF THE SHOW WAS SHOT IN LOS ANGELES. STILL!
LA!!!
I DIDN'T GET INTO COLUMBIA, EITHER.
NO!
NOEL!!!
(WELL, WHO WAS I KIDDING? MY GRADES WEREN'T HIGH ENOUGH.)
I DID, HOWEVER, GET INTO SYRACUSE UNIVERSITY, WHICH WAS TECHNICALLY IN NEW YORK. JUST FIVE HOURS FROM THE CITY BY CAR!
MIN! I GOT IN!
Yes!!
YAYY!!
SYRACUSE
NEW YORK CITY
CLOSE ENOUGH

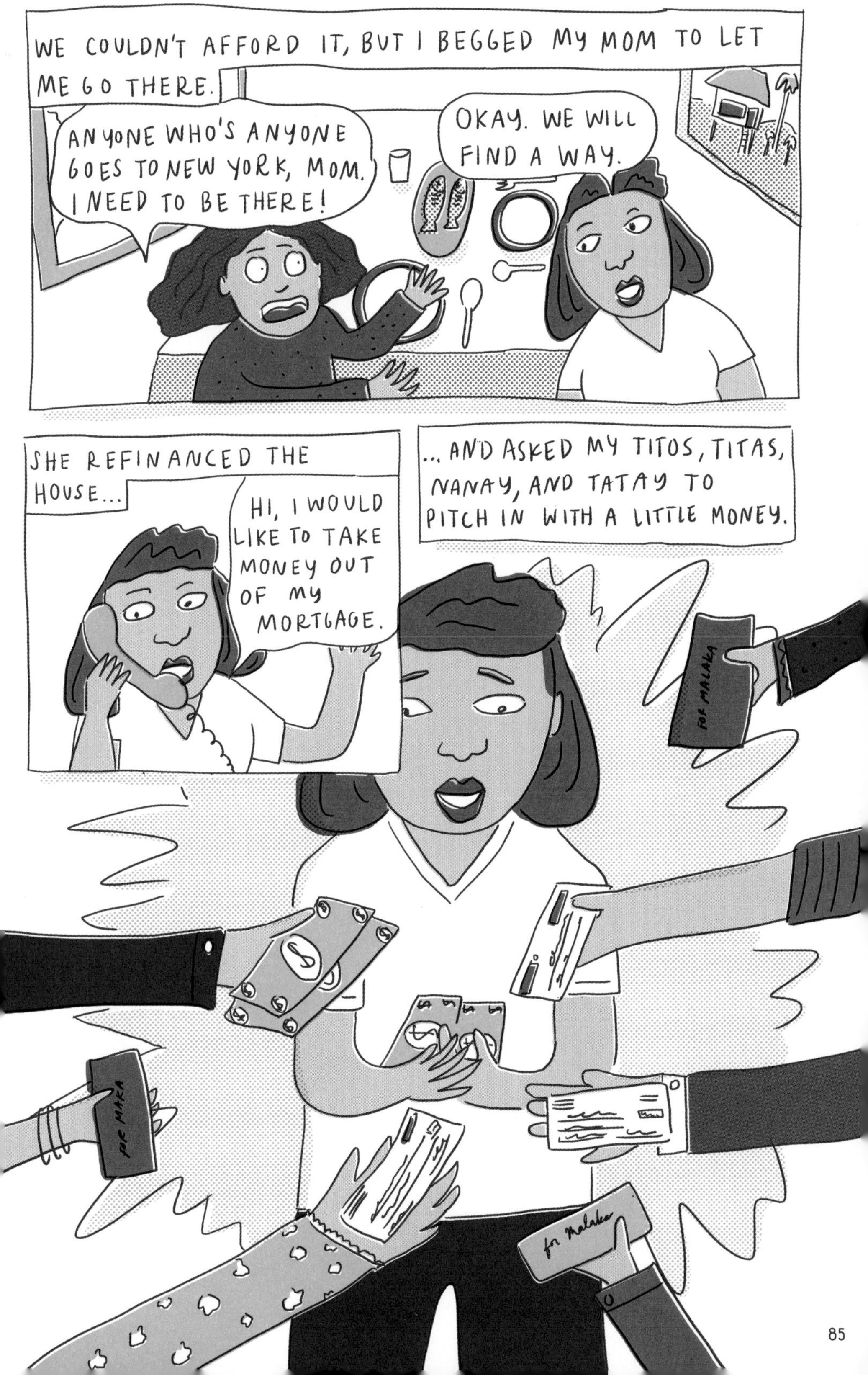
WE COULDN'T AFFORD IT, BUT I BEGGED MY MOM TO LET ME GO THERE.
ANYONE WHO'S ANYONE GOES TO NEW YORK, MOM. I NEED TO BE THERE!
OKAY. WE WILL FIND A WAY.
SHE REFINANCED THE HOUSE...
HI, I WOULD LIKE TO TAKE MONEY OUT OF MY MORTGAGE.
...AND ASKED MY TITOS, TITAS, NANAY, AND TATAY TO PITCH IN WITH A LITTLE MONEY.
FOR MALAKA
for Malaka

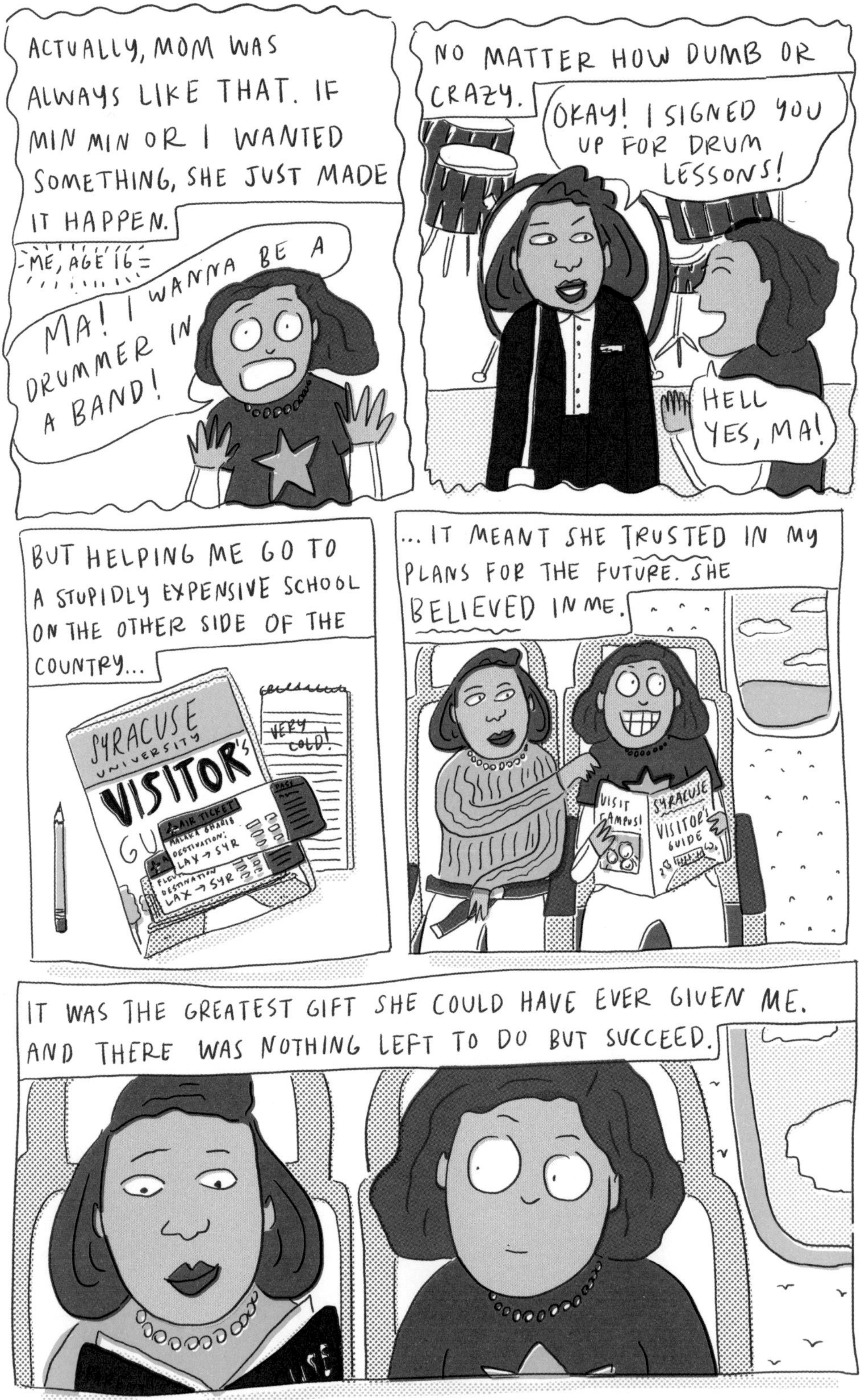
ACTUALLY, MOM WAS ALWAYS LIKE THAT. IF MIN MIN OR I WANTED SOMETHING, SHE JUST MADE IT HAPPEN.
ME, AGE 16
MA! I WANNA BE A DRUMMER IN A BAND!
NO MATTER HOW DUMB OR CRAZY.
OKAY! I SIGNED YOU UP FOR DRUM LESSONS!
HELL YES, MA!
BUT HELPING ME GO TO A STUPIDLY EXPENSIVE SCHOOL ON THE OTHER SIDE OF THE COUNTRY...
SYRACUSE UNIVERSITY
VISITOR'S
VERY COLD!
AIR TICKET
...IT MEANT SHE TRUSTED IN MY PLANS FOR THE FUTURE. SHE BELIEVED IN ME.
VISIT CAMPUS!
SYRACUSE VISITOR'S GUIDE
IT WAS THE GREATEST GIFT SHE COULD HAVE EVER GIVEN ME. AND THERE WAS NOTHING LEFT TO DO BUT SUCCEED.

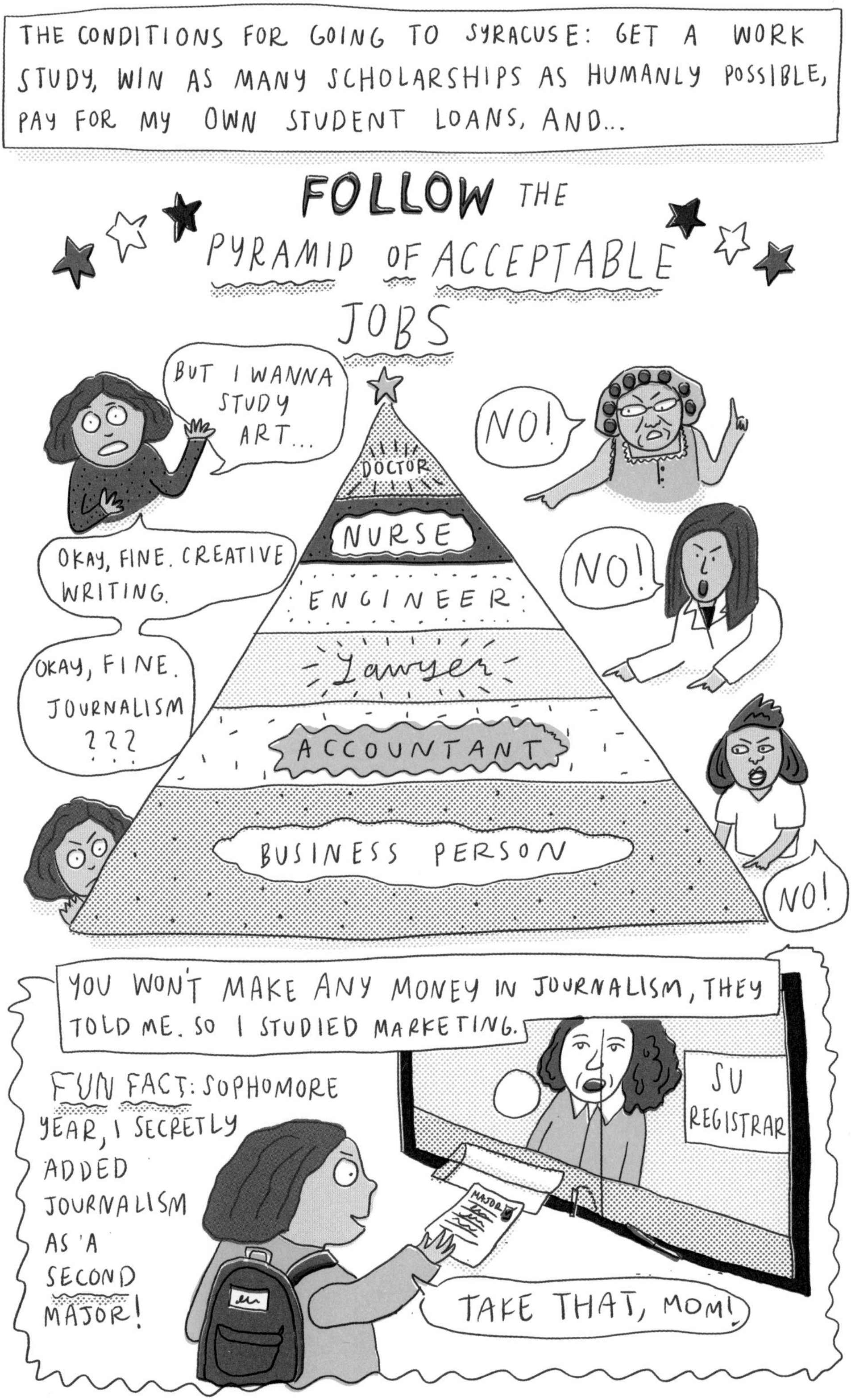
THE CONDITIONS FOR GOING TO SYRACUSE: GET A WORK STUDY, WIN AS MANY SCHOLARSHIPS AS HUMANLY POSSIBLE, PAY FOR MY OWN STUDENT LOANS, AND...
FOLLOW THE PYRAMID OF ACCEPTABLE JOBS
BUT I WANNA STUDY ART...
NO!
DOCTOR
NURSE
ENGINEER
Lawyer
ACCOUNTANT
BUSINESS PERSON
OKAY, FINE. CREATIVE WRITING.
NO!
OKAY, FINE. JOURNALISM ???
NO!
YOU WON'T MAKE ANY MONEY IN JOURNALISM, THEY TOLD ME. SO I STUDIED MARKETING.
FUN FACT: SOPHOMORE YEAR, I SECRETLY ADDED JOURNALISM AS A SECOND MAJOR!
SU REGISTRAR
MAJOR
TAKE THAT, MOM!

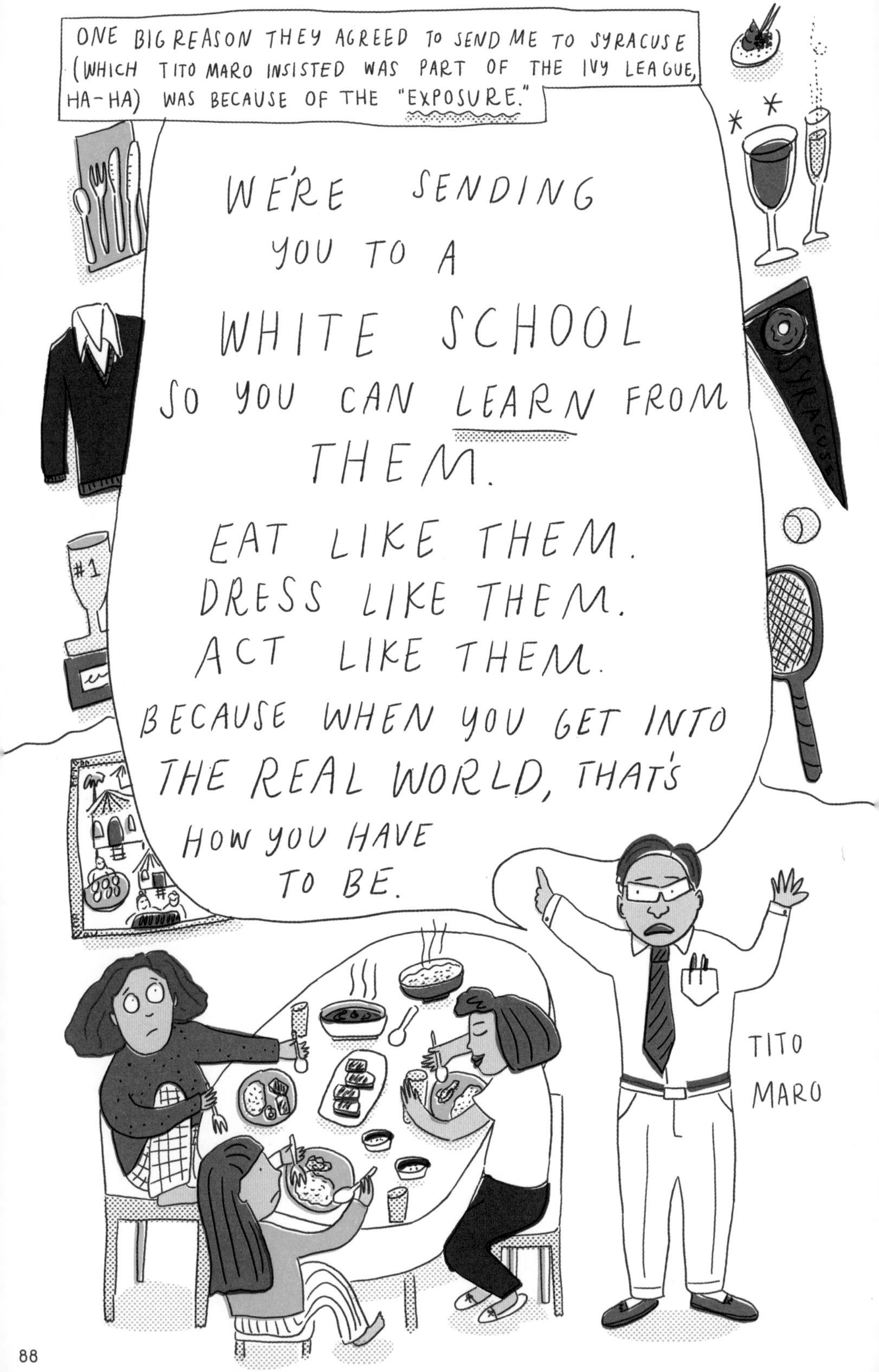

ONE BIG REASON THEY AGREED TO SEND ME TO SYRACUSE (WHICH TITO MARO INSISTED WAS PART OF THE IVY LEAGUE, HA-HA) WAS BECAUSE OF THE "EXPOSURE."
WE'RE SENDING YOU TO A WHITE SCHOOL SO YOU CAN LEARN FROM THEM. EAT LIKE THEM. DRESS LIKE THEM. ACT LIKE THEM. BECAUSE WHEN YOU GET INTO THE REAL WORLD, THAT'S HOW YOU HAVE TO BE.
SYRACUSE
#1
TITO MARO

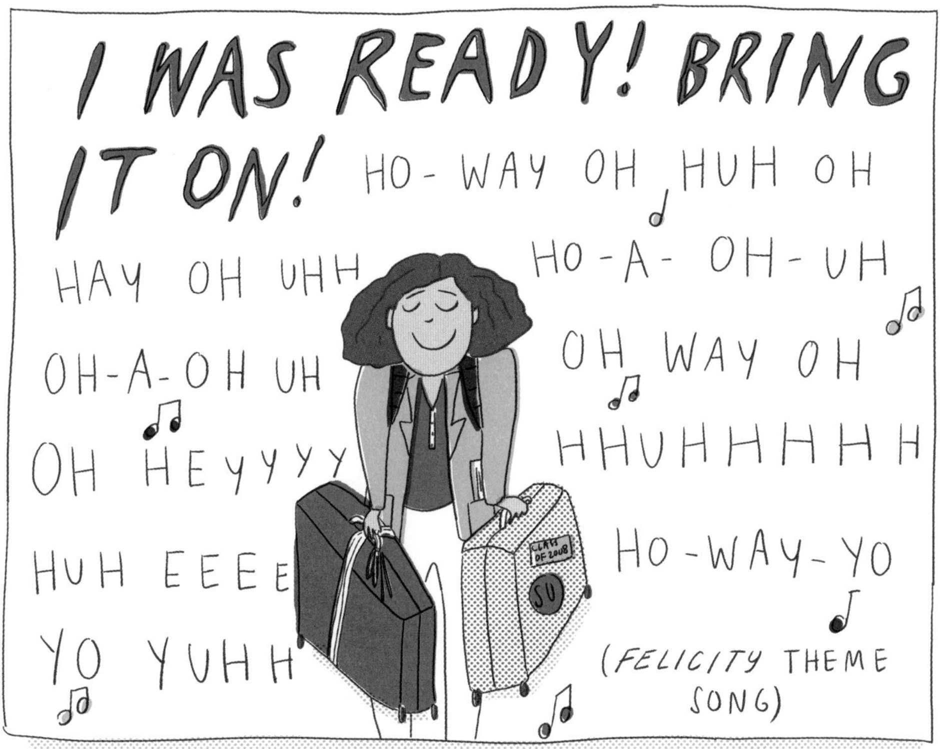
I WAS READY! BRING IT ON!
HO-WAY OH HUH OH
HAY OH UHH
HO-A- OH-UH
OH-A-OH UH
OH WAY OH
OH HEYYYY
HHUHHHHH
HUH EEEE
HO-WAY-YO
YO YUHH
(FELICITY THEME SONG)
CLASS OF 2008
SU

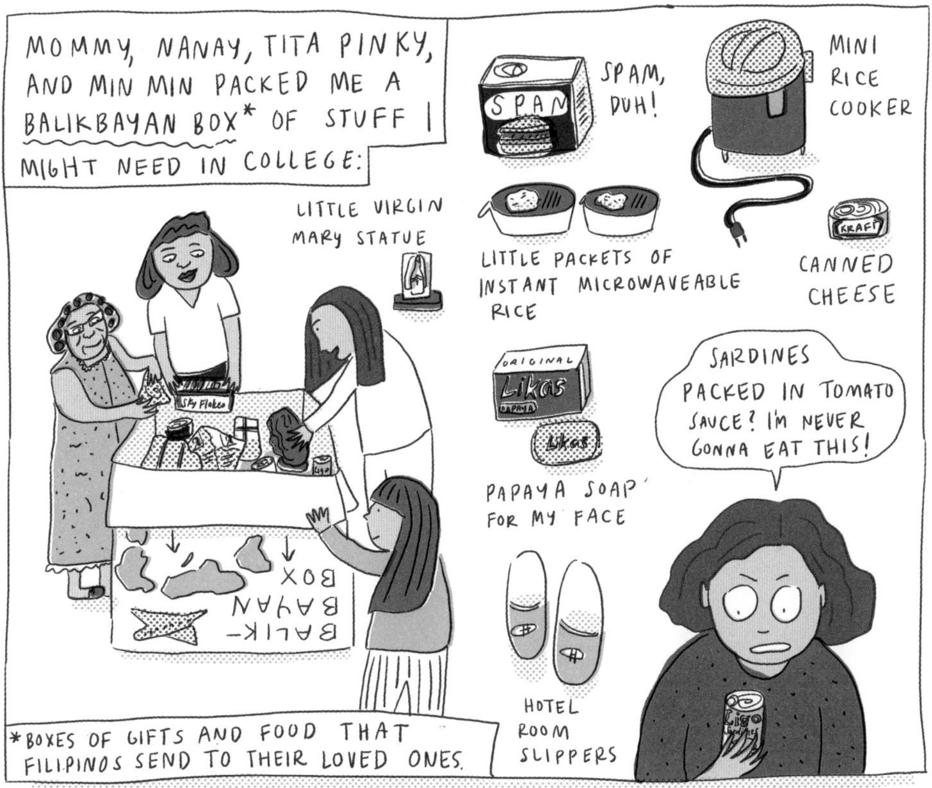
MOMMY, NANAY, TITA PINKY, AND MIN MIN PACKED ME A BALIKBAYAN BOX* OF STUFF I MIGHT NEED IN COLLEGE:
SPAM, DUH!
SPAM
MINI RICE COOKER
LITTLE VIRGIN MARY STATUE
LITTLE PACKETS OF INSTANT MICROWAVEABLE RICE
KRAFT
CANNED CHEESE
Sky Flakes
ORIGINAL
Likas
PAPAYA
PAPAYA SOAP FOR MY FACE
SARDINES PACKED IN TOMATO SAUCE? I'M NEVER GONNA EAT THIS!
BALIK-BAYAN BOX
HOTEL ROOM SLIPPERS
Ligo
*BOXES OF GIFTS AND FOOD THAT FILIPINOS SEND TO THEIR LOVED ONES.

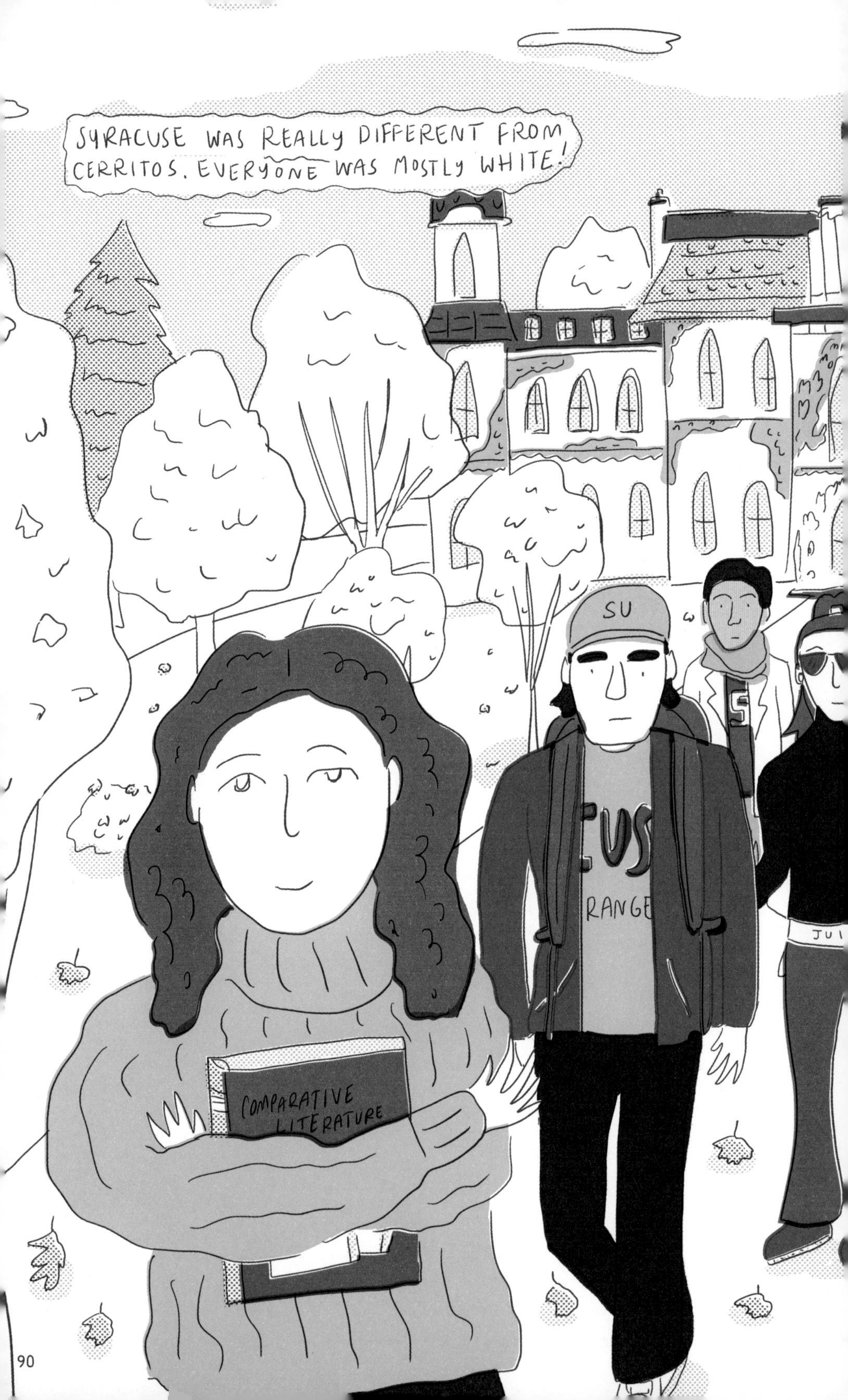
SYRACUSE WAS REALLY DIFFERENT FROM CERRITOS. EVERYONE WAS MOSTLY WHITE!
SU
RANGE
COMPARATIVE LITERATURE
JUI

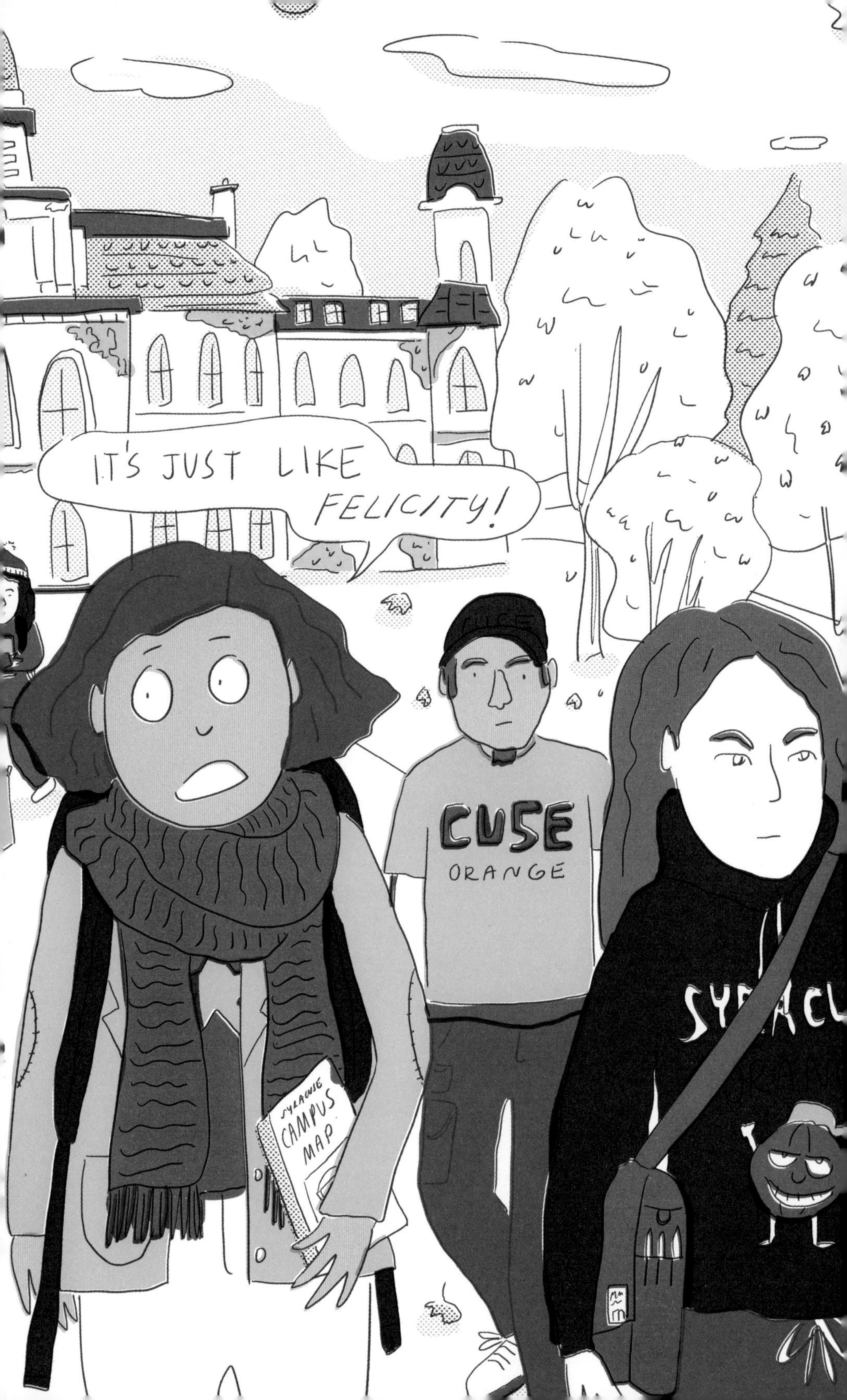
IT'S JUST LIKE FELICITY!
CUSE
ORANGE
CAMPUS MAP

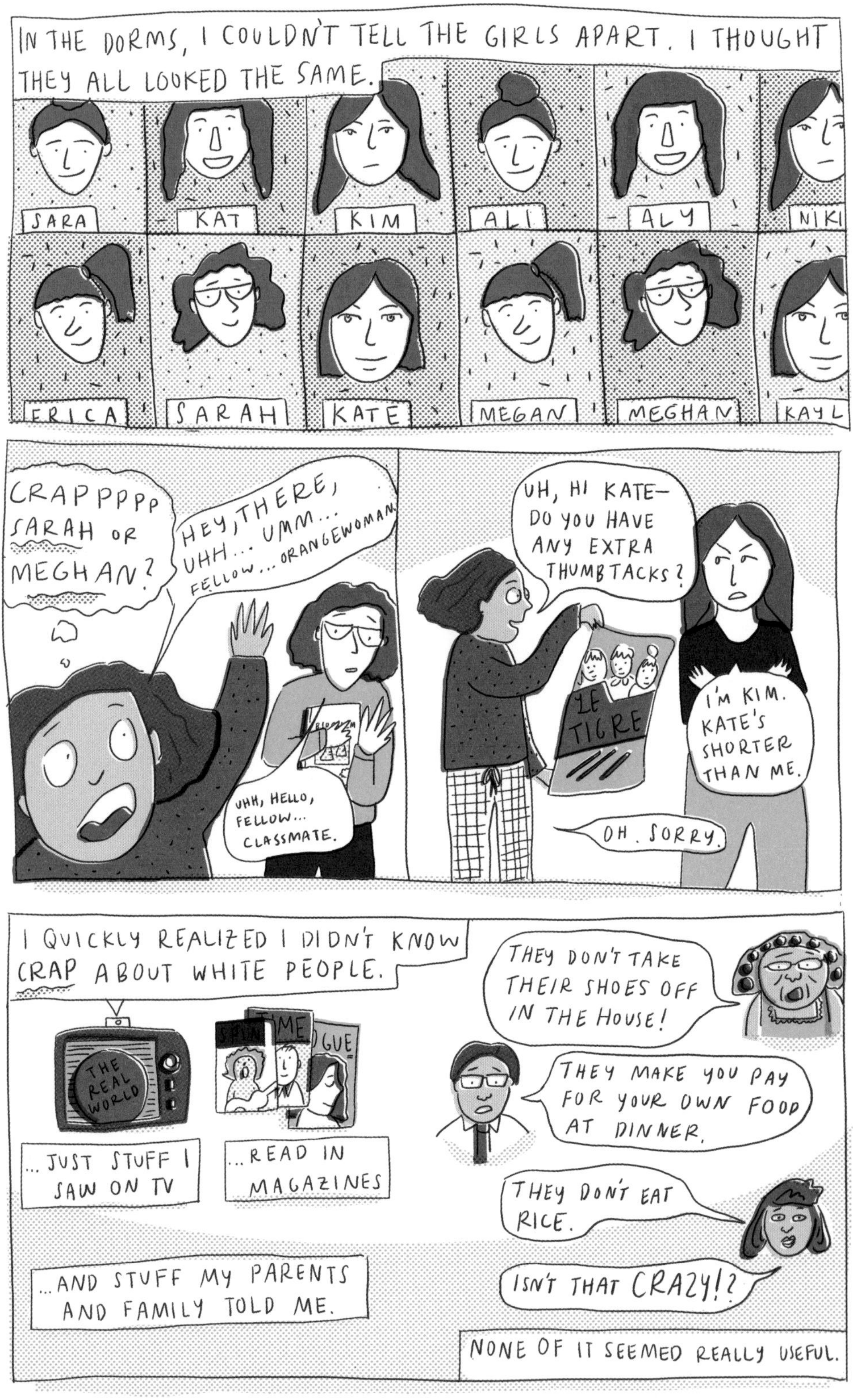
IN THE DORMS, I COULDN'T TELL THE GIRLS APART. I THOUGHT THEY ALL LOOKED THE SAME.
SARA
KAT
KIM
ALI
ALY
NIKI
ERICA
SARAH
KATE
MEGAN
MEGHAN
KAYL
CRAPPPPP SARAH OR MEGHAN?
HEY, THERE, UHH... UMM... FELLOW... ORANGEWOMAN.
UHH, HELLO, FELLOW... CLASSMATE.
UH, HI KATE— DO YOU HAVE ANY EXTRA THUMBTACKS?
LE TIGRE
I'M KIM. KATE'S SHORTER THAN ME.
OH. SORRY.
I QUICKLY REALIZED I DIDN'T KNOW CRAP ABOUT WHITE PEOPLE.
THE REAL WORLD
SPIN
TIME
VOGUE
...JUST STUFF I SAW ON TV
...READ IN MAGAZINES
...AND STUFF MY PARENTS AND FAMILY TOLD ME.
THEY DON'T TAKE THEIR SHOES OFF IN THE HOUSE!
THEY MAKE YOU PAY FOR YOUR OWN FOOD AT DINNER.
THEY DON'T EAT RICE.
ISN'T THAT CRAZY!?
NONE OF IT SEEMED REALLY USEFUL.

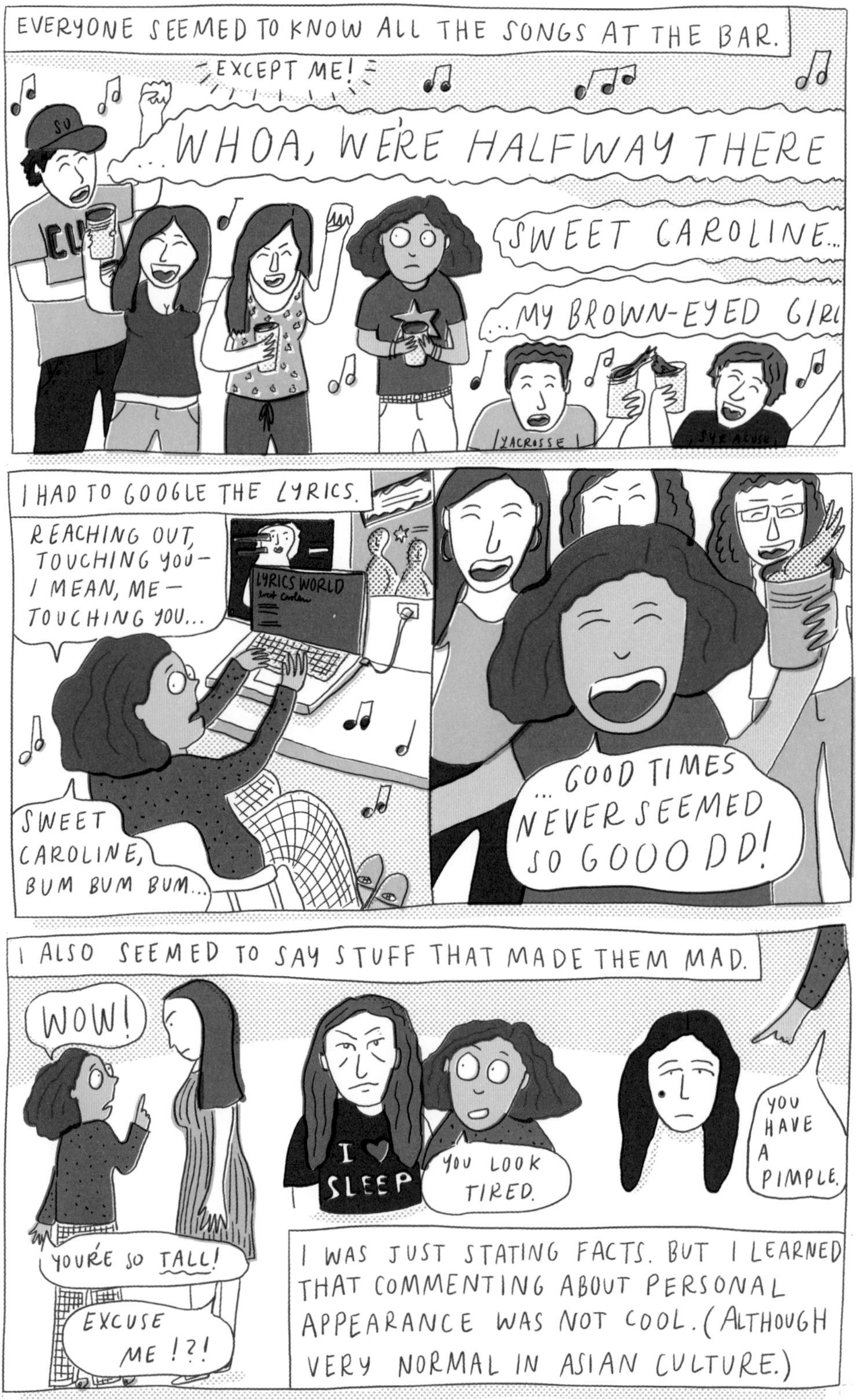
EVERYONE SEEMED TO KNOW ALL THE SONGS AT THE BAR.
EXCEPT ME!
...WHOA, WE'RE HALFWAY THERE
SWEET CAROLINE...
...MY BROWN-EYED GIRL
LACROSSE
SYRACUSE
I HAD TO GOOGLE THE LYRICS.
REACHING OUT, TOUCHING YOU— I MEAN, ME— TOUCHING YOU...
LYRICS WORLD
SWEET CAROLINE, BUM BUM BUM...
...GOOD TIMES NEVER SEEMED SO GOOOODD!
I ALSO SEEMED TO SAY STUFF THAT MADE THEM MAD.
WOW!
YOU'RE SO TALL!
EXCUSE ME!?!
I ♥ SLEEP
YOU LOOK TIRED.
YOU HAVE A PIMPLE.
I WAS JUST STATING FACTS. BUT I LEARNED THAT COMMENTING ABOUT PERSONAL APPEARANCE WAS NOT COOL. (ALTHOUGH VERY NORMAL IN ASIAN CULTURE.)

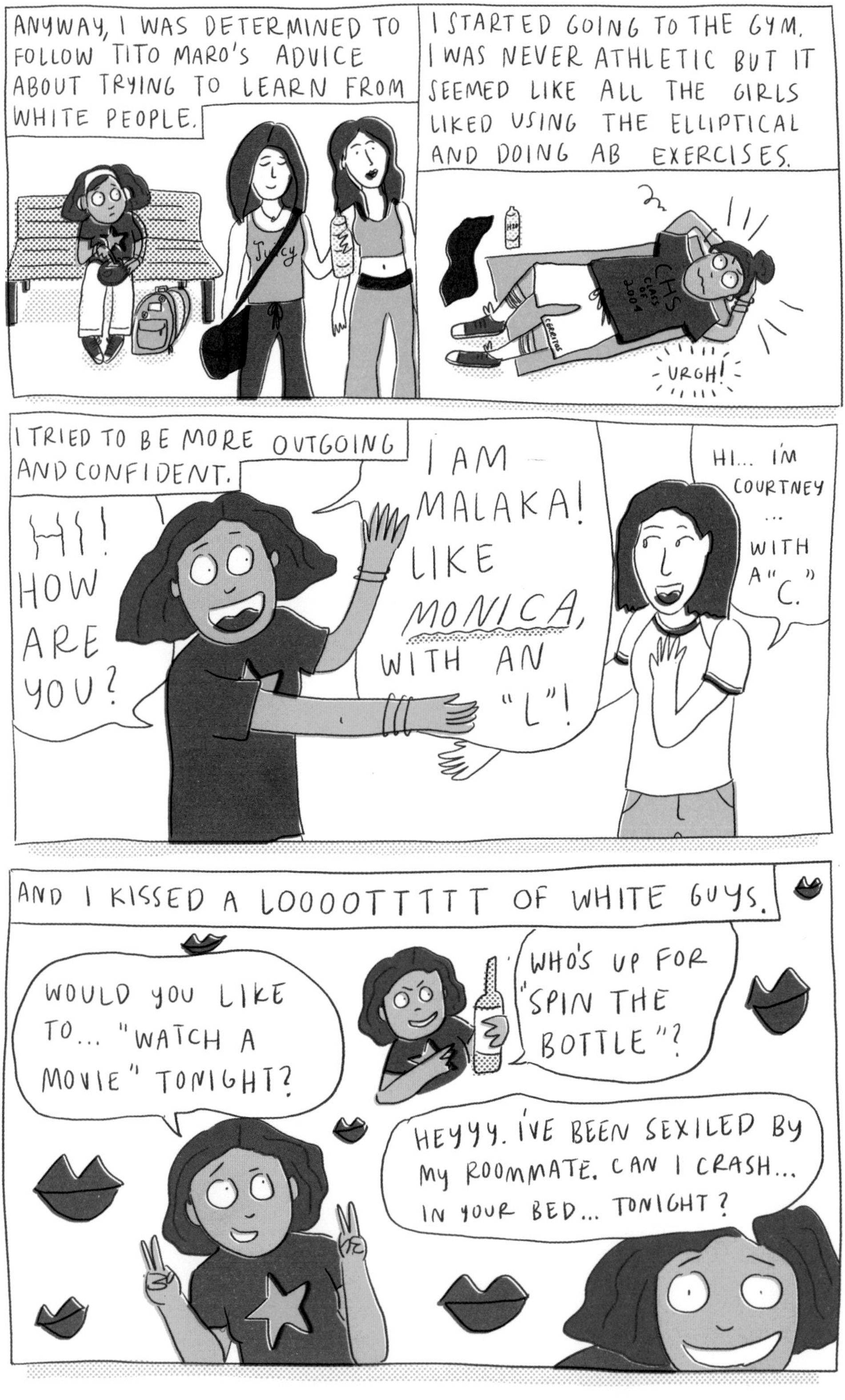
ANYWAY, I WAS DETERMINED TO FOLLOW TITO MARO'S ADVICE ABOUT TRYING TO LEARN FROM WHITE PEOPLE.
Juicy
I STARTED GOING TO THE GYM. I WAS NEVER ATHLETIC BUT IT SEEMED LIKE ALL THE GIRLS LIKED USING THE ELLIPTICAL AND DOING AB EXERCISES.
CHS CLASS OF 2004
CERRITOS
URGH!
I TRIED TO BE MORE OUTGOING AND CONFIDENT.
HI! HOW ARE YOU?
I AM MALAKA! LIKE MONICA, WITH AN "L"!
HI... I'M COURTNEY ... WITH A "C."
AND I KISSED A LOOOOTTTTT OF WHITE GUYS.
WOULD YOU LIKE TO... "WATCH A MOVIE" TONIGHT?
WHO'S UP FOR "SPIN THE BOTTLE"?
HEYYY. I'VE BEEN SEXILED BY MY ROOMMATE. CAN I CRASH... IN YOUR BED... TONIGHT?

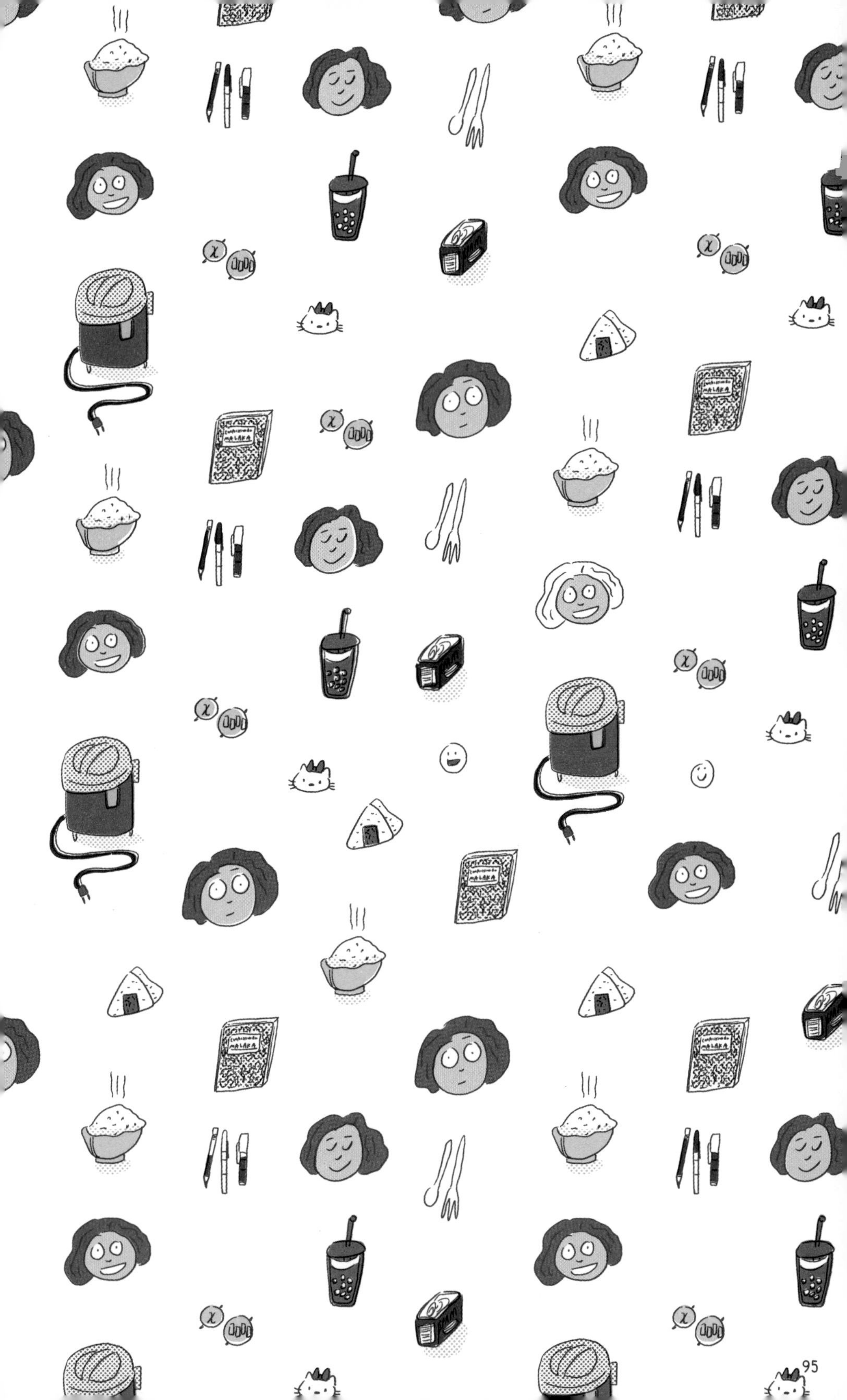

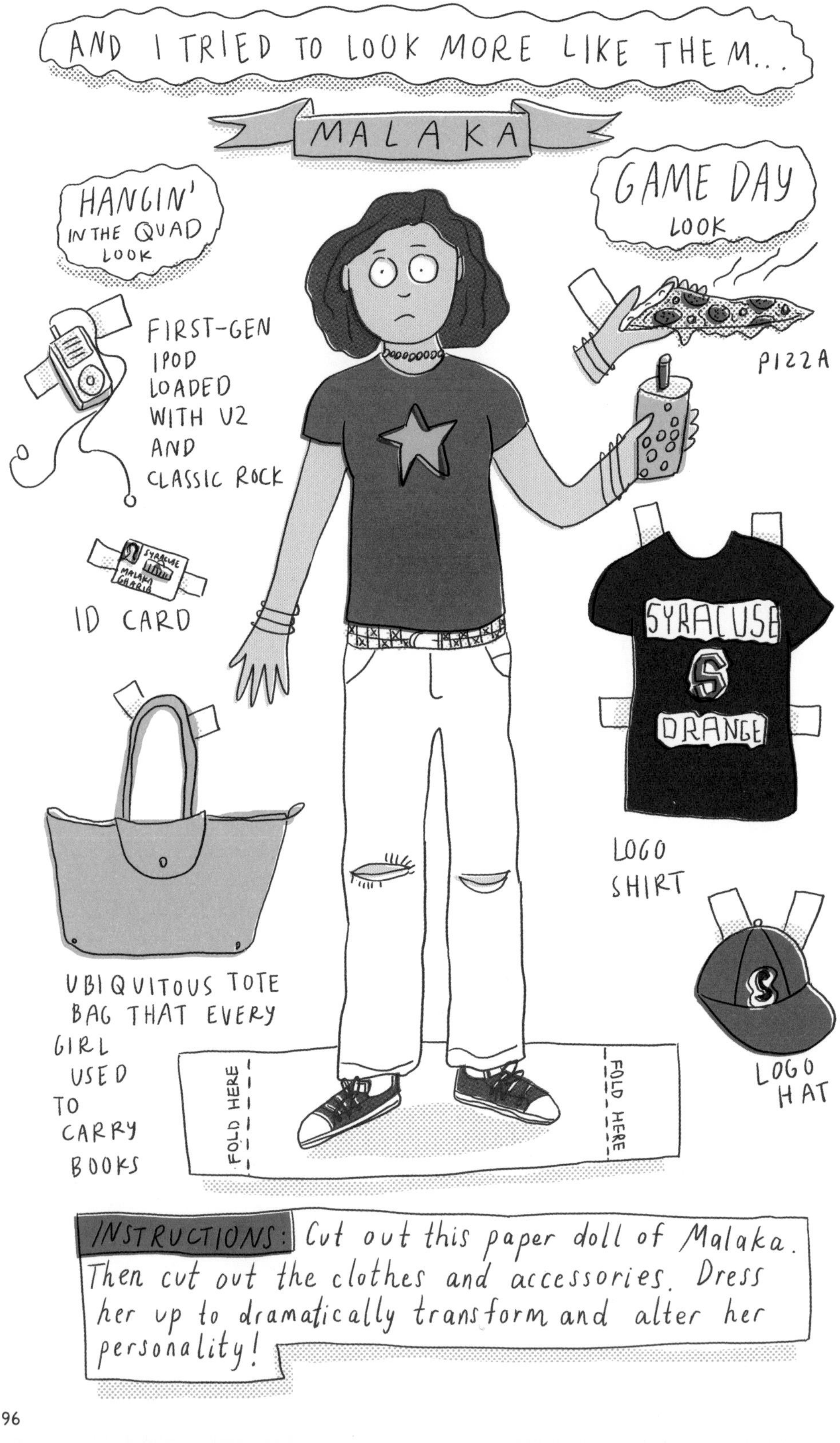
AND I TRIED TO LOOK MORE LIKE THEM...
MALAKA
HANGIN' IN THE QUAD LOOK
GAME DAY LOOK
FIRST-GEN IPOD LOADED WITH U2 AND CLASSIC ROCK
PIZZA
ID CARD
SYRACUSE
S
ORANGE
LOGO SHIRT
UBIQUITOUS TOTE BAG THAT EVERY GIRL USED TO CARRY BOOKS
FOLD HERE
FOLD HERE
LOGO HAT
INSTRUCTIONS: Cut out this paper doll of Malaka. Then cut out the clothes and accessories. Dress her up to dramatically transform and alter her personality!

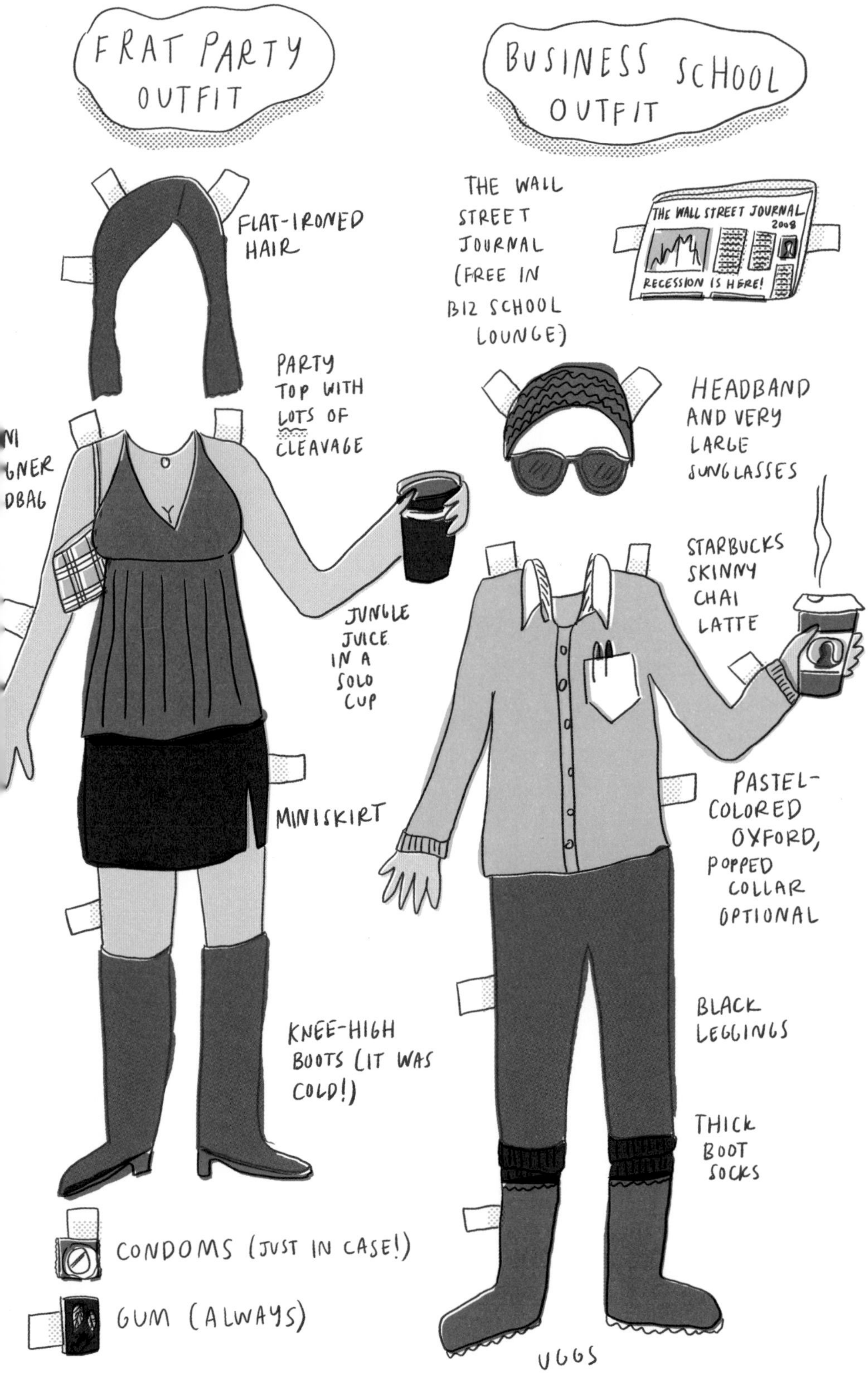
FRAT PARTY OUTFIT
FLAT-IRONED HAIR
PARTY TOP WITH LOTS OF CLEAVAGE
NI
GNER
DBAG
JUNGLE JUICE IN A SOLO CUP
MINISKIRT
KNEE-HIGH BOOTS (IT WAS COLD!)
CONDOMS (JUST IN CASE!)
GUM (ALWAYS)
BUSINESS SCHOOL OUTFIT
THE WALL STREET JOURNAL (FREE IN BIZ SCHOOL LOUNGE)
THE WALL STREET JOURNAL
2008
RECESSION IS HERE!
HEADBAND AND VERY LARGE SUNGLASSES
STARBUCKS SKINNY CHAI LATTE
PASTEL-COLORED OXFORD, POPPED COLLAR OPTIONAL
BLACK LEGGINGS
THICK BOOT SOCKS
UGGS

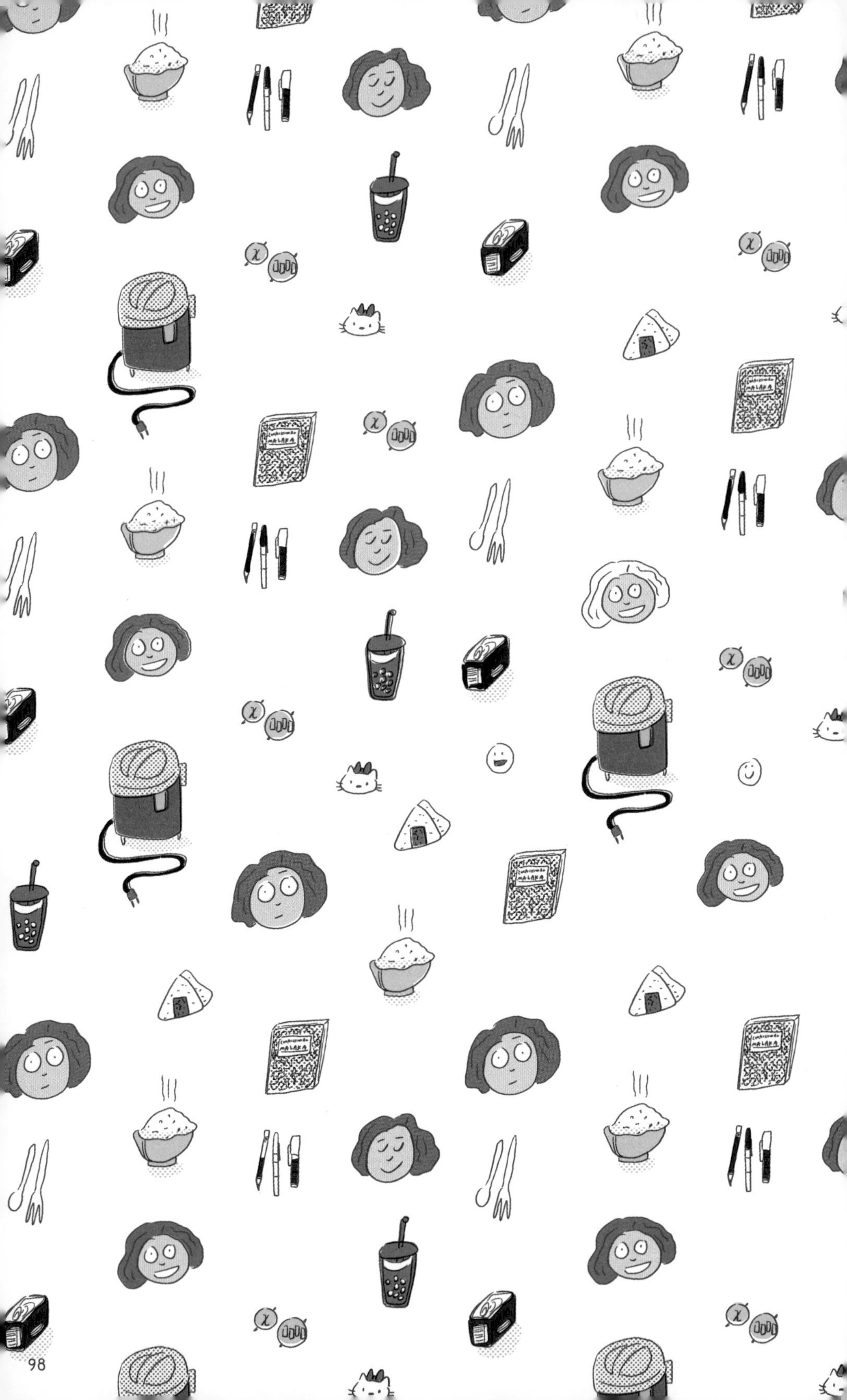

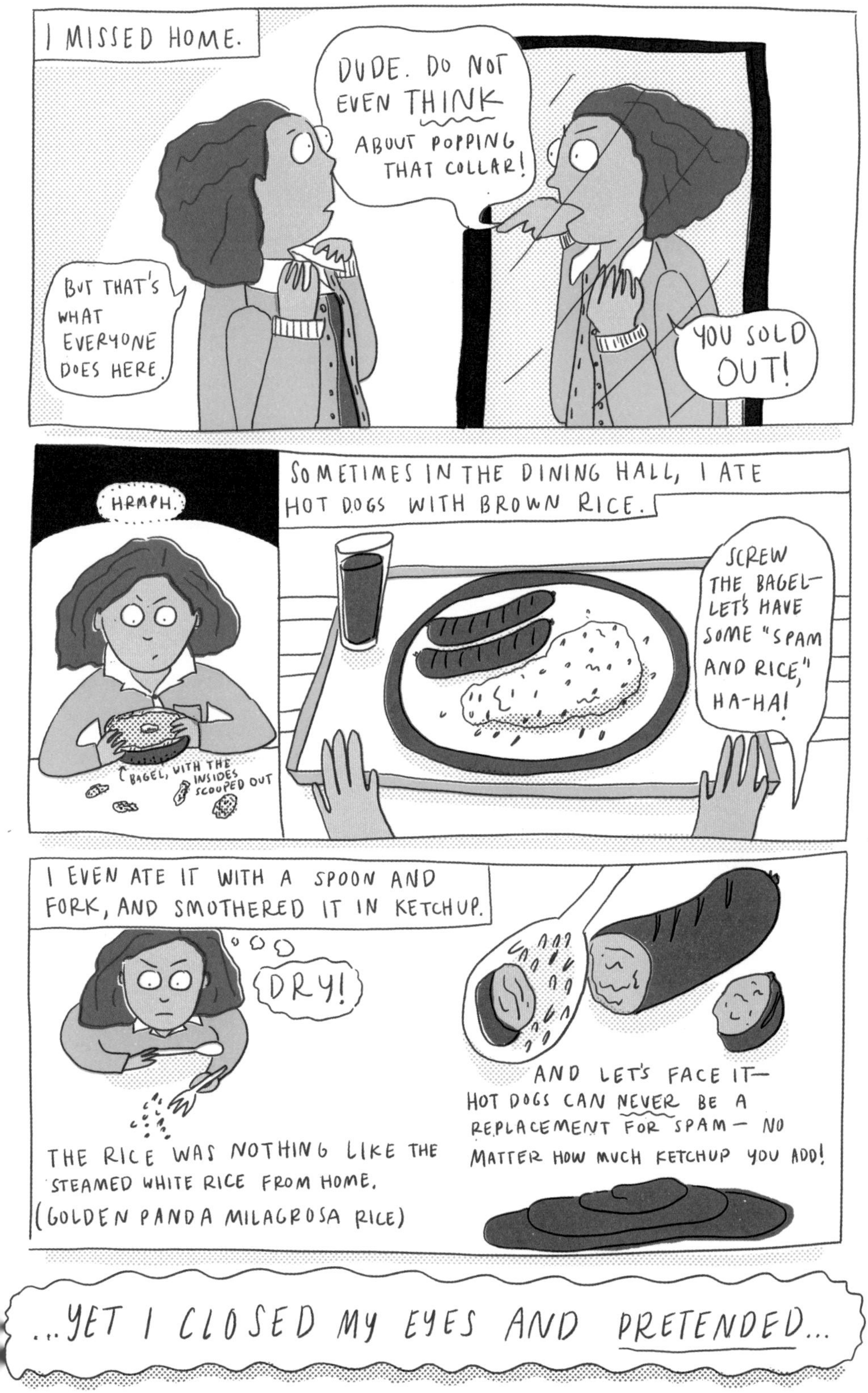
I MISSED HOME.
DUDE. DO NOT EVEN THINK ABOUT POPPING THAT COLLAR!
BUT THAT'S WHAT EVERYONE DOES HERE.
YOU SOLD OUT!
HRMPH.
SOMETIMES IN THE DINING HALL, I ATE HOT DOGS WITH BROWN RICE.
BAGEL, WITH THE INSIDES SCOOPED OUT
SCREW THE BAGEL- LET'S HAVE SOME "SPAM AND RICE," HA-HA!
I EVEN ATE IT WITH A SPOON AND FORK, AND SMOTHERED IT IN KETCHUP.
DRY!
THE RICE WAS NOTHING LIKE THE STEAMED WHITE RICE FROM HOME. (GOLDEN PANDA MILAGROSA RICE)
AND LET'S FACE IT- HOT DOGS CAN NEVER BE A REPLACEMENT FOR SPAM- NO MATTER HOW MUCH KETCHUP YOU ADD!
...YET I CLOSED MY EYES AND PRETENDED...

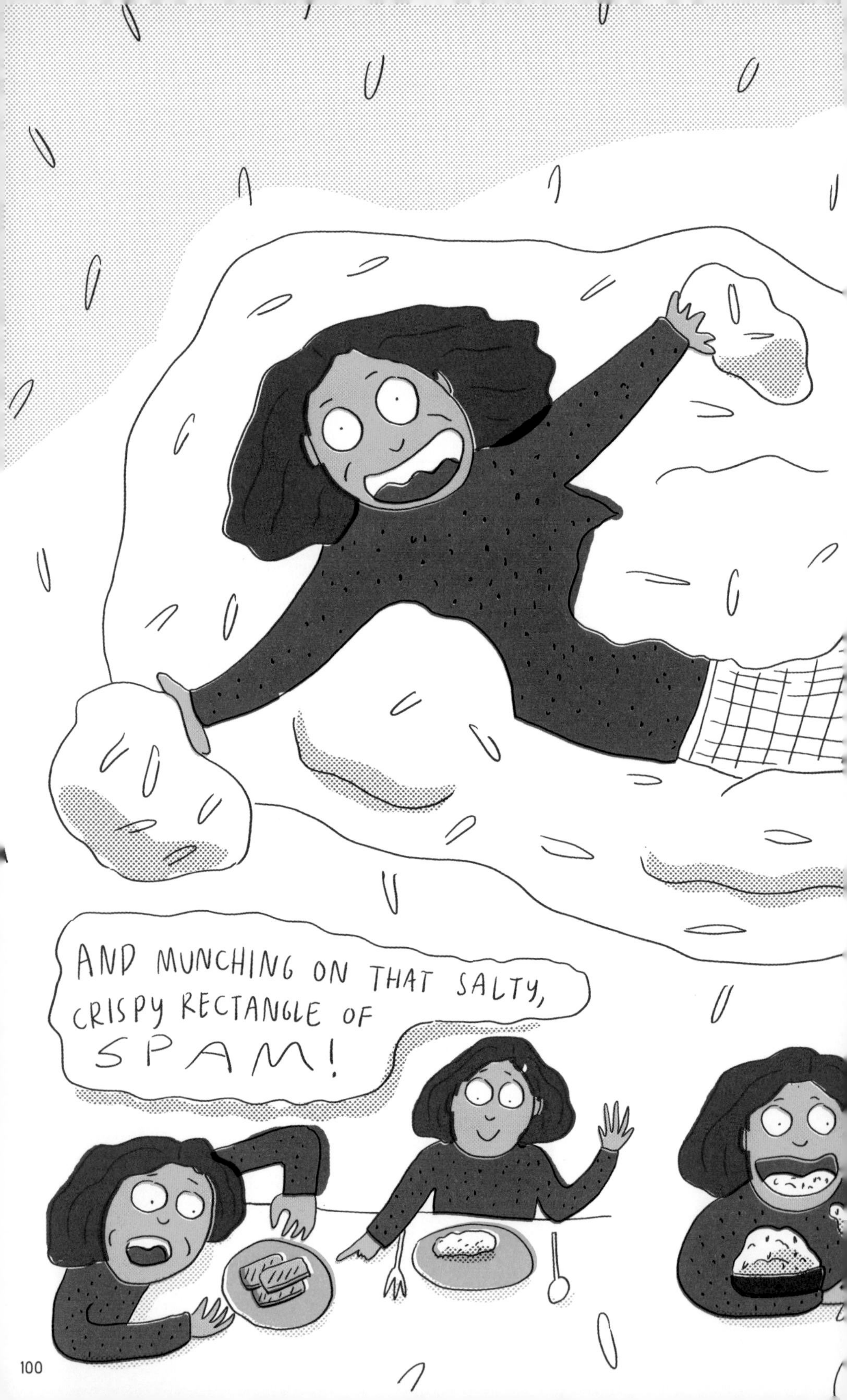
AND MUNCHING ON THAT SALTY, CRISPY RECTANGLE OF SPAM!

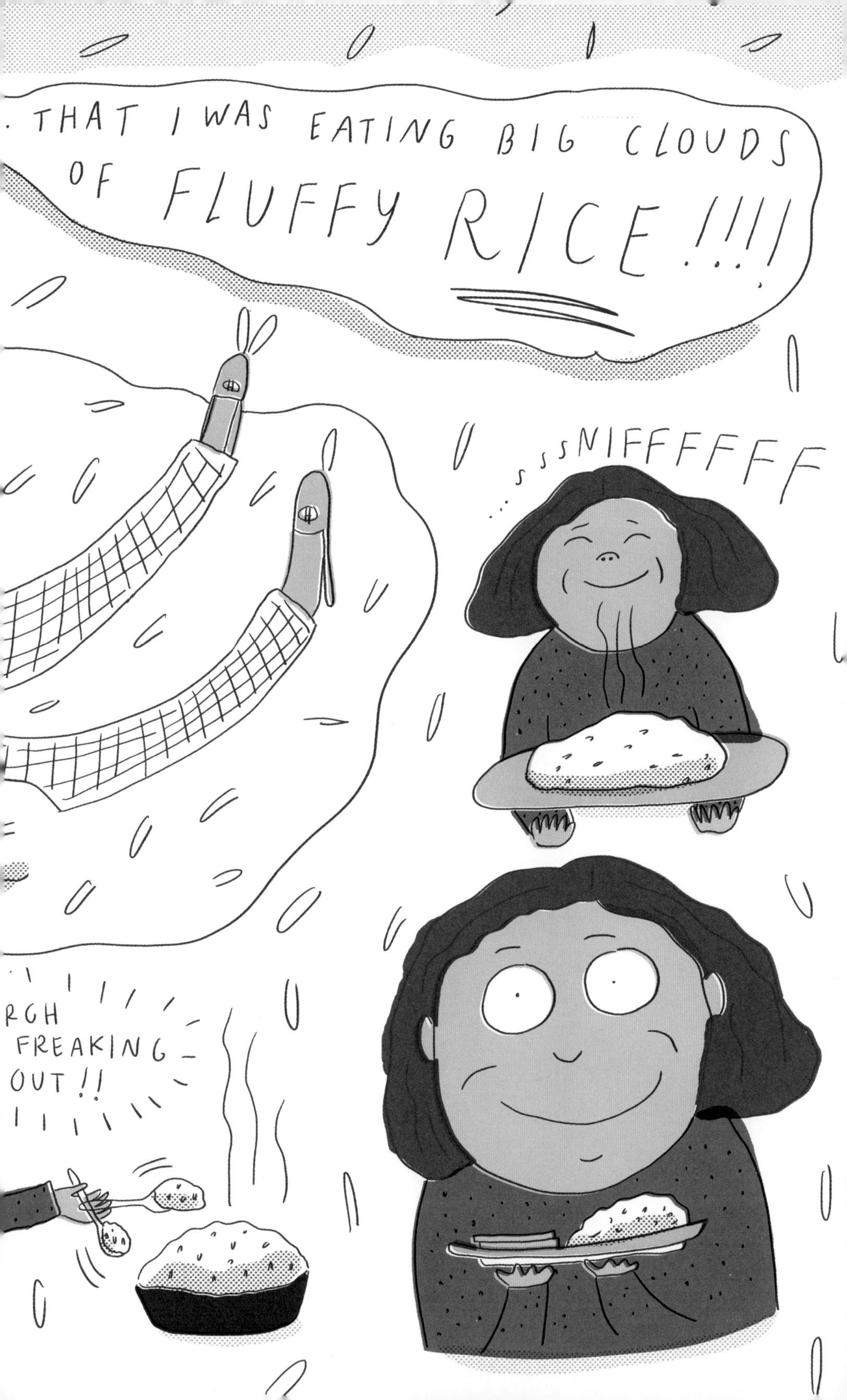

. THAT I WAS EATING BIG CLOUDS OF FLUFFY RICE!!!!
...sssNIFFFFFFF
RGH FREAKING OUT!!

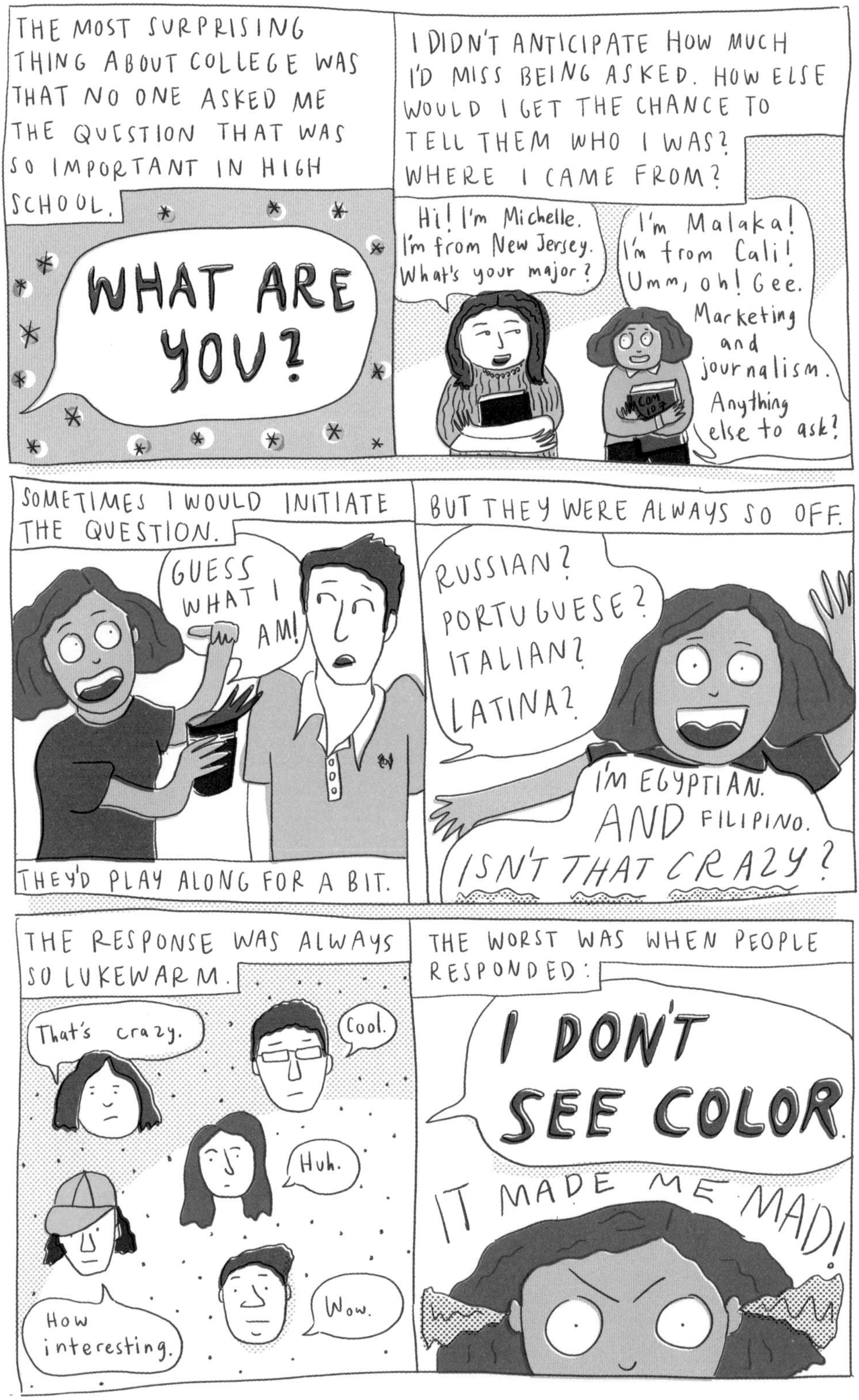
THE MOST SURPRISING THING ABOUT COLLEGE WAS THAT NO ONE ASKED ME THE QUESTION THAT WAS SO IMPORTANT IN HIGH SCHOOL.
WHAT ARE YOU?
I DIDN'T ANTICIPATE HOW MUCH I'D MISS BEING ASKED. HOW ELSE WOULD I GET THE CHANCE TO TELL THEM WHO I WAS? WHERE I CAME FROM?
Hi! I'm Michelle. I'm from New Jersey. What's your major?
I'm Malaka! I'm from Cali! Umm, oh! Gee. Marketing and journalism. Anything else to ask?
SOMETIMES I WOULD INITIATE THE QUESTION.
GUESS WHAT I AM!
THEY'D PLAY ALONG FOR A BIT.
BUT THEY WERE ALWAYS SO OFF.
RUSSIAN? PORTUGUESE? ITALIAN? LATINA?
I'M EGYPTIAN. AND FILIPINO. ISN'T THAT CRAZY?
THE RESPONSE WAS ALWAYS SO LUKEWARM.
That's crazy.
Cool.
Huh.
How interesting.
Wow.
THE WORST WAS WHEN PEOPLE RESPONDED:
I DON'T SEE COLOR.
IT MADE ME MAD!

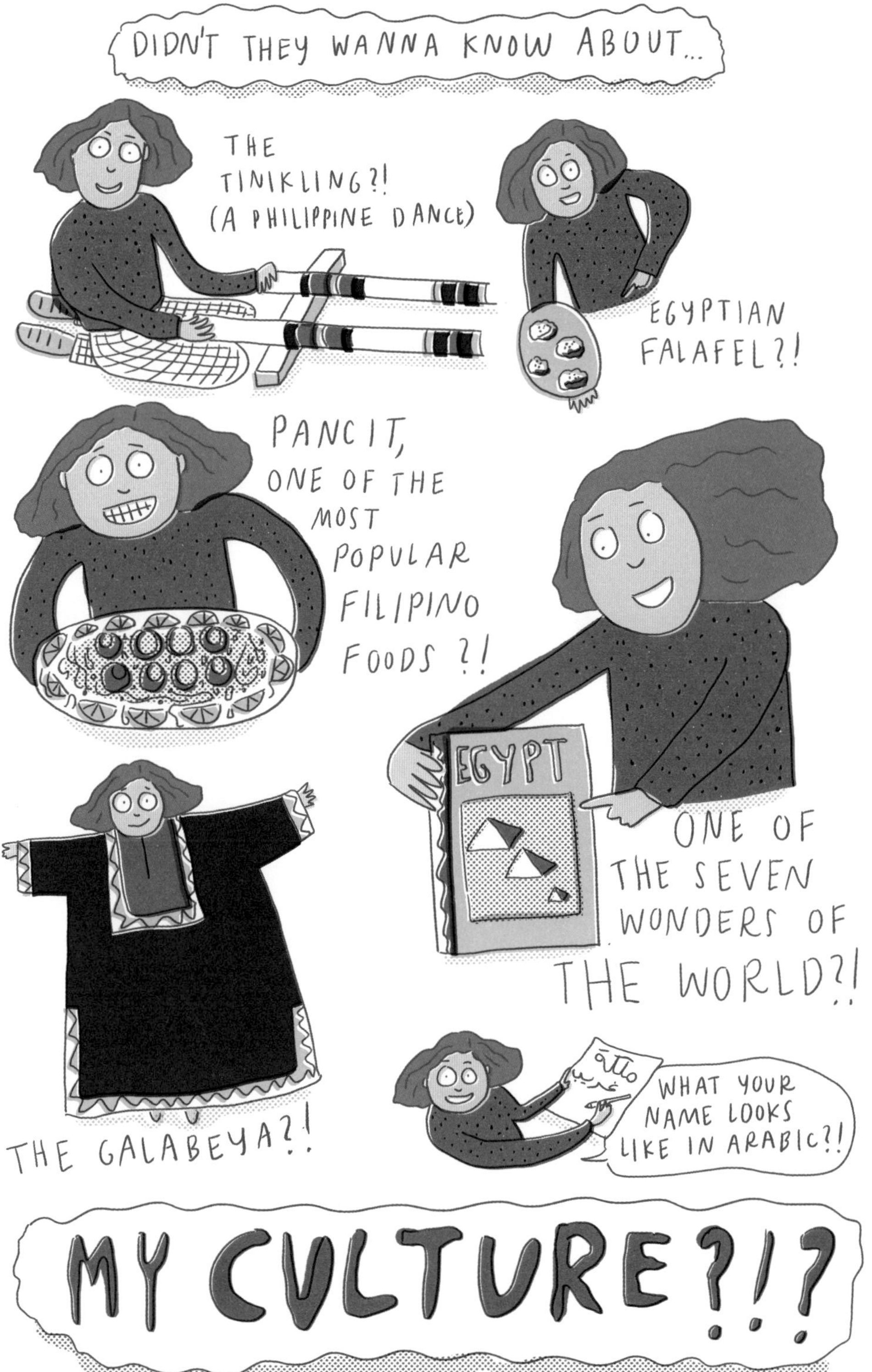
DIDN'T THEY WANNA KNOW ABOUT...
THE TINIKLING?! (A PHILIPPINE DANCE)
EGYPTIAN FALAFEL?!
PANCIT, ONE OF THE MOST POPULAR FILIPINO FOODS?!
EGYPT
ONE OF THE SEVEN WONDERS OF THE WORLD?!
THE GALABEYA?!
WHAT YOUR NAME LOOKS LIKE IN ARABIC?!
MY CULTURE?!?

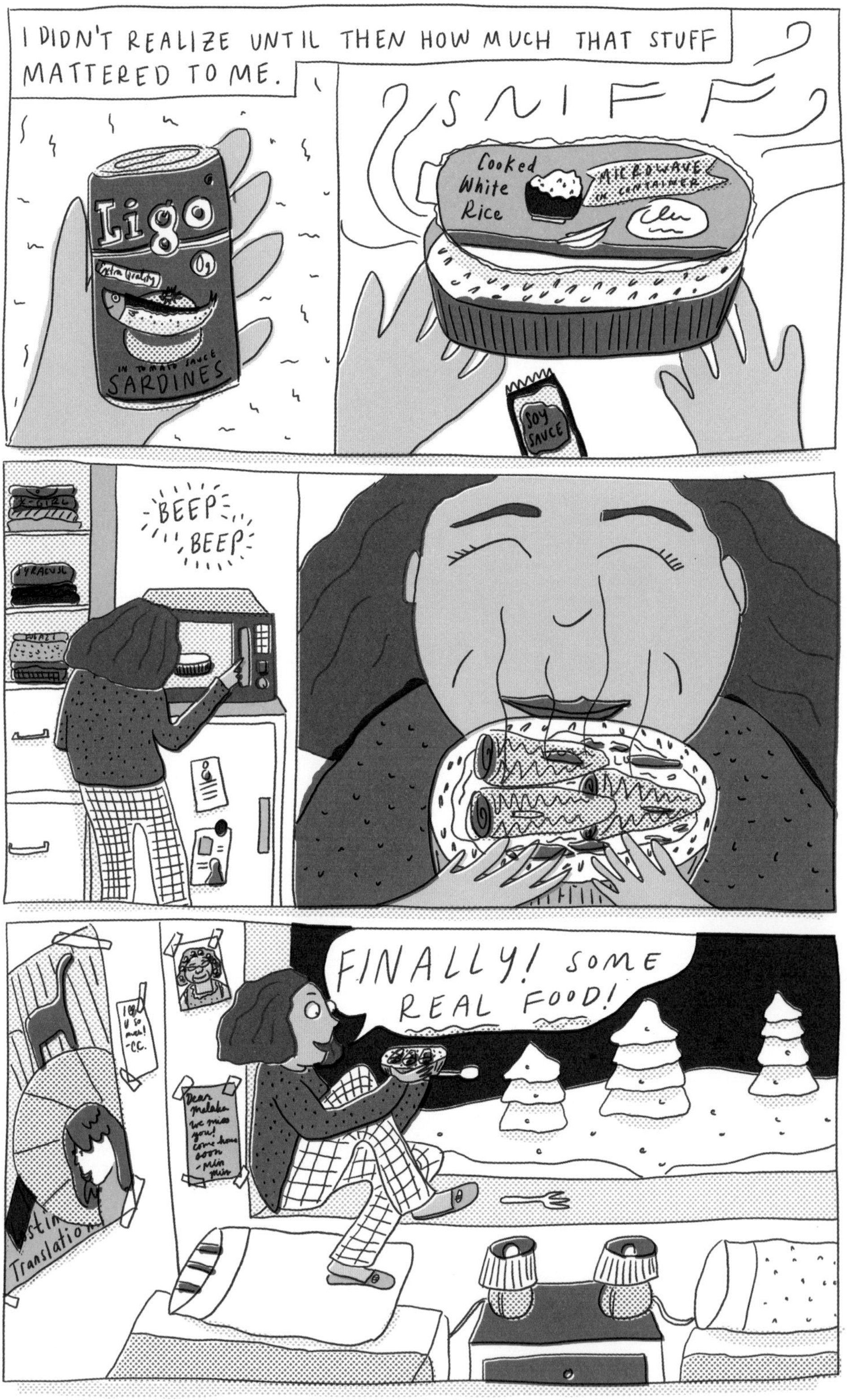
I DIDN'T REALIZE UNTIL THEN HOW MUCH THAT STUFF MATTERED TO ME.
Ligo
SARDINES
IN TOMATO SAUCE
SNIFF
Cooked White Rice
MICROWAVE IN CONTAINER
SOY SAUCE
X-GIRL
SYRACUSE
BEEP BEEP
FINALLY! SOME REAL FOOD!
Dear Malaka we miss you! come home soon - Min Min
Translation

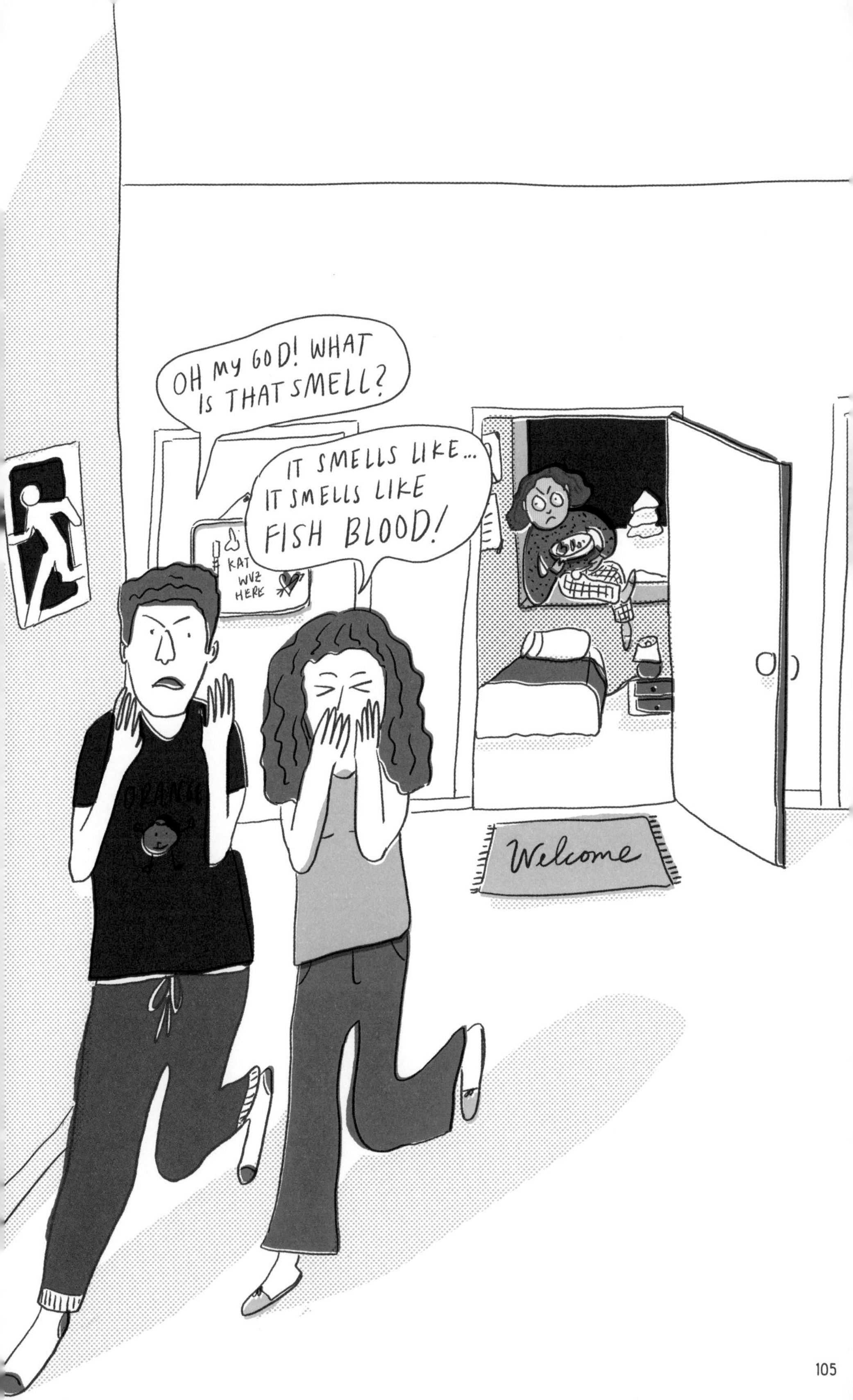
OH MY GOD! WHAT IS THAT SMELL?
IT SMELLS LIKE... IT SMELLS LIKE FISH BLOOD!
KAT WUZ HERE
Welcome

Chapter 6

TITO MARO WAS RIGHT
ABOUT THE REAL WORLD...

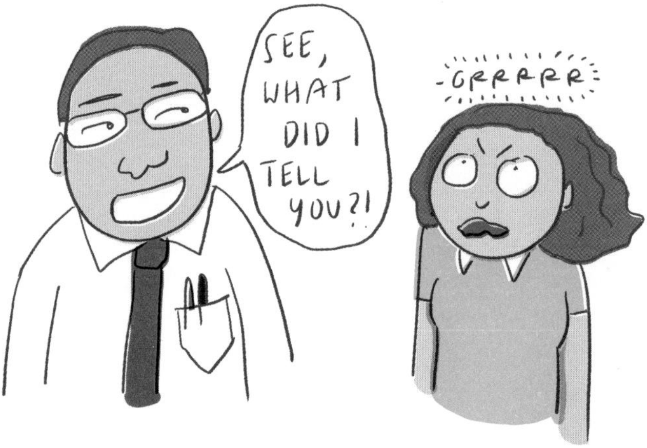
SEE, WHAT DID I TELL YOU?!
GRRRRR

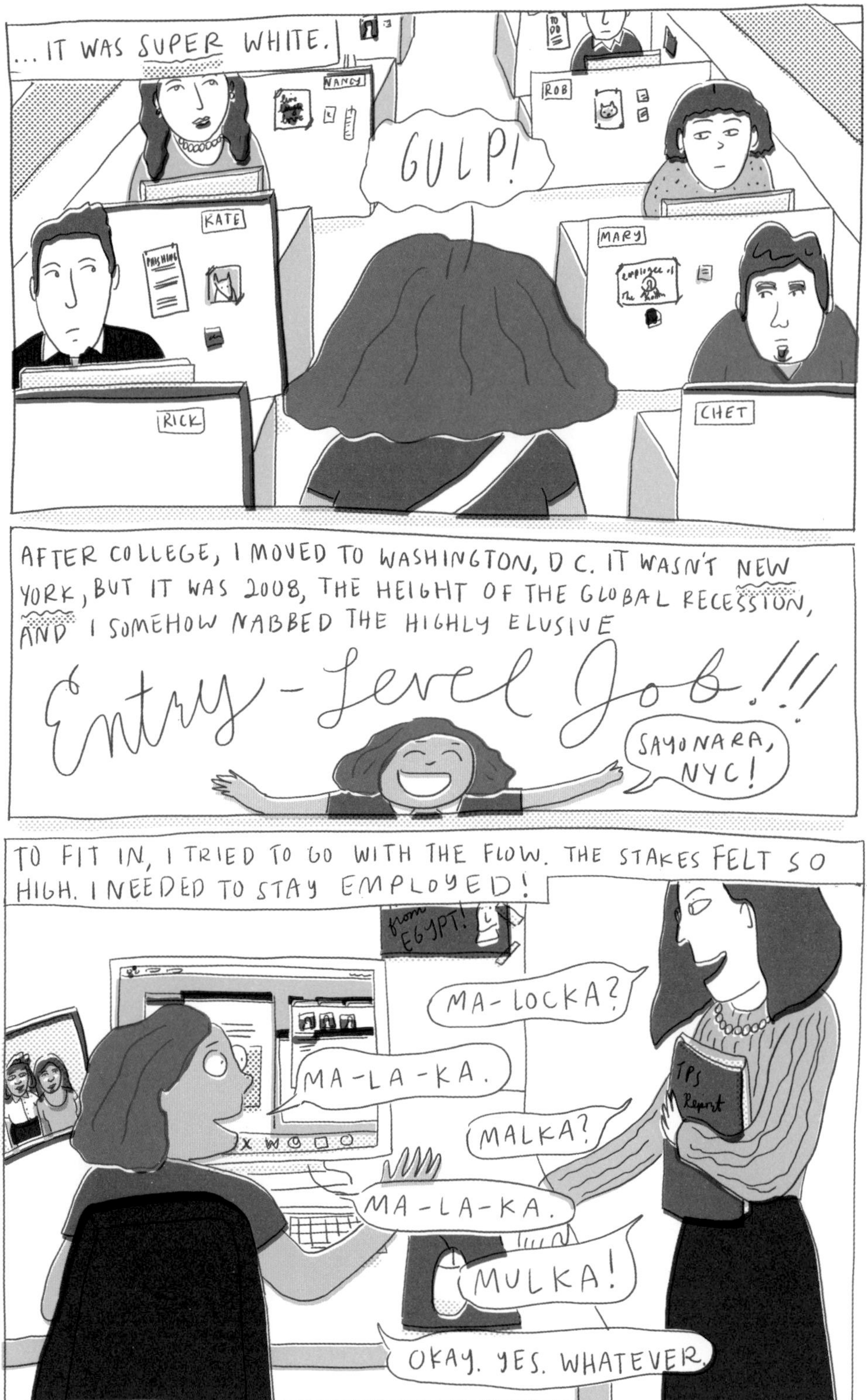
...IT WAS SUPER WHITE.
NANCY
ROB
GULP!
KATE
PHISHING
MARY
RICK
CHET
AFTER COLLEGE, I MOVED TO WASHINGTON, D.C. IT WASN'T NEW YORK, BUT IT WAS 2008, THE HEIGHT OF THE GLOBAL RECESSION, AND I SOMEHOW NABBED THE HIGHLY ELUSIVE
Entry-Level Job!!!
SAYONARA, NYC!
TO FIT IN, I TRIED TO GO WITH THE FLOW. THE STAKES FELT SO HIGH. I NEEDED TO STAY EMPLOYED!
from EGYPT!
MA-LOCKA?
MA-LA-KA.
MALKA?
MA-LA-KA.
MULKA!
OKAY. YES. WHATEVER.
TPS Report

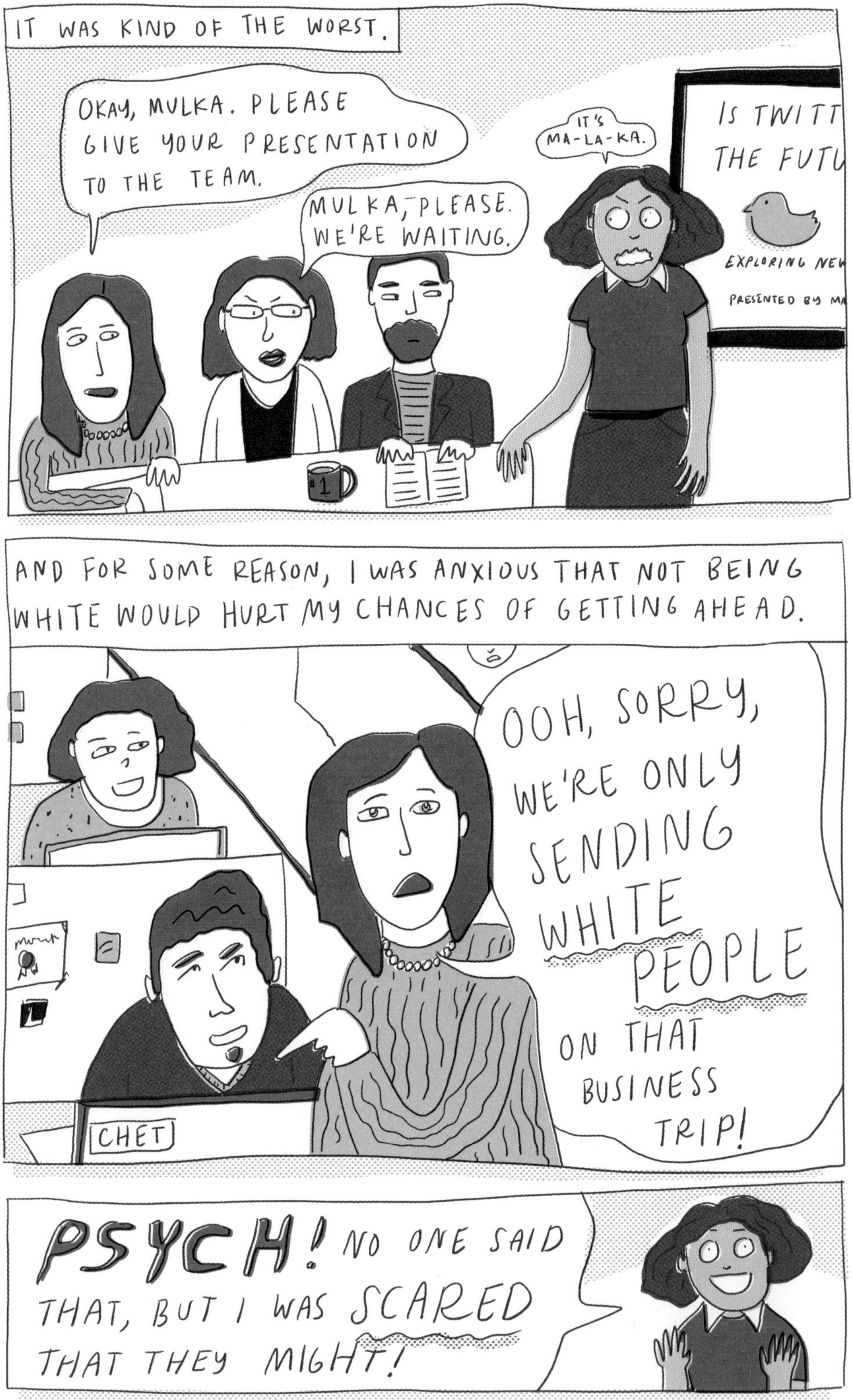
IT WAS KIND OF THE WORST.
OKAY, MULKA. PLEASE GIVE YOUR PRESENTATION TO THE TEAM.
MULKA, PLEASE. WE'RE WAITING.
IT'S MA-LA-KA.
IS TWITT
THE FUTU
EXPLORING NEW
PRESENTED BY MA
#1
AND FOR SOME REASON, I WAS ANXIOUS THAT NOT BEING WHITE WOULD HURT MY CHANCES OF GETTING AHEAD.
OOH, SORRY, WE'RE ONLY SENDING WHITE PEOPLE ON THAT BUSINESS TRIP!
CHET
PSYCH! NO ONE SAID THAT, BUT I WAS SCARED THAT THEY MIGHT!

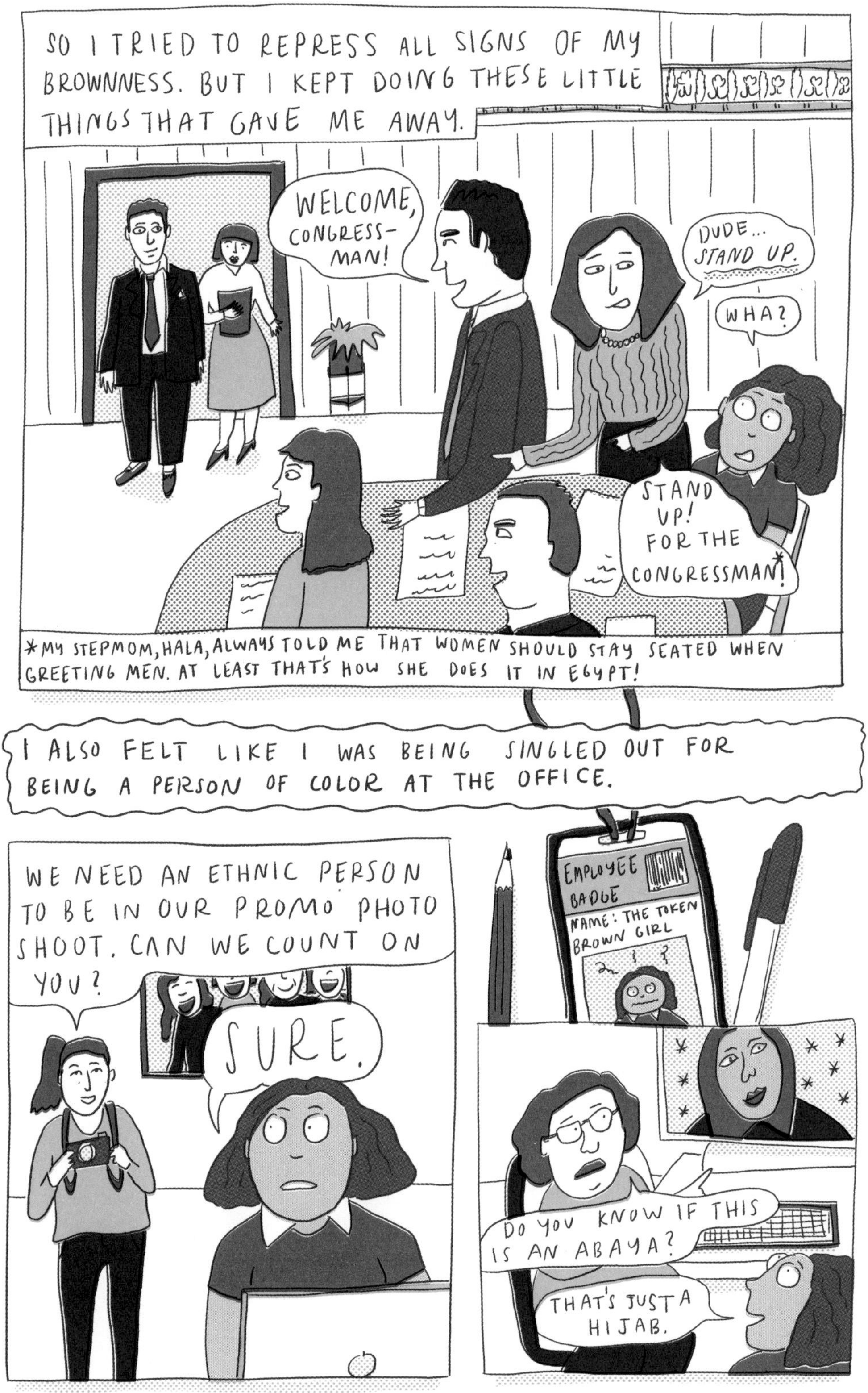
SO I TRIED TO REPRESS ALL SIGNS OF MY BROWNNESS. BUT I KEPT DOING THESE LITTLE THINGS THAT GAVE ME AWAY.
WELCOME, CONGRESS-MAN!
DUDE... STAND UP.
WHA?
STAND UP! FOR THE CONGRESSMAN!*
*MY STEPMOM, HALA, ALWAYS TOLD ME THAT WOMEN SHOULD STAY SEATED WHEN GREETING MEN. AT LEAST THAT'S HOW SHE DOES IT IN EGYPT!
I ALSO FELT LIKE I WAS BEING SINGLED OUT FOR BEING A PERSON OF COLOR AT THE OFFICE.
WE NEED AN ETHNIC PERSON TO BE IN OUR PROMO PHOTO SHOOT. CAN WE COUNT ON YOU?
SURE.
EMPLOYEE BADGE
NAME: THE TOKEN BROWN GIRL
DO YOU KNOW IF THIS IS AN ABAYA?
THAT'S JUST A HIJAB.

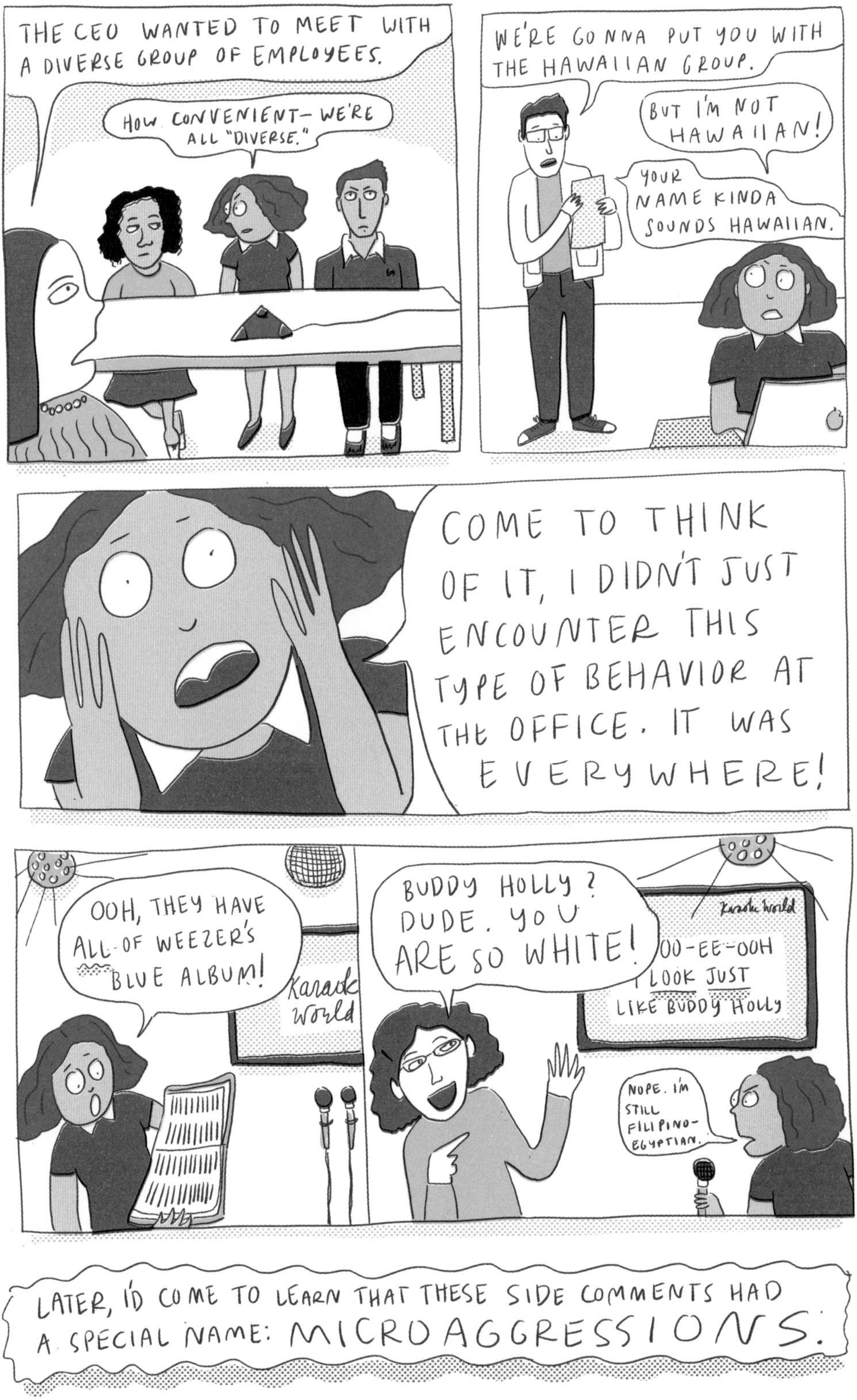
THE CEO WANTED TO MEET WITH A DIVERSE GROUP OF EMPLOYEES.
HOW CONVENIENT— WE'RE ALL "DIVERSE."
WE'RE GONNA PUT YOU WITH THE HAWAIIAN GROUP.
BUT I'M NOT HAWAIIAN!
YOUR NAME KINDA SOUNDS HAWAIIAN.
COME TO THINK OF IT, I DIDN'T JUST ENCOUNTER THIS TYPE OF BEHAVIOR AT THE OFFICE. IT WAS EVERYWHERE!
OOH, THEY HAVE ALL OF WEEZER'S BLUE ALBUM!
Karaoke World
BUDDY HOLLY? DUDE. YOU ARE SO WHITE!
Karaoke World
OO-EE-OOH I LOOK JUST LIKE BUDDY HOLLY
NOPE. I'M STILL FILIPINO-EGYPTIAN.
LATER, I'D COME TO LEARN THAT THESE SIDE COMMENTS HAD A SPECIAL NAME: MICROAGGRESSIONS.

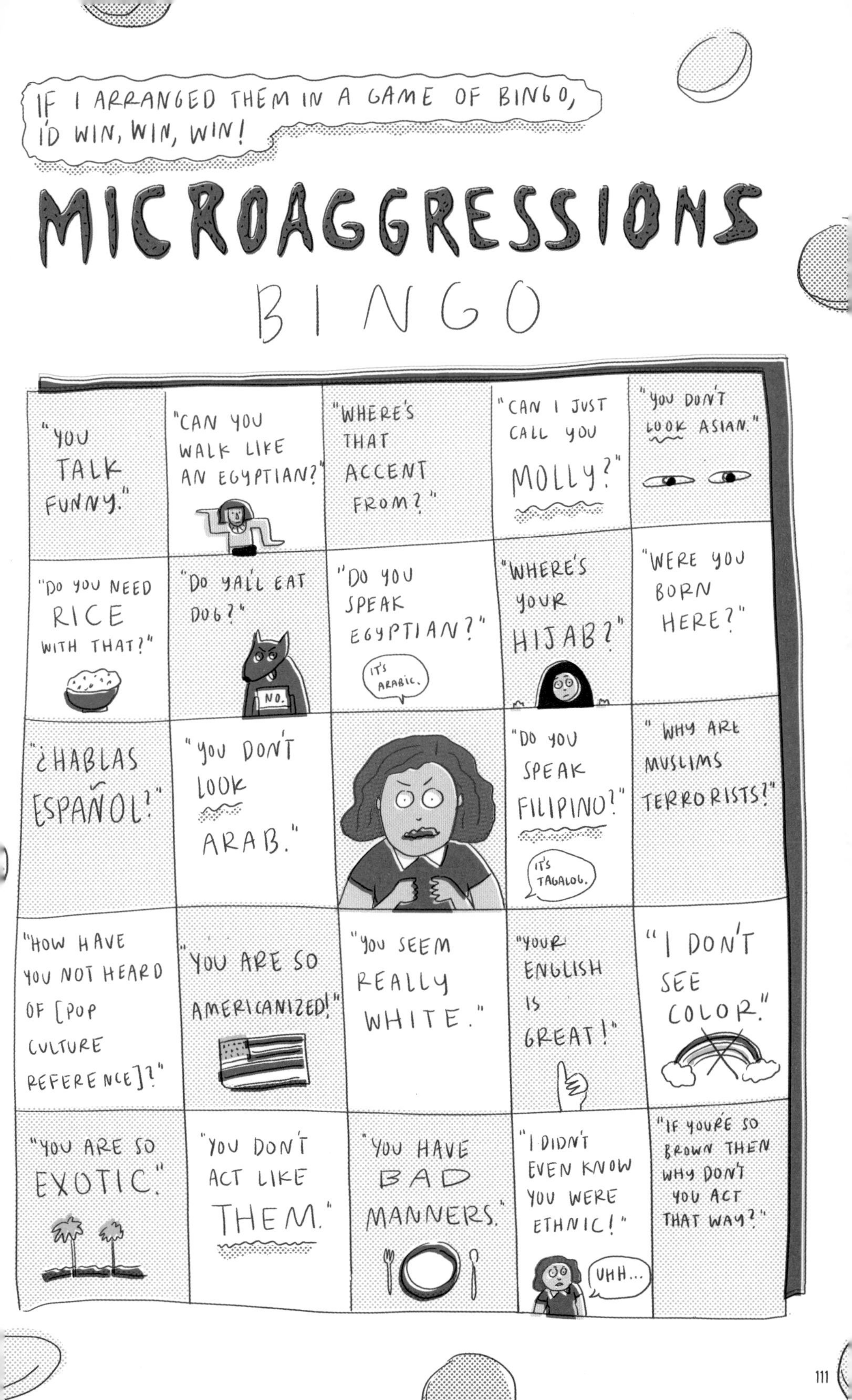
IF I ARRANGED THEM IN A GAME OF BINGO, I'D WIN, WIN, WIN!
MICROAGGRESSIONS
BINGO
"YOU TALK FUNNY."
"CAN YOU WALK LIKE AN EGYPTIAN?"
"WHERE'S THAT ACCENT FROM?"
"CAN I JUST CALL YOU MOLLY?"
"YOU DON'T LOOK ASIAN."
"DO YOU NEED RICE WITH THAT?"
"DO Y'ALL EAT DOG?"
NO.
"DO YOU SPEAK EGYPTIAN?"
IT'S ARABIC.
"WHERE'S YOUR HIJAB?"
"WERE YOU BORN HERE?"
"¿HABLAS ESPAÑOL?"
"YOU DON'T LOOK ARAB."
"DO YOU SPEAK FILIPINO?"
IT'S TAGALOG.
"WHY ARE MUSLIMS TERRORISTS?"
"HOW HAVE YOU NOT HEARD OF [POP CULTURE REFERENCE]?"
"YOU ARE SO AMERICANIZED!"
"YOU SEEM REALLY WHITE."
"YOUR ENGLISH IS GREAT!"
"I DON'T SEE COLOR."
"YOU ARE SO EXOTIC."
"YOU DON'T ACT LIKE THEM."
"YOU HAVE BAD MANNERS."
"I DIDN'T EVEN KNOW YOU WERE ETHNIC!"
UHH...
"IF YOU'RE SO BROWN THEN WHY DON'T YOU ACT THAT WAY?"

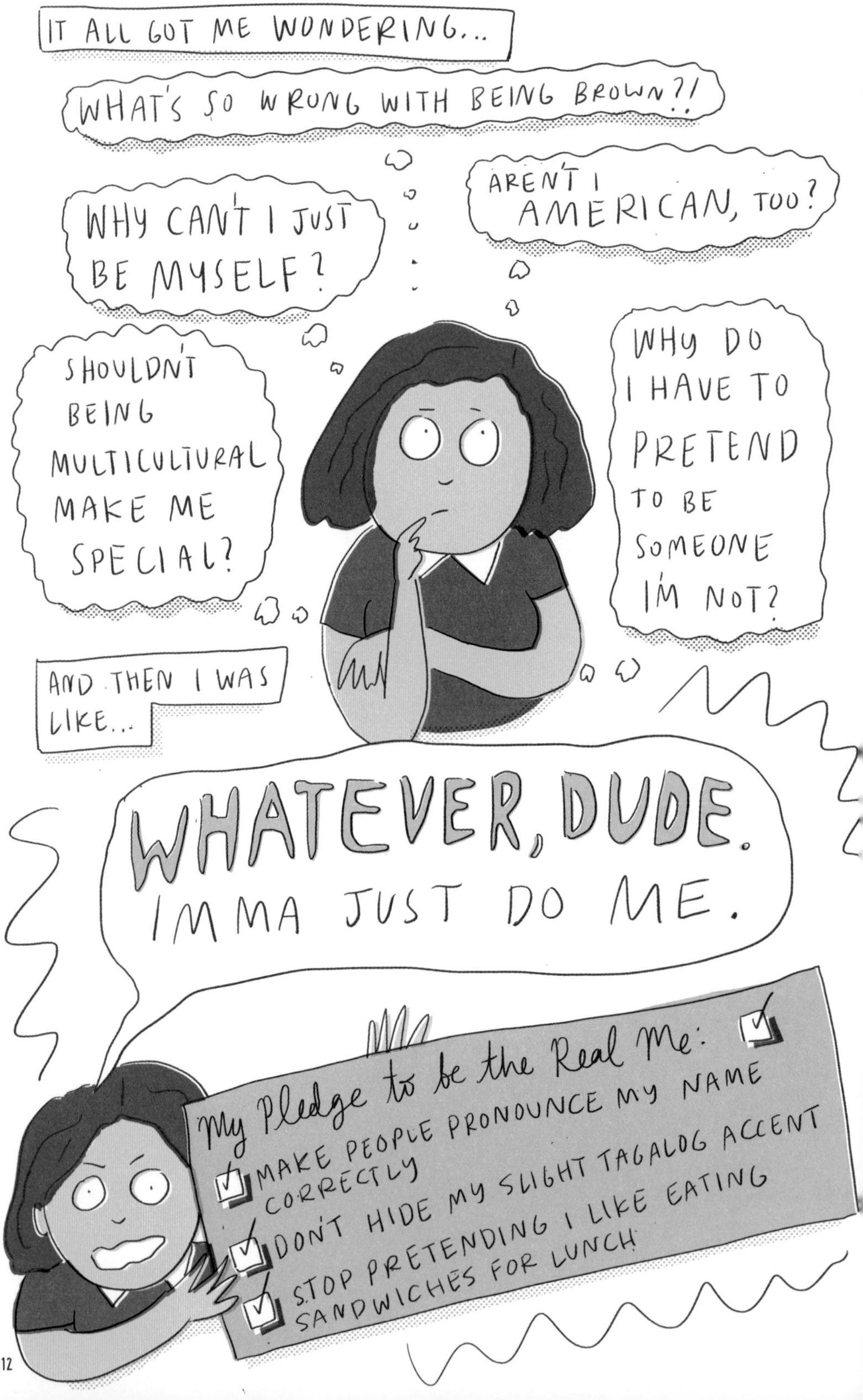

IT ALL GOT ME WONDERING...
WHAT'S SO WRONG WITH BEING BROWN?!
WHY CAN'T I JUST BE MYSELF?
AREN'T I AMERICAN, TOO?
SHOULDN'T BEING MULTICULTURAL MAKE ME SPECIAL?
WHY DO I HAVE TO PRETEND TO BE SOMEONE I'M NOT?
AND THEN I WAS LIKE...
WHATEVER, DUDE. IMMA JUST DO ME.
My Pledge to be the Real Me:
MAKE PEOPLE PRONOUNCE MY NAME CORRECTLY
DON'T HIDE MY SLIGHT TAGALOG ACCENT
STOP PRETENDING I LIKE EATING SANDWICHES FOR LUNCH

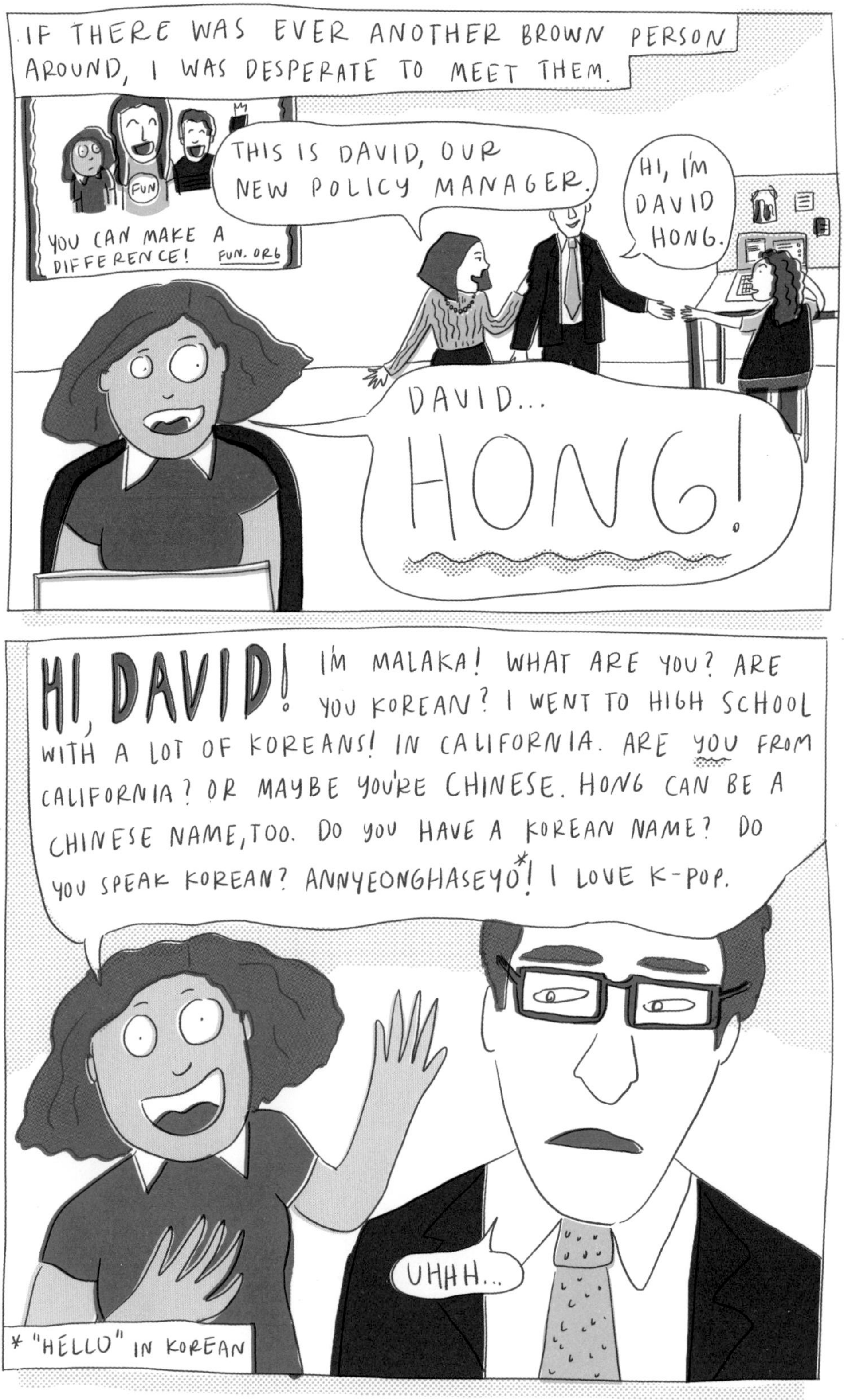
IF THERE WAS EVER ANOTHER BROWN PERSON AROUND, I WAS DESPERATE TO MEET THEM.
FUN
YOU CAN MAKE A DIFFERENCE! FUN.ORG
THIS IS DAVID, OUR NEW POLICY MANAGER.
HI, I'M DAVID HONG.
DAVID... HONG!
HI, DAVID! I'M MALAKA! WHAT ARE YOU? ARE YOU KOREAN? I WENT TO HIGH SCHOOL WITH A LOT OF KOREANS! IN CALIFORNIA. ARE YOU FROM CALIFORNIA? OR MAYBE YOU'RE CHINESE. HONG CAN BE A CHINESE NAME, TOO. DO YOU HAVE A KOREAN NAME? DO YOU SPEAK KOREAN? ANNYEONGHASEYO*! I LOVE K-POP.
UHHH...
* "HELLO" IN KOREAN

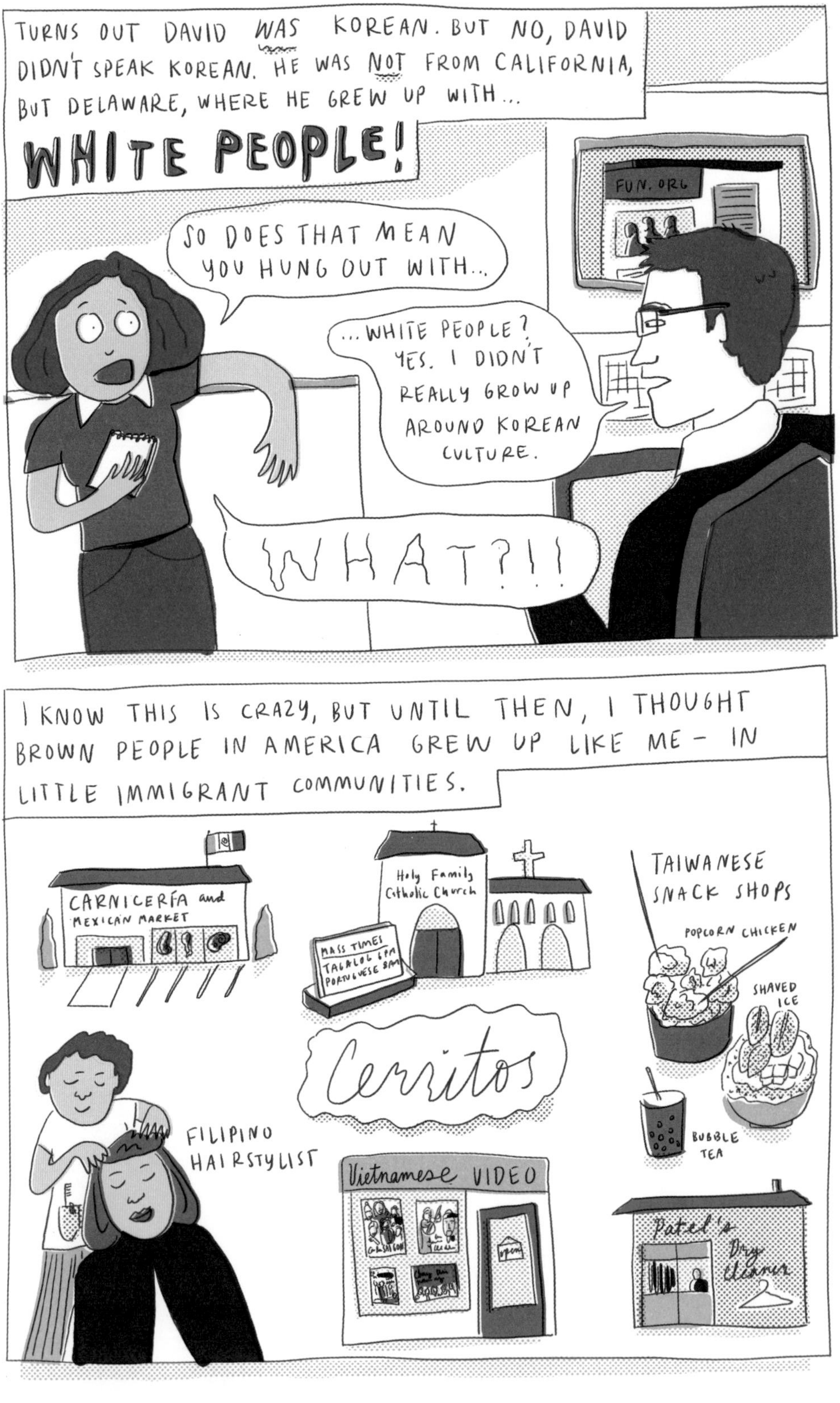
TURNS OUT DAVID WAS KOREAN. BUT NO, DAVID DIDN'T SPEAK KOREAN. HE WAS NOT FROM CALIFORNIA, BUT DELAWARE, WHERE HE GREW UP WITH...
WHITE PEOPLE!
FUN.ORG
SO DOES THAT MEAN YOU HUNG OUT WITH...
...WHITE PEOPLE? YES. I DIDN'T REALLY GROW UP AROUND KOREAN CULTURE.
WHAT?!!
I KNOW THIS IS CRAZY, BUT UNTIL THEN, I THOUGHT BROWN PEOPLE IN AMERICA GREW UP LIKE ME— IN LITTLE IMMIGRANT COMMUNITIES.
CARNICERÍA and MEXICAN MARKET
Holy Family Catholic Church
MASS TIMES
TAGALOG 6PM
PORTUGUESE 8AM
TAIWANESE SNACK SHOPS
POPCORN CHICKEN
SHAVED ICE
BUBBLE TEA
Cerritos
FILIPINO HAIRSTYLIST
Vietnamese VIDEO
open
Patel's Dry Cleaner

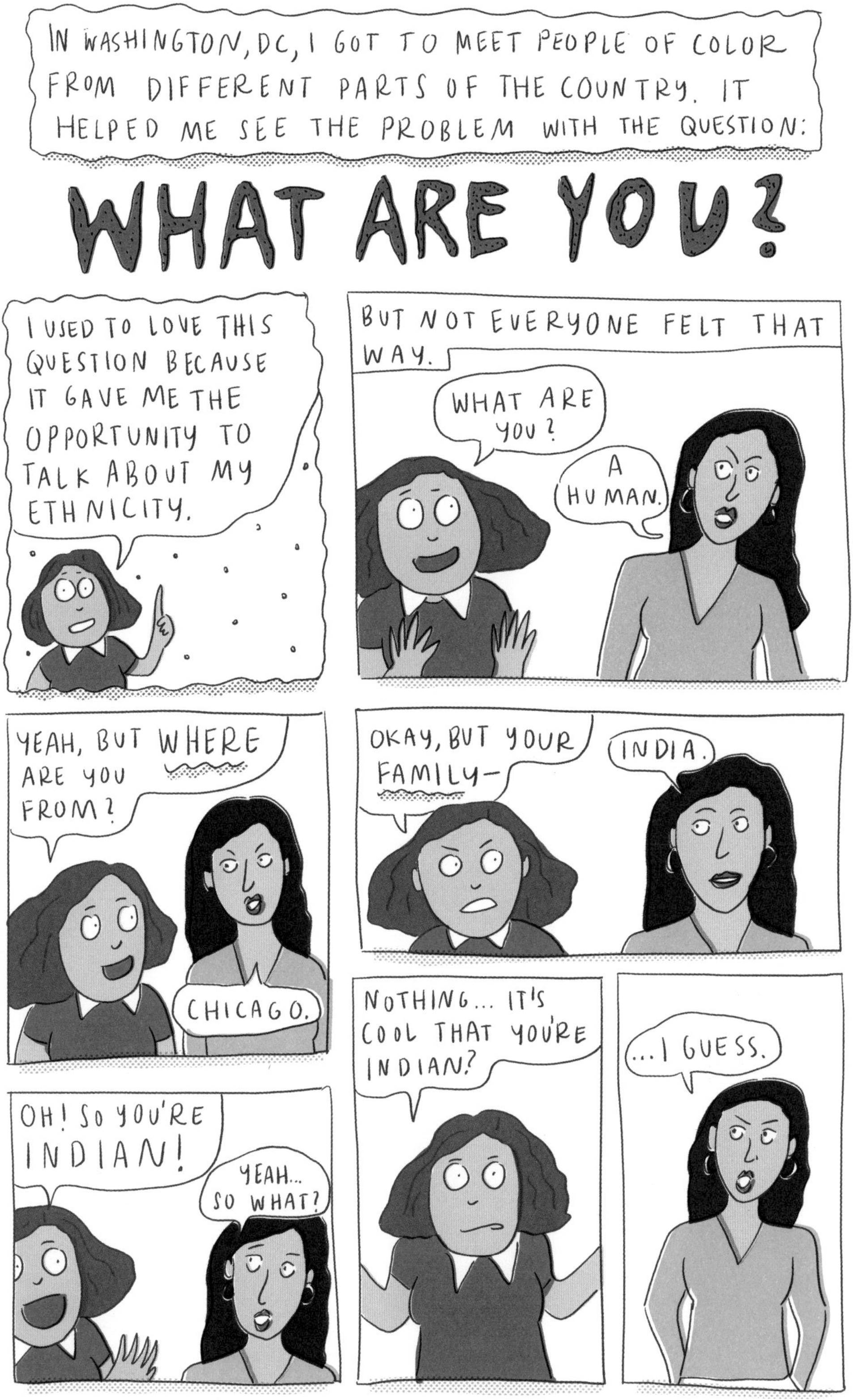
IN WASHINGTON, DC, I GOT TO MEET PEOPLE OF COLOR FROM DIFFERENT PARTS OF THE COUNTRY. IT HELPED ME SEE THE PROBLEM WITH THE QUESTION:
WHAT ARE YOU?
I USED TO LOVE THIS QUESTION BECAUSE IT GAVE ME THE OPPORTUNITY TO TALK ABOUT MY ETHNICITY.
BUT NOT EVERYONE FELT THAT WAY.
WHAT ARE YOU?
A HUMAN.
YEAH, BUT WHERE ARE YOU FROM?
CHICAGO.
OKAY, BUT YOUR FAMILY—
INDIA.
OH! SO YOU'RE INDIAN!
YEAH... SO WHAT?
NOTHING... IT'S COOL THAT YOU'RE INDIAN?
...I GUESS.

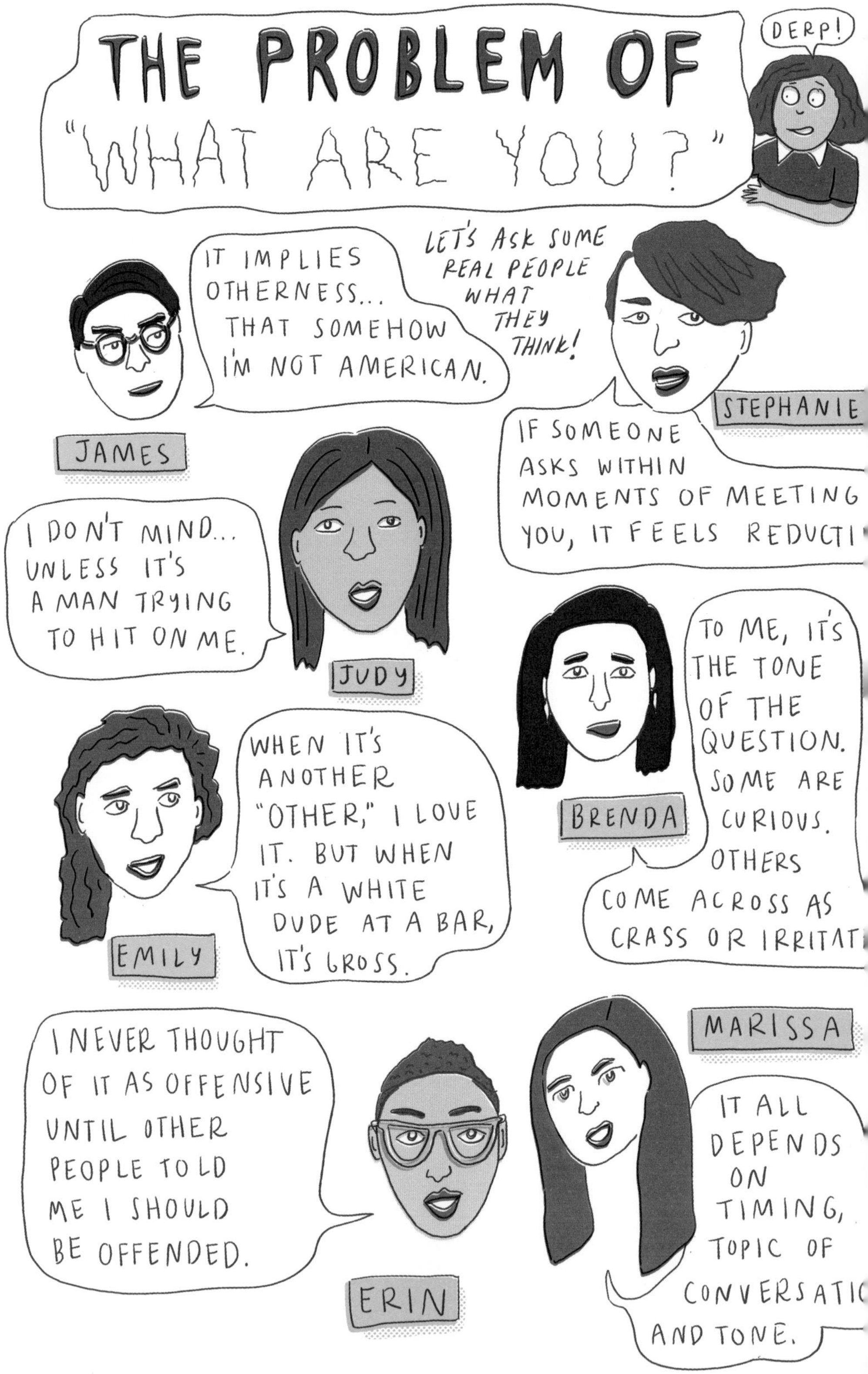
THE PROBLEM OF "WHAT ARE YOU?"
DERP!
IT IMPLIES OTHERNESS... THAT SOMEHOW I'M NOT AMERICAN.
JAMES
LET'S ASK SOME REAL PEOPLE WHAT THEY THINK!
STEPHANIE
IF SOMEONE ASKS WITHIN MOMENTS OF MEETING YOU, IT FEELS REDUCTI
I DON'T MIND... UNLESS IT'S A MAN TRYING TO HIT ON ME.
JUDY
TO ME, IT'S THE TONE OF THE QUESTION. SOME ARE CURIOUS. OTHERS COME ACROSS AS CRASS OR IRRITAT
BRENDA
WHEN IT'S ANOTHER "OTHER," I LOVE IT. BUT WHEN IT'S A WHITE DUDE AT A BAR, IT'S GROSS.
EMILY
I NEVER THOUGHT OF IT AS OFFENSIVE UNTIL OTHER PEOPLE TOLD ME I SHOULD BE OFFENDED.
ERIN
MARISSA
IT ALL DEPENDS ON TIMING, TOPIC OF CONVERSATI AND TONE.

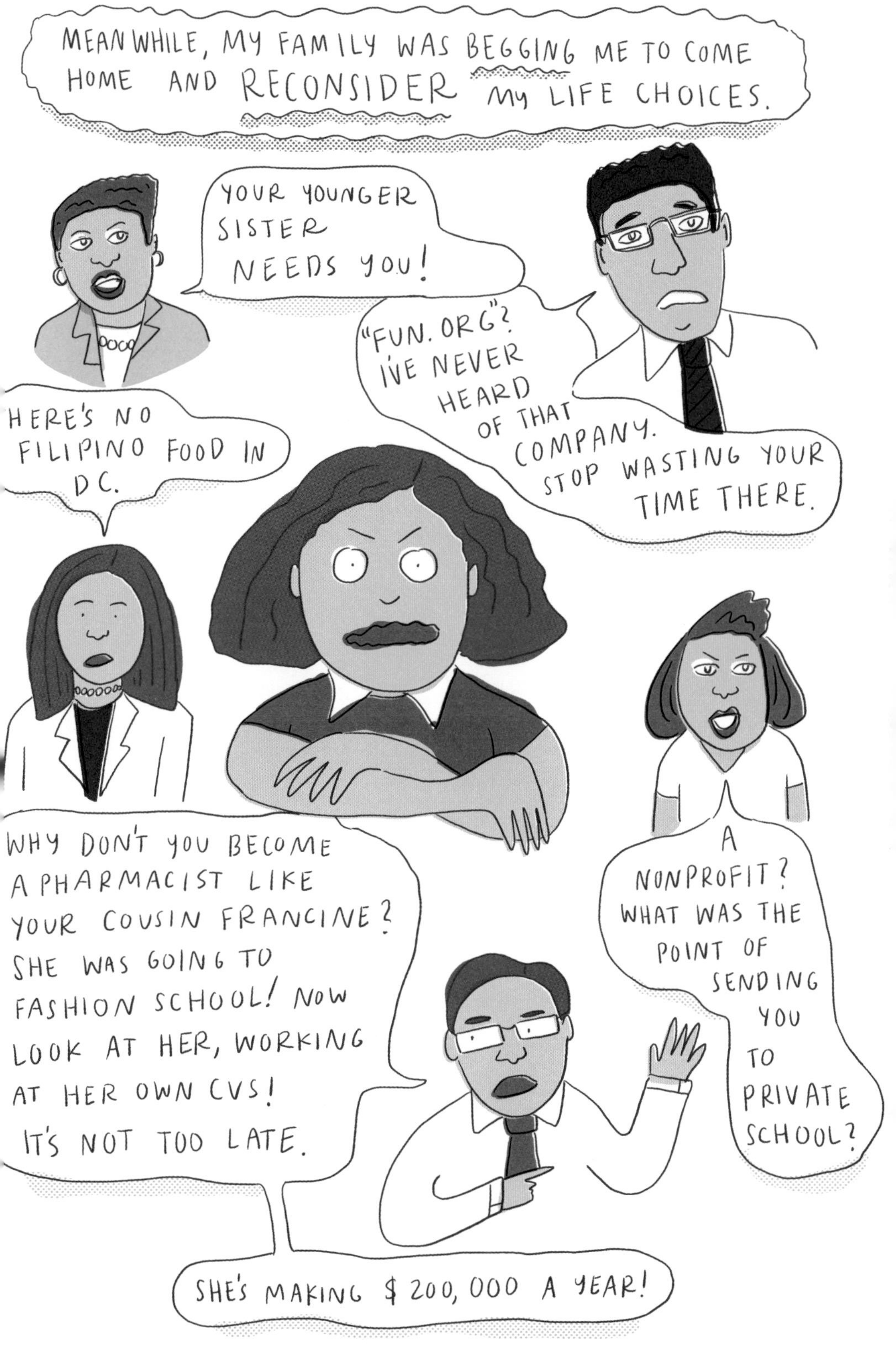
MEANWHILE, MY FAMILY WAS BEGGING ME TO COME HOME AND RECONSIDER MY LIFE CHOICES.
YOUR YOUNGER SISTER NEEDS YOU!
"FUN.ORG"? I'VE NEVER HEARD OF THAT COMPANY. STOP WASTING YOUR TIME THERE.
HERE'S NO FILIPINO FOOD IN DC.
WHY DON'T YOU BECOME A PHARMACIST LIKE YOUR COUSIN FRANCINE? SHE WAS GOING TO FASHION SCHOOL! NOW LOOK AT HER, WORKING AT HER OWN CVS! IT'S NOT TOO LATE.
A NONPROFIT? WHAT WAS THE POINT OF SENDING YOU TO PRIVATE SCHOOL?
SHE'S MAKING $200,000 A YEAR!

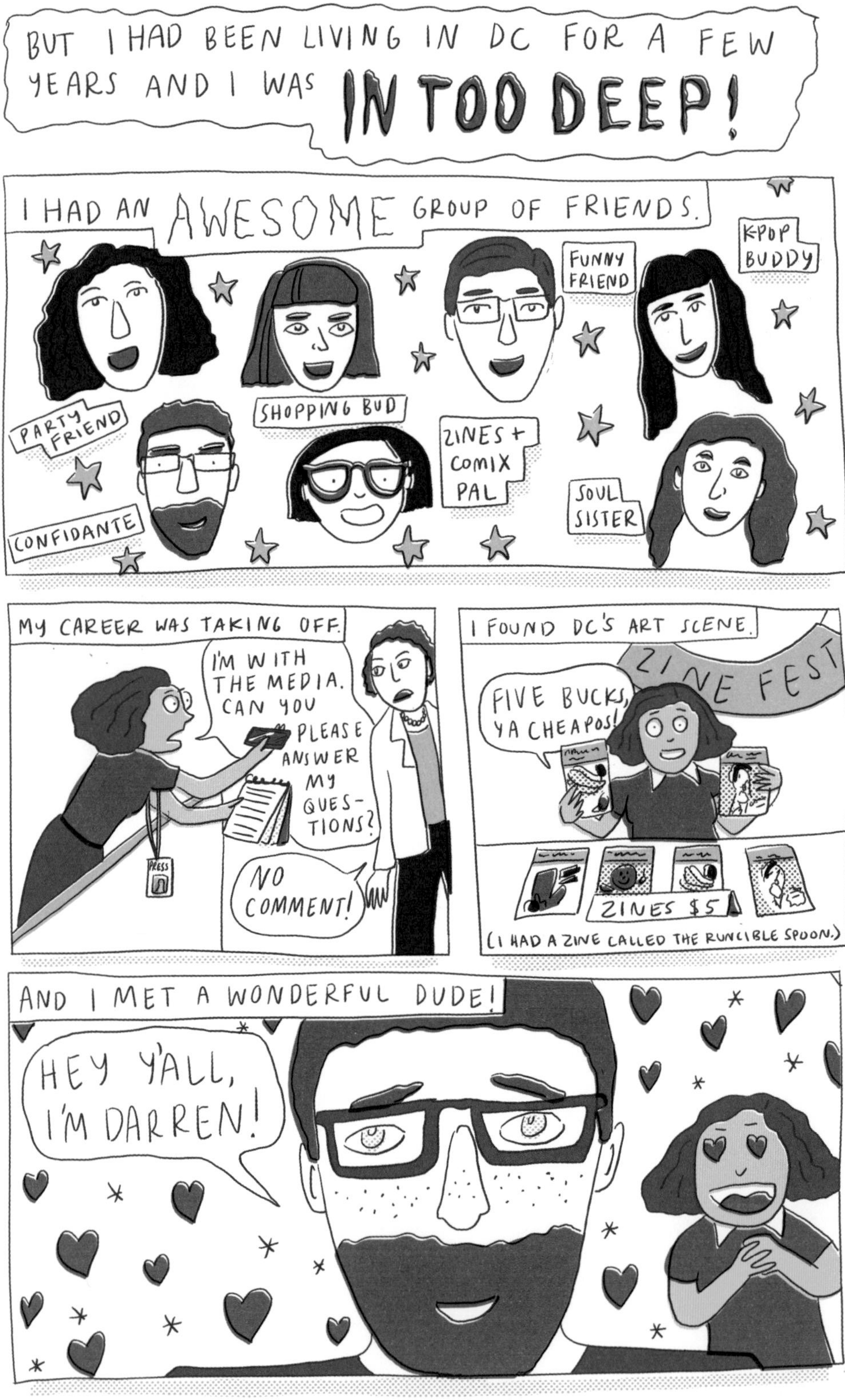
BUT I HAD BEEN LIVING IN DC FOR A FEW YEARS AND I WAS IN TOO DEEP!
I HAD AN AWESOME GROUP OF FRIENDS.
PARTY FRIEND
SHOPPING BUD
FUNNY FRIEND
KPOP BUDDY
CONFIDANTE
ZINES + COMIX PAL
SOUL SISTER
MY CAREER WAS TAKING OFF.
I'M WITH THE MEDIA. CAN YOU PLEASE ANSWER MY QUESTIONS?
PRESS
NO COMMENT!
I FOUND DC'S ART SCENE.
ZINE FEST
FIVE BUCKS, YA CHEAPOS!
ZINES $5
(I HAD A ZINE CALLED THE RUNCIBLE SPOON.)
AND I MET A WONDERFUL DUDE!
HEY Y'ALL, I'M DARREN!

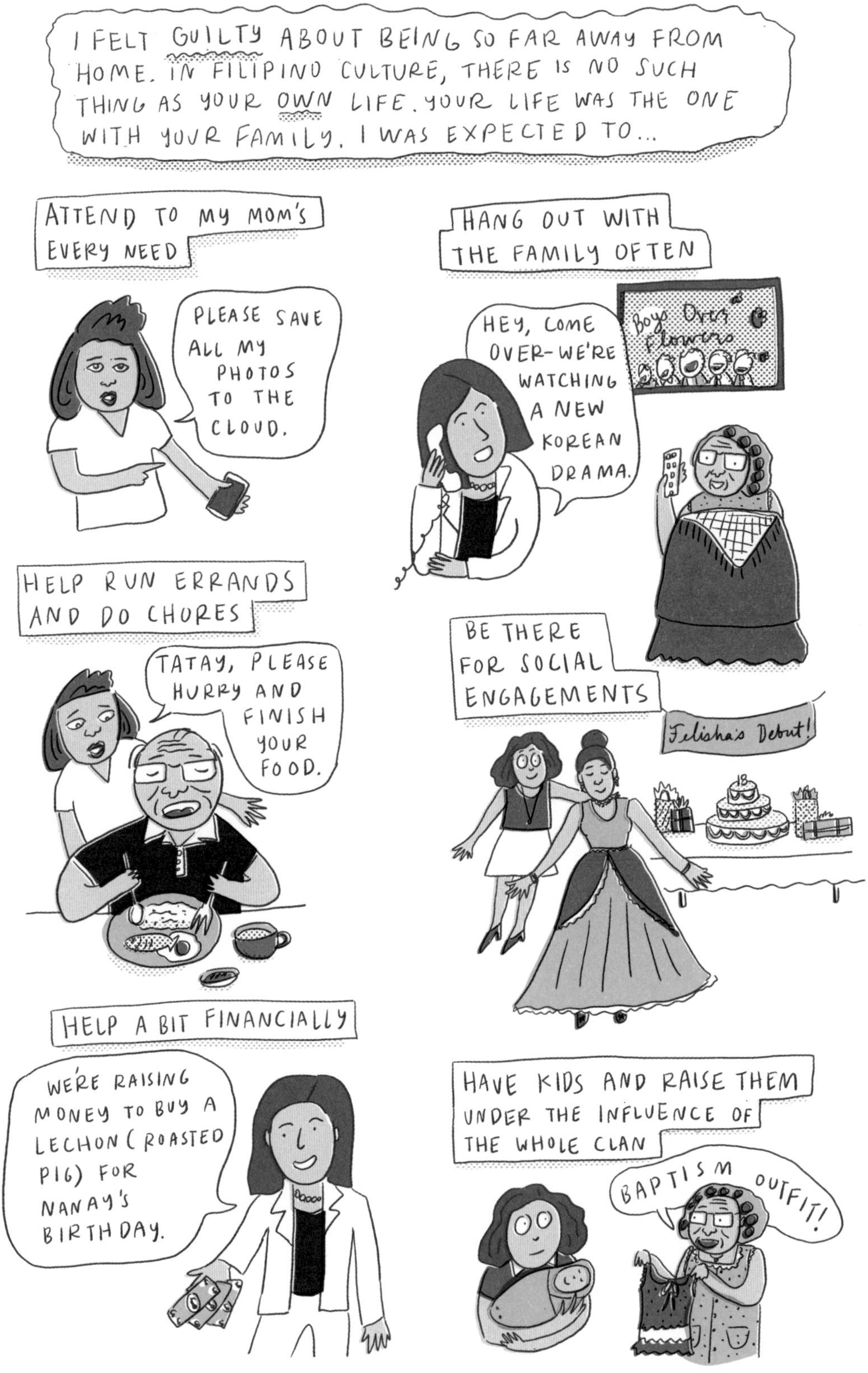
I FELT GUILTY ABOUT BEING SO FAR AWAY FROM HOME. IN FILIPINO CULTURE, THERE IS NO SUCH THING AS YOUR OWN LIFE. YOUR LIFE WAS THE ONE WITH YOUR FAMILY. I WAS EXPECTED TO...
ATTEND TO MY MOM'S EVERY NEED
PLEASE SAVE ALL MY PHOTOS TO THE CLOUD.
HANG OUT WITH THE FAMILY OFTEN
HEY, COME OVER—WE'RE WATCHING A NEW KOREAN DRAMA.
Boys Over Flowers
HELP RUN ERRANDS AND DO CHORES
TATAY, PLEASE HURRY AND FINISH YOUR FOOD.
BE THERE FOR SOCIAL ENGAGEMENTS
Felisha's Debut!
18
HELP A BIT FINANCIALLY
WE'RE RAISING MONEY TO BUY A LECHON (ROASTED PIG) FOR NANAY'S BIRTHDAY.
HAVE KIDS AND RAISE THEM UNDER THE INFLUENCE OF THE WHOLE CLAN
BAPTISM OUTFIT!

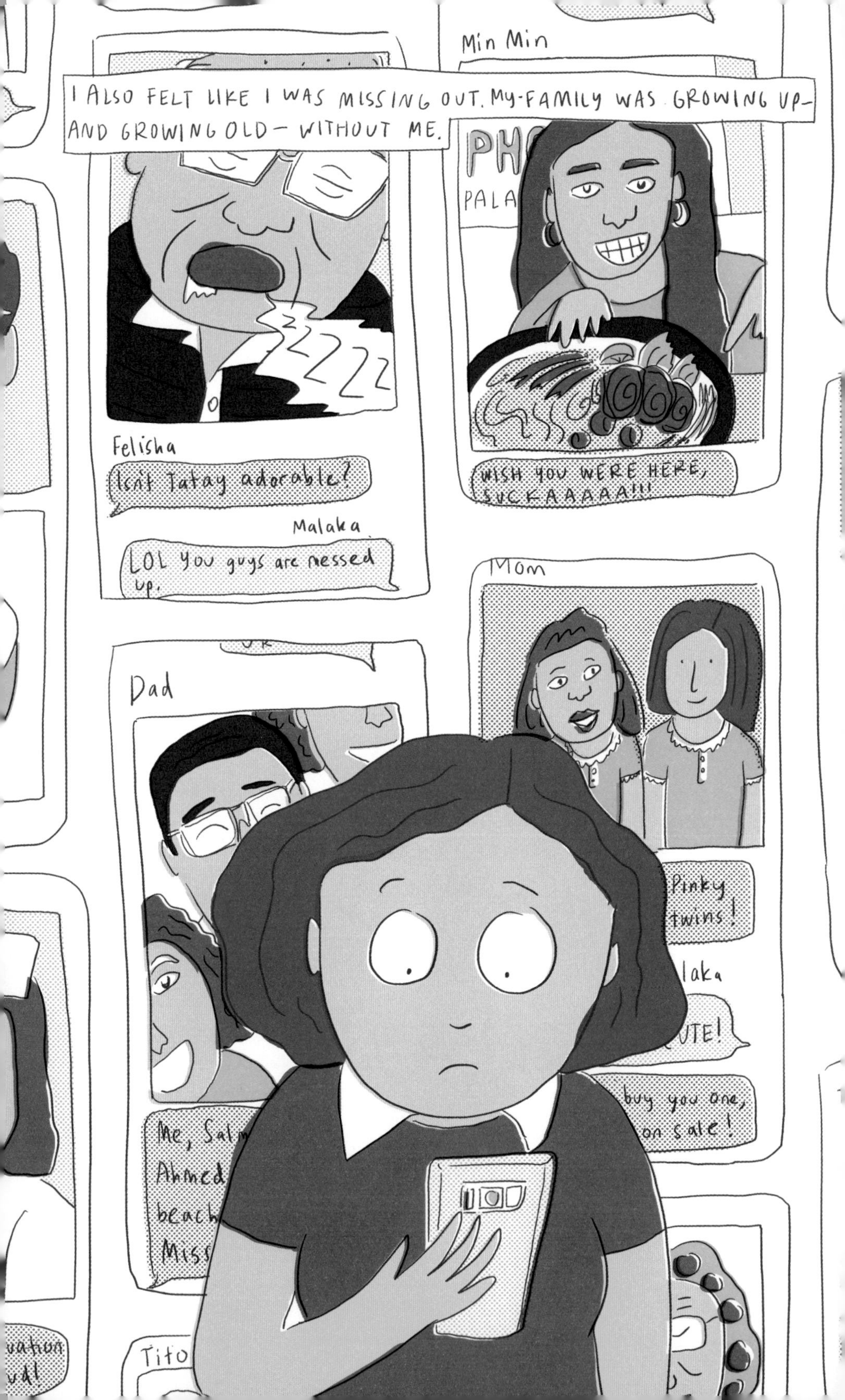

I ALSO FELT LIKE I WAS MISSING OUT. MY FAMILY WAS GROWING UP— AND GROWING OLD— WITHOUT ME.
Min Min
PHO
PALA
WISH YOU WERE HERE, SUCKAAAAA!!!
ZZZZZ
Felisha
Isn't Tatay adorable?
Malaka
LOL you guys are messed up.
Mom
Pinky twins!
Dad
Me, Salm
Ahmed
beach
Miss
UTE!
buy you one,
on sale!
Tito

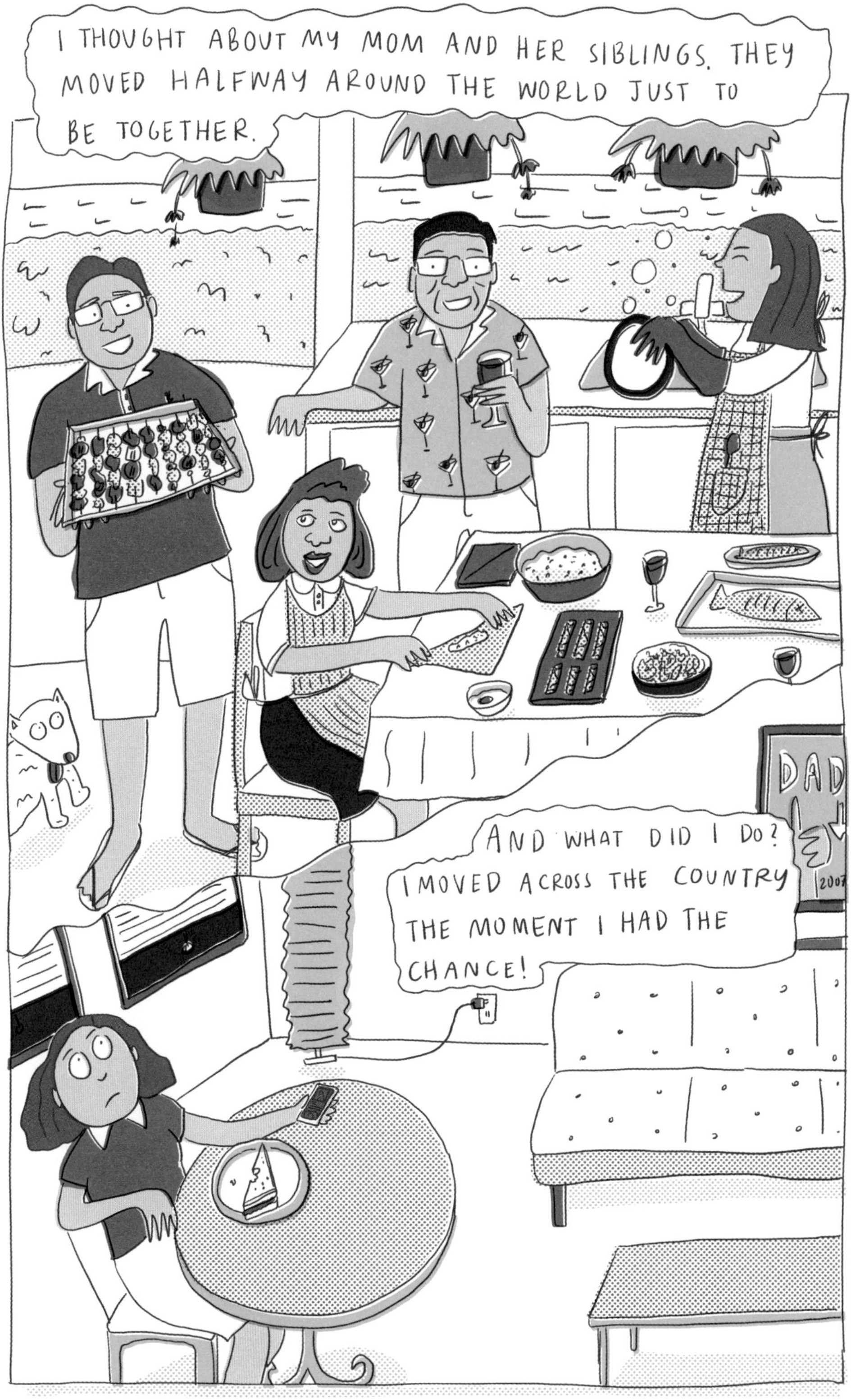
I THOUGHT ABOUT MY MOM AND HER SIBLINGS. THEY MOVED HALFWAY AROUND THE WORLD JUST TO BE TOGETHER.
DAD
2007
AND WHAT DID I DO? I MOVED ACROSS THE COUNTRY THE MOMENT I HAD THE CHANCE!

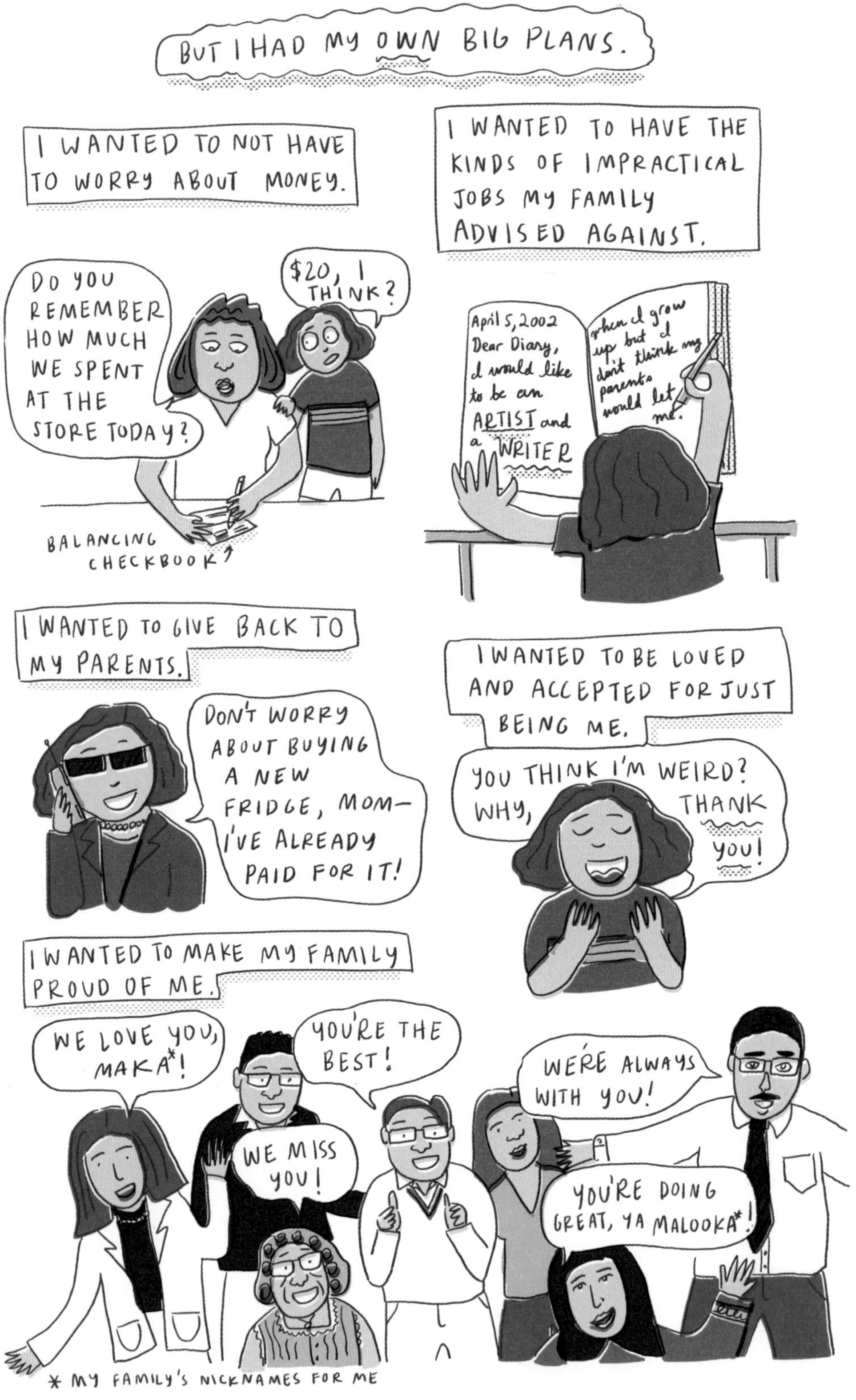
BUT I HAD MY OWN BIG PLANS.
I WANTED TO NOT HAVE TO WORRY ABOUT MONEY.
DO YOU REMEMBER HOW MUCH WE SPENT AT THE STORE TODAY?
$20, I THINK?
BALANCING CHECKBOOK
I WANTED TO HAVE THE KINDS OF IMPRACTICAL JOBS MY FAMILY ADVISED AGAINST.
April 5, 2002 Dear Diary, I would like to be an ARTIST and a WRITER
when I grow up but I don't think my parents would let me.
I WANTED TO GIVE BACK TO MY PARENTS.
DON'T WORRY ABOUT BUYING A NEW FRIDGE, MOM—I'VE ALREADY PAID FOR IT!
I WANTED TO BE LOVED AND ACCEPTED FOR JUST BEING ME.
YOU THINK I'M WEIRD? WHY, THANK YOU!
I WANTED TO MAKE MY FAMILY PROUD OF ME.
WE LOVE YOU, MAKA*!
YOU'RE THE BEST!
WE MISS YOU!
WE'RE ALWAYS WITH YOU!
YOU'RE DOING GREAT, YA MALOOKA*!
* MY FAMILY'S NICKNAMES FOR ME

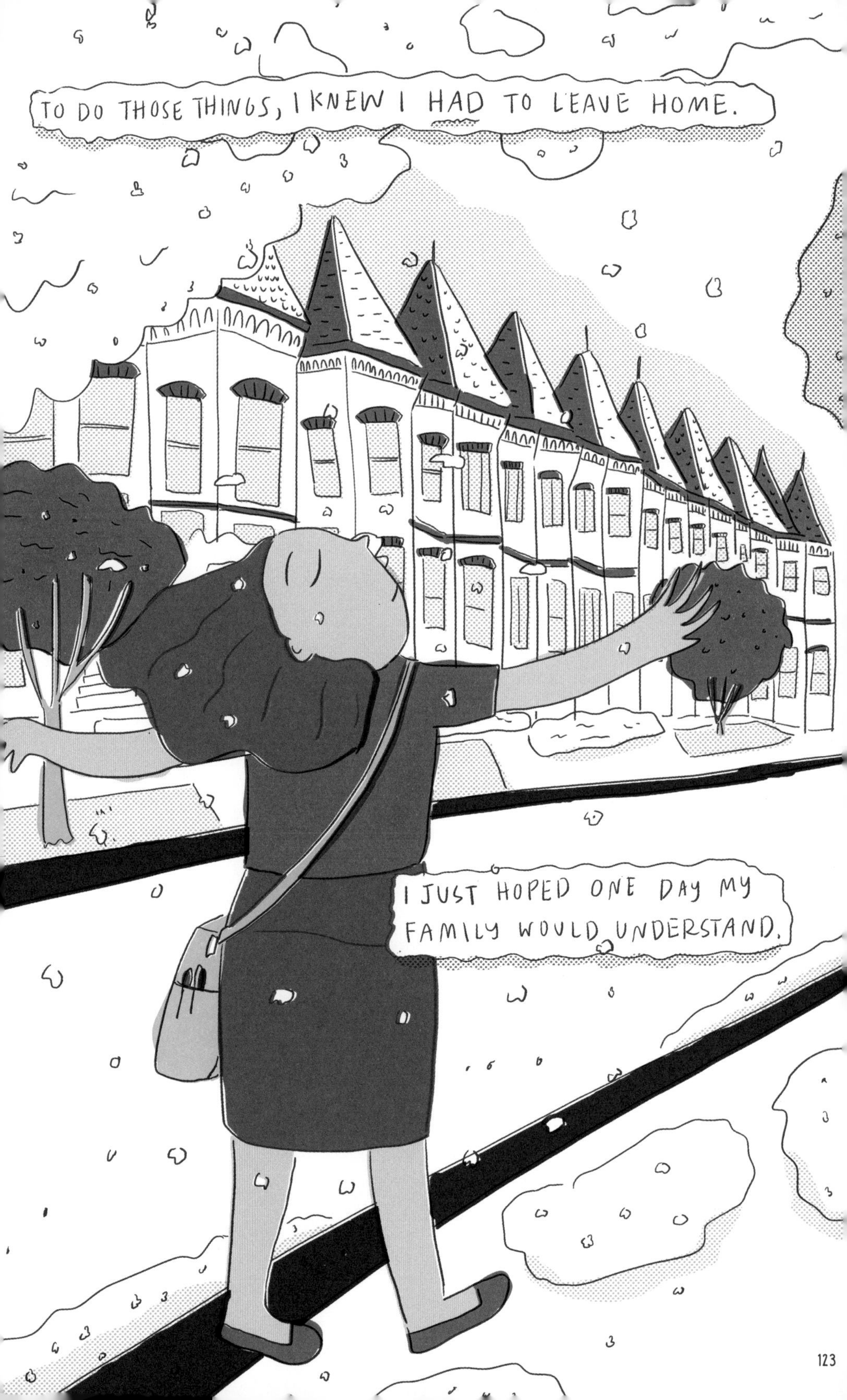
TO DO THOSE THINGS, I KNEW I HAD TO LEAVE HOME.
I JUST HOPED ONE DAY MY FAMILY WOULD UNDERSTAND.

Chapter 7

WHEN I WAS A KID,
MY DAD USED TO PLAY THIS
GAME WITH ME.

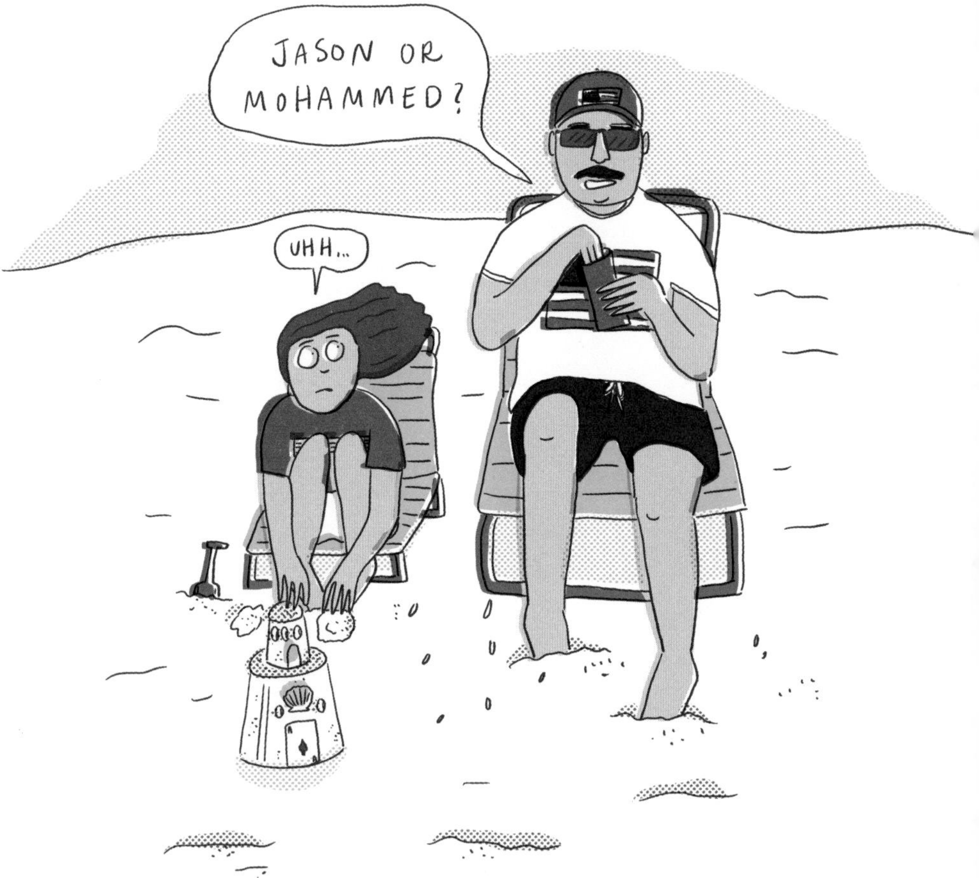

JASON OR MOHAMMED?
UHH...

MUSTAFA OR THOMAS?
UHH... MUSTAFA?
ROBERT OR MOHSEN?
MOHSEN?
ABDELRAHMAN OR GEORGE?
ABDELRAHMAN!
(THE ANSWER, IN CASE YOU DIDN'T GET IT, WAS ALWAYS THE MUSLIM NAME.)

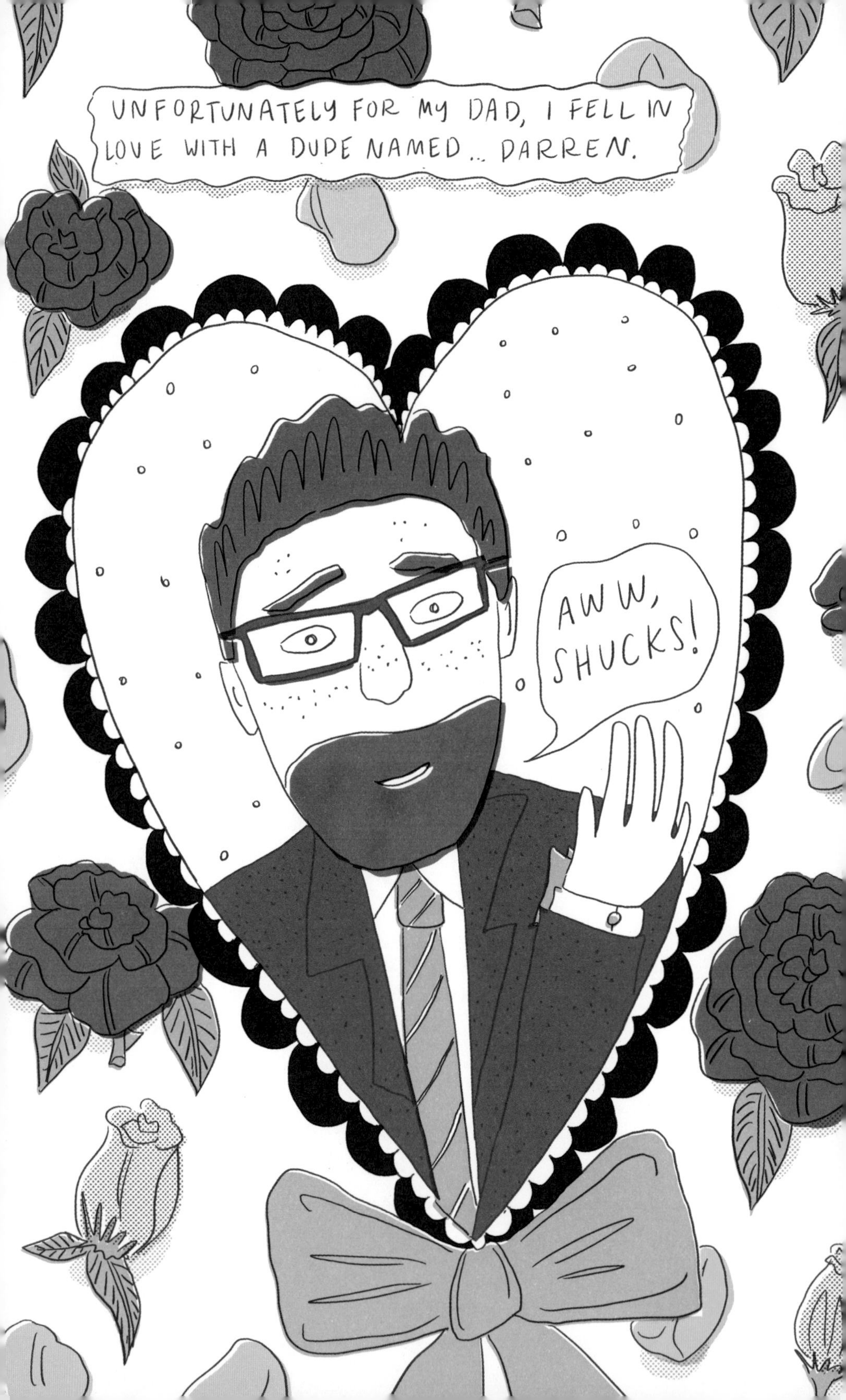
UNFORTUNATELY FOR MY DAD, I FELL IN LOVE WITH A DUDE NAMED... DARREN.
AWW, SHUCKS!

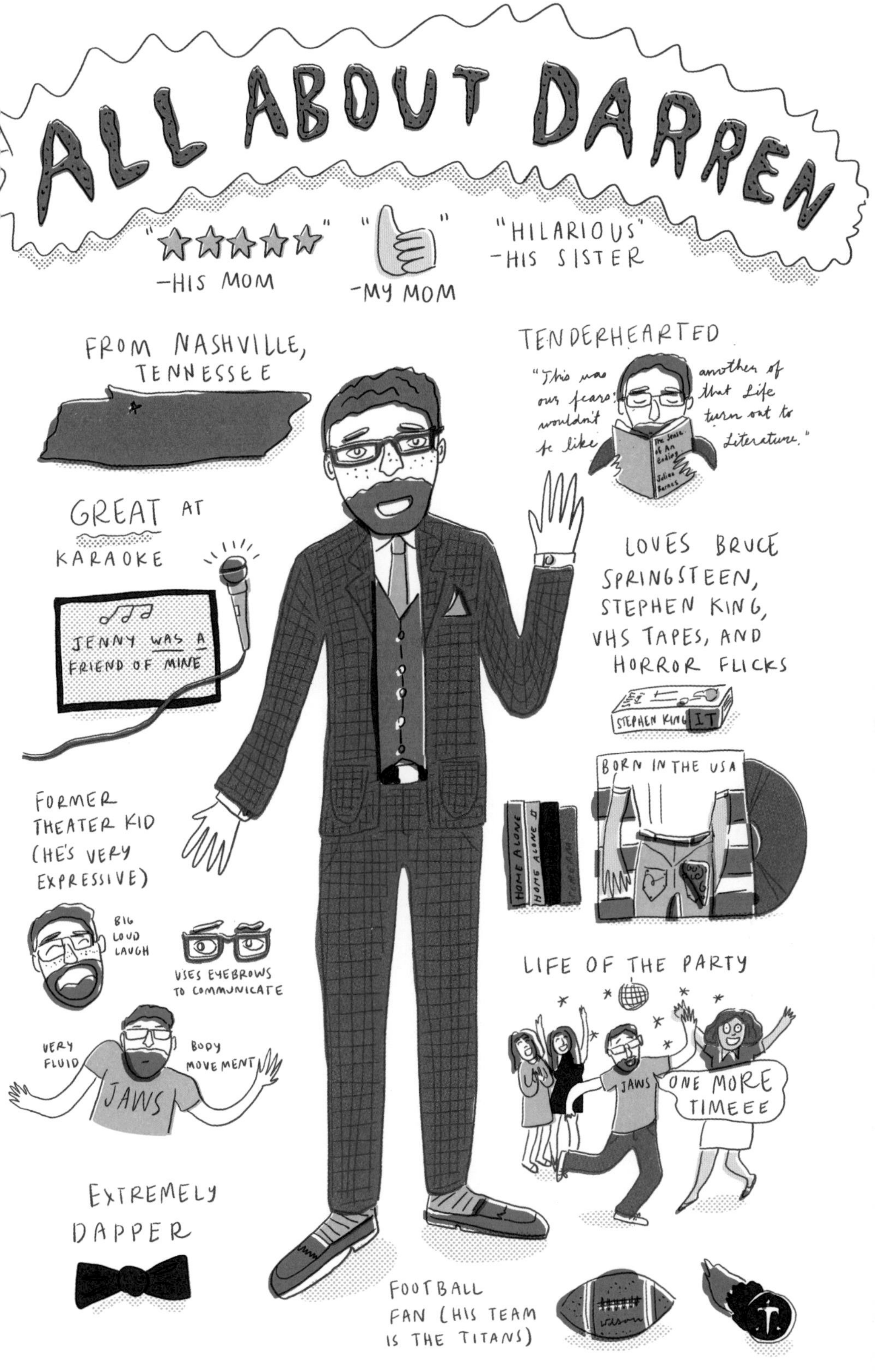
ALL ABOUT DARREN
"★★★★★" -HIS MOM
" " -MY MOM
"HILARIOUS" -HIS SISTER
FROM NASHVILLE, TENNESSEE
TENDERHEARTED
"This was another of our fears: that Life wouldn't turn out to be like Literature."
The Sense of An Ending
Julian Barnes
GREAT AT KARAOKE
JENNY WAS A FRIEND OF MINE
LOVES BRUCE SPRINGSTEEN, STEPHEN KING, VHS TAPES, AND HORROR FLICKS
STEPHEN KING IT
HOME ALONE
HOME ALONE II
BORN IN THE USA
FORMER THEATER KID (HE'S VERY EXPRESSIVE)
BIG LOUD LAUGH
USES EYEBROWS TO COMMUNICATE
VERY FLUID BODY MOVEMENT
JAWS
LIFE OF THE PARTY
JAWS
ONE MORE TIMEEE
EXTREMELY DAPPER
FOOTBALL FAN (HIS TEAM IS THE TITANS)

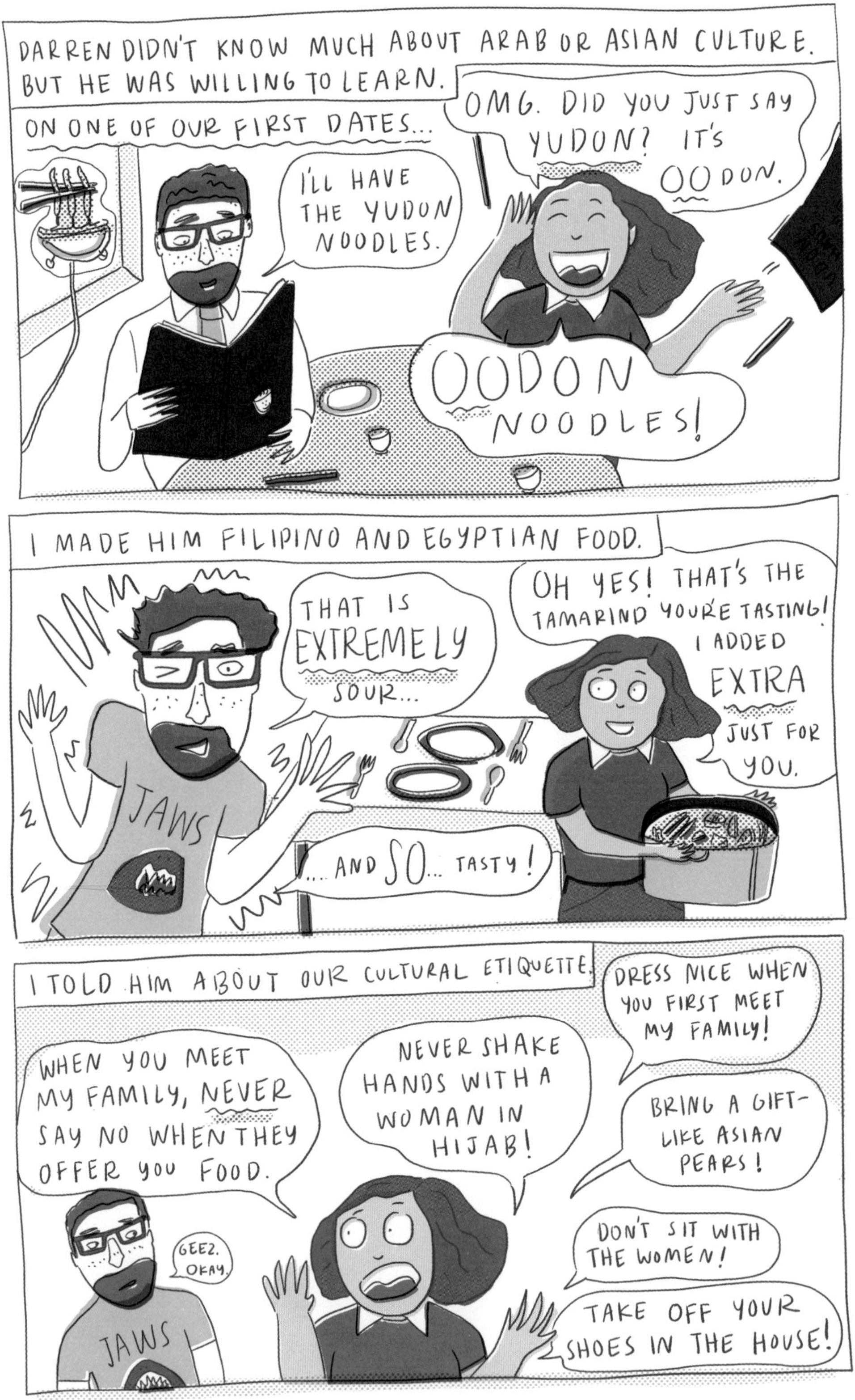
DARREN DIDN'T KNOW MUCH ABOUT ARAB OR ASIAN CULTURE. BUT HE WAS WILLING TO LEARN.
ON ONE OF OUR FIRST DATES...
I'LL HAVE THE YUDON NOODLES.
OMG. DID YOU JUST SAY YUDON? IT'S OODON.
OODON NOODLES!
I MADE HIM FILIPINO AND EGYPTIAN FOOD.
THAT IS EXTREMELY SOUR...
OH YES! THAT'S THE TAMARIND YOU'RE TASTING! I ADDED EXTRA JUST FOR YOU.
JAWS
....AND SO... TASTY!
I TOLD HIM ABOUT OUR CULTURAL ETIQUETTE.
DRESS NICE WHEN YOU FIRST MEET MY FAMILY!
WHEN YOU MEET MY FAMILY, NEVER SAY NO WHEN THEY OFFER YOU FOOD.
NEVER SHAKE HANDS WITH A WOMAN IN HIJAB!
BRING A GIFT- LIKE ASIAN PEARS!
GEEZ. OKAY.
DON'T SIT WITH THE WOMEN!
TAKE OFF YOUR SHOES IN THE HOUSE!
JAWS

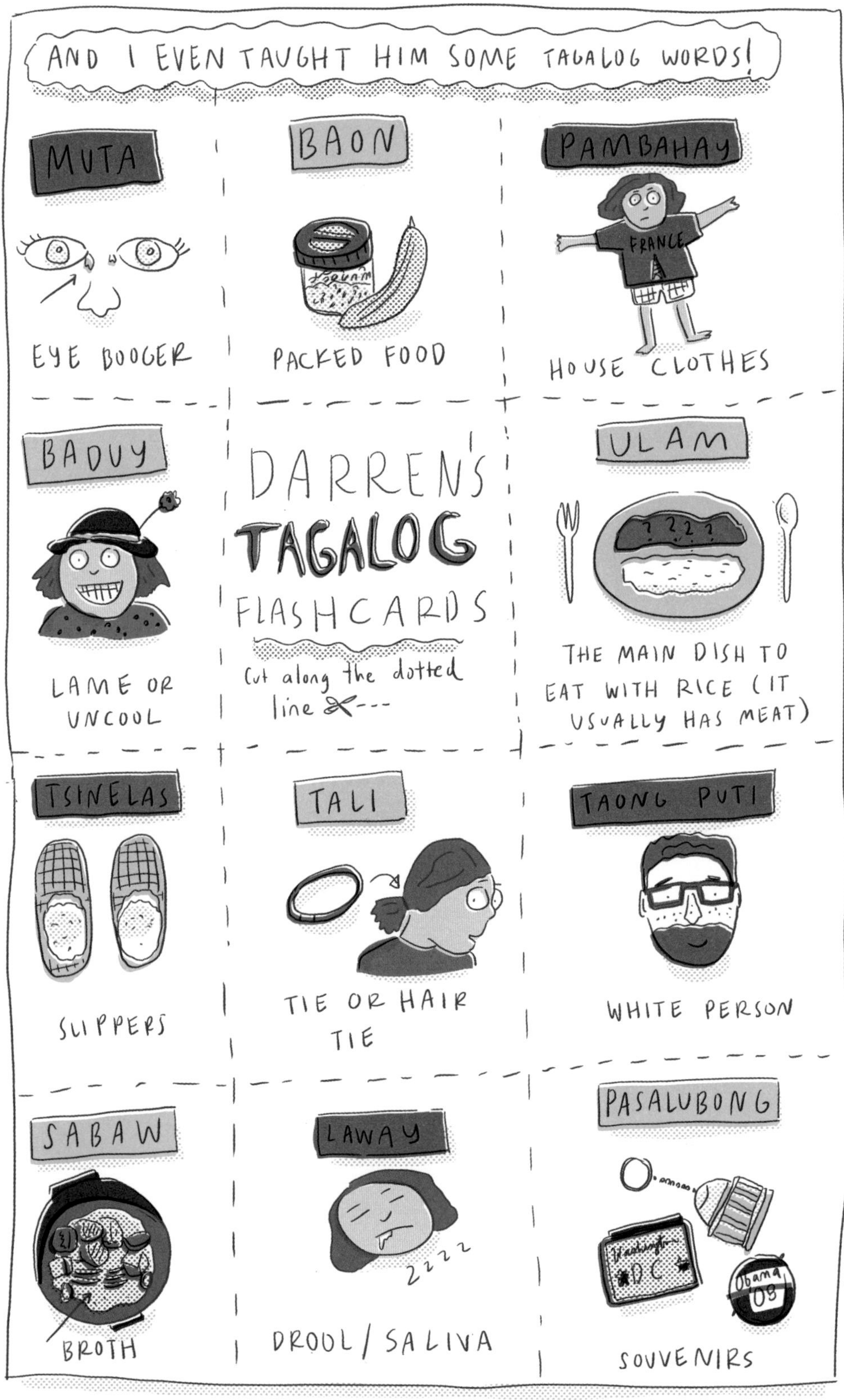

AND I EVEN TAUGHT HIM SOME TAGALOG WORDS!
MUTA
EYE BOOGER
BAON
PACKED FOOD
PAMBAHAY
FRANCE
HOUSE CLOTHES
BADUY
LAME OR UNCOOL
DARREN'S TAGALOG FLASHCARDS
Cut along the dotted line
ULAM
THE MAIN DISH TO EAT WITH RICE (IT USUALLY HAS MEAT)
TSINELAS
SLIPPERS
TALI
TIE OR HAIR TIE
TAONG PUTI
WHITE PERSON
SABAW
BROTH
LAWAY
DROOL / SALIVA
PASALUBONG
Washington DC
Obama 08
SOUVENIRS

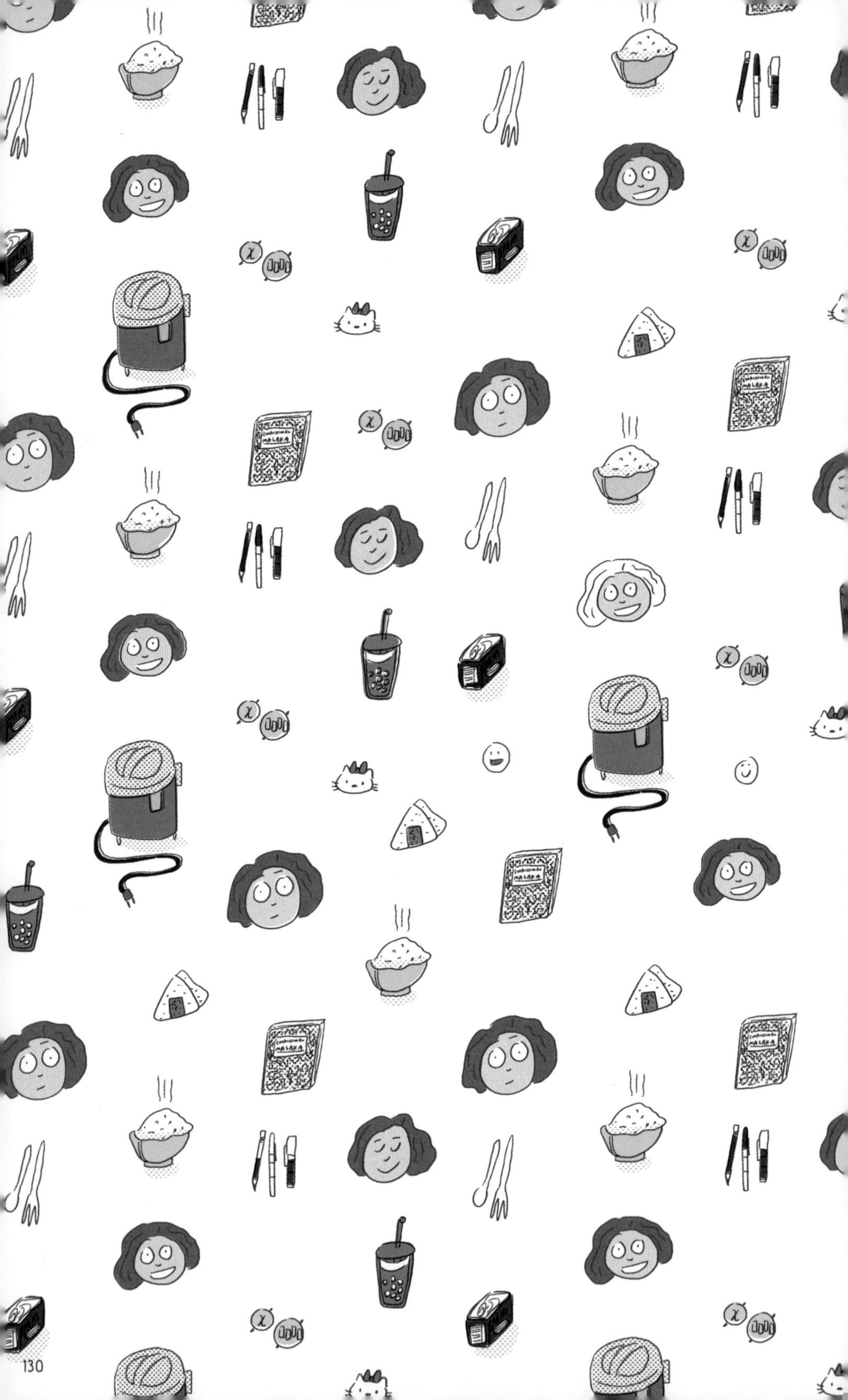

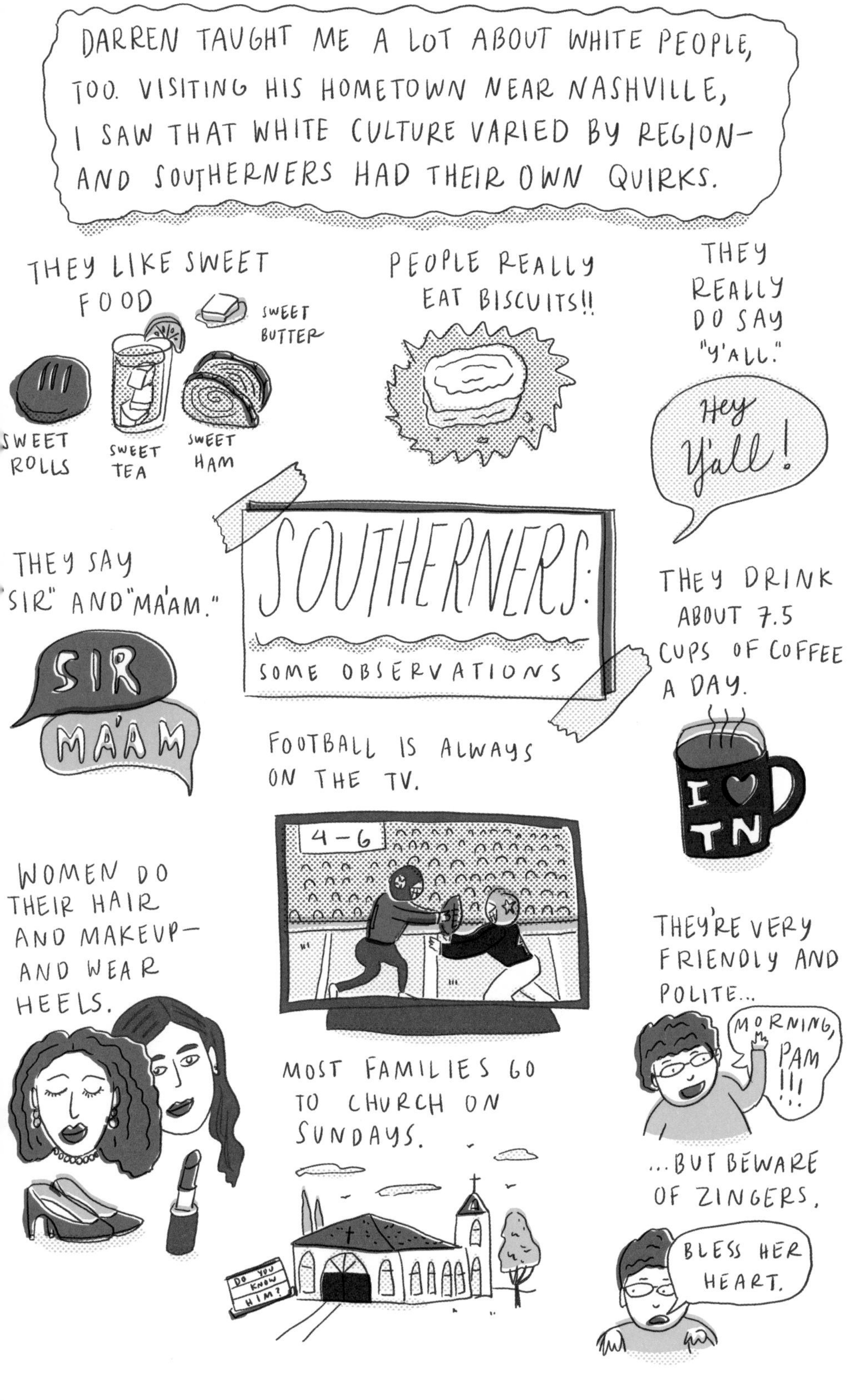
DARREN TAUGHT ME A LOT ABOUT WHITE PEOPLE, TOO. VISITING HIS HOMETOWN NEAR NASHVILLE, I SAW THAT WHITE CULTURE VARIED BY REGION— AND SOUTHERNERS HAD THEIR OWN QUIRKS.
SOUTHERNERS:
SOME OBSERVATIONS
THEY LIKE SWEET FOOD
SWEET BUTTER
SWEET ROLLS
SWEET TEA
SWEET HAM
PEOPLE REALLY EAT BISCUITS!!
THEY REALLY DO SAY "Y'ALL."
Hey Y'all!
THEY SAY "SIR" AND "MA'AM."
SIR
MA'AM
THEY DRINK ABOUT 7.5 CUPS OF COFFEE A DAY.
I ♥ TN
FOOTBALL IS ALWAYS ON THE TV.
4–6
WOMEN DO THEIR HAIR AND MAKEUP— AND WEAR HEELS.
MOST FAMILIES GO TO CHURCH ON SUNDAYS.
DO YOU KNOW HIM?
THEY'RE VERY FRIENDLY AND POLITE...
MORNING, PAM!!!
...BUT BEWARE OF ZINGERS.
BLESS HER HEART.

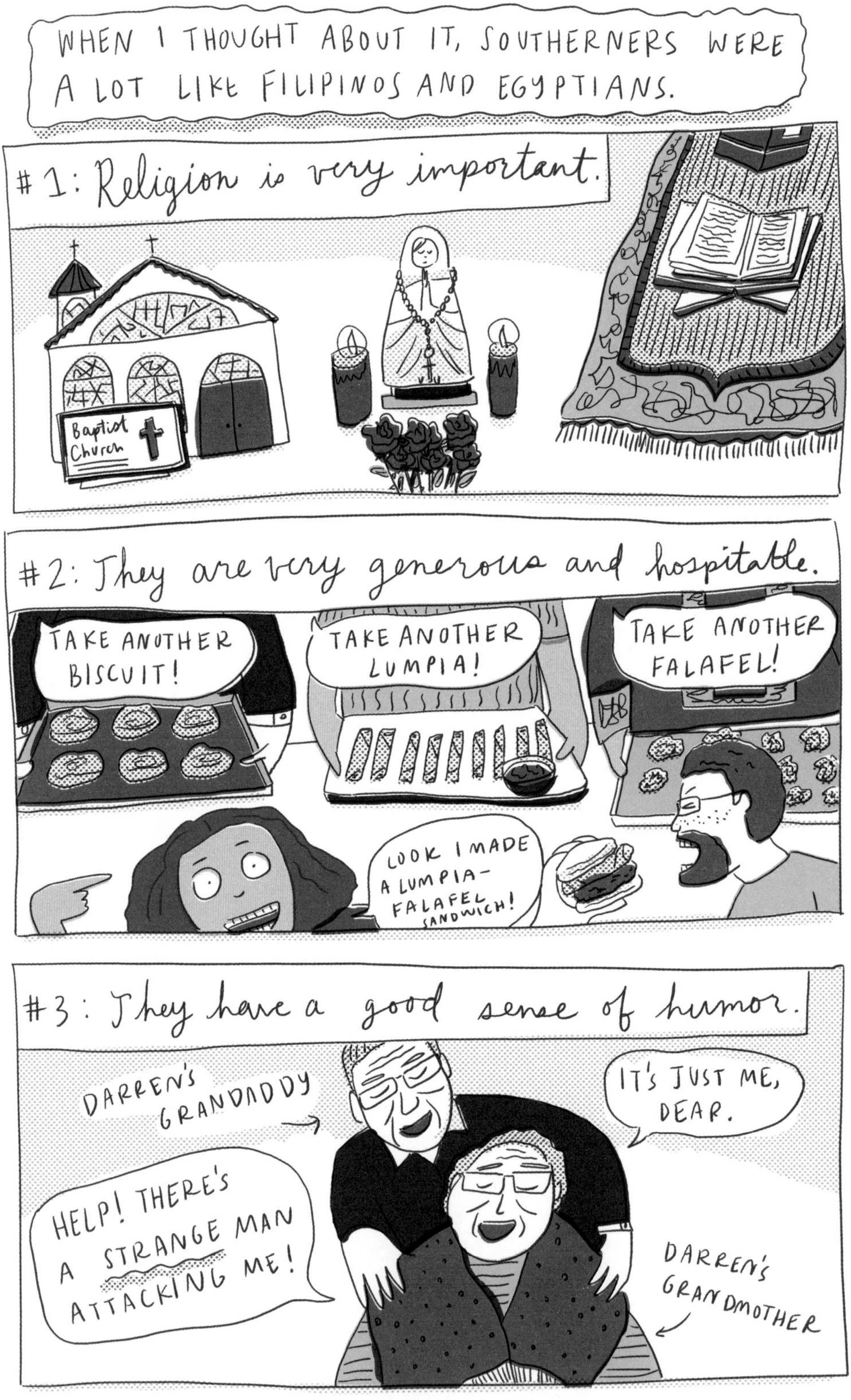
WHEN I THOUGHT ABOUT IT, SOUTHERNERS WERE A LOT LIKE FILIPINOS AND EGYPTIANS.
#1: Religion is very important.
Baptist Church
#2: They are very generous and hospitable.
TAKE ANOTHER BISCUIT!
TAKE ANOTHER LUMPIA!
TAKE ANOTHER FALAFEL!
LOOK I MADE A LUMPIA-FALAFEL SANDWICH!
#3: They have a good sense of humor.
DARREN'S GRANDDADDY
IT'S JUST ME, DEAR.
HELP! THERE'S A STRANGE MAN ATTACKING ME!
DARREN'S GRANDMOTHER

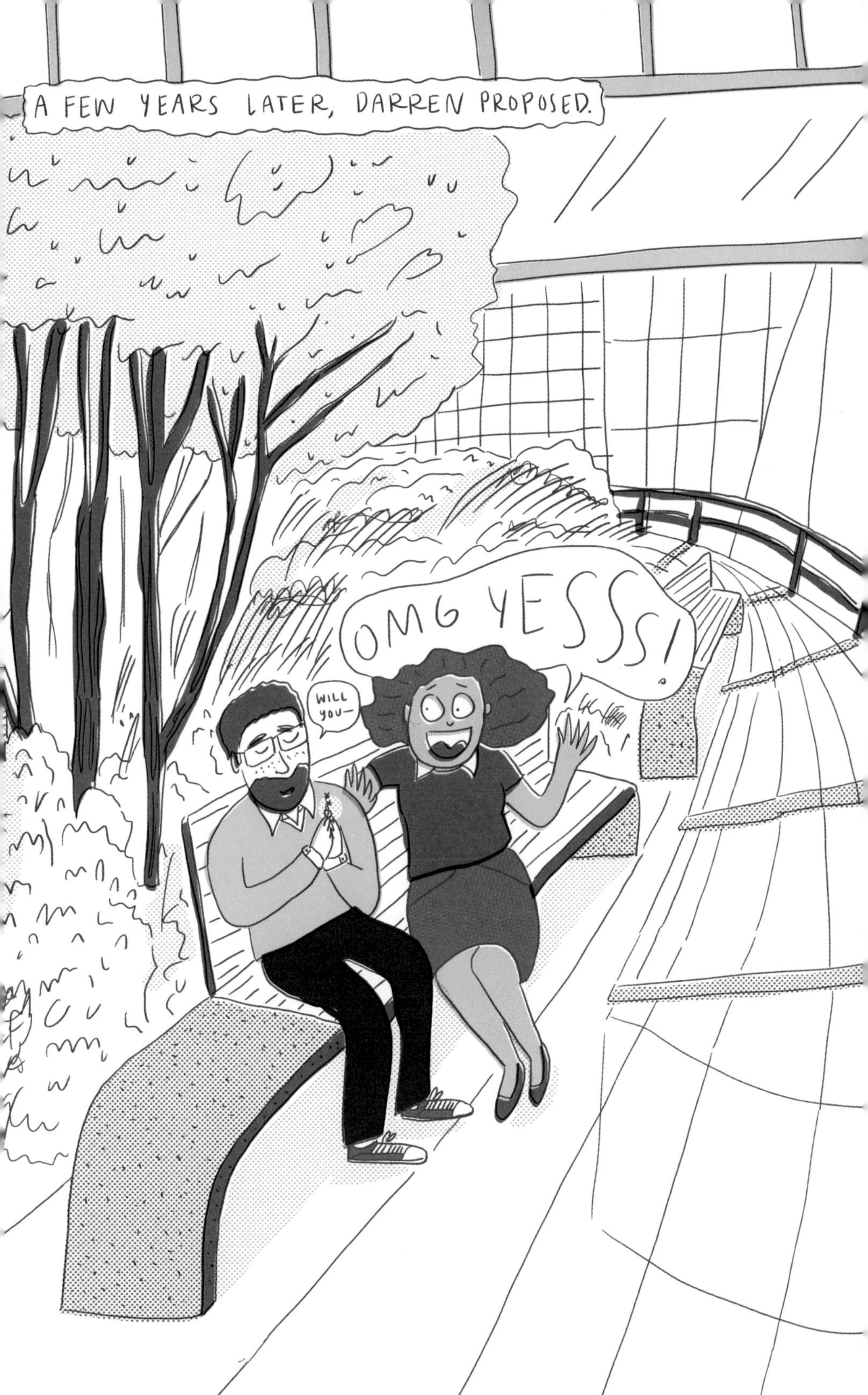

A FEW YEARS LATER, DARREN PROPOSED.
WILL YOU—
OMG YESSS!

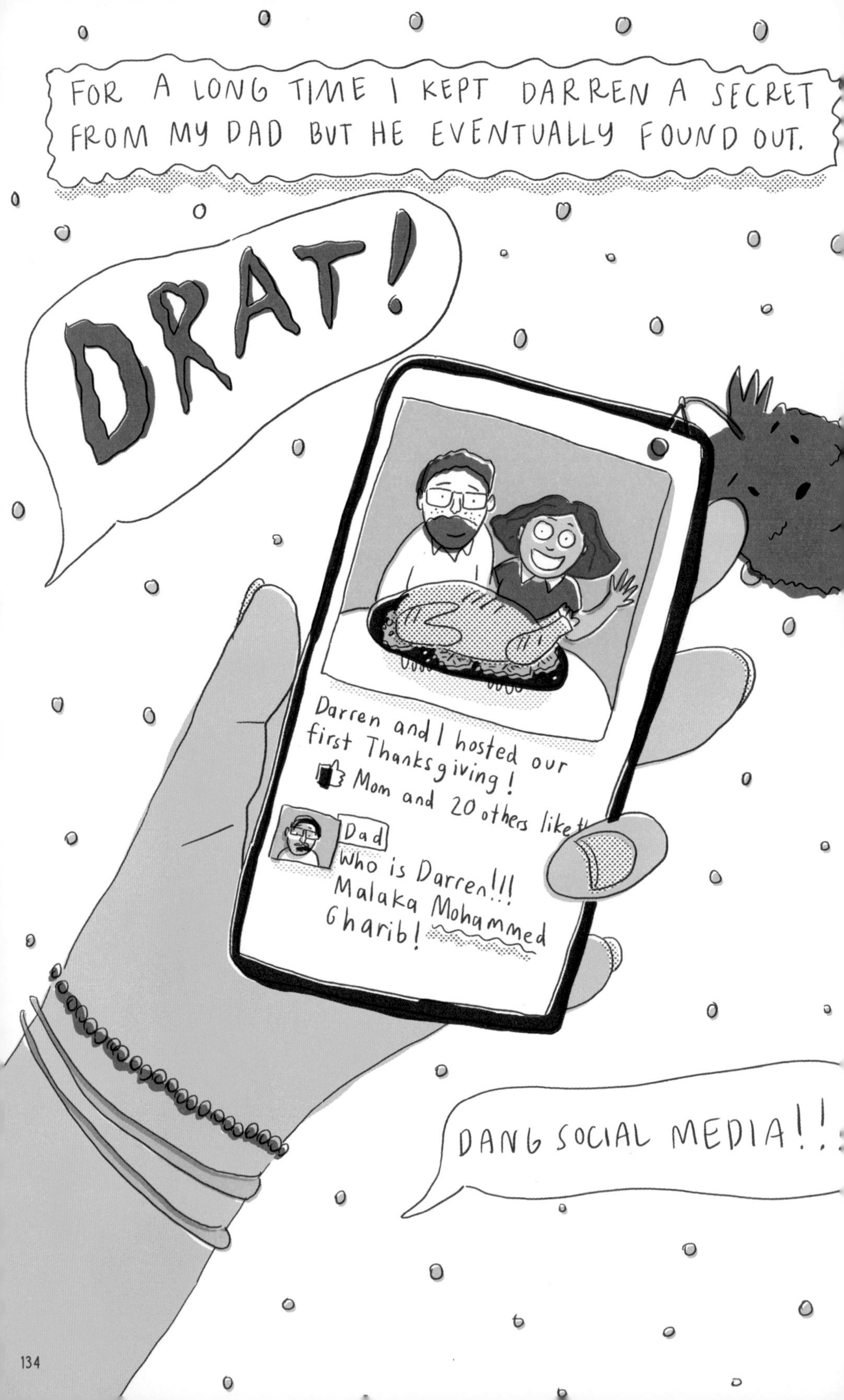
FOR A LONG TIME I KEPT DARREN A SECRET FROM MY DAD BUT HE EVENTUALLY FOUND OUT.
DRAT!
Darren and I hosted our first Thanksgiving!
Mom and 20 others like
Dad
Who is Darren!!! Malaka Mohammed Gharib!
DANG SOCIAL MEDIA!!

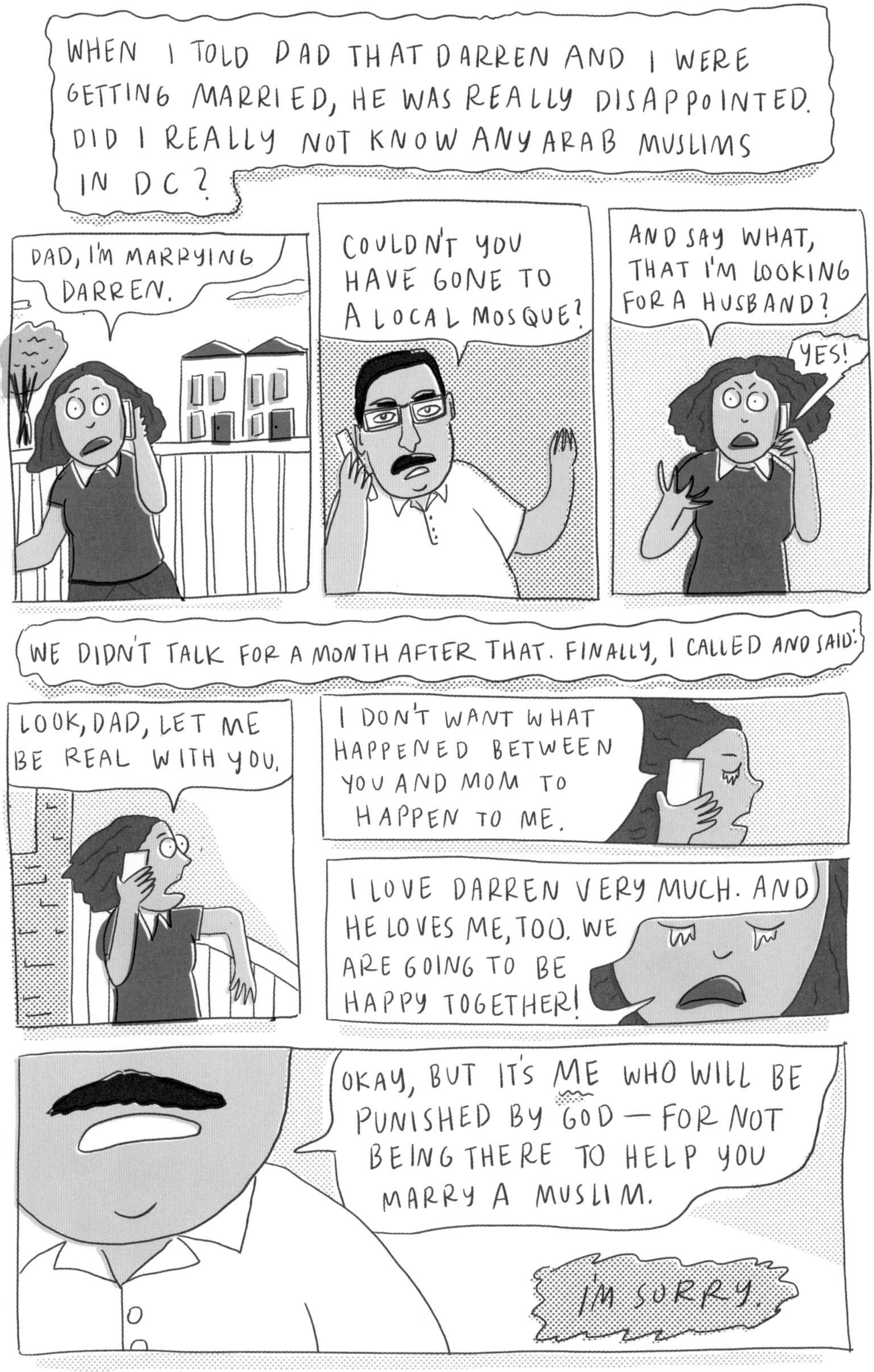
WHEN I TOLD DAD THAT DARREN AND I WERE GETTING MARRIED, HE WAS REALLY DISAPPOINTED. DID I REALLY NOT KNOW ANY ARAB MUSLIMS IN DC?
DAD, I'M MARRYING DARREN.
COULDN'T YOU HAVE GONE TO A LOCAL MOSQUE?
AND SAY WHAT, THAT I'M LOOKING FOR A HUSBAND?
YES!
WE DIDN'T TALK FOR A MONTH AFTER THAT. FINALLY, I CALLED AND SAID:
LOOK, DAD, LET ME BE REAL WITH YOU.
I DON'T WANT WHAT HAPPENED BETWEEN YOU AND MOM TO HAPPEN TO ME.
I LOVE DARREN VERY MUCH. AND HE LOVES ME, TOO. WE ARE GOING TO BE HAPPY TOGETHER!
OKAY, BUT IT'S ME WHO WILL BE PUNISHED BY GOD — FOR NOT BEING THERE TO HELP YOU MARRY A MUSLIM.
I'M SORRY.

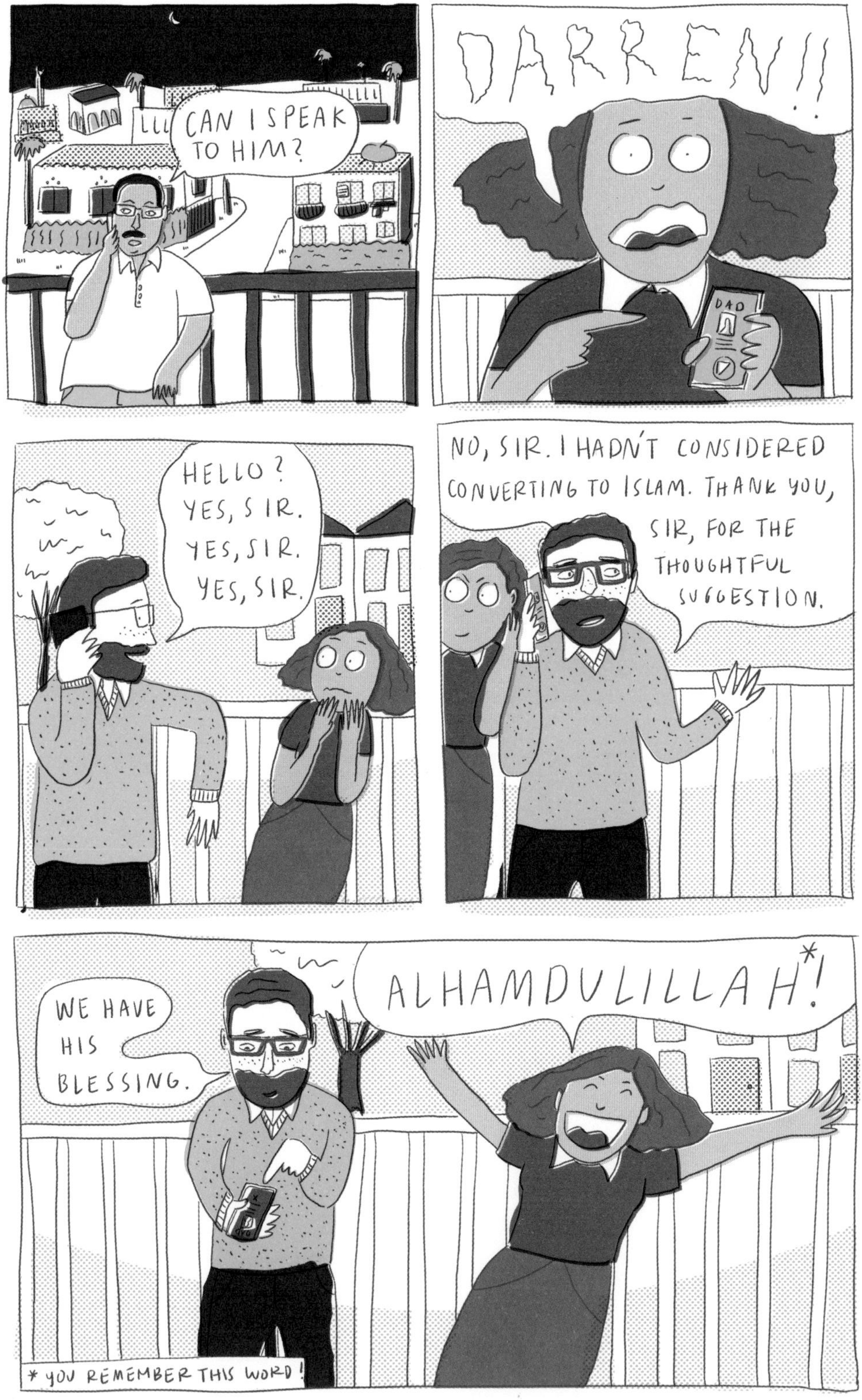
CAN I SPEAK TO HIM?
DARREN!!
DAD
HELLO? YES, SIR. YES, SIR. YES, SIR.
NO, SIR. I HADN'T CONSIDERED CONVERTING TO ISLAM. THANK YOU, SIR, FOR THE THOUGHTFUL SUGGESTION.
WE HAVE HIS BLESSING.
ALHAMDULILLAH*!
* YOU REMEMBER THIS WORD!

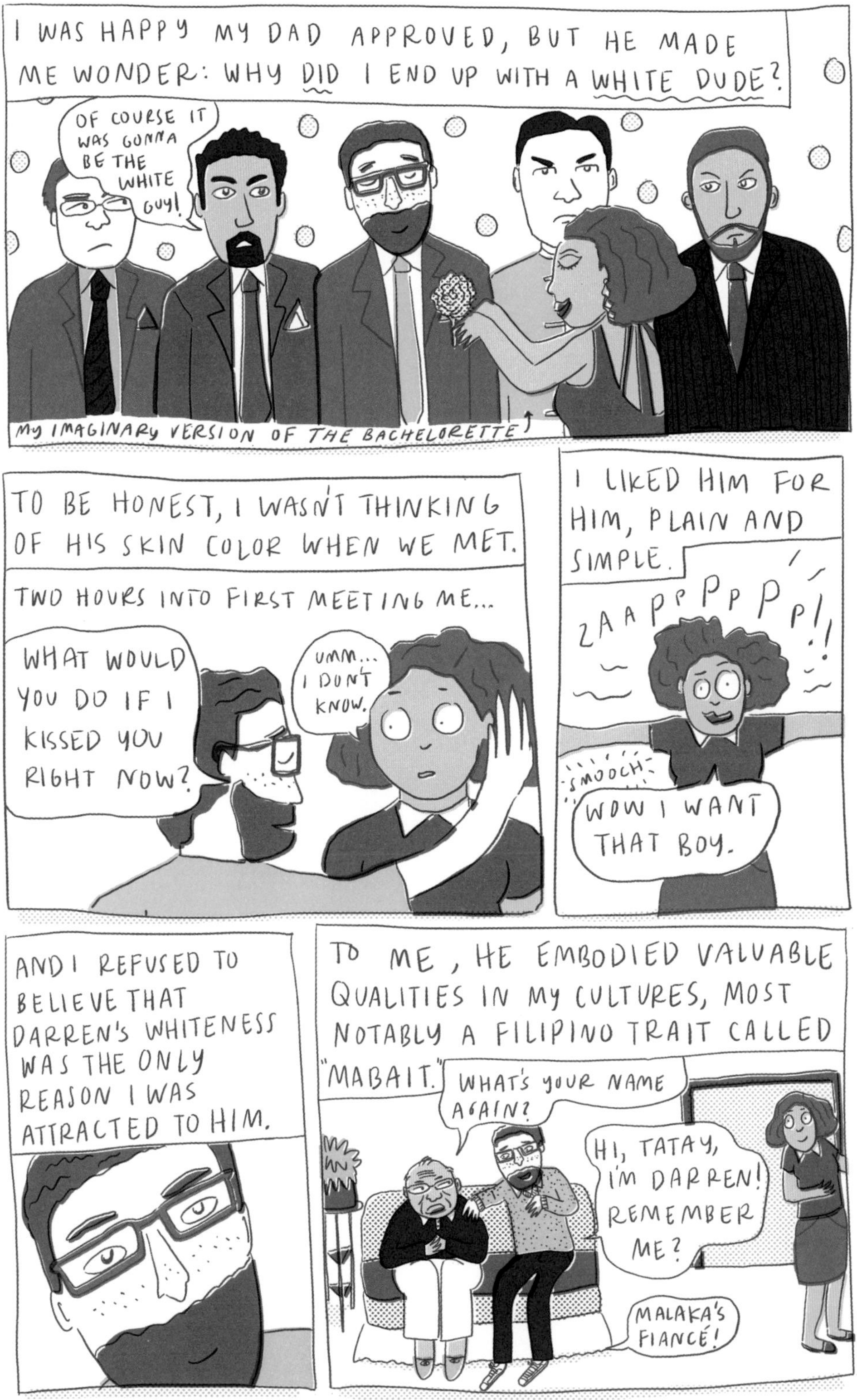
I WAS HAPPY MY DAD APPROVED, BUT HE MADE ME WONDER: WHY DID I END UP WITH A WHITE DUDE?
OF COURSE IT WAS GONNA BE THE WHITE GUY!
MY IMAGINARY VERSION OF THE BACHELORETTE
TO BE HONEST, I WASN'T THINKING OF HIS SKIN COLOR WHEN WE MET.
TWO HOURS INTO FIRST MEETING ME...
WHAT WOULD YOU DO IF I KISSED YOU RIGHT NOW?
UMM... I DON'T KNOW.
I LIKED HIM FOR HIM, PLAIN AND SIMPLE.
ZAAPPPPPP!
SMOOCH
WOW I WANT THAT BOY.
AND I REFUSED TO BELIEVE THAT DARREN'S WHITENESS WAS THE ONLY REASON I WAS ATTRACTED TO HIM.
TO ME, HE EMBODIED VALUABLE QUALITIES IN MY CULTURES, MOST NOTABLY A FILIPINO TRAIT CALLED "MABAIT."
WHAT'S YOUR NAME AGAIN?
HI, TATAY, I'M DARREN! REMEMBER ME?
MALAKA'S FIANCÉ!

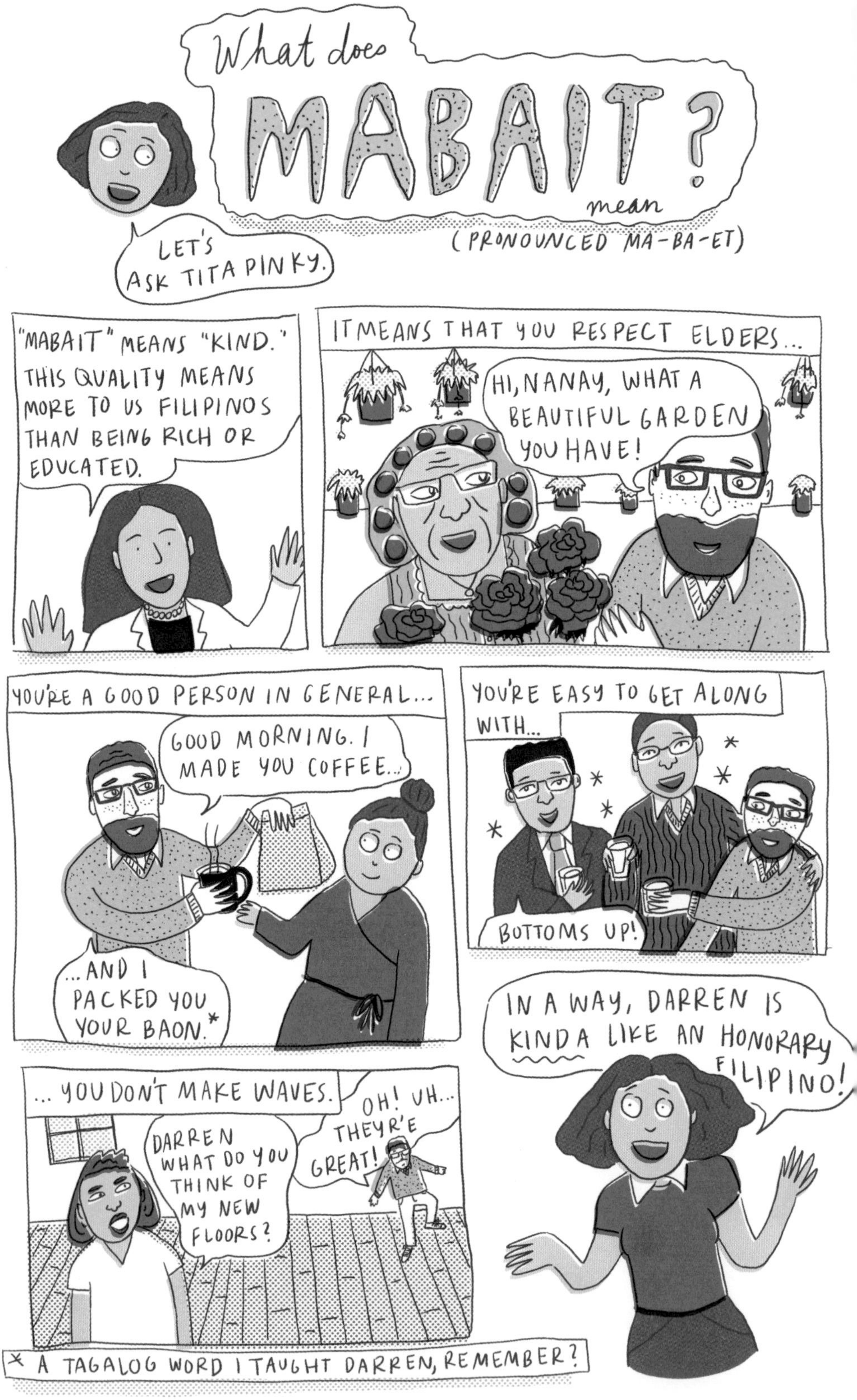
What does MABAIT? mean
(PRONOUNCED MA-BA-ET)
LET'S ASK TITA PINKY.
"MABAIT" MEANS "KIND." THIS QUALITY MEANS MORE TO US FILIPINOS THAN BEING RICH OR EDUCATED.
IT MEANS THAT YOU RESPECT ELDERS...
HI, NANAY, WHAT A BEAUTIFUL GARDEN YOU HAVE!
YOU'RE A GOOD PERSON IN GENERAL...
GOOD MORNING. I MADE YOU COFFEE...
...AND I PACKED YOU YOUR BAON.*
YOU'RE EASY TO GET ALONG WITH...
BOTTOMS UP!
... YOU DON'T MAKE WAVES.
DARREN WHAT DO YOU THINK OF MY NEW FLOORS?
OH! UH... THEY'R'E GREAT!
IN A WAY, DARREN IS KINDA LIKE AN HONORARY FILIPINO!
* A TAGALOG WORD I TAUGHT DARREN, REMEMBER?

AND SO WE HAD

OUR BIG, FAT, FILIPINO-EGYPTIAN-AMERICAN SOUTHERN BAPTIST-MUSLIM WEDDING!

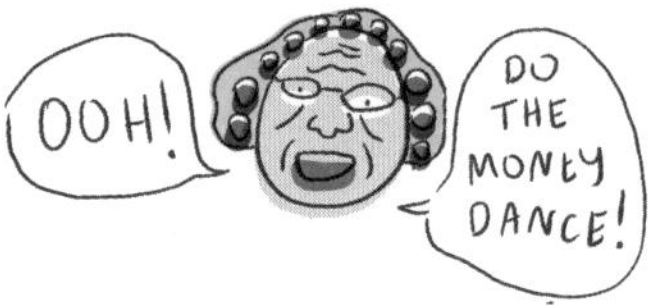
OOH!
DO THE MONEY DANCE!

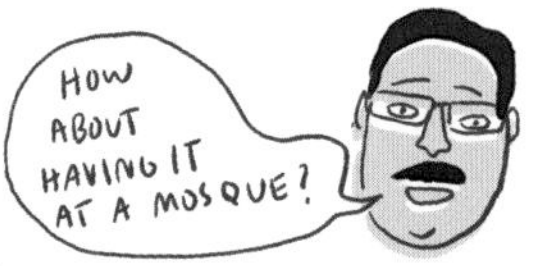
HOW ABOUT HAVING IT AT A MOSQUE?

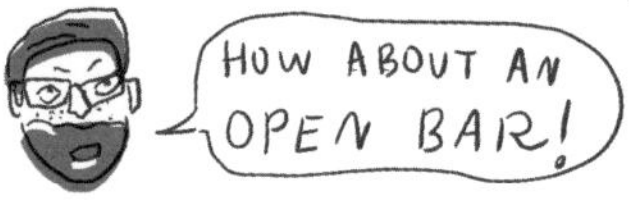
HOW ABOUT AN OPEN BAR!

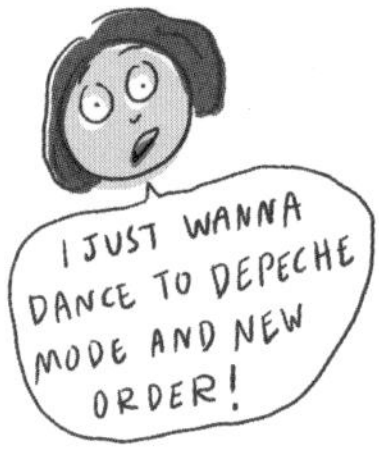
I JUST WANNA DANCE TO DEPECHE MODE AND NEW ORDER!

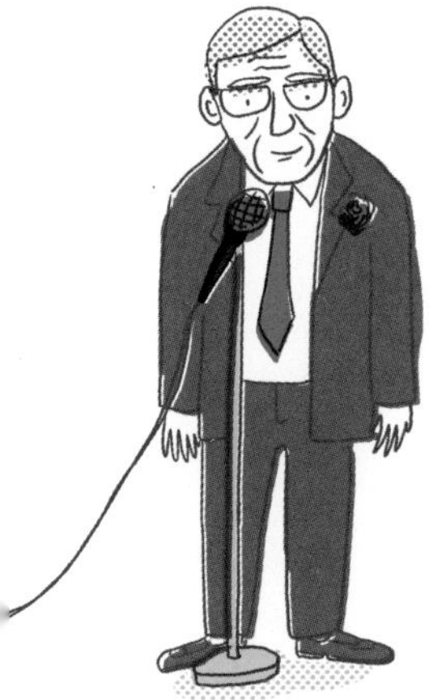

DARREN'S GRANDADDY, A SOUTHERN BAPTIST PASTOR, OFFICIATED THE WEDDING WITH A CEREMONY SCRIPT THAT DREW FROM THE KORAN AND THE BIBLE.

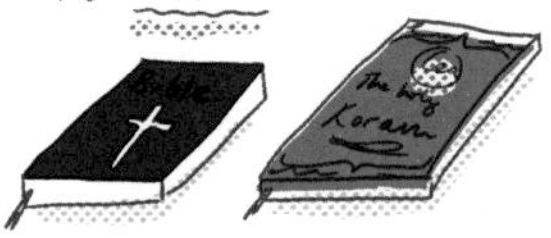
Bible
The Holy Koran

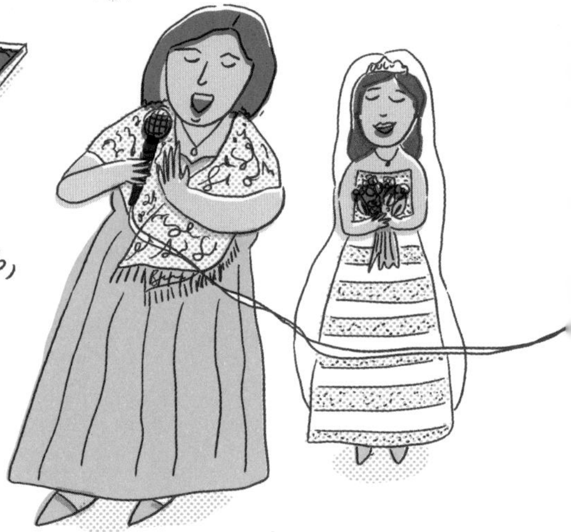

MY SISTER SALMA SANG A BEAUTIFUL ARABIC SONG, "I SWEAR YOU DESERVE IT" BY SAYED DARWÎSH.

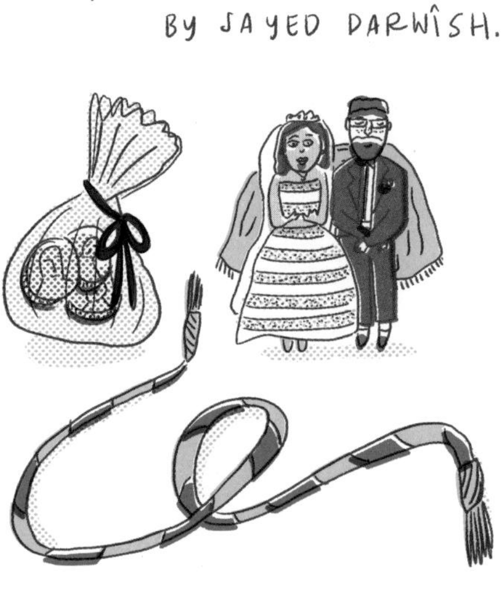

WE PERFORMED THE FILIPINO COIN, VEIL, AND CORD CEREMONY. THE COIN REPRESENTS FUTURE CHILDREN; THE VEIL, UNITY; AND THE CORD, THE COUPLE'S BOND.

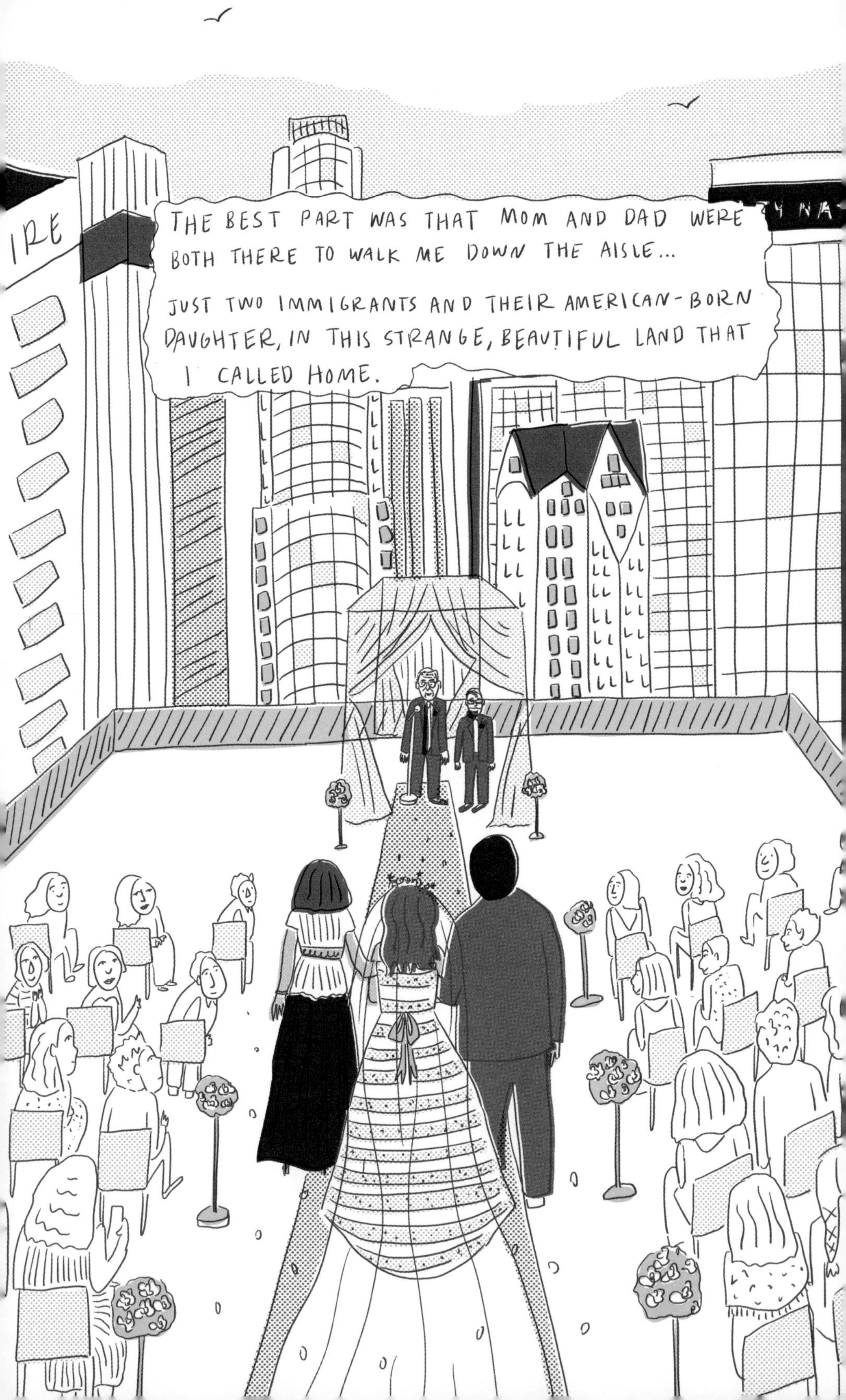
THE BEST PART WAS THAT MOM AND DAD WERE BOTH THERE TO WALK ME DOWN THE AISLE...
JUST TWO IMMIGRANTS AND THEIR AMERICAN-BORN DAUGHTER, IN THIS STRANGE, BEAUTIFUL LAND THAT I CALLED HOME.

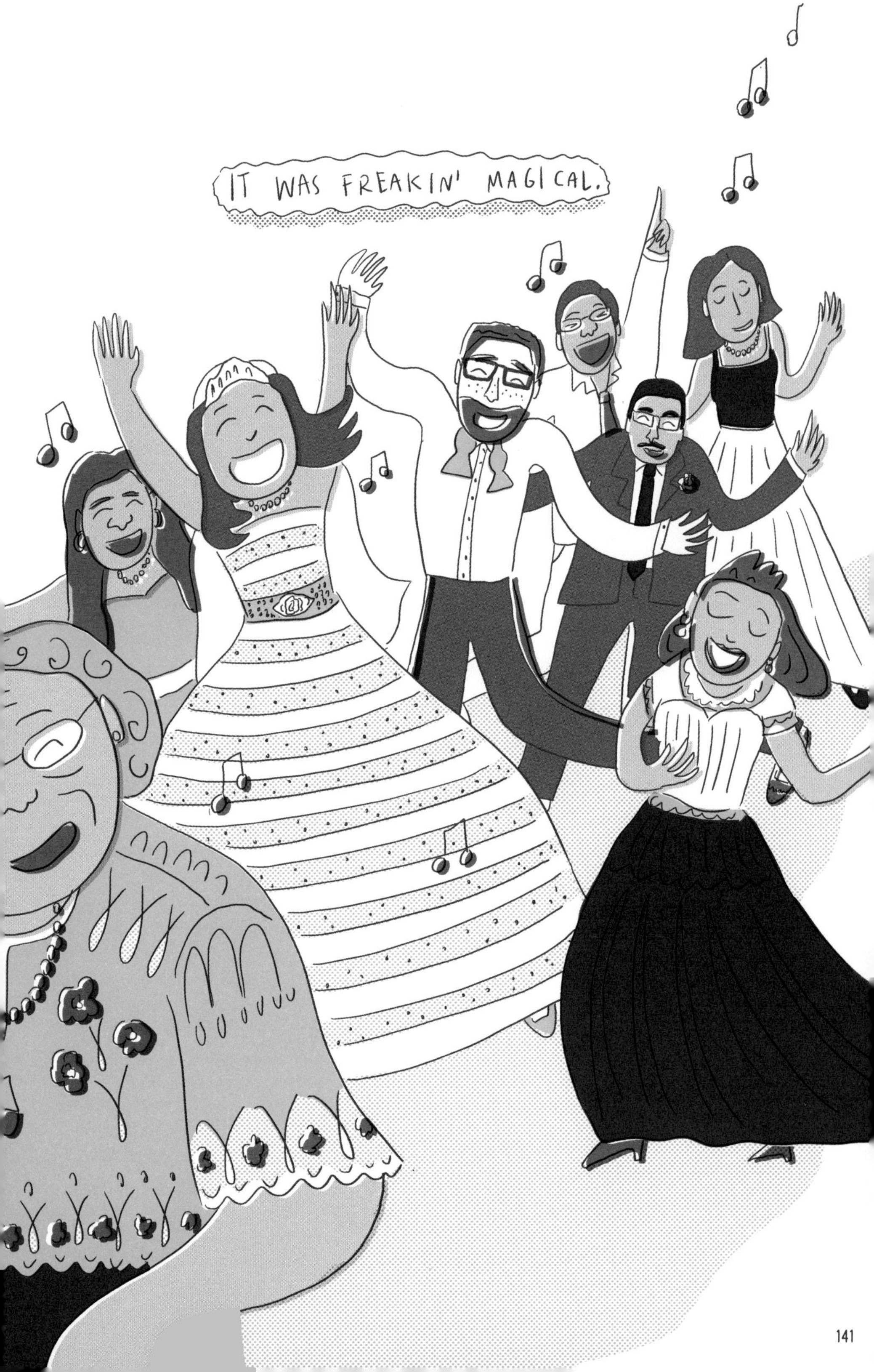
IT WAS FREAKIN' MAGICAL.

Chapter 8

SO HERE WE WERE, LIVING OUR CUTE LITTLE LIFE IN DC.

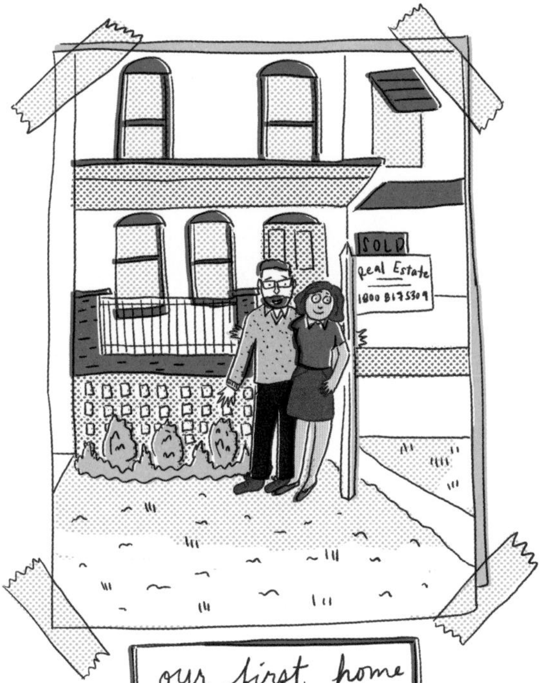
SOLD
Real Estate
1800 8675309

our first home

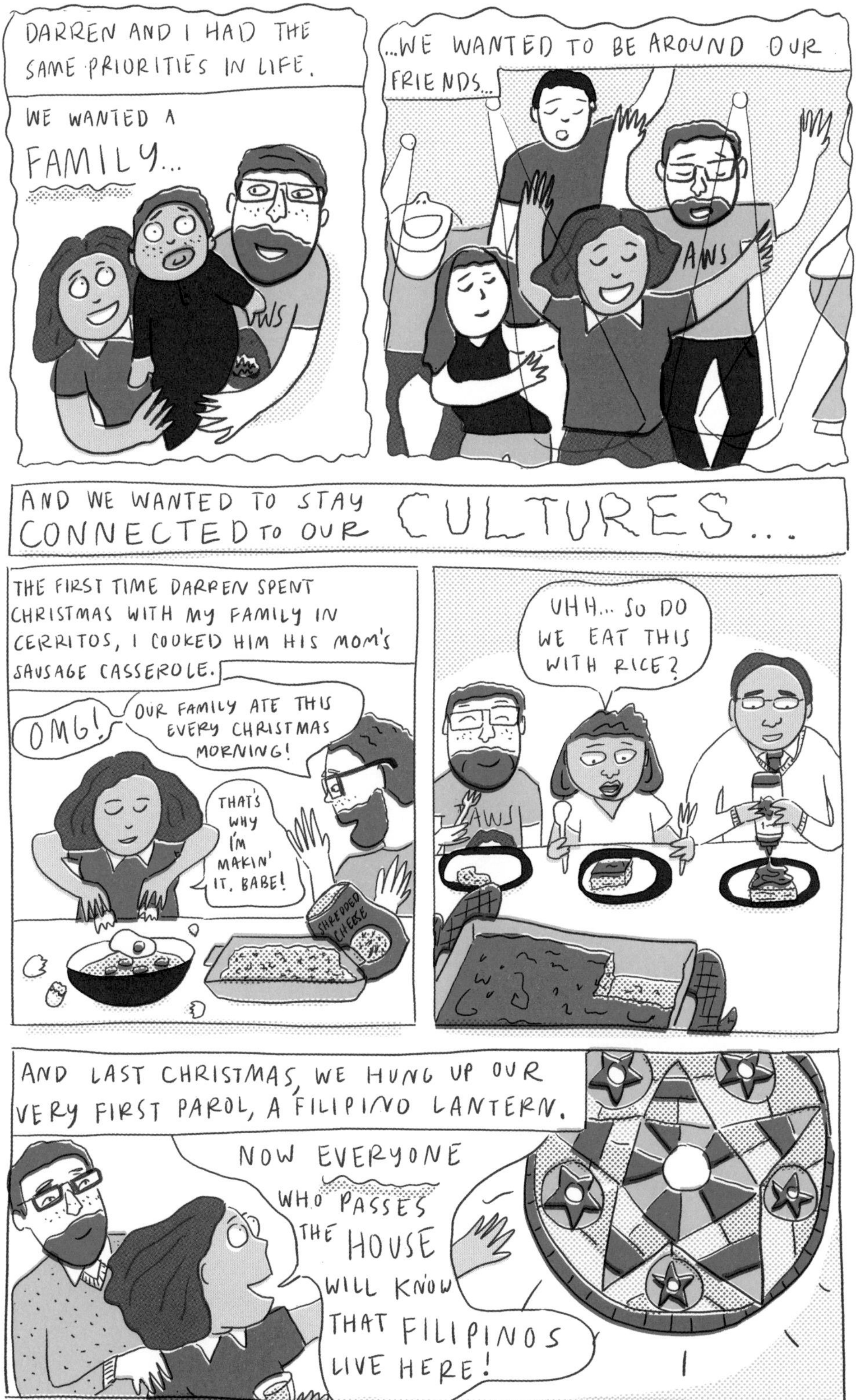
DARREN AND I HAD THE SAME PRIORITIES IN LIFE.
WE WANTED A FAMILY...
...WE WANTED TO BE AROUND OUR FRIENDS...
AWS
AND WE WANTED TO STAY CONNECTED TO OUR CULTURES...
THE FIRST TIME DARREN SPENT CHRISTMAS WITH MY FAMILY IN CERRITOS, I COOKED HIM HIS MOM'S SAUSAGE CASSEROLE.
OMG!
OUR FAMILY ATE THIS EVERY CHRISTMAS MORNING!
THAT'S WHY I'M MAKIN' IT, BABE!
SHREDDED CHEESE
UHH... SO DO WE EAT THIS WITH RICE?
AND LAST CHRISTMAS, WE HUNG UP OUR VERY FIRST PAROL, A FILIPINO LANTERN.
NOW EVERYONE WHO PASSES THE HOUSE WILL KNOW THAT FILIPINOS LIVE HERE!

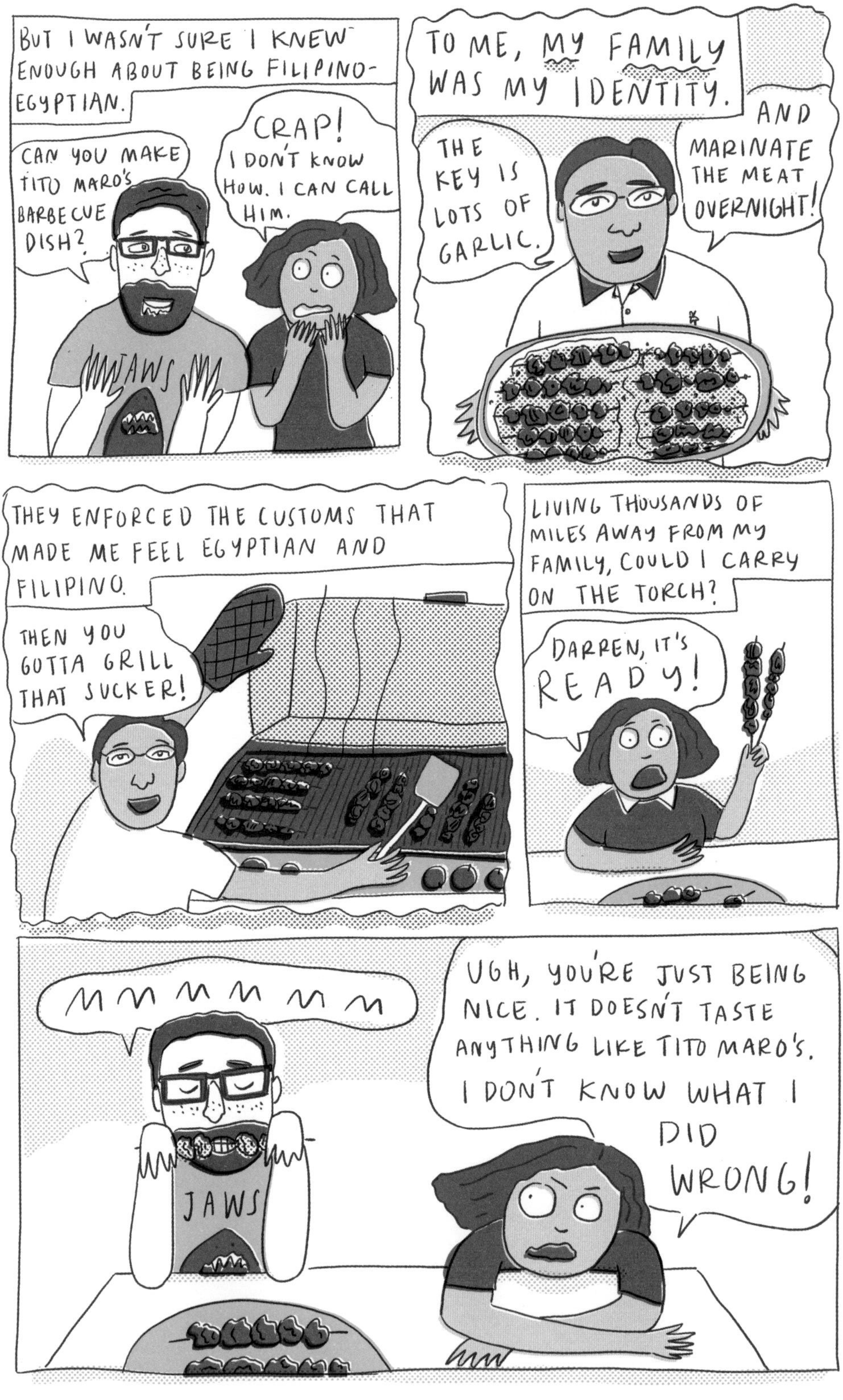
BUT I WASN'T SURE I KNEW ENOUGH ABOUT BEING FILIPINO-EGYPTIAN.
CAN YOU MAKE TITO MARO'S BARBECUE DISH?
CRAP! I DON'T KNOW HOW. I CAN CALL HIM.
JAWS
TO ME, MY FAMILY WAS MY IDENTITY.
THE KEY IS LOTS OF GARLIC.
AND MARINATE THE MEAT OVERNIGHT!
THEY ENFORCED THE CUSTOMS THAT MADE ME FEEL EGYPTIAN AND FILIPINO.
THEN YOU GOTTA GRILL THAT SUCKER!
LIVING THOUSANDS OF MILES AWAY FROM MY FAMILY, COULD I CARRY ON THE TORCH?
DARREN, IT'S READY!
MMMMMMM
UGH, YOU'RE JUST BEING NICE. IT DOESN'T TASTE ANYTHING LIKE TITO MARO'S. I DON'T KNOW WHAT I DID WRONG!
JAWS

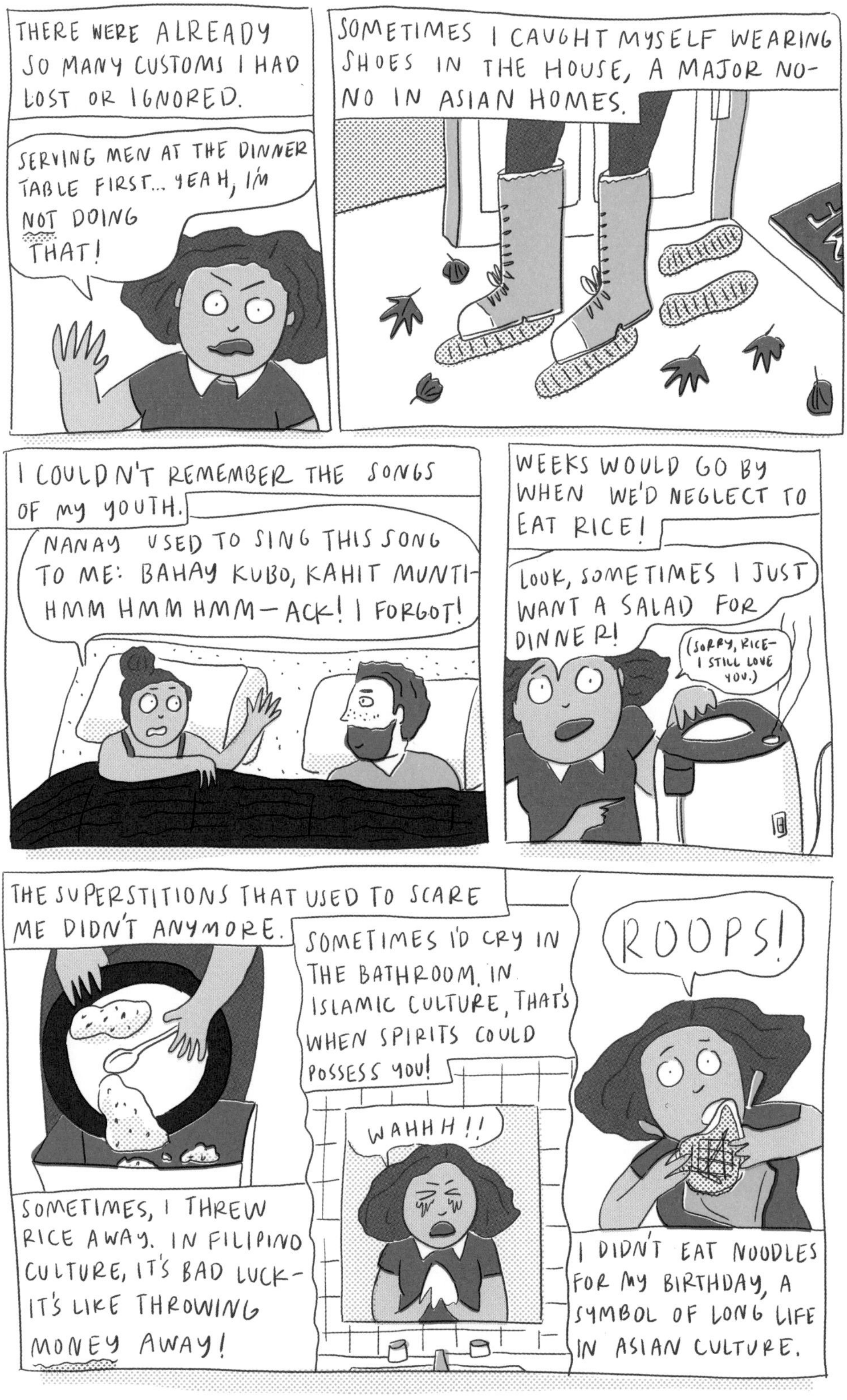
THERE WERE ALREADY SO MANY CUSTOMS I HAD LOST OR IGNORED.
SERVING MEN AT THE DINNER TABLE FIRST... YEAH, I'M NOT DOING THAT!
SOMETIMES I CAUGHT MYSELF WEARING SHOES IN THE HOUSE, A MAJOR NO-NO IN ASIAN HOMES.
I COULDN'T REMEMBER THE SONGS OF MY YOUTH.
NANAY USED TO SING THIS SONG TO ME: BAHAY KUBO, KAHIT MUNTI- HMM HMM HMM—ACK! I FORGOT!
WEEKS WOULD GO BY WHEN WE'D NEGLECT TO EAT RICE!
LOOK, SOMETIMES I JUST WANT A SALAD FOR DINNER!
(SORRY, RICE- I STILL LOVE YOU.)
THE SUPERSTITIONS THAT USED TO SCARE ME DIDN'T ANYMORE.
SOMETIMES, I THREW RICE AWAY. IN FILIPINO CULTURE, IT'S BAD LUCK- IT'S LIKE THROWING MONEY AWAY!
SOMETIMES I'D CRY IN THE BATHROOM. IN ISLAMIC CULTURE, THAT'S WHEN SPIRITS COULD POSSESS YOU!
WAHHH!!
ROOPS!
I DIDN'T EAT NOODLES FOR MY BIRTHDAY, A SYMBOL OF LONG LIFE IN ASIAN CULTURE.

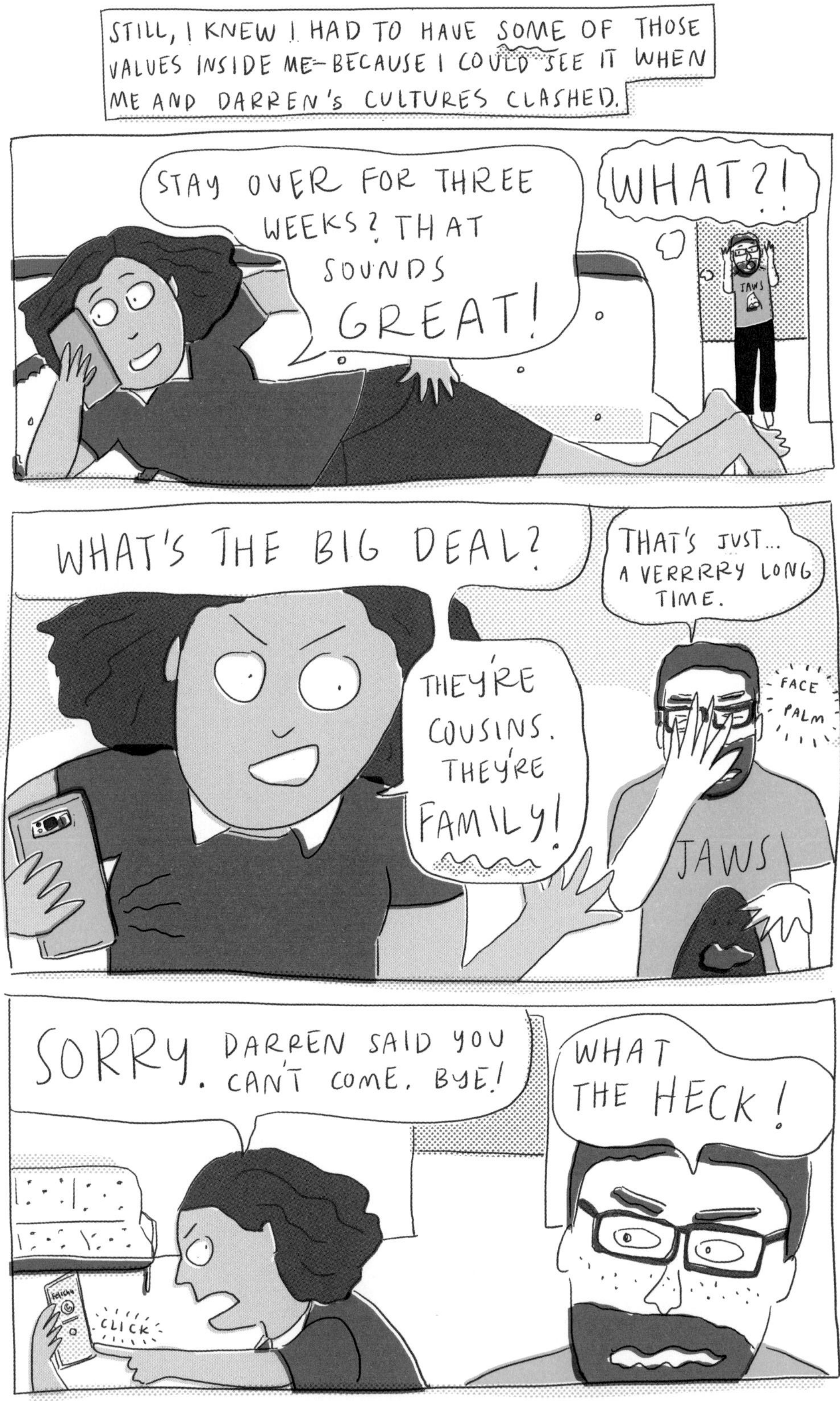
STILL, I KNEW I HAD TO HAVE SOME OF THOSE VALUES INSIDE ME—BECAUSE I COULD SEE IT WHEN ME AND DARREN'S CULTURES CLASHED.
STAY OVER FOR THREE WEEKS? THAT SOUNDS GREAT!
WHAT?!
JAWS
WHAT'S THE BIG DEAL?
THEY'RE COUSINS. THEY'RE FAMILY!
THAT'S JUST... A VERRRRY LONG TIME.
FACE PALM
JAWS
SORRY. DARREN SAID YOU CAN'T COME. BYE!
WHAT THE HECK!
CLICK

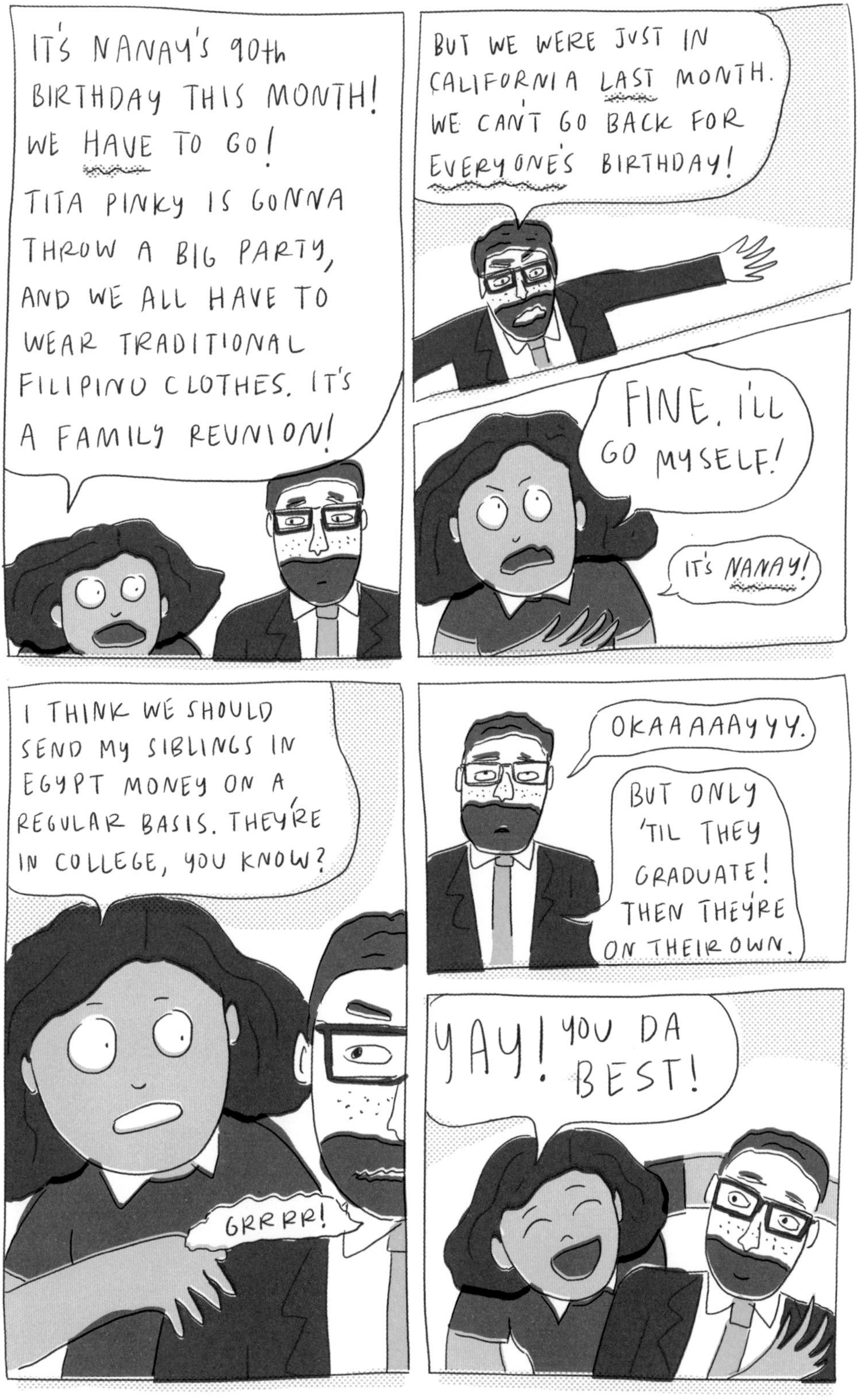
IT'S NANAY'S 90th BIRTHDAY THIS MONTH! WE HAVE TO GO! TITA PINKY IS GONNA THROW A BIG PARTY, AND WE ALL HAVE TO WEAR TRADITIONAL FILIPINO CLOTHES. IT'S A FAMILY REUNION!
BUT WE WERE JUST IN CALIFORNIA LAST MONTH. WE CAN'T GO BACK FOR EVERYONE'S BIRTHDAY!
FINE. I'LL GO MYSELF!
IT'S NANAY!
I THINK WE SHOULD SEND MY SIBLINGS IN EGYPT MONEY ON A REGULAR BASIS. THEY'RE IN COLLEGE, YOU KNOW?
GRRRR!
OKAAAAAYYY.
BUT ONLY 'TIL THEY GRADUATE! THEN THEY'RE ON THEIR OWN.
YAY! YOU DA BEST!

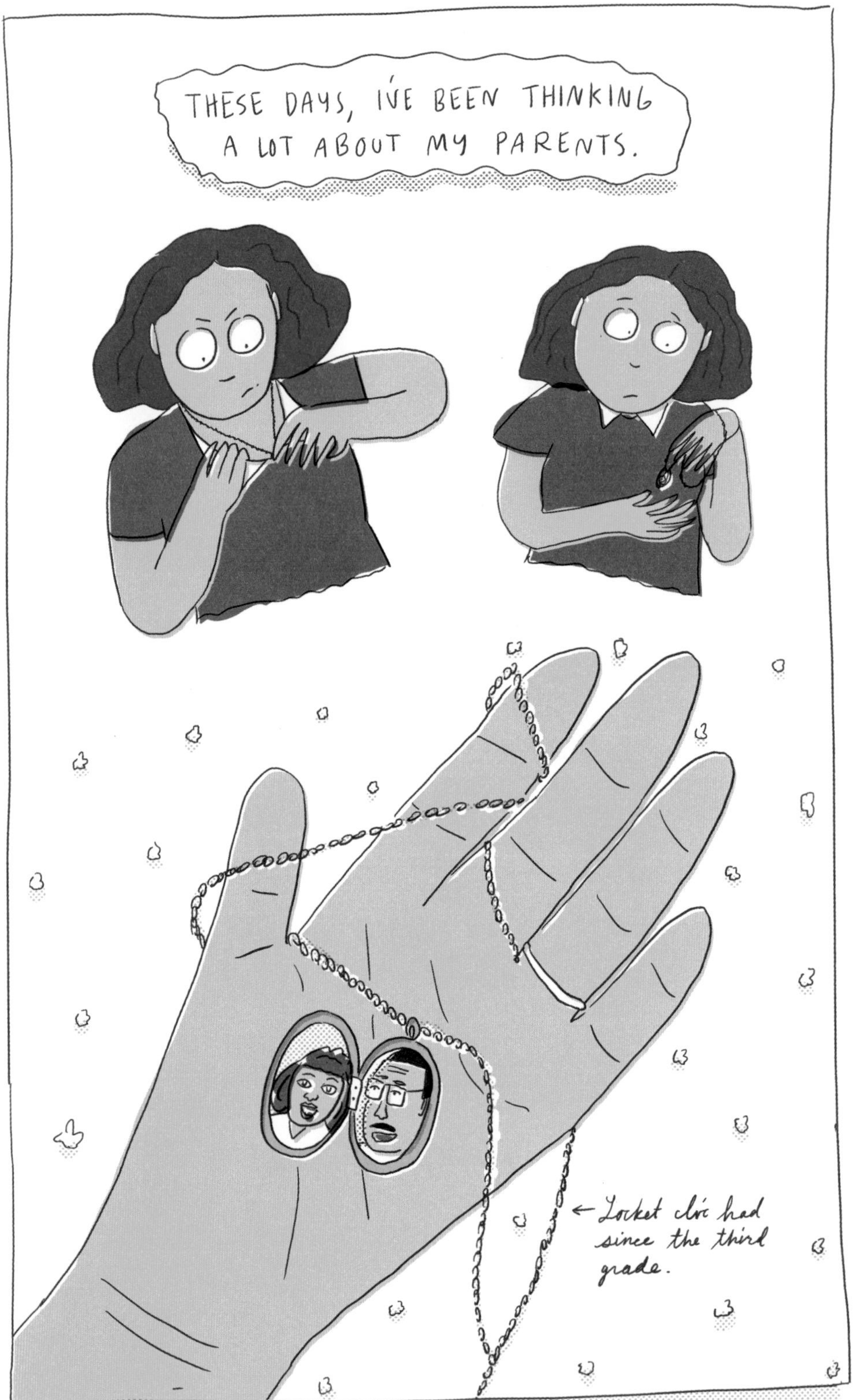
THESE DAYS, I'VE BEEN THINKING A LOT ABOUT MY PARENTS.
← Locket I've had since the third grade.

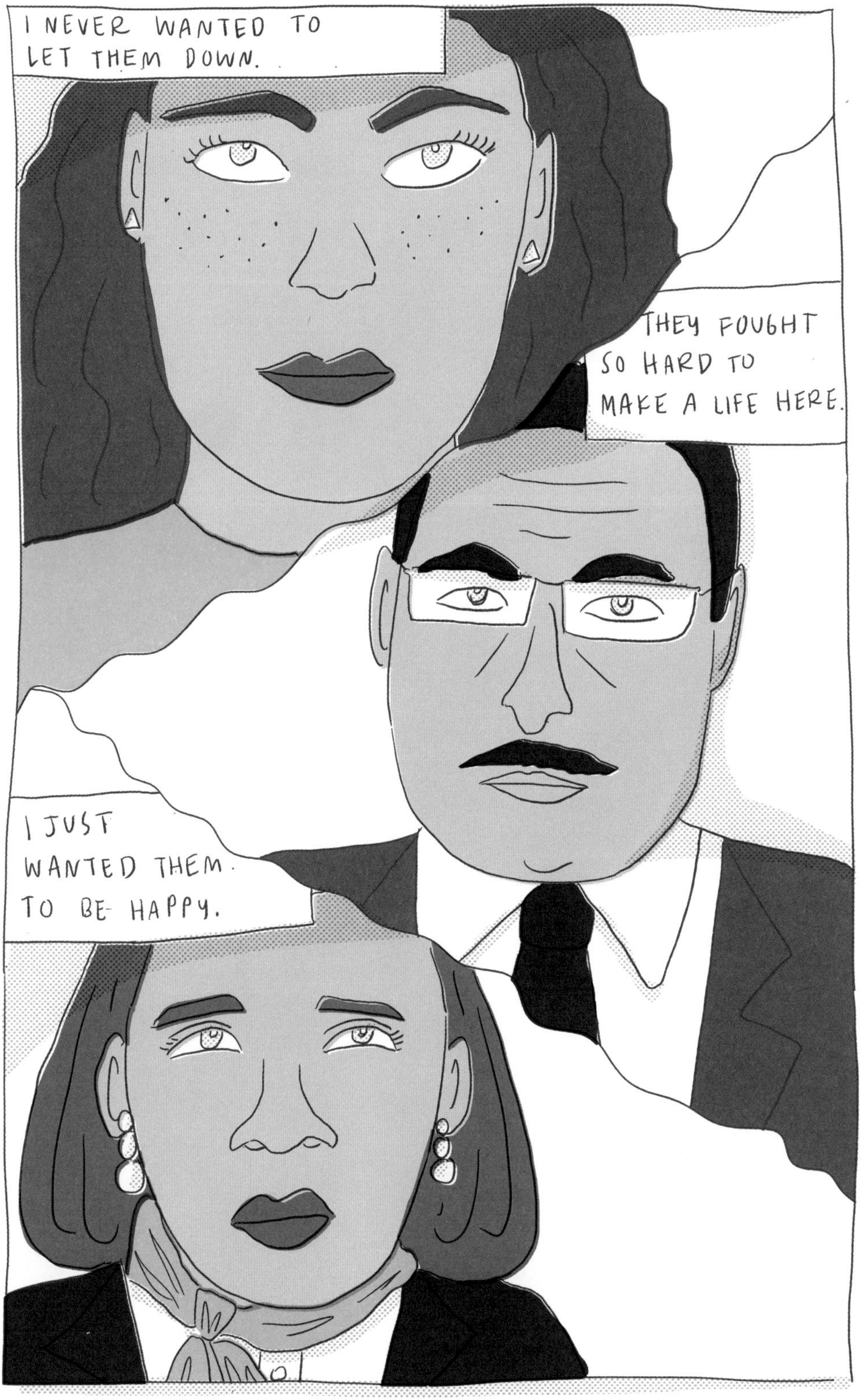

I NEVER WANTED TO LET THEM DOWN.
THEY FOUGHT SO HARD TO MAKE A LIFE HERE.
I JUST WANTED THEM TO BE HAPPY.

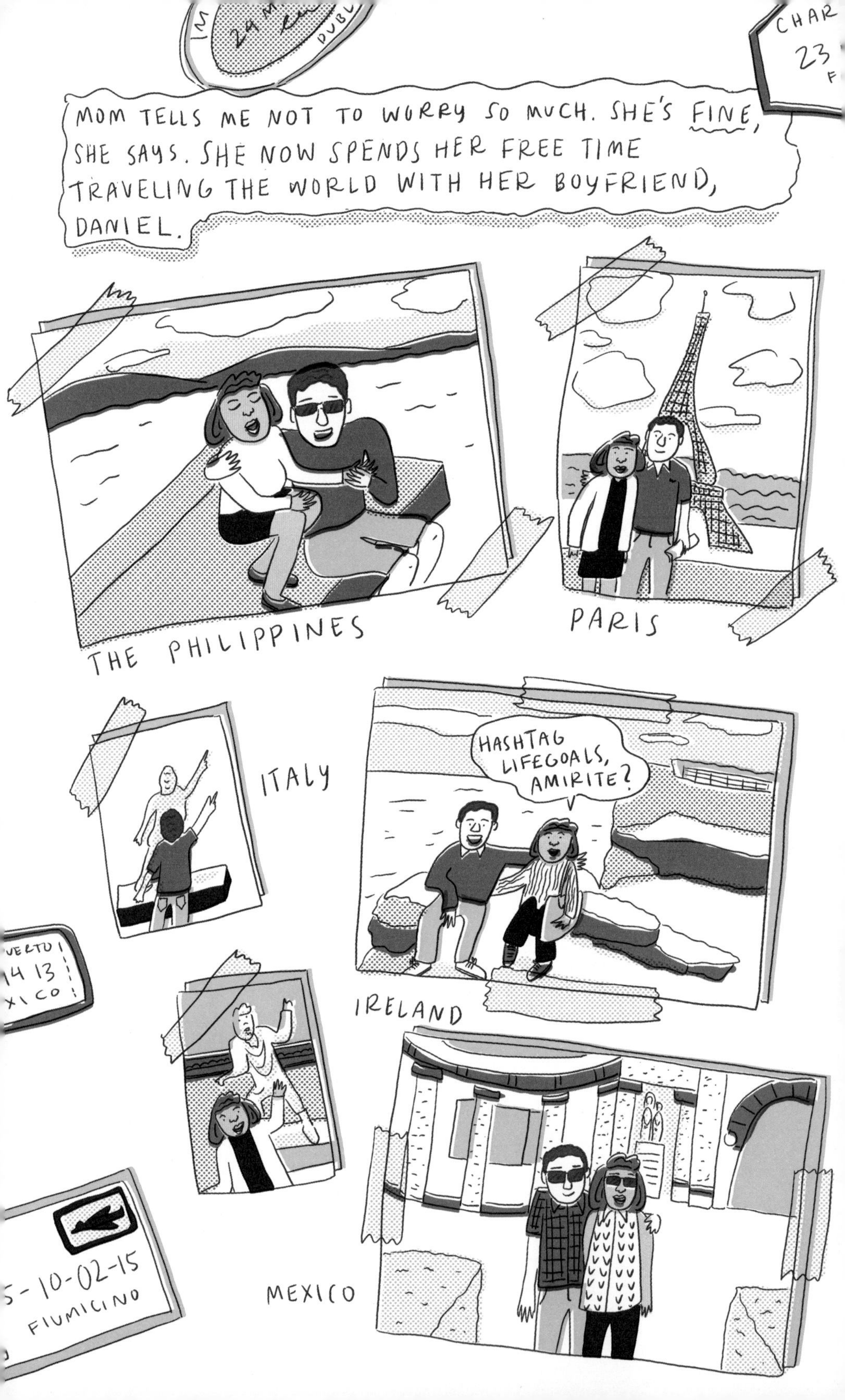

MOM TELLS ME NOT TO WORRY SO MUCH. SHE'S FINE, SHE SAYS. SHE NOW SPENDS HER FREE TIME TRAVELING THE WORLD WITH HER BOYFRIEND, DANIEL.
THE PHILIPPINES
PARIS
ITALY
HASHTAG LIFEGOALS, AMIRITE?
IRELAND
MEXICO
CHAR
23
14 13
5-10-02-15
FIUMICINO

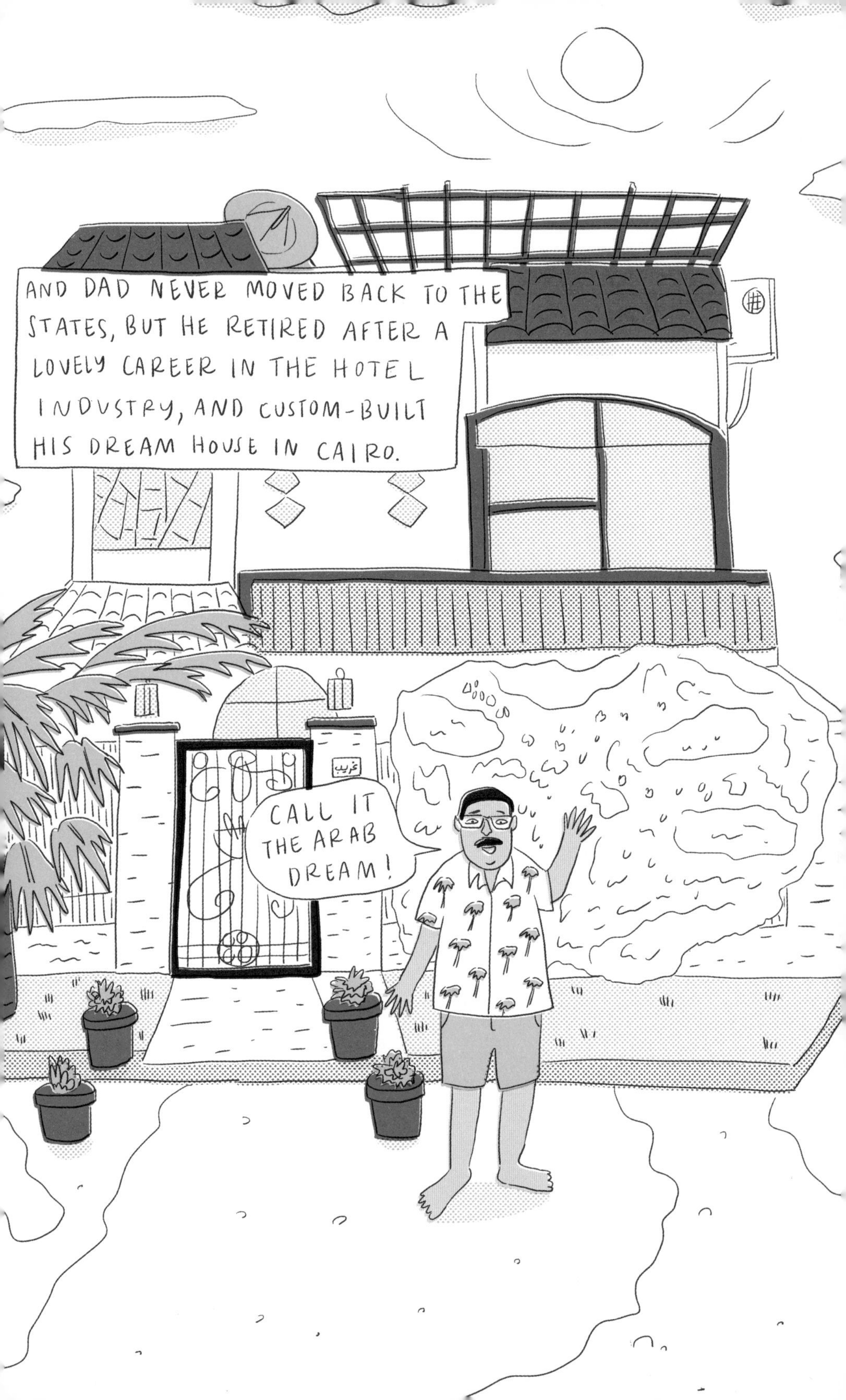
AND DAD NEVER MOVED BACK TO THE STATES, BUT HE RETIRED AFTER A LOVELY CAREER IN THE HOTEL INDUSTRY, AND CUSTOM-BUILT HIS DREAM HOUSE IN CAIRO.
CALL IT THE ARAB DREAM!

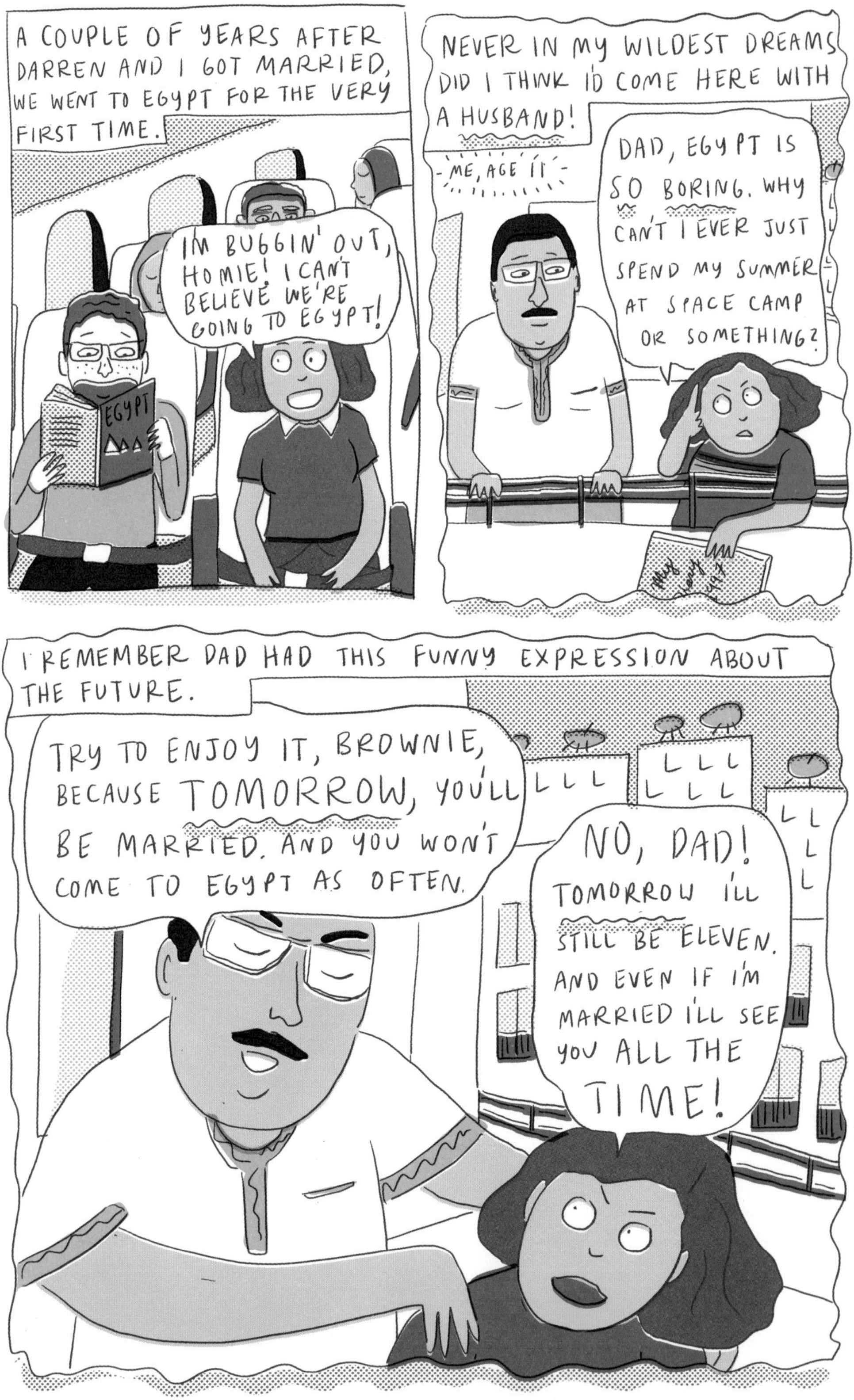
A COUPLE OF YEARS AFTER DARREN AND I GOT MARRIED, WE WENT TO EGYPT FOR THE VERY FIRST TIME.
EGYPT
I'M BUGGIN' OUT, HOMIE! I CAN'T BELIEVE WE'RE GOING TO EGYPT!
NEVER IN MY WILDEST DREAMS DID I THINK I'D COME HERE WITH A HUSBAND!
-ME, AGE 11-
DAD, EGYPT IS SO BORING. WHY CAN'T I EVER JUST SPEND MY SUMMER AT SPACE CAMP OR SOMETHING?
I REMEMBER DAD HAD THIS FUNNY EXPRESSION ABOUT THE FUTURE.
TRY TO ENJOY IT, BROWNIE, BECAUSE TOMORROW, YOU'LL BE MARRIED. AND YOU WON'T COME TO EGYPT AS OFTEN.
NO, DAD! TOMORROW I'LL STILL BE ELEVEN. AND EVEN IF I'M MARRIED I'LL SEE YOU ALL THE TIME!

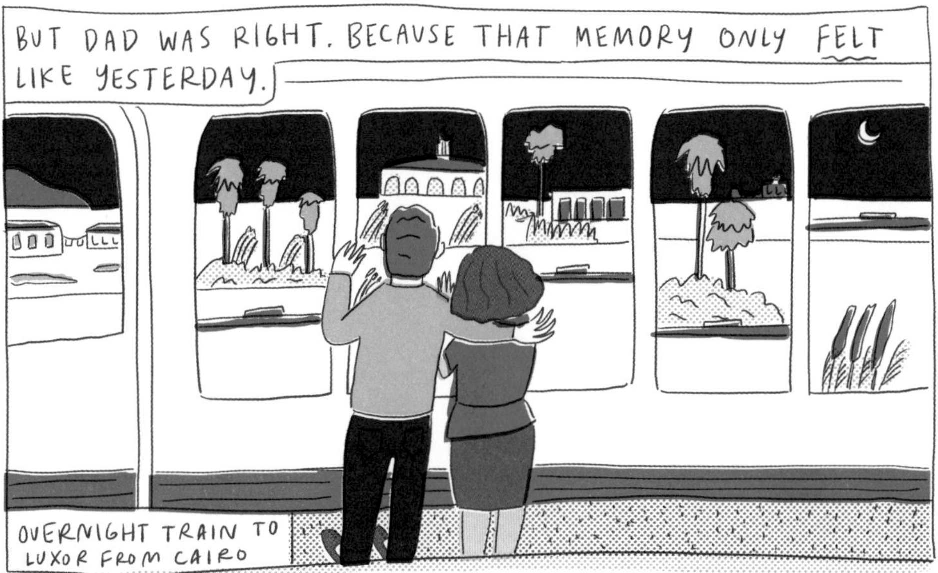
BUT DAD WAS RIGHT. BECAUSE THAT MEMORY ONLY FELT LIKE YESTERDAY.
OVERNIGHT TRAIN TO LUXOR FROM CAIRO

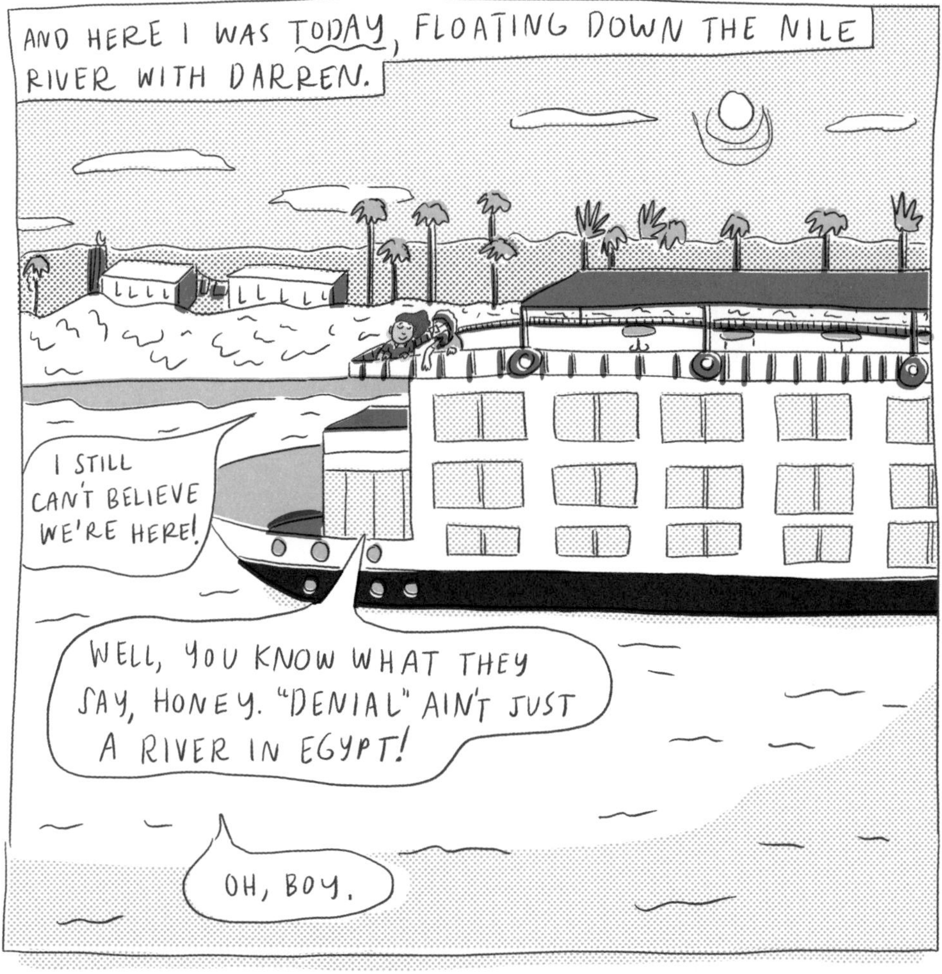
AND HERE I WAS TODAY, FLOATING DOWN THE NILE RIVER WITH DARREN.
I STILL CAN'T BELIEVE WE'RE HERE!
WELL, YOU KNOW WHAT THEY SAY, HONEY. "DENIAL" AIN'T JUST A RIVER IN EGYPT!
OH, BOY.

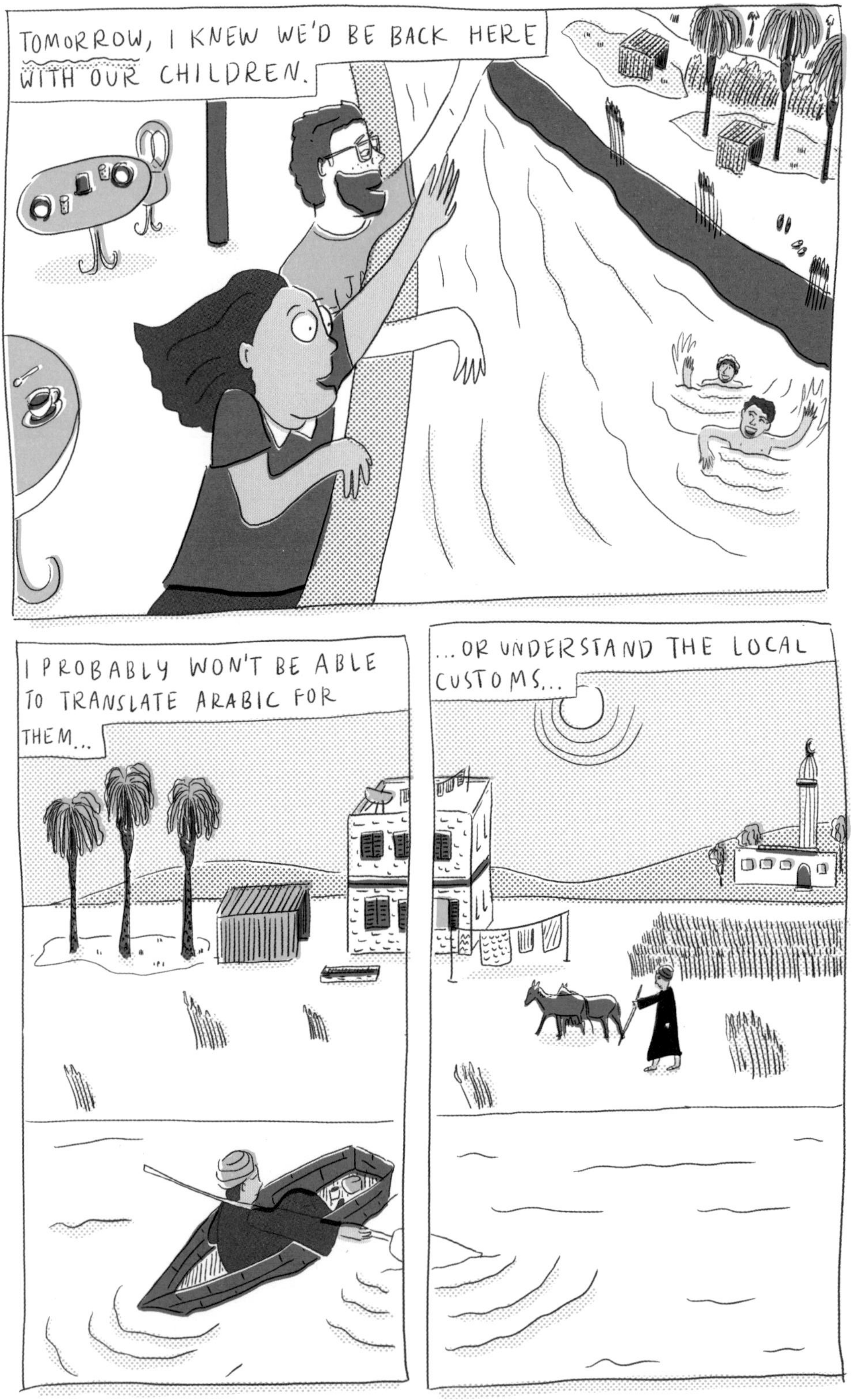
TOMORROW, I KNEW WE'D BE BACK HERE WITH OUR CHILDREN.
I PROBABLY WON'T BE ABLE TO TRANSLATE ARABIC FOR THEM...
...OR UNDERSTAND THE LOCAL CUSTOMS...

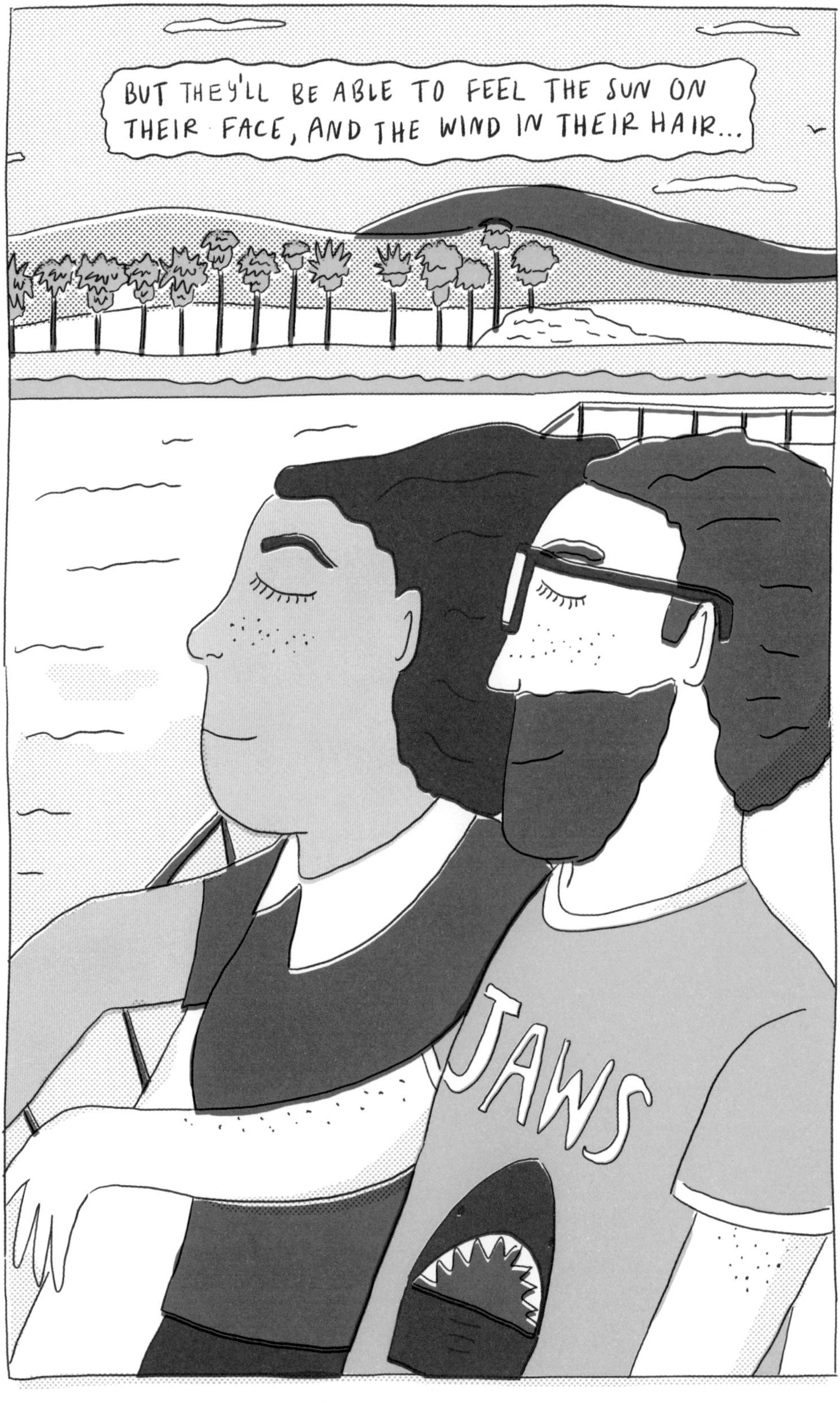
BUT THEY'LL BE ABLE TO FEEL THE SUN ON THEIR FACE, AND THE WIND IN THEIR HAIR...
JAWS

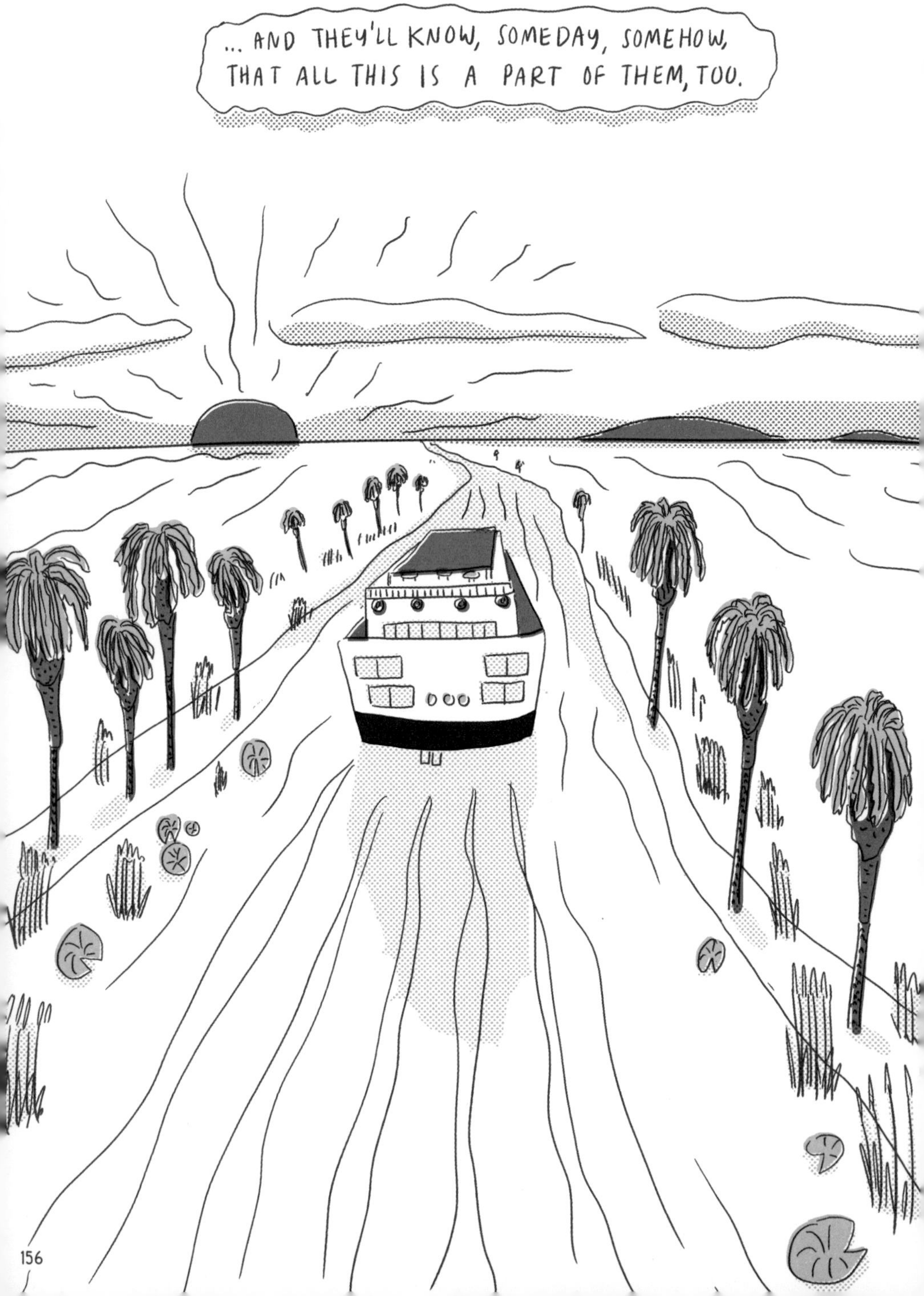
... AND THEY'LL KNOW, SOMEDAY, SOMEHOW, THAT ALL THIS IS A PART OF THEM, TOO.

Acknowledgments

THANK YOU TO MY EDITOR, SARA NEVILLE, WHO'S BEEN WITH ME THROUGH THICK AND THIN. TO DARREN, FOR BEING MY ROCK.

TO THE AMAZING PEOPLE WHO MADE THIS BOOK POSSIBLE: BEN DE LA CRUZ, LA JOHNSON, KAT CHOW, JESS GOLDSTEIN, DANIEL GREENBERG, AND THE TEAM AT CLARKSON POTTER, ESPECIALLY TERRY DEAL, DANIELLE DESCHENES, JENNIFER JIMENEZ, AND JOHN TOMASELLI.

TO MY BACKREADERS: JUSTIN CLARAVALL, BRENDA ABDELALL, CHARITA CASTRO, MICHAEL HAEDERLE, JORDAN ZAKARIN, KATIE RUST, MALLORY YU, CLAIRE O'NEILL, BETTINA MAKALINTAL, AND JOHN WIE.

BIG THANKS TO DENNIS VILLA JUAN PEREZ, SALLY ABDELMAGEED, JAMES CUARTERO, GABBIE IBARRA, HARSH SHAH, DAVID HONG, CAITLIN MURPHY, STEPHEN HERMES, AND NISHANT SHRIKHANDE, FOR THE CONVERSATIONS THAT HELPED SHAPE THIS BOOK.

SHOUT-OUT TO MY CERRITOS HIGH FRIENDS: KADI, YALDA, VRINDA, KYLE, SWATI, HENNA, JAMES, ERIC, MIKE F., RAEIDA, ALBERT, EMIL, JOSH, NATE, AND JORGE. TO MY IG FAM, ESPECIALLY STEPHANIE S., JUDY G., EMILY, MARISSA S., AND ERIN. TO MY DC FAMILY FOR THE ENDLESS LOVE AND SUPPORT.

TO MOMMY, DADDY, MIN MIN, TITO MARO, NANAY, TATAY, TITA PINKY, TITO ARNEL, TITO OVID, TITA JEAN, FELISHA, AHMED, SALMA, DUNNIA, HALA, AMITO MONA, AND DARREN, FOR TRUSTING ME TO TELL YOUR STORIES.

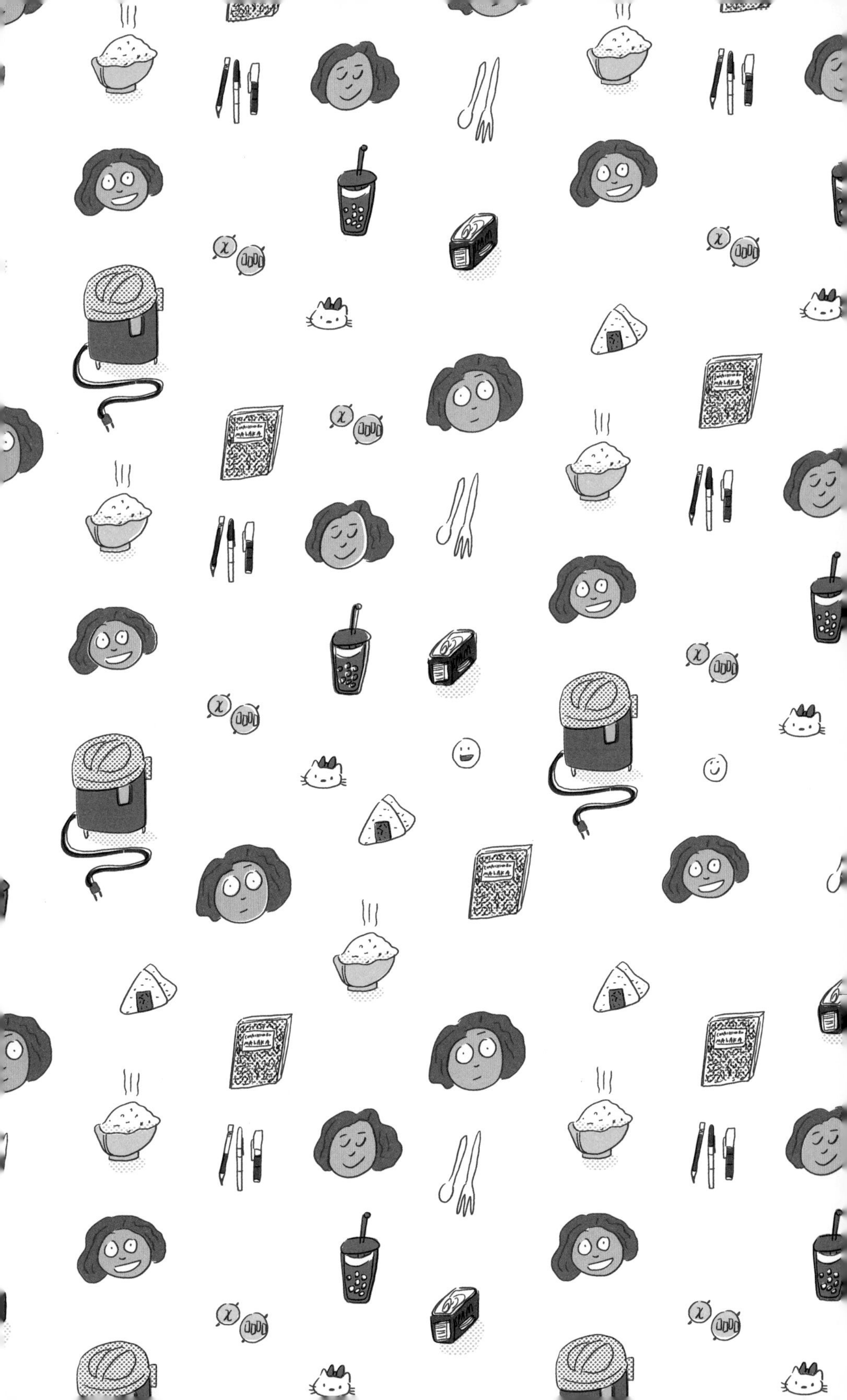

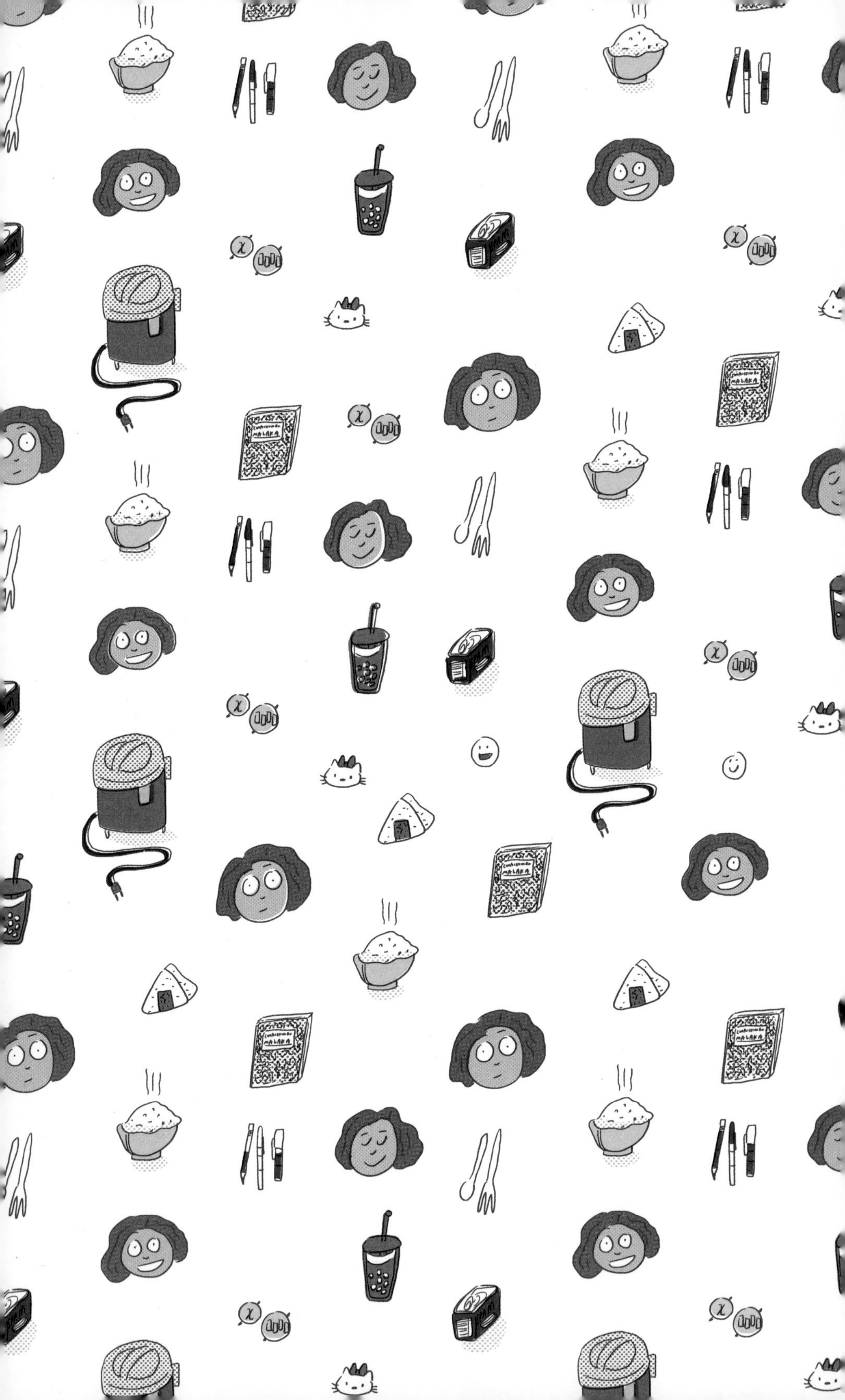